INSIGHT GUIDE

Los angeles

APA PUBLICATIONS
Part of the Langenscheidt Publishing Group

INSIGHT GUIDE
Los angeles

ABOUT THIS BOOK

Editorial

Update Editor
Sarah Hudson
Editorial Director
Brian Bell

Distribution

UK & Ireland
GeoCenter International Ltd
The Viables Centre, Harrow Way
Basingstoke, Hants RG22 4BJ
Fax: (44) 1256-817988

United States
Langenscheidt Publishers, Inc.
46–35 54th Road, Maspeth, NY 11378
Fax: (718) 784-0640

Canada
Prologue Inc.
1650 Lionel Bertrand Blvd., Boisbriand
Québec, Canada J7H 1N7
Tel: (450) 434-0306. Fax: (450) 434-2627

Worldwide
Apa Publications GmbH & Co.
Verlag KG (Singapore branch)
38 Joo Koon Road, Singapore 628990
Tel: (65) 865-1600. Fax: (65) 861-6438

Printing

Insight Print Services (Pte) Ltd
38 Joo Koon Road, Singapore 628990
Tel: (65) 865-1600. Fax: (65) 861-6438

CONTACTING THE EDITORS
Although every effort is made to provide accurate information, we live in a fast-changing world and would appreciate it if readers would call our attention to any errors or outdated information that may occur by writing to: **Insight Guides, P.O. Box 7910, London SE1 1WE, England. Fax: (44 20) 7403-0290. e-mail: insight@apaguide.demon.co.uk**

www.insightguides.com

This guidebook combines the interests and enthusiasms of two of the world's best known information providers: Insight Guides, whose titles have set the standard for visual travel guides since 1970, and Discovery Channel, the world's premier source of nonfiction television programming.

The editors of Insight Guides provide both practical advice and general understanding about a destination's history, culture, institutions and people. Discovery Channel and its website, www.discovery. com, help millions of viewers explore their world from the comfort of their own home and also encourage them to explore it first hand.

This fully updated edition of *Insight: Los Angeles* is

carefully structured to convey an understanding of the city and its culture as well as to guide readers through its sights and activities:

◆ The **Features** section, with a yellow bar at the top of each page, covers the history and culture of the city through informative essays.

◆ The main **Places** section, indicated by a blue bar, is a complete guide to all the sights and areas that are worth visiting. Places of special interest are clearly coordinated by number with the maps.

◆ The **Travel Tips** section, identified with an orange bar, provides a handy point of reference for information on travel, hotels, shopping, restaurants, and more.

EXPLORE YOUR WORLD'

The contributors

This edition has been comprehensively revised by writer/director **Mix Ryan**. After two degrees at USC and over a decade of filmmaking in every reach of LA, Ryan knows the city inside out and shares it in "Muscles – Why They Grow Here Like Oranges", a new chapter on Theme Parks, and features on Inventions, Hollywood, and Universal Studios. His latest film is *Wings* for Discovery Channel.

Edited by **Sarah Hudson**, this edition of the guide has retained much of the work produced by contributors to previous editions and the original visual flair that was the work of managing editor **Martha Ellen Zenfell**.

John Wilcock was the previous editor and a major contributor to most parts of the guide. The author of a number of travel guides, he began his career on British newspapers, and was co-founder of *The Village Voice* and Andy Warhol's *Interview* in New York. After editing the *Los Angeles Free Press*, he realized that California was more interesting than his fellow New Yorkers believed. So he swapped coasts.

Nancy Gottesman was Wilcock's appointed assistant editor. She attended UCLA and has written or edited for a variety of publications, including the *Los Angeles Magazine*, *Los Angeles Reader* and *LA Style*.

Other contributors included: **Liz Brody**, who wrote "Earthquakes and Other Calamities"; **Merrill Shindler**, who wrote the "Valleys and Canyons" chapter; **Tania Martinez-Lemke**, who did much of the research for the "Automania" feature; **Stanley Young**, writer of the feature on "Alternative Altars", and who co-wrote the history section with **William M. Mason**; **Duane Byrge**, member of the LA Film Critics Association, wrote the feature "No Business But Show Business"; **Michael Tennesen** has been a contributing editor to the *Los Angeles Magazine* and wrote the "South Bay" chapter; **Oliver Johnson** wrote the feature on William Mulholland; and **Barbara Horngren** and **Judith Blocker** co-wrote the "Day Trips" chapter.

Leading US photographer **Catherine Karnow** set up an office and appointed an assistant especially for this book and didn't stop working from dawn to dusk to capture many of the great images reproduced here. Many new images for this edition came from British photographer **Glyn Genin**, who shot *Insight Compact Guide: Los Angeles*.

This latest edition was proofread by **Lisa Cussans** and indexed by **Elizabeth Cook**.

Map Legend

— ·· —	International Boundary
— — —	State Boundary
— · —	National Park/Reserve
— — —	Ferry Route
Ⓜ	Subway
✈ ✈	Airport: International/ Regional
🚌	Bus Station
❶	Tourist Information
✉	Post Office
⛪ † ⛪	Church/Ruins
†	Monastery
☾	Mosque
✡	Synagogue
🏰 🏚	Castle/Ruins
∴	Archaeological Site
∩	Cave
🗽	Statue/Monument
★	Place of Interest

The main places of interest in the Places section are coordinated by number with a full-color map (e.g. ❶), and a symbol at the top of every right-hand page tells you where to find the map.

CONTENTS

Maps

The famous Hollywood
sign overlooks equally
famous Los Angeles

Travel Tips

Insight on ...

Information panels

Places

L.A. LORE

Almost everybody has a preconceived notion of what the
Big Orange is all about – but they're often mistaken

Los Angeles rarely lives down to people's worst expectations: the smog is (usually) bearable, the gangs (mostly) stay in areas seldom seen by tourists, and even the intimidating freeways prove to be more negotiable than the wary visitor may fear. Despite its problems with pollution, urban sprawl and more or less 24-hour gridlock on many of its boulevards, plus all the troubles of a city that is still growing too fast, Los Angeles nevertheless remains a location where people come to start a new life, to begin anew, to make themselves over.

Unlike most places, it's a city with no clearly defined focal point, no spot that all would agree is the center. So finding your own center – of LA in general or of Hollywood in particular – can offer an interesting subtext to any exploration, even a personal one. What makes this odyssey especially captivating in Los Angeles is the wide variety of sets and settings with which to construct one's scenario. Only a city whose best-known product is illusion could offer so many different backdrops to those anxious to play make-believe. Choose your era and open your eyes to the magic of everyday life.

Movie settings

Downtown Los Angeles is like a carnival with little bits of everything: nostalgia (Angels' Flight funicular railway), futuristic architecture, a tranquil Japanese garden, the 1920s and 1930s grandeur of Broadway theaters, exuberant Grand Central Market, and the adobe street where the city began. North and west of Downtown are scores of movie settings: beautiful Spanish patios, architecture that inspired Walt Disney, the Witches' House, glittering Rodeo Drive, the canals of Venice, Santa Monica Pier, astonishing homes and awesome views from the hills, a lakeside shrine – and even what is arguably America's most beautiful museum.

Is Hollywood's center the Hollywood sign? And, as the sign itself is virtually inaccessible, where is the best setting from which to see it? (Hint: there's water in the picture.) Once a city in its own right, Hollywood celebrated its incorporation with a 1903 party in the old Hollywood Hotel; when Lillian Gish stayed there 10 years later, she noted the sweet aroma of orange blossoms all around her. The hotel is long gone, but the site (Sunset at Highland) is still a mecca to some. "I've seen people stand and stare at the corner for five minutes at a time," says the former curator of the Max Factor museum, itself for a time a repository of movie history.   ▷

PRECEDING PAGES: blondes having more fun; beauty at the beach; restaurateur Ed Debevic's starry staff; pool with a view.
LEFT: commercial artist in Pasadena.

Maybe the places where the early stars lived, worked, played and died are your vision of what Hollywood is all about? If so, you'll want to inspect Whitley Heights, an early rival to Beverly Hills; Gower Gulch; the canyon homes of John Gilbert or Rudolph Valentino; or wander around Will Rogers' charming ranch or through the terraced ruins of Harry Houdini's old house. One of movieland's most enduring love affairs ended in a mansion on Beverly Drive with the death of publisher William Randolph Hearst and, a decade later, that of Marion Davies, the chorus girl for whom he founded a notable movie company.

Powerful players

It must surely have entered the mind of media tycoon Rupert Murdoch, a powerful player in Hollywood after he bought 20th Century-Fox, that publishing is not enough to be truly influential in what is still perceived as being a largely one-industry town. For the people in that rarefied world, "Morton's on Monday night" might be the center of things. Or the Beverly Hills Hotel, in whose $1,000-a-night bungalows some of them stay while the $10 million house they bought is being torn down to make room for the new $15 million home they have planned to put in its place.

Reshaped anew by every generation, the short stretch of Sunset Boulevard known as "the Strip," with its music clubs and giant billboards, is a center to many. In the movies' golden era between the two world wars, it housed the spots where the stars met and played – Ciro's, the Trocadero, Mocambo, the Garden of Allah, Schwab's – all gone today but preserved in photographs in the equally historic Hollywood Roosevelt Hotel. Some things are as durable as ever: thousands throng the portals of the Chinese Theater, opened by Sid Grauman in 1927, to admire cement signatures of the stars as well as their often grateful inscriptions.

For some visitors and many more residents, the "center" is not a single place but, in the word of the old Irish proverb, "where you are sitting" – in this case, in their automobiles. It is impossible to overstate the significance that the car plays in the life of the average Los Angeleno. The driver is master of his or her own fate, free to roam and to dream, to escape to a private world sheltered from the vibrant street life which is the focus in other cities. To be a car owner in LA is to realize not only how immense the city is but why the very name has become a synonym for a lifestyle as much as a location. ❏

RIGHT: truckin' through LA County.

Decisive Dates

Circa **9000 BC**: The first nomads reach what is today California.

Pre-1700s: Indian tribes inhabit the Los Angeles region, including Gabrieleno, Chumash, Cahuilla, and Tataviam.

1771: San Gabriel Mission is founded by the Spanish.

1781: Don Felipe de Neve, the Mexican Governor of California, founds Los Angeles. A Franciscan monk, Junípero Serra, dedicates the

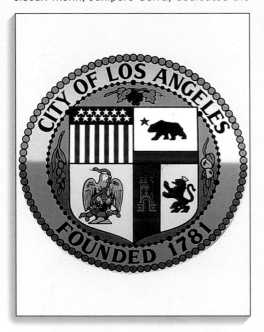

town, naming it after St Francis of Assisi's first church, St. Mary of the Angels – El Pueblo de Nuestra Senora la Reina de Los Angeles.

1790: The community's first census reports 70 families living in a total of 30 adobe dwellings.

1840s: The first orange groves are planted.

1842: The first California gold is discovered by Francisco Lopez in Placerita Canyon.

1847: Mexican General Andres Pico surrenders California to US General John Fremont at the Cahuenga Pass.

1848: The Treaty of Guadalupe is signed, fixing present US/Mexico borders.

1849: Gold is discovered at Sutter's Fort in the Sierra foothills – the gold rush begins.

1850: Limits of Los Angeles County mapped out. Population: 1,500. California becomes the 31st state in the Union.

1850s: Under successive treaties with the Federal government, native Indian tribes sign away 90 percent of their 7½ million acres.

1851–60: Chinese population grows, coming to LA to build railroad and search for gold.

1852: 100,000 miners pass through Los Angeles – it becomes a lawless western town.

Late 1850s: The gold rush ends – and economic depression sets in.

1857: The Fort Tejon earthquake (estimated 8.0 on today's Richter scale).

1860–80: Enlarged irrigation systems are constructed to keep Los Angeles watered.

1867: Gas lamps illuminate the city's streets.

1871: The Chinese Massacre – in response to the murder of a white policeman, mass shooting and lynching leaves more than 24 dead.

1874: The first navel orange trees are planted at Riverside.

1876: Southern Pacific Railway arrives. Waves of immigrants follow.

1882: The first Los Angeles phone book is issued – all three pages of it.

1887: Harvey Wilcox files to form subdivision of his ranch, wife Daieda names it Hollywood.

1890: Orange County divided from LA County. Population of Los Angeles: 50,000.

1893: Edward Doheny and C.A. Canfield strike oil near the site of today's MacArthur Park.

1904: Hollywood passes legislation to prohibit drunkenness and enforce speed limit of 12 miles an hour (19 km/h).

1905: Abbott Kinney opens his Venetian-style resort near Santa Monica.

1907: Oil derricks proliferate in LA – Echo Lake so polluted it catches fire for three days. First house in Beverly Hills is built – lots on Sunset Boulevard cost $1,000.

1908: Ex-Chicago filmmaker William Selig completes *The Count of Monte Cristo*, Southern California's first commercial film.

1910: Los Angeles annexes Town of Hollywood.

1911–20: The Martin, Lockheed, and Douglas aviation companies begin production.

1911: Hollywood's first movie, *The Law of the Range,* is filmed in a former tavern at Sunset and Gower. The *Los Angeles Times* building is destroyed by a bomb.

1913: William Mulholland opens his new aqueduct, bringing water from the Owens Valley.

1920: Prohibition hits the US, but proximity to Mexico and offshore bootleggers keeps up-spirits in Los Angeles.

1921: Hollywood's first national scandal hits, as Roscoe "Fatty" Arbuckle is accused of rape and murder. After acquittal, his career is over.

1923: Beverly Hills becomes a movie colony.

1926: Warner Studios adds sound to its feature *Don Juan* and the following year gives Al Jolson some dialogue in *The Jazz Singer*.

1927: The first Academy of Motion Pictures awards – the Oscars – presented at the Hollywood Roosevelt hotel.

1928: The St Francis Dam in San Fransquito Canyon bursts, sending a 180-ft (55-meter) wall of water from Santa Clarita to Oxnard, killing 400. Los Angeles City Hall is dedicated.

1931: Los Angeles International Airport (LAX) is opened.

1932: The Olympic Games are staged in what is then the world's largest stadium, the Coliseum in Los Angeles.

1933: The Long Beach Earthquake (estimated 6.3 on Richter scale) kills 120 in Los Angeles.

1939: Union Station, last of the great railroad terminals, opens.

1941: December 7 – Pearl Harbor attacked. US enters World War II. Night blackouts begin.

1943: Zoot Suit Riots as sailors and Latinos clash in coastal beach communities. Downtown LA becomes a battlezone for several nights.

1947: The California legislature passes a law against smog.

1950–65: 31,000 acres (12,500 hectares) of orange groves fall to housing development.

1952: Alien Land Act denying land ownership to Orientals is declared unconstitutional.

1955: Disneyland opens.

1959: A citizen group saves Watts Towers from the wrecking ball.

1963: California's population becomes the largest of all US states, with the Los Angeles County population hitting 9 million. The Beach Boys form in the South Bay.

1965: Civil unrest erupts as the Watts Riots, lasting five days, kill 34 people.

1968: Presidential candidate Robert F. Kennedy is assassinated at the Ambassador Hotel.

1971: An earthquake measuring 6.6 in the San Fernando Valley claims the lives of 64 Southern Californians.

1974: The oil tycoon J. Paul Getty donates his Malibu home as a museum.

1980: Former actor and state governor Ronald Reagan becomes the 39th US President.

1987: The Whittier Earthquake – varied structural damage throughout Downtown, East LA, and Hollywood.

1988: Los Angeles Dodgers win World Series.

1990: Water rationing imposed for the first time.

1992: The controversial acquittal of several LA police officers, charged with beating Rodney

King, a black motorist, starts riots which leave 51 people dead.

1994: Earthquake measuring 6.6 in the San Fernando Valley kills 44 people in the LA area.

1995–97: The football star O. J. Simpson is accused (and eventually acquitted in criminal court, found guilty in civil court) of murdering his wife and her friend. His trial enthralls the world.

1998: The Getty Center opens to great fanfare, giving Los Angeles the cultural lead over San Francisco.

2000: Renovations and new attractions are announced for Downtown and Hollywood Boulevard area; Disney announces its intention to open a new California adventure park. ❑

PRECEDING PAGES: *The Bear Dance*, a hand-colored lithograph by George Catlin, 1832.
LEFT: the Seal of Los Angeles.
RIGHT: Mickey Mouse and friends.

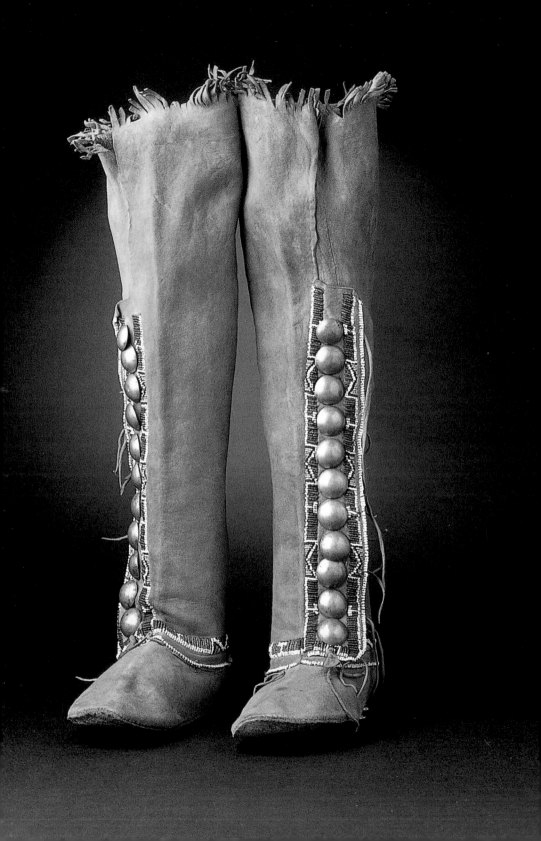

BEGINNINGS

In less than a century the fastest city in the West has become the cradle of a culture exported all over the world

California, as yet unnamed, was a peaceful place when the white men arrived. The land and sea provided all that was needed for nourishment, and for 10,000 years Indians had lived along its sunny shores following the cycle of the seasons. Historians estimate that there were as many as 200,000 indigenous peoples, divided into a rich variety of tribes and nations – the Indians of California spoke more distinct languages than the rest of the continent combined.

In the larger settlements they lived in large buildings covered with boards over lashed beams, but for the most part the small groups of 120 individuals lived in simple dwellings made of local reeds, breezy huts which could be easily rebuilt in case of infestation or dirt. The region had an abundance of game and fish as well as the staple food, acorn flour, which was laboriously harvested and processed from the local oak forests.

Tribes traded with each other using strings of seashell currency *(wampum)* to buy stone tools, obsidian knives, and the woven reed baskets in which they carried almost everything. Religious ceremonies centered around the sweat lodge *(temescal)*, used for cleansing and communion with the Great Spirit. Later these proved to be deadly efficient places for the spreading of white men's diseases.

Finding little to exploit or acquire, the Spanish all but ignored this wild frontier for more than two centuries after 16th-century New World explorers Vizcaino and Cabrillo had first claimed the territory: at best, it was considered little more than a place to find harbors in which to shelter and replenish the treasure-laden galleons on the seven-month journey between the Orient and Europe. Their rich cargo of silks, spices, sandalwood and mercury would be worth as much as $8 million today.

It was only when the Dutch, English and French began to show interest that the Spanish

Crown grew concerned. Further impetus for the Spanish colonization of California was the Russians' advance from Alaskan bases farther and farther south in their quest for the lucrative pelts of sea otters. These could be acquired for just a few cents and then resold to Chinese buyers for more than $100.

The missionaries

From the king of Spain came the order to develop Alta California, establishing ports, outposts, and missions. The Spanish had a well-tested technique for implanting their influence: priests, usually accompanied by just a handful of foot soldiers, served as the colonial vanguard, founding missions, converting Indians and, through education, changing the locals into surrogate Spaniards.

The Jesuits had been in Baja California since 1697, turning that peninsula into virtually their own dominion; but in 1767, seeking to diminish their growing political power, the Spanish Crown replaced them with Franciscans (or the

---

LEFT: Apache boots.
RIGHT: detail from the San Gabriel Mission.

greyfriars, as they were known for the habits they wore). Aware of the need for a strong-willed and determined man to be in charge of the new missions in Alta California, the Spanish viceroy chose Majorcan-born Junípero Serra, who was already 56 years old.

Serra first arrived on July 1, 1769, with General Gaspar de Portolá to found the Mission San Diego de Alcala in California's first city. One month later Portolá and some of his men came upon a friendly group of Indians with whom they

FOUNDING MISSIONS

Junípero Serra covered several thousands of miles on foot and by mule along the Camino Real, and founded nine more missions.

Fermin de Lasuen, then aged 66, established eight more missions before his death 18 years later. (The final two missions, San Rafael and Solano – both north of the Golden Gate – were late additions in 1817 and 1823.) These 21 missions were the dominant feature of Spanish influence in California until secularized in the 1830s by Mexico's government. After this, with one or two exceptions, the missions fell into disrepair for more than half a century. In 1880, the publication of a book by Helen Hunt Jackson about govern-

exchanged trinkets. Portolá called the stream where they met El Rio de Nuestra Señora la Reina de Los Angeles de Porciuncula. But the city that would bear the same name – Los Angeles – would have to wait another 12 years before its founding.

Portolá continued on his way north, following the Indians' well-worn path along which the missions were later founded. This trail came to be known as "El Camino Real," the Royal Road. It is now more or less the highway known as California State Route 1.

After Junípero Serra's death and a one-year stint as leader of the missionaries by his biographer Francisco Palou, the redoubtable

ment mistreatment of the Indians (*A Century of Dishonor*) revived interest in restoring them. California's "mission-style" architecture dates from this period.

Today there is considerable controversy over the role of the missions and Serra's contribution. Some historians, in retrospect, see the revered priest as assisting a repressive colonial government in order to subjugate and enslave a native population.

Two years after Serra's death a visiting French sea captain wrote: "The moment an Indian allowed himself to be baptized, [from] that moment he relinquished every particle of liberty and subjected himself body and soul to a tyranny from which there was no escape. The Church then claimed as its own himself, his creed and his obedience, and enforced its claims with the strong hand of power... If he ran away and attempted to regain his native independence, he was hunted down by the soldiers, brought back and lashed into submission."

One defender of the mission system, however, has written that in 1769 "the California Indians were living in the Stone Age, raised no crops, herded no flocks and practiced no other form of food production. They ate birds, small game, fish and insects."

In the fall of 1781, six weeks before the British surrendered at Yorktown, Felipe de Neve, then governor of Spanish California, founded the new *pueblo* – or settlement – of Los Angeles. The settlers (or *vecinos pobladores*), most of them African, Indian and Hispanic in origin, named the embryo colony El Pueblo de Nuestro Señora de la Reyna de Los Angeles del Río Porciùncula – something of an extended name for a small village that would become the center of Los Angeles. Within three years the founding fathers had started construction on a church to serve as the centerpiece of the town's main plaza.

Each mission used Indian converts to set up large-scale "industries" – operations making olive oil, citrus fruit growing, cattle raising (for the hides, not the meat), and soap and tallow manufacture. San Gabriel Arcangel, founded in 1771, at the edge of an inhospitable desert some 8 miles (13 km) from the present-day downtown of Los Angeles, turned out to be one of the most agriculturally productive in the chain, and by 1811 was reaping the largest wheat crop ever recorded by any of the missions.

LEFT: Indian pictographs (and preceding photographs) from LA's Southwest Museum.
ABOVE: an Indian basket maker.

By 1790, with its population recorded as 139 residents, Los Angeles presented a very pleasing sight. Aside from a few fields cleared for planting between the town and the river, the countryside was pretty much as it had looked when General Portola had passed through 30 years previously.

The terrain was what geographers call savanna country, grassland interspersed with groves of California live oak, willow and sycamore trees beside the river and streams with marshland south of town. The Los Angeles River had been selected as a promising townsite because, unlike the desert washes, it did not dry up in summer. Here, as elsewhere, the settlers learned the hard way how fickle Californian winters can be: the placid river flooded in 1818, forcing the relocation of the town's first square.

Following a 1786 law, the governor became empowered to give land grants, grazing rights and 2,000 head of cattle to the settlers, and thus the early founders were awarded huge "ranchos" to develop. Many of them went to individuals whose names survive in the modern city. Los Feliz, Las Virgenes, the Verdugos, Sepulveda – now better known as freeway off-ramps or "surface" streets – were once huge haciendas.

California's ranchos

In some ways the ranchos followed the pattern of the missions, with scores of Indians working in the main house and tending the large herds. Any excuse was used to stage a fiesta or a *merienda* (picnic) and visitors were always welcome. Life was lived largely in the saddle, and nothing was more highly respected than a graceful steed and the consummate skill to ride it. Horsemanship was a passion among the *rancheros*, and in the early days it was not uncommon for an entire herd of cattle to change hands as the result of a horse-race.

Rodeos, where all the cattle were divided according to their rancho brand, were the high point of the year. Here the local *vaqueros*, their horses decked out in ornate saddles and twisted rawhide reins with silver mountings, would compete to see who was the best in various contests of horsemanship.

In 1821 Mexico declared itself a republic, an act that would eventually lead to the secularization of the missions in the following decade. All Spanish-born priests were ordered out of California and 8 million acres of mission land were broken up into 800 privately owned ranches and handed out like party favors by the newly installed Mexican governors.

About 25 families settled on the common land of the two nearest missions to Los Angeles, San Gabriel and San Fernando. In the course of time these areas became, in effect, the city's first suburbs.

Although also eligible for land title, converted Indians were mostly swindled out of their rights by unscrupulous new Mexican *rancheros*. Many mission Indians simply went to work for the new *ranchos*, unable to return to the way of life they had long ago left. At the height of the mission era (1805–10), 20,000 Indians were tied to the system as unpaid laborers and some were literally worked to death. Many missions had stocks, irons and whipping posts in constant use.

The missions completely disrupted the Indians' way of life by destroying their traditional hunting skills and the complicated network of tribal relationships that served as the fabric of their culture. While the Franciscans may have arrived with the purest of hearts and the highest of ideals, their intrusion into California served to set off a cultural and physical genocide of the indigenous peoples.

In 1846 a succession of disagreements along the Rio Grande prompted a war between the United States and Mexico, the ultimate prize being possession of Texas. The *Californios* put up a good resistance, considering the size of the forces sent against them.

At the Battle of San Pascual later that year the Angelenos defeated the American column led by Stephen W. Kearney, although they were evidently outnumbered in the early part of the engagement.

But this was the high-watermark of their

LIFE CAN BE CHEAP

At one point the murder rate in lawless, western-style Los Angeles reached almost one a day, and that was not even counting the Indians.

county seat, a mayor replaced the *alcalde*, and the first Protestant church was founded.

But Los Angeles was still just a small and dusty agricultural hamlet with a meager population of 1,500. An 1849 US government report states: "The town consists of an old adobe church and about a hundred adobe houses scattered about a dusty plaza and along three or four broad streets leading thereto." This was all to change within a few months with the discovery of gold at Sutter's Mill and the 1849 Gold Rush.

attempt to drive the *Yanquis* (Yankees) from California. A relief column from San Diego reached San Pascual, and by January 1847 the American flag was to be found flying over Los Angeles. The Mexican forces capitulated a few days later at Cahuenga Pass. The Treaty of Guadalupe was signed in 1848 and fixed the present borders.

The Gold Rush

Los Angeles quickly became Americanized. By 1850 the city was accorded the status of

LEFT: the Seal of California.
ABOVE: Pio Pico, governor in 1832 and 1845.

Gold has played a large part in LA history – not only the metal, which of course brought adventurers from all over the world to the goldfields in the northern part of the state and had its obvious spillover effect on the city to the south, but also the "liquid" gold of the oil discoveries which peppered the whole region with oil derricks and pretty much shaped the automobile-obsessed California culture of today.

And then, stretching the metaphor only slightly, historians talk of the "golden" oranges, a bountiful crop that did so much to familiarize out-of-staters with "the golden state" back in the 19th century. The commercial orange crop dates to the 1840s, when the earliest groves were planted near to where Union Station stands today.

Although many Angelenos ventured into the gold country, the real wealth lay in selling food to the miners. Their numbers had reached 100,000 by 1852 and food was at a premium, with potatoes going for 40 cents a pound. The wildly inflated prices finally created a market for the beef which had once been so much less valuable than the hide. Cattle prices, jumping tenfold in a matter of months, reached $40–$50 per steer. Enterprising *rancheros* employed a single trail boss and four or five *vaqueros* to drive large herds 400 miles (640 km) along the rugged trail north. At one point the animals even had to splash through the surf above San Buenaventura.

New money flowed into Los Angeles and, although the Gold Rush produced the city's first population boom, most of the newcomers were the human jetsam of the mining fields. Los Angeles quickly turned into a lawless western town where street killings, shootouts and lynchings became commonplace. In 1855 the mayor quit his position to take part in a lynching, after which he was immediately re-elected.

Vigilante law

The boom was soon over, however, and Los Angeles, like the rest of the state, fell into a severe economic depression: banks failed, and merchants went bankrupt. But Los Angeles had grown sixfold in a decade, and racial tension was high between Mexicans and whites as resentment against the Yankee domination grew. By 1860 bullfighting was banned in the city and the first baseball club was formed (at a girls' school), a sure indication of the underlying cultural shift.

Latinos suffered with the onset of the depression of the 1850s. Vigilantes drove 10,000 Mexican miners from the southern mines, aided by a cadre of eager lawyers and a handful of greedy Anglo merchants. The merchants, who had advanced credit at exorbitant interest rates, foreclosed on many of the ranchos, ensuring the impoverishment of the Mexican majority in the town. All Spanish land-grants were reviewed, and each case had to be heard five times, ensuring that legal fees were suitably exorbitant. ❑

RIGHT: detail of Downtown mural.

AFTER THE GOLD RUSH

Following a period of immense wealth, California hit some problems,
but the arrival of oranges and movie stars saved the day

The Latino population's anger over the discrimination against them soon expressed itself in violence. Many of the overland stagecoaches from San Francisco were preyed upon by roving bands of Mexican outlaws, who came to be thought of as folk heroes to the local Latino population; in one 14-year period the Wells Fargo stages were held up 313 times for a loss of $400,000.

The most famous of these *banditos*, Tiburcio Vasquez, who hid out in what is now Laurel Canyon, was captured after having been betrayed, but, once in jail, was visited by scores of well-wishers and supporters. A set of famous rocks where he held off the posse that captured him (on the road to Lancaster) now bears his name, and has been used as the classic Western shootout backdrop in hundreds of movies.

Between 1851 and 1860 the Chinese population increased enormously. Many were laborers imported to help build the transcontinental railroad, and others were drawn by the search for gold. But, after the gold ran out and the railroads had been completed, many moved down to Los Angeles where they became merchants or laborers on the local water-irrigation ditches. On October 23, 1871, touched off by the murder of a white policeman, a mob invaded Chinatown, shooting and lynching at random. By day's end, more than two dozen Chinese had been murdered, constituting one of the bloodiest incidents in the history of the state.

Agriculture – a new industry

In so many other ways, the city's fast-growing Oriental population had already made an indelible mark on this evolving polyglot society. It is impossible to visualize how the railroads could have been completed or the vast market gardens of southern Californian could have evolved without their contribution. Japanese and Chinese market gardens in particular bene-

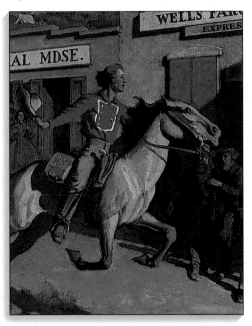

fited the city; enlarged irrigation systems between 1860 and 1880 not only helped supply the local demand for fresh vegetables but also produced a surplus of food to ship north.

Los Angeles and its environs became a major agricultural region. Sheep-raising, which had superseded the cattle culture of previous years, was badly hit when thousands of sheep died after the 1877 drought. But sheep and cattle continued to be a mainstay for the area, even as fruits and vegetables grew in importance.

Oranges, in particular, started to become the region's major crop. The fruit had been cultivated as early as 1804 at the San Gabriel Mission, and in 1841 William Wolfksill planted a 70-acre (28-hectare) orchard in what is now downtown Los Angeles. But a new seedless variety – the navel orange, brought to the area from remote Brazil – fuelled the fruit's popularity.

Within a decade oranges were being shipped to San Francisco and other parts of the state and, although in the 1870s experimental ship-

---

PRECEDING PAGES: Central Pacific Railroad, 1867.
LEFT: gold mines by artist William McIllvain.
RIGHT: Pony Express rider brings the news.

ments were being sent as far afield as St Louis (they took two months to arrive), it was the invention of the refrigerated rail car that made oranges a viable crop for shipping far afield. In 1911, promoters at San Bernardino offered 50-acre groves, already planted, for $5,000.

Orange production peaked in the 1940s. Thereafter, the demand for land for housing development – ironically much of the demand had been created by people attracted to the state by publicity about the oranges – gradually sent real estate prices too high for growers to afford. Most of the beautiful orange-crate labels, lithographed with acid-etched granite plates, date

from 1885 to the 1950s, and were intended for the gaze of the distributor rather than the consumer. Today some of these crate labels are worth as much as $2,000.

Orange groves eventually filled much of the land between Alameda Street and the Los Angeles River, where there were still some vineyards (as the name Vignes Street reveals) and vegetable gardens.

The *zanjas*, as the irrigation ditches were still called, watered the area and at the same time served the little city as a sewage disposal system. For almost a century, until 1878, a large waterwheel carrying 13 gallon buckets just north of Elysian Park raised water 36 ft (11 meters)

from the *zanja madre*, or mother ditch, to flumes that transferred it to LA's plaza.

With the realization that its growth would be limited unless it improved communications with the rest of the continent, and spurred on by the example of San Francisco, which had earlier become the terminus of the first transcontinental railroad, LA became determined to connect with the rail system. Despite competition from San Bernardino, which had easier access, the Southern Pacific Railroad was persuaded to extend a track to Los Angeles. As predicted, the boom followed.

The region's agriculture was by now its economic mainstay, with grapes and wine becoming primary products, as well as wheat, corn barley, potatoes, and other vegetables and fruits. The Southern Pacific reached Los Angeles in 1876; by 1877 New Yorkers were enjoying California oranges.

Southern Pacific had been receiving $118 for each first-class ticket, $85 for second-class, Chicago to Los Angeles. By the close of 1876 the highest fare from the Pacific Coast to Missouri was $15. Later it dropped to $10 and, for one day only, to a single dollar bill.

As a result, waves of new settlers, including European immigrants, flooded the city: 100,000 on the Southern Pacific railroad in one year. The *Santa Fe* was bringing in three to four trainloads a day. Land prices jumped tenfold as speculators preyed on the wide-eyed newcomers, drawn by idyllic pictures of boundless orange groves against gloriously clear skies.

Grand hotels were built to form the nexus of still unformed communities, and tourism boomed. "We hired the most imaginative liars we could find," said the spokesman for one real estate company. Newcomers were met off the train with music and dancing. And not to disappoint would-be buyers, speculators were not above sticking oranges on thorny Joshua trees to demonstrate the ubiquity of the fruit.

Hollywood is born

Subdividers had barely stepped off the Southern Pacific before they were establishing new towns. One of these entrepreneurs, Horace Wilcox, planned a community around his 120-acre (48-hectare) orchard at the edge of the mountains. Chamber of Commerce publicists like to think that Hollywood began with the movies, but the word first appeared in print when

Wilcox lettered it on the gate of his farm in 1886. He would have preferred the name "Fig-wood" himself, figs being the major produce of the orchard spreading around what is now the junction of Hollywood and Cahuenga boulevards, but he acceded to the choice of his young second wife, Daeida, who had acquired the name from a stranger she met on a train.

Topeka-born Wilcox, a paraplegic who relied on crutches, subdivided the property, sold lots, unsuccessfully tried to grow holly, planted pepper trees, and dreamed of a serene, temperance community like that of his native Kansas.

"And then we came," mused Cecil B. De

sequent building boom brought another wave of bricklayers, carpenters, painters and other craftsmen. Tent cities sprang up on the fringes of town. But the boom was to last only a further couple of years.

After the difficult adjustment between 1888 and 1890, Los Angeles' population stabilized at 50,000, and the city embarked on a much-needed public works program. The new cadre of City Fathers, under the inimitable Harrison Gray Otis, later founder of the *Los Angeles Times*, were determined to make Los Angeles succeed. Boosterism was in the air: streets were paved, numerous public buildings were con-

Mille years later, "and Wilcox saw his dream disappear the minute the first camera crews came in. Show people! What a disaster!"

The major factor in the visitors' interest in Los Angeles was climate. Having confirmed that, as the posters claimed, Southern California was a "Semi-Tropical Paradise," many of those who came on brief visits decided to stay. By the end of the 1880s the wooden sidewalks were crowded with people, night and day; hotel rooms were double-booked; and the sub-

structed, and many more parks were initiated.

The discovery of oil, which eventually ushered in the automobile age and turned Wilshire Boulevard – for more than a century, it had been the La Brea Trail – into a major highway, was not taken seriously until the final years of the century. At first, the black sticky stuff that oozed to the surface at the La Brea tar pits and in a handful of other spots had found use as water-proofing for boats, huts, and sometimes drinking vessels, and experiments demonstrated that this tar could be burned in furnaces as a possible replacement for wood. Mixed with sand, it also seemed to provide a good paving material. But even when distilled into a

LEFT: an orange-crate label.
ABOVE: Temple Block, in peaceful downtown Los Angeles, around 1871.

flammable spirit, it looked like a product in search of a purpose.

A former gold prospector, Edward L. Doheny, and his partner Charles Canfield put up $400 for a vacant lot near West-lake. Using a pick and shovel, then a wooden drill, they sank a pit 160 ft (49 meters) before reaching a black liquid much like the substance that seeped out of the La Brea tar pits, the kind of heavy oil that "took a week to ooze downstairs." Using a hand pump, the two men brought up seven barrels

THE DANGERS OF OIL

In 1907 Echo Park Lake, north of downtown Los Angeles, became so polluted due to oil production in the area that it caught fire and burned for three days.

bile had arrived and Earl stationed himself at the corner of Wilshire Boulevard and La Brea with a red and yellow painted farm wagon holding a large tank full of gasoline. "Fill 'er up, Earl," yelled the drivers of the new-fangled cars as they stopped to wipe their dusty windscreens. They paid 50 cents for 5 gallons.

A better way to deliver gas was needed, however. On a trip to France another Los Angeleno, Earle C. Anthony, spotted a vendor delivering his product through a hose rather than a fun-

a day. (Doheny was worth around $100 million when he died in 1935.)

Black gold

As derricks shot up throughout the city (2,300 in a five-year period) the black ooze suffered from overproduction and the price fell to 15 cents a barrel. The automobile had yet to arrive.

At about this time Arthur Freemont Gilmore arrived in Los Angeles from Illinois, and bought 256 acres of what had once been Rancho La Brea. Finding the land ideal for grazing his cows, he sank a well to find water and instead struck oil. By the time his son Earl graduated from Stanford in 1909 the automo-

nel. On his return, he set to work with his partner Don Lee and invented the gas pump.

With the coming of the railroad, the discovery of oil, and the acquisition of a reliable flow of water, Los Angeles tripled in population between 1900 and 1910, from 102,000 to over 320,000, and nearly doubled in area (compare that to today's estimate of 14 million in Greater Los Angeles). Neighboring communities, such as the little town of Hollywood, were annexed.

The city also annexed a long strip of territory that snaked south to the new port of San Pedro. This was a small fishing village that had miraculously won out as the city's harbor despite a heavy-handed campaign by Henry

Huntington; he had already completed a three-quarter-mile (1,200-meter) wharf at Santa Monica, serviced exclusively – naturally – by his own Southern Pacific Railroad.

Despite Huntington's Byzantine politicking in Washington, a party celebrating the new port's location at San Pedro was held in 1899. Twenty thousand cheering participants ate barbecued beef and 5 tons of clams. For 10 years trains continued to bring in massive quantities of rock needed for the 2-mile (3-km) long breakwater that protected the city's new deep-water port.

Los Angeles continued to swallow up separate cities to the south and the west until, by

the area turned into a wasteland as the water was drained away by the 233-mile (375-km), gravity-fed California aqueduct, a $24.5-million public works spectacular approved by Los Angeles voters in 1907.

The addition of a parallel conduit to the aqueduct (in 1941 at a cost of $200 million) and of supplemental water from Parker Dam on the Colorado River 206 miles (332 km) away, in addition to other sources, brings today's total to well over 500 million gallons a day, a supply that is threatened by drought, environmental degradation, agricultural waste, and competing users in Arizona, Colorado and Mexico.

1920, the city's population had increased to nearly 600,000.

The crucial catalyst that made possible Los Angeles' extraordinarily rapid growth was water. Rain is infrequent and unpredictable in Southern California, and the burgeoning population quickly outstripped the region's rivers and meager supply of ground water. Under the leadership of William Mulholland (see page 217), the city greedily sucked water from other parts of the state. The farmers of the fertile Owens Valley saw their water rights stolen and

LEFT: oil wells at First and Temple streets.
ABOVE: Hill and Fourth streets, in around 1905.

Getting about

Despite its size, getting about Los Angeles in the early part of the century was not a problem. In 1905 it took just 38 minutes to reach Venice Beach from the city center. LA had one of the nation's best public transport systems when the famous Red Car Line blanketed the region, spurring further decentralization as the communities sprang up along its tracks.

But, gradually, automobiles strangled the transit system, slowing it down and drawing away passengers. By raising fares to make up for declining revenues, the systems drove away even more passengers. As buses moved in, the trolley tracks were torn up, leaving blighted rights-of-way, many of which still remain in place to this day.

In the 1950s, the designers of Southern California's freeway system were forced to follow many of the trolleys' routes to the communities that had sprung up along the lines, and today's regional governments are being forced to spend billions of dollars re-establishing light railway services, in most cases on the original rights-of-way.

During World War I, Los Angeles expanded rapidly and annexed land in all directions,

OFF YOUR TROLLEY

At their peak the trolley companies, with thousands of miles of tracks and 600 Big Red Cars, served 42 towns and carried over 225,000 passengers a day.

formal elections in 1904 drunkenness was prohibited, the sale of liquor was forbidden, and a speed limit of 12 miles an hour (19 km/h) was rigidly enforced. As late as 1909 the garden town was still the sort of place where Carrie Jacobs Bonds, while staying in her suite at the Hollywood Hotel, could write her famous song *The End of a Perfect Day*.

"No dogs or actors," proclaimed a sign at the hotel before the movie folk transformed this quiet community forever.

including the now well-watered San Fernando Valley. Most of the beach communities resisted for a time, fearing that LA's "blue laws," which banned liquor sales on Sunday, would ruin their best business day of the week. But, finally, they too were absorbed into what was becoming, geographically at least, a mega-city.

Hollywood was one of these towns soon to fall within the grasp of the Los Angeles City Council. At the beginning of the 20th century it was a sedate country-club town, the perfect manifestation of Horace and Daeida Wilcox, the two paragons of propriety who had founded this serene community on 200 acres (80 hectares) of land in the late 1880s. After the town's first

Wilcox himself never actually saw paradise lost. He was dead by the 1890s and his dream was pursued by Daeida and her new husband until her death in 1914, just in time to prevent her from the ignominy of seeing what befell her precious little Hollywood.

The Nestor Film Company arrived in 1911 and shot *The Law of the Range* in the Blondeau Tavern – available, as it happened, by virtue of the Prohibition ordinances which had been passed at Daeida Wilcox's urging.

Two years later Cecil B. De Mille, Jesse Lasky, Samuel Goldwyn and Arthur Friend arrived and shot *The Squaw Man*, the first full-length feature movie made in Hollywood.

Within 18 months Lasky's studio occupied an entire city block.

In the early days it wasn't easy for film people to settle in the good neighborhoods. "They thought we were tramps," recalled screenwriter Anita Loos who, still in her teens, was earning the stupendous sum of $800 a week. "They saw themselves as being invaded and supplanted as elegant ladies and gentlemen, so they ganged up on us."

By 1910 the city had five fiercely competitive newspapers and five years later there were already 15,000 automobiles. As yet, there was still no major industry in the area except for real estate. Once here, prospective buyers – many of them suffering from ill-health and here for the rejuvenating climate – received free bus trips and free lunches to entice them to visit planned subdivisions where they might become customers.

The real estate rush

"Nearly everybody in Southern California is more or less in the real estate business," observed one writer in 1948, though it pertains to any time in the city's history. "That is, nearly everyone figures on what profit he could sell out for and what he could do with the money in some other neighborhood. The homestead handed down from generation to generation is nearly unknown."

A couple of miles south of Hollywood one enterprising young realtor, A.W. Ross, had purchased 18 acres of land on the south side of Wilshire Boulevard for $54,000. He set up his office in a white, one-story building at the corner of Ogden Drive and began to sell off lots for $100 per foot of frontage. It was hard going at first, but within just a few years retailers who had turned down corner sites for $6,000 were pleading with Ross to accept $600,000 for the same parcels of land.

Some of the suburban developments began with a bang, some with barely a whimper, but an early fanfare was no guarantee of eventual success. Tobacco heir Abbott Kinney reconstituted Venice as a sort of American residential theme park built on what had been marshes and wetlands south of Santa Monica (*see page 198*). Gondolas plied the waters of the newly con-

structed Grand Lagoon in which all the new community's canals terminated. Building lots overlooking the canals were sold for $2,700 a piece.

WHAT'S IN A NAME?

The movie and media tycoon Samuel Goldwyn changed his name from Samuel Goldfish – probably a smart move.

Kinney was determined to inject a high level of culture into his ersatz Venice, but after a $16,000 loss on his ambitious first season of opera he was forced to lowered his cultural sights.

By 1915, when Barney Oldfield won the first and only Venice Grand Prix, a 300-mile (480-km) car chase through local streets, the fledgling movie industry had discovered Los

Angeles. But Kinney's grand architectural folly eventually went bankrupt and fell on half a century of hard times. In the 1950s, Orson Welles used the then-decrepit Venice as the backdrop for *A Touch of Evil*. Most of Los Angeles agreed: the seedy area had become an enclave of beatniks and artists.

Though tidier now, Venice retains a hint of its earlier attitude of nonconformity. By contrast, Beverly Hills was sedate. When the area was named in 1907, a single house went up quietly at Crescent Drive and Lomitas. The four original streets – Park Way, Carmelita, Elevado and Lomitas – still traverse the community east to west, but the four original north–south drives

LEFT: Hollywood's first map.
RIGHT: early 20th-century steam car.

– Rodeo, Canon, Crescent and Beverly – have been supplanted with others. Original residential lots along Sunset cost around $1,000, with a 10 percent discount for cash and an additional 10 percent discount if the property was improved (i.e. built on) within six months. Only six homes were built north of Santa Monica Boulevard in the first three years.

By 1923, however, Beverly Hills had become the movie colony's bedroom and the celebrity residents were able to wage and win a campaign to preserve their exclusivity by foiling an annexation attempt by Los Angeles. Long before the advent of the Miracle Mile in the

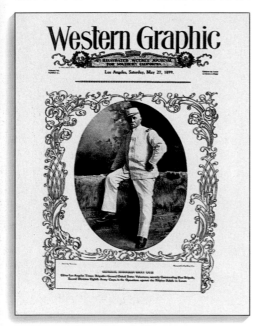

late 1920s, Wilshire Boulevard had been a prestige address: the venerable Ambassador Hotel (where Robert Kennedy was assassinated and which multi-millionaire Donald Trump later bought) was erected on pastures where future oil baron Arthur Gilmore had once grazed his cattle.

Another tycoon, Edwin Tobias Earl, who invented the refrigerated railway car, built a large mansion with some of the money he made by selling his business in 1900. Earl, who later founded the *Los Angeles Express*, saw his rival become his neighbor when Colonel Harrison Gray Otis of the *Los Angeles Times* bought a corner lot on Wilshire at Parkview.

During the 1920s, Los Angeles experienced another oil boom as wells were sunk at Huntington Beach, Signal Hill and Santa Fe Springs. Eventually a forest of derricks stretched from the mountains to the sea. Even Venice, with its canals and gondolas, became an oil city. Once again, confidence men and investors rushed to take advantage of the bonaza by selling shares in non-existent drilling companies to plenty of unwitting victims.

Apart from oil, there was little industry in Southern California. Los Angeles was famous as one of the most productive agricultural regions in the US, and agriculture would remain paramount right up until the beginning of World War II.

Despite being hampered by a 1913 law that prohibited "aliens" from owning land, Japanese truck farmers aroused the jealousy of their neighbors by becoming incredibly productive. (Their industriousness was ill rewarded after Pearl Harbor when President Roosevelt's Executive Order 9006 sent 112,000 of them, the majority American-born, to internment camps; at the end of the war, they saw their property sold for taxes and "fees.") Chinese produce brokers, along with Italians, Armenians, Slavs, and Anglos, created a very diverse ethnic agricultural mix.

The sky's the limit

Aviation, which would become a major Southern California industry, got an early start in 1883 when the country's first glider took off near San Diego. Many of the most famous names in aviation made their fortunes in Southern California: Glenn Martin, who assembled his first plane in an abandoned church in Santa Ana and flew the first seaplane to Santa Catalina; the Lockheed brothers, who started operations in Santa Barbara in 1916; and Donald W. Douglas, who fabricated his first transport in a shack behind a Santa Monica barbershop four years later.

Following in this pioneering tradition was the eccentric Howard Hughes, whose wooden *Spruce Goose*, the world's largest cargo plane, made its only flight in Los Angeles Harbor in the late 1940s. A major tourist attraction, the giant plane was long berthed in Long Beach next to the *Queen Mary*, which was living out its old age as a floating hotel. ❏

LEFT: Colonel Harrison Gray Otis, editor of the *Los Angeles Times*.
RIGHT: California welcomed early aviation pioneers.

FROM THE MOVIES TO THE MODERN AGE

The first local movie was made on a downtown rooftop. Now Los Angeles – and in particular Hollywood – has become the world center of filmmaking

Besides oranges, oil and good weather, Los Angeles became synonymous during the 1920s as the center of the film industry. Although the first California movie was made on a downtown rooftop and movie-making spread east and south before the studios settled temporarily on what is now Glendale Boulevard, many early westerns were shot in the hills of Griffith Park, and in many of the surviving one-reelers, such as those featuring the Keystone Kops and Laurel and Hardy, the topology of Silverlake is still recognizable. By 1915 Hollywood procured its reputation as the home of film studios and film production. Four years later it was turning out 80 percent of the world's feature films.

D. W. Griffith, the film-directing titan, had been a stage actor before he started directing in 1907. He arrived in Los Angeles in 1908, with Mack Sennett and a 16-year-old Mary Pickford among his retinue, around the time that the first of what would be over 10,000 five-cent peep shows began opening in store fronts around the country.

Before *Birth of a Nation* and *Intolerance,* the epic motion pictures that made his reputation, Griffith directed 142 one-reelers for Biograph, gradually developing the technique – long shot/medium shot/close-up sequence – that is the foundation of filmmaking. Little credit has been given to his chief cameraman Billy Bitzer, who crawled along the ground under fire to film the battle scenes in *Birth of a Nation* and ascended in a balloon for the overhead shots in *Intolerance.*

By the end of 1919, Cecil B. De Mille, Charlie Chaplin and W. C. Fields were already living in splendid homes on a street now grandly called De Mille Drive. But they had all been preceded in the neighborhood by Mack Sennett, at whose Glendale Boulevard studio the Keystone Company had ground out 140 one-reelers in the year before World War I, making stars out of Mabel Normand, Ben Turpin,

JESSE L. LASKY présente une production DE GEORGE MELFORD LE CHEIK cénario de MONTE M. KATTERJOHN l'après la nouvelle de E. M. HULL avec AGNÈS AYRES & RUDOLPH VALENTINO

Fatty Arbuckle, Gloria Swanson and the famous Keystone Kops.

Here, Mabel Normand tossed the first custard pie and Chaplin developed the tramp character who was eventually to earn him $10,000 a week. Hollywood soon turned into a new and chaotic Babylon. "It was a world," wrote one observer, "in which everybody was caught with their pants down."

Hollywood Babylon

Over the years, many of Hollywood's citizens were caught in just such compromising positions. Even in the early days Hollywood produced scandals as well as movies: Olive

---

PRECEDING PAGES: Dolores del Rio, one of the first Hollywood film stars.
LEFT: Gloria Swanson in *Sunset Boulevard.*
RIGHT: French poster of Valentino's *The Sheik.*

Thomas, Mrs Jack Pickford, a heroin addict, a suicide, 1920; Roscoe "Fatty" Arbuckle, ruined after an accusation of rape – he was later acquitted – which ended a starlet's life in 1921; William Desmond Taylor, mysteriously murdered in 1922; Wallace Reid, a fatal victim of morphine addiction; Charlie Chaplin, satyr; romantic lover Rudolph Valentino, tagged as a homosexual; Eric von Stroheim, orgiast; Marie Provost, killed by her own dogs; Mary Astor, self-confessed adulterer; Cheryl Crane, Lana Turner's daughter, killer; and countless other drunks, drug addicts and suicides right to the present day.

The first round of Hollywood scandals prompted Adolph Zukor, William Fox, Sam Goldwyn and the other moguls to look for a censor to protect filmdom's image. They settled on Will Hays, who had been Republican Party chairman in 1920.

The next year, Hays had to deal with the murder of Paramount director William Desmond Taylor, who was shot in his Westlake apartment. Among the suspects were Mabel Normand, Mary Miles Minter, and Minter's mother, each of whom had been Taylor's lover. After *Birth of a Nation* star Wallace Reid's death at 33 the following year, Hays insisted on morality clauses in future contracts and the censoring of scripts.

Hollywood wasn't big enough for the movie industry – it spilled over into Carl Laemmle's Universal City (where a producer could rent a western town, a mansion, or a farm), Burbank, Century City and Culver City. By the mid-1920s, the movie industry employed more than 20,000 people, who between them took home $1.5 million weekly in salaries.

One big speakeasy

Los Angeles did not take the arrival of Prohibition on January 16, 1920, very seriously. Close proximity to the Mexican border and a sprawling coastline made it easy for small ships to land liquor at Malibu and other secluded beaches, and a fair amount of homemade alcohol was manufactured in the city itself. With its long tradition of pre-Prohibition unlicensed liquor parlors, known as "blind-pigs," speakeasies were not a radical step for the locals to accept. In fact, several places downtown on Spring Street featured alcohol and gambling. They were seldom raided by police.

Tony Cornero, who became one of the biggest bootleggers along the coast, ran a lumber schooner that could handle 7,000 cases of liquor. He would load up in Vancouver with papers showing his destination as Mexico or Central America. As one of the industry's top wholesalers, he would park off the coast. His distributors, buying "over the rail," would evade customs with the 1920s' equivalent of high-speed cigarette boats. Distributors, police, customs agents and hijackers competed with each other for the cargoes, so everyone was armed to the teeth. Sometimes a load would be hijacked several times on its journey between the schooner and the speakeasy.

By 1920, *The New York Times* reported that California was wide open to the whims of gangsters and racketeers: "Alcohol is cheap and plentiful; hijacking is a favorite outdoor sport; gang murders are becoming episodical; and the police, fettered by political interference, espionage and other harassments, seem to be helpless." Fifty federal agents policed 198,000 sq. miles (513,000 sq. km) of Southern California landscape, with a population of 2.3 million. They were also expected to patrol 539 miles of coastline and 500 miles (800 km) along the Mexican border. They were supposed to discover alcohol in ships whose interiors had been

effect has there been any difficulty here about securing whatever in the liquor line that may be desired by anybody."

California's image as a land of plenty served as a magnet throughout the 1930s for the troubled Dust Bowl farmers of Oklahoma, Arkansas, Missouri, and northern Texas. By 1940, 365,000 "Okies" had limped westward in caravans of overloaded automobiles. Just as in many parts of the city today, three generations of a family would eat, sleep and live for months in a car or – if they were lucky – a garage.

The California boom that began in 1940 was fueled by wars: hot (World War II), lukewarm

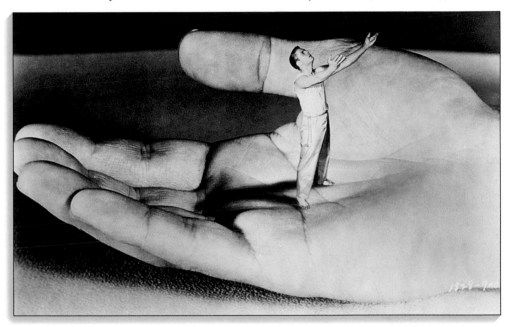

thickly covered with red carpeting to absorb odors, and in subterranean passages of canyons and farms where it was hidden. In addition, they had to regulate wineries where the legal sacramental wines were made, and to visit the hundreds of bogus congregations that sprang up to buy the blessed vintages (one congregation grew to 1,200 members in a single year).

Los Angeles became known as a great town for conventions. According to *The New York Times*, "At no time since Prohibition went into

LEFT: Stan Laurel and Oliver Hardy pose in the Hollywood Wax Museum.
ABOVE: still from *The Incredible Shrinking Man.*

(Korea and Vietnam), and Cold. The taxes on the $100 billion defense that poured into the state between 1940 and 1970 resulted in a system of highways, schools, housing, agriculture, and social welfare that was second to none, contributing to an increase in population of over 39 million during the same 30 years. In 1941, contracts between the federal government and the California Institute of Technology alone totaled $83 million. Even with 750,000 Californians in uniform, the number of wage earners in the state increased by nearly a million.

A great many of the war dollars raining down from Washington landed on Henry J. Kaiser, who built warships in such numbers that he was dubbed "Sir Launchalot." When they got up to speed, the Lockheed and North American factories were producing planes in a non-stoppable stream at twice the rate Roosevelt had called for in 1940.

Racism and riots

Despite wartime propaganda and post-war romanticizing, the home market was not all wine and roses and Rosie the Riveter. There was rationing of gasoline, tires, sugar and meat, which created a raging black market. Prejudice against women and blacks was rampant in the unions, industry and the military; in LA, rioting

With the explosion in population came problems: further water shortages, declining services, environmental crises, and racial strife. The black population exploded tenfold after 1940, and blacks were plagued by discriminatory housing and employment restrictions that were familiar elsewhere.

On a sweltering summer evening in 1965, the Watts ghetto in south-central Los Angeles erupted in widespread rioting. By the time the National Guard restored order six days later, $40-million worth of damage had been caused by vandalism, looting and fire, 4,000 people had been arrested and 34 were dead.

soldiers and sailors attacked Mexican-American "zoot-suiters." The family in particular, and moral precepts in general, were endangered by social and economic disruption.

After the war, soldiers returning from the Pacific and workers who had been brought in to staff the war factories stayed on, creating pressure for housing that resulted in another land boom. Schools and libraries, post offices and police stations, freeways and airports were constructed to service the hundreds of square miles of housing developments that sprang up to take care of them. The $1.75 billion Feather River project brought more much-needed water into the Southern California region.

Later, in the 1960s busing to achieve integration drove a further wedge between the black and white communities. At UCLA, two members of the Black Panthers were killed during demonstrations over the future of the Black Studies program.

Three years later, in his controversial book *The Last Days of the Late, Great State of California*, Curt Gentry would quote one disenchanted black: "Everywhere they say, 'Go to California! California's the great pot of gold at the end of the rainbow!' Well now we're here in California and there ain't no place else to go and the only pot I see's the kind they peddle at Sixth and Avalon."

In 1963, California became the most populous state in the Union, and Southern California continued to be the most populous region in the state. The city of Los Angeles has more than 3 million residents; the population of Los Angeles County is heading past 10 million. Orange and San Bernardino counties account for another 3½ million. San Diego is already well over 2 million and counting.

This may be too many people. From 1910 to the 1950s, Southern California led the nation in agricultural production. But water shortages, environmental degradation and over-development have cut into the agricultural business.

center and the country's busiest port, the needs of its residents are going unaddressed. As its minority populations, especially Latins and Asians, increase, the city presides over a crumbling infrastructure of overburdened roads, schools, hospitals, and social services.

Los Angelenos, already claiming with a sense of irony, that their "seasons" consisted of floods, fires and earthquakes, added a fourth – "riots" – after a substantial part of the black community exploded in 1992. The trouble flared following the beating of a black motorist, Rodney King, by officers of the Los Angeles Police Department, after he had been stopped

Thirty-one thousand acres of orange groves alone fell before the bulldozers between 1950 and 1965. Severe controls on air pollutants are expected to cost billions over the next decade. In 1990, Los Angeles was forced to impose water rationing for the first time.

The sad truth is that, although it has a growing class of super-rich entertainment moguls and merchants involved in foreign trade, Los Angeles is no longer the land of milk and honey. Despite the fact that it is the capital city of the Pacific Rim, with a burgeoning financial

for speeding. The police action had been caught on videotape and was screened endlessly on TV worldwide. Three years later the black and white communities were polarized again over the trial of O. J. Simpson, a black football star who was tried and acquitted of the murder of his wife and her male friend.

Despite a school population that is increasing by 15,000 students a year, a mere handful of schools have been built in Los Angeles since the 1970s. And lack of leadership has conspired to create one of the tightest, most segregated and most expensive housing markets, and to make Los Angeles home to more homeless people than any other US city. ❑

LEFT: bandleader Jack Conrad's space bus.
ABOVE: a movie set being constructed.

CALIFORNIA DREAMIN':
THE INVENTIVE CITY

Where the Last Frontier meets the Pacific Rim,
cultures and styles kill conformity. As entrepreneurs
say: "If I can make it here, I'll make it anywhere..."

Sorry, New York – you're not even in the top four of invention capitals in the US, judging by the average number of patent applications received each year by the Patent Office. Not that LA can make claim to the top spot – that goes to San Jose, where the line of patent attorneys runs out the door.

But Los Angeles can lay claim to the title of Trend Capital, where even if it wasn't born here, it moved here to become famous. Since the California Gold Rush days dreamers have come through LA looking for anything to hitch their dream to – real or flaky.

SUNSHINE COMMERCE

LA sunshine has incubated many an idea and entrepreneur – the warmth created a natural spawning ground for the health and fitness revolutions; the movie industry fled its New Jersey roots and sprouted in the year-round sunny locations of LA; and aviation pioneers found the mild weather ideal for empire-building.

Not everything invented in LA was weather driven (like the Zamboni ice-rink machine), and many products, if not actually invented in LA, were at least exploited here, and became synonymous with LA innovation.

Fads. Trends. Celebrity. The friction of these intangibles often heats up into a hot product – some catch fire around the world, and some go down in flames. Here are a few that were once dreams, but are still burning bright.

△ **THE NET**
In 1969, UCLA was the first node on the ARPANET, which was the predecessor to the Internet.

◁ **THE BIKINI**
The bikini was introduced by French designer Louis Reard in 1946. The swimwear was banned in much of Europe, and it was the 1960 Hollywood *Beach Party* films that finally made the bikini acceptable.

BARBIE, WOMAN OF THE WORLD

△ **HEALTHY EATING**
LA has originated such staples as the oxygen bar, the smoothie, herbal tea baths, wheat grass cocktails, and the Pritikin diet.

▽ **DETROIT WEST**
Tail-fins and convertibles were just a couple of California aftermarket creations that Detroit picked up on.

▷ **THE SPACE SHUTTLE**
Aviation's deep roots in Los Angeles are evident in this program awarded by NASA to Rockwell International.

◁ **ROLLERBLADES**
Inventor Scott Olson of Minnesota says, "When I first started selling Rollerblades, the sport shops laughed me out of their stores, but packing up and moving to California made it more maiinstream."

LA born and raised, Barbie has become an international star. She even has her own Hall of Fame. Her "management" company, the El Segundo Mattel toy company say, "in every second of every day, two Barbie dolls are sold somewhere in the world." . Some models trade for thousands of dollars.

It all started when Ruth Handler, partner in Mattel, noticed her daughter Barbara playing with dolls and imagining them in grown-up roles. Ruth spotted the need for a doll that would inspire little girls to think about what they wanted to be when they grew up. The all-male executive team at Mattel said it would be too expensive to produce. Ruth ignored them and Barbie made her debut at the 1959 Toy Fair in New York. Some felt her black-and-white swimsuit was "scary, sleazy, spellbinding." However, a few felt she had a "fresh face, with fashions to fit a girl's daydreams."

Most importantly, Barbie earns an average of $1.5 billion a year for Mattel, has a longtime, stable boyfriend, and never ends up in the tabloids.

THERE'S NO BUSINESS BUT SHOW BUSINESS

You can't escape it. Just think of the number of mundane businesses in LA which include the words "star" or "celebrity" in their names

The unofficial motto of the University of Southern California School of Cinema and Television is "Reality Ends Here." And that is the inscription that once hung above the entrance of the school famous for launching such hot filmmakers as George *(Star Wars)* Lucas and Steven *(Jurassic Park)* Spielberg into superstar orbit. It was enough to attract eager, young neophytes from all over the country with dizzying notions of fame, fortune and multi-picture deals swirling unrealistically in their starstruck heads.

It might be a good idea for Los Angeles County to post the same warning, "Reality Ends Here," at the County line. Once you step across the border, no matter how well screwed on your head may be, this place is going to infect you if you're at all smitten by the entertainment bug. The All-American myth, that any young man or woman can pull themselves up by the bootstraps and become a success, automatically seems to take on stellar qualities in the land of the lotus. All types of people – chefs, accountants, dog trainers, caterers – seek that five-pointed distinction that comes from being a star. And all with varying degrees of seriousness and success, admittedly.

Even those so new to Hollywood they're applying for a driver's license will sense the pervasiveness of this particular mania. The Department of Motor Vehicles in Hollywood, its walls bedecked with autographed pictures of famous license plates, prides itself on its photographic savvy.

While a driver's license may not count for much on the vanity scale, ownership of a small business can allow you to be a star in your own right. All you need do is look in the West Los Angeles phone book, for example,

under "Star" or "Celebrity" and you'll find: Star Camera, Star Deli and Donut Show, Star Kosher Meat Market, Star Liquors, Star Nails and Hair No. 2, Star Strip Theater, Celebrity Airport Livery, Celebrity Hot Dog, Celebrity

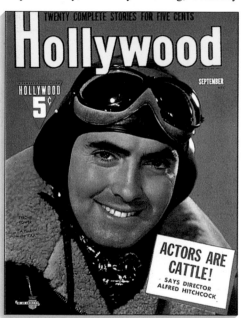

Look-A-Likes, Celebrity Dry Cleaners, Celebrity Sound, etc., etc., etc.

Looney notoriety

There are, of course, stars created from merely making TV commercials. Local yokel car dealers, mainly, have achieved a level of loony notoriety for themselves. Cal Worthington, a resident of Long Beach, regularly appeared on nighttime TV with his dog Spot, who is always a different animal, but never a dog. A garrulous fellow named Ralph Williams, another car dealer celeb, was long a source of jest in talk show host Johnny Carson's late-night monologues.

PRECEDING PAGES: stars of yesterday lined up for their portrait; stars of today are cut out for fame.
LEFT: the Del Rubio singers, on their shared bed.
RIGHT: the Hollywood hunk smolders happily.

"When you go out to even the most obscure mom-and-pop grocery store to ask if you can use the store to shoot a TV or movie location, they're likely to pull out a contract agreement from under the till," notes *The Hollywood Reporter*'s Robert Osborne.

"They are all so steeped in it," says Osborne, who has covered Hollywood, its stars and folklore for more than a decade for the entertainment industry's trade paper. "Even the most normal and well-adjusted people can get kind of carried away by it all."

Among the more notorious and well-known Hollywood spots to incorporate a star package

into its line is lingerie shop Frederick's of Hollywood. Now sporting a bra museum, Frederick's boasts the unmentionables of such mentionables as Cher, Mae West, Madonna, Diana Ross, and even Lassie's mom, June Lockhart.

"The movie business itself is a caste system," says Osborne. "It's important what car you drive, what you wear, what seat you get at the restaurant Spago, if you're trying to put together a multi-million dollar deal. That kind of thing is very important and taken very seriously. If you're going to get a 'go' on that picture, those kinds of perceptions are very important, and it carries over into the way people think out here."

Indeed, if "reality ends here," what or who is the barometer of this reality? Why do otherwise normal people get caught up in this? Why? Because this is a one-factory town: the Entertainment Industry is simply referred to in LA as "the industry."

The most important man in town stands at a mere 13½ inches (34 cm) tall. He is bald and owns not a stitch of Armani. But despite his complete lack of stature, most people are in awe of him. That is because he is Oscar, the gold statuette awarded annually by the Academy of Motion Picture Arts and Sciences for great, "artistic" achievement.

Being star-conscious

In this town where status and recognition often substitute for actual power, and where images are created, cultivated and carved into the public's mind, it's hard not to be star-conscious. Even the generally staid *Los Angeles Times* always leads its Sunday real estate section with a column called "Hot Property," accompanied by a color photograph of the hottest star who has sold his or her home or bought a new one, usually to tear down and replace with an even more opulent and bigger one. And at least once or twice a month month, the *Los Angeles Times*' Calendar section will carry a cover story about some star's new contract, health-food philosophy, beef with Hollywood, new designer dress, or about something similarly abstruse and esoteric.

As often as not, the *Times* focus is on a really big name, but sometimes even relatively minor TV stars receive coverage, people who are now essentially doing nothing except moving from one house to another.

But in this image-conscious area, even doing nothing can be made to appear as if it is something. Thanks to Hollywood publicists, stars and their antics do not have to be hard news. They don't even have to be soft news. Publicists create an awareness – more of a whiff and essence, something sprayed unceasingly into the heavy, star-scented Los Angeles air.

FAME AT LAST

An arrest, a sojourn at the Betty Ford alcoholism clinic or a divorce will keep one's name in the public eye almost indefinitely.

It may seem immodest and downright arrogant to folks in Middle America that people in Hollywood actually hire people to think of ways to get their names into the paper or promoted on television, but the fact is that every actor or actress who's had 15 minutes of fame can bask in it practically forever.

awash in movie ads: a menacing and squinting Clint Eastwood; a manic Jack Nicholson smile; a toothpaste commercial Tom Cruise; or the recumbent pink-spandexed Angelyne.

Who's that? Angelyne is a self-promoting, busty, Jayne Mansfield type who took out a billboard extolling her availability. "Call Angelyne" is the admonition, and presumably people do, even though there is nothing to indicate that Angelyne has ever performed any other role than the one you are seeing. It is entirely possible, however, that she

Somehow, time hasn't changed the Hollywood image of neon, pink Cadillacs, red lipstick, white tuxedoes, roaring lions and laconic heroes riding into the sunset. Reality, however, is that such a Hollywood exists only on the billboards of Sunset Boulevard. In Sunset Boulevard's teeming mid-section – the 7000 to 9000 blocks, called "the Strip" – the Boulevard is

LEFT: the all-important Oscar.
ABOVE: *Revenge of the Creature*, a classic early Hollywood creation.

has achieved some measure of success as a traffic hazard, and it is a fact she now charges for photographs and interviews. For a close-up of Angelyne in her full glory, turn to the photograph on page 166.

Stars on the ground

Stars are not just in the phone book and on billboards, but also underfoot. Hollywood's Walk of Fame, on Hollywood Boulevard and some connecting streets like Vine Street, is renowned. It's the one spot that tourists flock to, often bending over fully to take photos. While it's easy to find stars for Orson Welles, Lawrence Welk, Humphrey Bogart and Gene Autry (he's on the Walk four times for radio, TV, music and the movies) underfoot on the Walk of Fame, other stars are noticeably absent. Don't expect to step on Paul Newman or Dustin Hoffman. Like so many other awards, recognition here is largely self-anointed. Stars are not selected so much as endorsed – once, that is, their publicists have made overtures to a special committee headed by Hollywood's "honorary mayor", Johnny Grant.

Meeting several times a year to consider applications for the Walk of Fame, which anyone can submit, the committee considers professional accomplishment and longevity, even

ally one star on the boulevard, Maurice Diller, who seems unknown to everybody. There's some speculation that it was a mistake and the inscription actually should read Mauritz Stiller, the Russian-Swedish director who brought Greta Garbo to Hollywood and who died there in 1928. But because of the misspelling nobody knows for sure.

"There are other stars, the Max Factor star, for instance, where the honor reflects more cooperation with the Chamber of Commerce than stardom," says Wells. "It's true that Max Factor makeup was instrumental in movies and that a lot of stars used it, but it's also true that

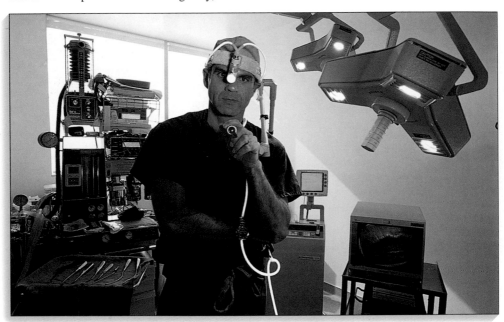

community service. In return, the honoree, if still alive, must agree to show up at the actual star-installation ceremony and pay a fee of around $5,000.

One who has heeded the New Testament message "Ask and ye shall receive" and later found his star shining brightly on the Walk is evangelist Billy Graham. "There was a constant push from Billy Graham's people. They were relentless. Eventually, he got his star and it was justified that he was a TV personality of sorts," says Therese L. Wells, a former publicist for the Chamber of Commerce's Walk of Fame.

"It sometimes seems the smaller the star, the bigger the push," notes Wells. "There is actu-

the Max Factor company has been very active with the Hollywood Chamber of Commerce and its activities."

Out-of-town visitors who arrive expecting to see the glamorous Hollywood of Fred Astaire and Cary Grant movies are in for a rude surprise. Despite the Hollywood Chamber of Commerce's ongoing refurbishment, Hollywood Boulevard is not exactly a black-tie area or even – after dark, at least – a place to stroll with the family. In fact, if you're in search of the mindless, the drifters, and some of the most wacked-out people in the world, Hollywood Boulevard on a Saturday night is on a par with any big-city bus station.

Los Angeles has even spawned such lesser walks of fame as the Avenue of Athletes (Silverlake), the Walk of Western Stars (Newhall), the Rock Walk (Hollywood) and the Orange County Walk of Stars (Anaheim).

Real heart

Despite the somewhat phony self-promotion and dubious shine to many entities, there is a real heart that beats beneath modern Hollywood's mean streets where, according to legend, everybody is only too willing to step on everybody else.

> ### FIRST IMPRESSIONS
>
> When Charlie Chaplin arrived in LA, aged 21, he was not impressed: "an ugly city, hot and oppressive, and the people looked sallow and anemic."

Desi avoided the party scene and that they never told their jokes to industry people. They invented this mythical guy in Nebraska and directed their jokes at him. These were the people they were trying to entertain, not the Beverly Hills cocktail crowd."

Today's corporate/conglomerate/multi-national movie and TV industry is vastly different from the old studio days. So different, in fact, that some people think that "the real" Hollywood no longer exists.

"The movie industry is loaded with honest, down-to-earth people who make it all work, but you don't hear about them," *The Hollywood Reporter's* Osborne says. "Many of the ones who have endured seem to have a place somewhere else, another residence in the mountains somewhere, like Clint Eastwood or Robert Redford.

"The ones who stay close get caught up in it too much and lose their creative bearings," Osborne notes. "Lucille Ball told me she and

LEFT: plastic surgeons are stars, too.
ABOVE: Betty Boop, the famous cartoon character, holds court at Universal Studios.

Tycoons to lawyers

The biggest changes have occurred at the top of the executive ladder, where such immigrant empire builders as Louis B. Mayer, Samuel Goldwyn, Harry Cohn, Jack Warner and Darryl M. Zanuck have been succeeded by a generation of lawyers, MBAs and powerful agents. Walk into a studio with Jack Nicholson's name on a contract and a copy of your local phone book as the script and you're talking "bankable project." Admittedly the current moneyman may suggest a car chase or two, a big gun shootout and some "tasteful" sex, but generally speaking they will not interfere very much with the "integrity" of your project.

"Right now, it's only a notion. But I think I can get money to make it into a concept and later turn it into an idea," ran a line of Beverly Hills party talk in Woody Allen's *Annie Hall*. Here, in these structured times, there is little of the kind of analysis that Columbia boss Harry Cohn was talking about half a century ago when he said his butt itched – which meant that for him, the movie he was viewing wasn't working. Today's lawyers seemingly have less sensitive asses, and instead twitch to graphs and demographics to select their projects.

The studios themselves have hopscotched all over the place, with new owners and new premises, faster than a director can yell "Cut." For instance, Columbia Studios started out in Hollywood, moved to Burbank and then spent time in Culver City at the once-renowned MGM lot, overseen from across the street by MGM/ UA's huge glass office complex, which looks like a modern European train station. MGM, in the mid-1990s, had no less than three owners in two years, one of them being the state bank of France.

Naturally, the wonderful world of showbiz is not totally populated by stars, even if stardom might be everyone's aspiration, including those who support the dreams: the legion of

THE ULTIMATE MOVIE

Sunset Boulevard, which portrayed the pathos of a former silent superstar in her declining years in a broken-down Hollywood mansion, struck a chord with critics as the ultimate inside-Hollywood movie.

It won three Oscars, but not everyone was pleased with the way the industry was depicted. "You bastard," shouted an angry Louis B. Mayer to Billy Wilder, the director, at a preview screening. "You have disgraced the industry that made and fed you. You should be tarred and feathered and run out of Hollywood." Andrew Lloyd Webber's success with a musical version 50 years later demonstrated the timelessness of the story.

photocopiers, résumé typists, answering service operators, messengers, script readers and gofers of every variety.

There are divorce lawyers, nutritionists, and entertainment lawyers (law students call it "punk law"), as well as publicists, personal managers, personal trainers, swamis and psychics. Many of these people, if not directly looking for a break, know how to take advantage of opportunities that might in time present themselves.

Macho movie star Steven *(Hard to Kill)* Seagal, for example, got the attention of the industry by serving as a personal trainer to one of the town's top agents.

Always "on"

Waiters, waitresses and that guy who came to deliver balloons for your office party are always "on." Sometimes it seems that half the local populace is auditioning and the other half is trying to write a script about it all. And if they don't make it to the podium of the Dorothy Chandler Pavilion to accept an Oscar or land a walk-on part in a soap opera, they somehow manage to display their thespian skills in some other way. One former entertainer offers his servic-

chance of actually getting a speaking part, and a 1-in-15 chance of getting a walk-on. And I'm talking only about the talented, qualified people. It's the old Catch-22 situation, you can't get a union card without a part and you can't get a part without a union card."

Still, hardly any of the young hopefuls fail to keep up with the industry production charts in the trade papers – *The Hollywood Reporter, Daily Variety* – to see what movies are being shot and when and where.

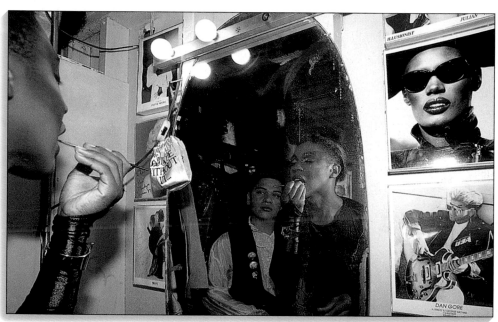

es as a Shakespeare impersonator, showing up with a rose, a hand-penned sonnet and the fragrant gift of romance in a routine imaginatively entitled Bard-O-Gram.

But even for those strip-a-grammers, muscle pumpers, and aerobics queens, just how easy is it to get that first break?

"It's extremely difficult," says James Ulmer, who has covered the local labor scene for *The Hollywood Reporter*. "Just off the top of my head, I'd say they've got about a 1-in-50

This interest extends to the general public as well. Watching a movie or television show getting made is not difficult. For 10 years Jack Weinberg, a former attorney, ran a service called Hollywood on Location which listed the shows that were shooting on the city streets on any given day.

"Let's face it," Weinberg said, "everybody who comes out here, no matter how sophisticated they are, wants to see stars. When Queen Elizabeth visited they didn't give her a dinner at the Jet Propulsion Lab; they held it at 20th Century-Fox."

Today's visitors can get a similar (free) list by calling in at the Film & Video Permit Office,

LEFT: Clark Gable's grandchildren with their mother.
ABOVE: female impersonators performing at the Cage aux Folles nightclub.

6922 Hollywood Boulevard, which prints up a daily list of the average of 50 productions that are being shot on LA streets most days of the week.

Star-gazing spots

Restaurants are still the most likely places to see the few stars who are likely to make unscheduled public appearances. Movieland's equivalent of New York's erstwhile Algonquin Round Table is Musso & Frank's Grill on Hollywood Boulevard, just across from the Pussycat Theater *(see page 163)*. It's an old-style gathering place with wooden booths, white

tablecloths, brash yet gentlemanly waiters and a no-nonsense menu that has barely changed since the restaurant opened in 1919. Ernest Hemingway, Faulkner, Scott Fitzgerald and Nathanael West all sought solace here, sipping martinis and grousing about how they were treated by philistine producers.

The Polo Lounge at the Beverly Hills Hotel remains the all-round best bet for star gazing. It epitomizes both the old Hollywood and the current version where power breakfasts of oat bran, yogurt and wheat toast reflect today's fitness-crazed entertainment types. Until he sold it to the Sultan of Brunei, immensely rich oilman Marvin Davis owned the Beverly Hills

Hotel. He dabbles in film studios (he once owned Fox) and rumors constantly persist that he will pounce on another studio. Davis owns the Carnegie Deli, one of the Beverly Hills in-spots, where customers while away their waiting time by voting for a picture or actor in a number of movie categories such as Turkey of the Decade, the Overall Wurst of the Year, Cheesecake of the Year, Big Baloney (as in jerk) of the Year, Tongue of the Year (who talked the most and said the least) and Borscht of the Year (the film or TV person who left them the coldest).

Other celebrity hangouts include Le Bistro, Mr Chow's Restaurant, Cine Bar and Grill, The Columbia Bar and Grill, Spago, L'Ermitage, Morton's, Trump and, in Beverly Hills, Trader Vic's and the Ivy.

Sports and showbiz

The Los Angeles sports scene is also full of celebrities. Athletic heroes such as Magic Johnson enticed moviedom's royalty to the Great Western Forum where the Lakers basketball team and the Kings ice-hockey team played (they now play at the Staples Center). The most famous Laker fan is Jack Nicholson, but Dyan Cannon and Michael Douglas can also be seen sitting at or near courtside. These star-studded crowds have not gone unnoticed either. Aware of the Forum's industry-heavy audience, the Illinois Film Commission shrewdly bought an eye-catching advertisement in the stadium extolling the virtues of filming in their state.

During the six-year tenure of peerless Wayne Gretzky with the previously neglected Los Angeles Kings (he left in 1996), hockey attendance skyrocketed. The Kings' fans include Sylvester Stallone, Kevin Costner, Rob Lowe, Peter (*Columbo*) Falk and Tom Hanks.

And the office of Dodgers' manager Tommy Lasorda is plastered with the mugs of such fans as Frank Sinatra and Don Rickles. Sports and showbiz are often one and the same, and crossover is not infrequent. The University of Southern California's Marion Morrison was a stand-in offensive linesman for the Trojans long before he became the somewhat more famous John Wayne.

Wayne's teammate, silent screenstar Ward Bond, also made it big on the Hollywood scene. USC's more recent crop of celluloid heart-throbs includes Tom Selleck, a volleyball and basketball star Trojan; the late Michael Landon, who threw the javelin; and once-famous, but now of course notorious, sportsman, announcer and star court witness, O. J. Simpson.

The University of California (USC), however, does not have the collegiate monopoly on Los Angeles stars. The University of California, Los Angeles (UCLA) and its Bruins have boasted Mike *(Hill Street Blues)* Warren on its basketball team and Mark ("Sexiest Man in America") Harmon on its football team. In this town, even animals can

HUMBLE BEGINNINGS

The inventor of the moving picture was the eccentrically named Englishman Eadweard Muybridge, who took five years to film a horse galloping in 1877.

one tour line has gone a step farther: "See the Stars' Last Stops," beckons the promo flyer of the Grave Line Tours, which specializes in the macabre sites of (usually sudden) death. See the motel where Janis Joplin overdosed on drugs; the hotel where John Belushi met a similar fate; the spot where a famous costume designer leaped from her hotel room, only to die unnoticed in the canvas awning above the sidewalk.

Oh, there's lots to do here in the Big Orange, affectionately nicknamed to chime with New

become stars. Rin Tin Tin and Lassie types play supporting roles in today's "buddy" flicks and they, too, get the red-carpet treatment. If you're a couch potato, you've probably caught *Dogs of the Rich and Famous* on the tube. In this show, stars show up with their special canine sidekicks.

There's always some new wrinkle in the search for stars. While the often-obsolete maps to star homes are still a draw for some visitors,

York's Big Apple monicker. And as innocent as you may be on arrival, if you hang around long enough, you may find yourself "taking a meeting," "doing lunch," or "pacting a pic." You'll know which films have great "b.o." (that's "box office" to you and me) and – the keenest test of all – you'll even understand the headlines in *Daily Variety*. "Stix nix hix pix." If that makes sense to you, you're in with a chance, babe.

So, once you're up to snuff, there's one last thing you just have to do before you leave: apply to the Hollywood Chamber of Commerce to see if you, too, can get your very own sidewalk star. ❏

LEFT: the murder trial of O.J. Simpson became a television drama on news bulletins all over the world.
ABOVE: Tom Cruise and Nicole Kidman, today's golden Hollywood couple.

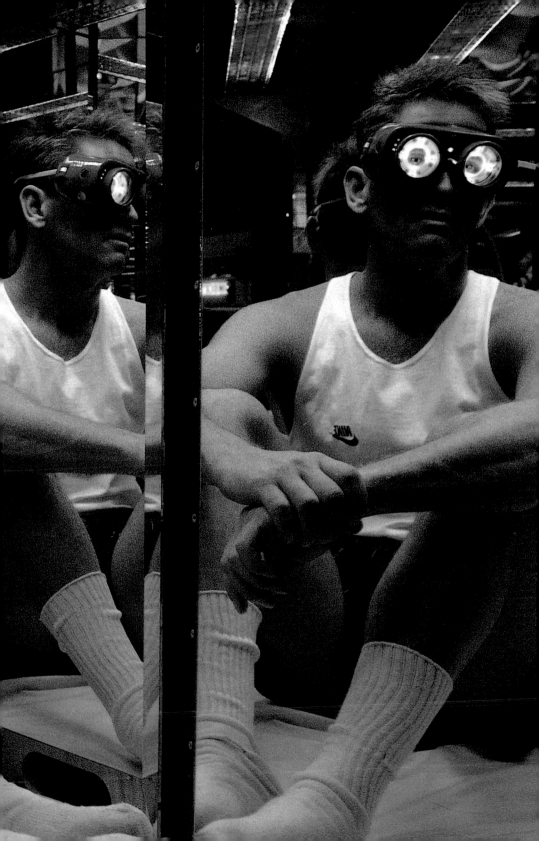

ALTERNATIVE ALTARS

Wacky, way off beat, weird – call it what you will –
the alternative is celebrated in the land of milk and honey

You never know where you'll find a church or house of worship in Los Angeles. The city has a reputation for openness towards the unconventional and is often considered one of the nation's centers of offbeat religions, sects, cults and alternative altars.

Tolerance has its limits, however, as Mary Ellen Tracy discovered in 1989. The woman claimed to be the high priestess of an ancient church that worshipped sex and fecundity; the Municipal Court claimed she had indeed worshipped sex – with 2,000 men – and had done so for money. They found her guilty of running a house of prostitution.

Offbeat altars

Not all alternative houses of worship are as controversial as Ms Tracy's, but they do indeed abound in gaudy profusion in this city of the Angels. "We found that alternative religions grow where established religion is the weakest," says J. Gordon Melton, visiting scholar at the University of California Santa Barbara, and author of *Encyclopedia of American Religions*. In fact, established *anything* is a rarity in this city, the bulk of whose population is from outside the state, if not outside the country. (In any case, many of those practicing unconventional faiths in Los Angeles claim to have come from another planet entirely.)

The problem in Los Angeles is deciding just what is conventional and what is alternative. Other parts of the US may justly point to their "eccentrics" and "offbeat movements." In LA the eccentric is the norm, and, as for offbeat, the entire population often appears to move in cultural syncopation. Demographers and politicians throw up their hands when it comes to LA; the population and the culture here are, as they put it, "California-skewed."

PRECEDING PAGES: giving the brain a spin at the Altered States Mind Gym.
LEFT: Hindu procession at Venice.
RIGHT: Crystal Cathedral, the world's first drive-in church.

In fact, New Mexico and Arizona have more unconventional religions per capita than Southern California, but it is here they tend to engage in high-profile acts, like the mass suicide in Rancho Santa Fe near San Diego in 1997, when around 40 members of a non-Californian sect "beamed themselves to a better life" in what

has become widely known as the "Heaven's Gate Incident."

Off-center religious persuasions are growing apace in all large urban areas, and in LA they tend to be visible, exotic, kooky, and usually, benign. "California prophets, like its geraniums, grow large, rank and garish," wrote one commentator on the religious scene over 40 years ago, and that statement is still true. In the new millennium, LA hosts a constellation of New Age operations that Angelenos indulge in: quasi-religious, self-help institutions into which the participants actively throw themselves.

In many ways, these groups are the most Californian of all, combining a mixture of health-consciousness, metaphysics, psychology and business. Even a cursory glance at the notice boards of one of the many metaphysical bookstores reveals a thriving community of these smaller, more exotic parlors and salons of worship of the New Age.

For around $150 you can attend a Playshop in Re-Creation with Robert L. Brown, Re-Creationist, "a blend of ancient metaphysics, mysticism, practical health and fitness, creative Play and Love." Sean Michael, a "Visionary Therapist," invites the public to

> ### CONVENTIONAL ALTARS
>
> In LA's sprawling metropolitan areas it has often been the churches and temples that have served as the spiritual, social and political center of a community.

Hallowed hotels

Many Angeleno temples, it is true, were once garish neon structures fit for a Cecil B. De Mille film. In these days of corporate youth, however, quasi-religious New Age gatherings are more likely to be held in the hallowed realms of meeting rooms in airports.

"Channeling," the ability to allow a non-corporeal entity to talk through a human, is often a staple of these gatherings. Kevin Ryerson, the channel that Shirley Maclaine brought to fame in books such

evenings of group channelings, creating space (this involves physical and intuitive exercising, electromagnetic balancing, meditation and toning) as well as "blowing through the Sound Barrier," an aural exercise that can "alter structure and matter."

If you want to "Turn on your Dream Machine" with Don Ginn, you can "find that special mate, triple your income, attain greater spiritual unfoldment, become a professional artist or musician, rejuvenate your body or take that much needed trip to Tahiti" – all through visualization.

All of this comes to you in exchange for a rather large fee, of course.

as *Out on a Limb*, holds weekends in Los Angeles on subjects such as "Prophecy and Your Future Self." For a few hundred dollars per person, Mr Ryerson goes into a drowsy trance and the "invisible staff" speaks through him. What Shirley knew is now available to the public: the audience often reaches hundreds of believers.

Less expensive channeling sessions can be had all over Los Angeles. Taryn Krivé, for example, is an expert in "Time Travel, Future Selves and Past Life Regression" – the latter being "one of the most powerful tools on this (or any other) [*sic*] planet for healing." Krivé, a pretty and pert erstwhile-actress, once held Thursday channeling sessions in the San Fernando Valley where you could ask questions of some of the characters who spoke through her, including Bel-Bel, a five-year-old child from Atlantis, and Barking Tree, a spokes-entity for a committee of five disembodied personalities. Today Krivé focuses on a new area of therapy: psychic counseling. "Is your life filled with unanswered questions? A reading can give you a clear perspective."

Other clear perspectives are offered at the Atlantean Discoveries Discount Book and Gift Shop in Chatsworth where Group Trance Channeling Sessions are held with a different guest channeler each week. Don't be surprised if some of the "entities" that are channeled through the participants not only come from a different historical time but also a different galaxy and dimension.

In the City of the Angels there is decidedly an audience for such other-worldly thought. The Association for Past-Life Research and Therapies, Inc. holds a weekend encounter with Dr R. Leo Sprinkle in a Claremont hotel to investigate the relationship between reincarnation and UFO encounters. Saivahni Sharma-Singh holds "Starseed Sessions" involving "extraterrestrial, celestial, mission, master level activations, and dimensional shift preparations. (Appointments are taken daily.)"

Metaphysical fads

Those less inclined to leave this planet, if not this plane, can always delve into the latest chic metaphysical fad – "City Shamans." The "Neo-Pagan movement," as it has come to be known, is in full swing in Los Angeles. The most famous example of these urban medicine men and women is Lynn Andrews, known as the "Shaman of Beverly Hills." Andrews came to fame through her books, starting with *Medicine Woman* in 1981 and continuing with *Jaguar Woman*, *Star Woman* and *Crystal Woman*. A member of the Rodeo Drive designer set, Andrews had a paranormal vision of an Indian wedding basket and promptly romped off to Manitoba. "I wondered if I had the right clothing?" queried this Beverly Hills spiritual seeker. "I was wearing Sassoon jeans, boots, and a khaki jacket from Kerr's."

Andrews, clothes notwithstanding, found her basket in the hands of Agnes Whistling Elk, a Cree woman in Manitoba who initiated her into the ways of the shamans. The tale struck some sort of spiritual nerve in Los Angeles. She now gives popular weekend seminars on shamanism, complete with initiations and the granting of new spiritual names. For those less inclined to mass earth rituals, Andrews can also be consulted privately in her chic Beverly Hills home.

As with channeling, there is also shamanic counselling for the less well-to-do. The Healing Light Center Church holds classes in "City Shamanism" in Santa Monica on Sundays. Alexandra, a well-dressed blonde psychic, has a center

LEFT: a man with a cross to bear, Venice.
RIGHT: stretching the imagination.

in Los Angeles, but around $400 will garner you a place in her seminars "with a small group of people on the most powerful areas on vortex sites in Sedona, Arizona." Dael Walker, Crystal Master, holds lectures in "Medicine Bags and Healing Devices," and Lois Marten – otherwise known as Rainbow Star Dancer of Hacienda Heights – uses a variety of tools in her Native American medicine path seminars, including crystals and colors. Seminars are open, by the way, only to eight evolved persons who are selected by personal vibrations.

We may not be able to pinpoint what constitutes the offbeat in Southern California, but rest

plified by the film industry's early and, to a greater degree, public excesses and Los Angeles became a very comfortable environment for the flourishing of Eastern thought.

Frostless belt theosophy

Theosophy, a blend of Eastern and Western wisdom and culture, was founded by Madame Blavatsky and Colonel Henry Steel Olcott in New York in 1875. It arrived in Southern California shortly after. By 1912 – before the influx of movie people – the Krotona lodge was established in the Hollywood Hills and for the next 10 years a theosophical community flourished

assured that, however we define that realm, it is alive and well in numbers and profusion in Los Angeles as nowhere else.

The propensity for the metaphysical – and most of what constitutes the popular cults and alternative religions in Los Angeles *is* metaphysical – has a mundane explanation: Los Angeles faces the Pacific. During the 20th century this area accepted the largest number of immigrants from Asia. Even at the beginning of the 20th century the railroad-building Chinese and new Japanese arrivals were already practicing what was for America highly exotic religions: Buddhism and Shintoism. Combine this with a sense of the unconventional exem-

in the famed "frostless belt." It was here that Alice Bailey, an English adherent, was contacted by a Master called "The Tibetan" to write a number of books in his name. In the 1920s, the Krotona lodge moved to Ojai, a small town some 50 miles (80 km) north of the city to await the evolution of a new sub-race in California as predicted by Dr Ales Hrdlicka, an anthropologist. To this day the Theosophy Hall at 33rd and Grand in Los Angeles is the scene of lectures and classes.

The "I Am" experience

In 1930, Guy W. Ballard and his wife Edna were contacted by the Ascended Master St

Germain, an epochal meeting that marked the founding of the "I AM" church. St Germain took the Ballards on a "white flame which formed a circle about 50 ft [15 meters] in diameter" and whisked them on an odyssey through time and space, to buried cities of the Amazon, to lost Inca cities in the Andes and to Yellowstone National Park. At each point of their journey the blessed couple were shown a wealth of treasures – hoards that Ballard was never again able to rediscover, even though the man was a mine promoter.

OUT-OF-TOWN FRIENDS

Sightings of three-fingered, glowing beings stocking up on supplies at the Joshua Tree National Monument have fueled UFO speculation.

Divining the future

Following in the Ballards' steps come a host of groups such as the Church Universal and Triumphant, headed by Elizabeth Clare Prophet. Ms Prophet, a Messenger for the Ascended Masters, is, as her name humbly suggests, an individual who can divine the future. "I think that earthquakes are geological events on the planet whose time has come," she said. (The theme of imminent disaster is usually dear to any Angeleno's heart.) "The probability is

there, the prophecies are there, the scientific statements are there."

Ms Prophet, however, is not there, not anymore; she moved her entire congregation and well-endowed church from Malibu, where it had been since 1961, to Montana, where she "holds the balance in terms of earth changes, earthquakes and so forth" with mantras and Violet Flame decrees. Just in case the balance fails, Ms Prophet's followers have also built giant underground fallout shelters where they will all sit out Armageddon.

The tale of their wondrous trip captured the imagination of their fellow Angelenos, who bought thousands of copies of their magical story at $2.50 each. Not long thereafter the Ballards built a garish church replete with a magnificent neon sign flashing out "I AM" and began selling charts of the "Magic Presence," "I AM" signet rings, the "Flame in Action," an expensive electric device with colored lights and other celestially ordained doodahs, including "New Age Cold Cream."

The Ballards and their ilk are clearly precursors of the present New Age groups in Los Angeles, combining as they do elements of

LEFT: Hindu Temple at Malibu Canyon.
ABOVE: a scene from the Hare Krishna festival in Venice.

Eastern thought, science fiction and huckster-ism in an unconventional cocktail that has long been a staple of this city.

A strong strain of unconventional churches has also formed in this city around charismatic and entertaining leaders, such as Aimée Semple McPherson. Ms McPherson arrived in the early 1920s with just $100 in cash in her pocket and within four years was the leader of the 30,000-strong congregation of the Four Square Gospel sect *(see page 143)*.

And today there is the Reverend Robert Schuller and his magnificent Crystal Cathedral, a glass monstrosity in Orange County at Lewis

and Chapman boulevards in Garden Grove. It was the world's first drive-in church. Schuller, a pastor in one of the country's oldest denomi-nations, the Reformed Church of America, delivers feel-good messages of inspiration wrapped up in show business, from symphony concerts to massive celebrations of Christmas and Easter with a cast of hundreds, including animals. (Tel: 1-714-54-GLORY for tickets.)

Established alternatives

Set beside the Ms Prophets and the Ballards of this city are groups and churches which consti-tute American outposts of ancient and long-established Eastern religions. The oldest of

these in Los Angeles is the Vedanta Temple, dating back to 1923 when Swami Prabha-vananda came to California, and, with uncom-mon prescience, proclaimed that Hollywood should be the center of Vedanta in America. And so it became. Lectures were given in an alabaster replica of the Taj Mahal on Ivar Street, and by the 1930s Vedanta in Hollywood included the writers Aldous Huxley and Christopher Isherwood among its illustrious ad-herents. A large new Vedanta temple now sits in the Malibu hills in Calabassas.

The Self-Realization Fellowship was found-ed in Los Angeles in 1923 by Paramahansa Yogananda, the Hindu author of the perennial spiritual best-seller *Autobiography of a Yogi*. This gentle guru left his earthly body in 1952, but the organization he founded continues as a respected place of worship. The SRF's Lake Shrine, on Sunset Boulevard not far from the Pacific Ocean, is a beautiful and peaceful oasis of flowers and water *(see page 155)*. Yoga has become so commonplace in LA that no self-respecting health club is without a full slate of well-attended yoga classes.

Why has Los Angeles become a center for so many varied and exotic forms of worship? Is it because of the "wonderful transparency of the air" and the heavy charge of mineral magnetism from the gold-mines and "emana-tions" from the miners of yore, as Emma Hard-ing wrote in her history of spiritualism? Or is it because the sandy soil of the Los Angeles Basin offers little resistance to propagating roots and the warm climate is particularly amenable to the rapid flowering of almost any plant, weed and orchid alike?

We may never know, but indubitably South-ern California has always been a repository of dreams and dreamers, prophets and vision-aries. The earliest accounts of the area held that this "island" – as it was then thought to be – was under the domination of the beauti-ful queen Califia who ruled a nation of black-skinned Amazons. From the first, California was cloaked in a patina of the exotic and all those offbeat forms of worship, from UFOs to city shamans, are all part of the mystique of this city that celebrates the gaudy and the unconventional. ❏

LEFT: a sidewalk salesman in tune with the times.
RIGHT: putting your faith in mud.

MUSCLES – WHY THEY GROW HERE LIKE ORANGES

What is it about Los Angeles that draws the weird, the wacky, the wonderful
– or, for that matter, the innovator, the outsider, the pioneer?

L ike moths to a flame, people have come to Los Angeles by the thousand for sunshine, oil, movies, land, and muscles. As the Los Angeles population grew, the railroads and eventually the telephone arrived, and word spread of the health benefits of life in the sun. Refugees from cold eastern winters came seeking long days of sunshine – hoping this solar elixir would encourage good health and good fortune, as well as plain relief from arthritis, constant colds, and shoveling sidewalks.

Surrounded by mountains, desert, and ocean, the recreational opportunities screamed health and vigor, and many health enthusiasts and eccentrics followed the cry.

Fitness in the beginning

In the 1890s, fitness was more about staying alive and illness free than about working out, and diets often meant putting on weight, not taking it off. Physical fitness was something admired, but not entirely understood. Muscles were more for legends like Samson, Ulysses, Tarzan, Atlas, and Hercules, who had inspired dreams of strength – but these dreams were pursued more in weightlifting contests and circus sideshows, not by common man.

This was soon about to change, and many fitness historians point to the emergence of Eugene Sandow as ground zero in the fitness revolution. Billed as "The World's Strongest Man," Sandow arrived from Europe as more than the ordinary sideshow – what set him apart was the aesthetic quality of his physique. Men and women considered him a perfect combination of muscular development and attractiveness, so much so that his embodiment of brawn shifted the focus on extraordinary strength to the aesthetics of muscularity. Sales of barbells and dumbbells rose dramatically.

PRECEDING PAGES: Surfer Moms learn in a surf class.
LEFT: posing in Gold's Gym in Venice.
RIGHT: rollerblading is not as easy as it may look.

Contests began in which the physical measurements of competitors were compared – the start of the bodybuilding industry. In 1899, this rise in interest in health and fitness was boosted by a new magazine called *Physical Culture*,

which sold for 5 cents and was an instant success. It was published by fitness guru Bernarr Macfadden, a New York man ahead of his time. Having developed a superb physique through a vegetarian diet and daily workouts, Macfadden was written up in *Time* and *Newsweek,* and at the mere sight of a press camera he would strip to his underwear to show off his muscles.

Some people thought Macfadden was a nut – but once in LA he became just one of a number of eccentric, self-proclaimed health experts. Like Otto Carque (1867–1936), considered the grand old man of LA food and health gurus, he prescribed exercise, fresh air and nude sunbathing as the cure for nearly every ailment.

Similarly Arnold Ehret, who prescribed a diet of only grape juice, believing it gave "supernatural strength," held that a healthy, fasting individual could broadcast and receive electrical "love vibration" through the hair.

Already LA was developing a reputation as an accepting home to those on the cutting edge (or slightly off it), but it was the confluence of a new growing industry that would solidify its claim as the health and fitness leader.

"This is my good side…"

Motion pictures created a totally new kind of celebrity. If you were the most famous actor on

Broadway, perhaps tens of thousands of people had seen you, but even a middling movie star was known to millions. Sadly, this dizzying mass of adulation was fickle. The camera has no pity; a close-up shows flaws nobody would ever get close enough to notice in a stage actor.

So while the many Midwestern retirees who fled to LA seeking health thought in terms of comfort and warmth, for actors health was a matter of career survival – once you lost your looks, you were on the scrap heap. Hollywood's feverish quest for youth had begun, and so had a symbiotic relationship – stars flocked to the newest and greatest health fads in an effort to retain their beauty and youth, while health and

fitness gurus touted celebrity use and endorsement to promote their latest products.

By the late 1920s, you could get fig coffee, grain-free uncooked pies, alkaline bread, non-devitalized vegetable salt, and even bubbling oxygenated tooth powder. Health-food gurus like Paul C. Bragg cultivated Hollywood and numbered quite a few entertainers among their followers – but they also drew devotees from another new form of culture and entertainment growing in LA, which was attracting health and fitness advocates from around the nation.

The Legend of Muscle Beach

To begin with, it really wasn't about muscles. It was about fitness and fun. Muscle Beach, in Santa Monica, was just a patch of sand south of the pier. But with the addition of a tumbling platform and gymnastics equipment, it became the birthplace for the modern fitness movement. A haven for health nuts, Muscle Beach attracted the best bodies of the day: Jack LaLanne, John Grimek (a protege of Bernarr Mcfadden's and the first "Mr America"), Vic Tanny, Charles Atlas, and Joe Gold. All would go on to fitness fame, fortune, or both.

The focus of attention at the original Muscle Beach, through the 1930s, '40s and '50s, was acrobats – strong men and women who built human towers and threw each other around. It began as a place where friends could work out in the sand, and grew to include athletes, circus performers, wrestlers, college gymnasts, and movie stunt people. On weekends the crowd of spectators numbered 10,000, watching stunts and incredible acts, like Paula Boelsems, who taught an elephant how to water-ski; George Eiferman, who played a trumpet with one hand while lifting weights with the other; and Abbye "Pudgy" Stockton, a dainty acrobat who was the first great female weightlifter.

Movie stars such as Clark Gable and Tyrone Power hung out there; Mae West found her chorus boys there, and Jayne Mansfield met her husband there (and so did Jane Russell). It was only a matter of time before one of the Muscle Beach athletes became a movie star. The first one was Steve Reeves, discovered by Cecil B. DeMille and star of many films as Hercules. "He was the most beautiful human to ever walk the sand of Muscle Beach," recalls Harold Zinkin, author of *Remembering Muscle Beach* and the first "Mr California."

Eventually, by the late 1950s Santa Monica had tired of the act. Rumors were alleged of the pier owners complaining that the free Muscle Beach shows drew paying customers away from them, and some found the whole thing offensive. After five weightlifters were found partying with underage girls, the city claimed Muscle Beach had become a magnet for "perverts and narcissistic parasites," and it was bulldozed. Use of the name Muscle Beach was forbidden, as were weightlifting and any events not approved by the city recreation department.

In the 1960s, the echoes of Muscle Beach took shape, literally, about 2 miles (3 km) south

A rush to the millennium

Through the 1980s and '90s, LA continued to be at the vortex of fitness trends and innovators. Local fads become national phenomenons – in the 1980s, the Beverly Hills-centered *Jane Fonda Workout* spread aerobics from a housewives fad into an entertainment industry status and networking event. With great foresight, Fonda began the craze in the capital of body-worship; and with great timing, the *Workout* hit on the tidal wave of videotape and VCRs that broke across the world that decade. Also in the 1980s, Nathan Pritikin's revolutionary diet plan marched out of Santa Monica and across the

at "The Pen," an outdoor weight park on Venice Beach. Smaller and exclusively for weightlifting, this new hangout became the providence of champion bodybuilders such as Frank Zane, Franco Columbo, and Dave Draper. In 1965, Joe Gold opened what has since become "The Mecca" of bodybuilding – Gold's Gym. It was here that the next movie stars of bodybuilding, Schwarzenegger and Lou (*Incredible Hulk)* Ferrigno, were featured in the 1975 documentary *Pumping Iron*. Once again, LA was at the center of the health and fitness universe.

LEFT: Muscle Beach: *the* place for pumping iron.
ABOVE: rollerblading football.

nation, eventually promoting a low-cholesterol diet and structured exercise to the world.

The 1990s were fast and furious in LA: a riot that left the city in flames, an earthquake that left many unsettled, and a sizzling economy that put more money in most pockets, but with less time to enjoy it. Is it any wonder that the fierce workouts of Spinning, which is basically a stationary bike race, and Tae-Bo, a combination of TaeKwonDo and boxing, have become so popular? High intensity, they burn off a lot of stress, as well as calories, in a relatively short amount of time, and these homegrown workouts are enjoying outrageous popularity across the globe. The folks behind Spinning now claim to have licensees on six out of seven continents; Billy Blanks, the master behind TaeBo, is recognized around the world – in 1999, the Tae-Bo workout tape was No. 2 on the Billboard video sales charts, beating most Hollywood films of that year. Blanks, a devout Christian, has also tried to encourage a positive calming effect from these fierce workouts, telling his devotees to change their life through "will – strength – belief – perseverance."

As always, Angelenos also sort out their spiritual side in many different ways, often working it in through meditation and/or yoga, which is more popular than ever. Generally, there has

been a push toward healthier eating. According to a study reported in the *Los Angeles Times*, Californians are drinking less alcohol – a 79-million gallon decline over the past decade. Perhaps they're replacing it with more nutrition – some of the fastest growing franchises in California are purveyors of juice and smoothies, and the most successful of these started in LA.

Health gurus and celebrities continue to feed off each other – the herbal tea bar Elixir, on Melrose, is a popular spot for stars like Susan Sarandon, Winona Ryder, Kevin Bacon, and Julia Roberts, who seem to need a fix to fend off everything from flu to stress to hangovers;

and according to the folks at Robert's American Gourmet, the *Seinfeld* gang used to keep up their energy on the set by munching on Power Puffs, a cheese-puff impostor loaded with ginseng and bee pollen (they also claim Ziggy Marley, Brooke Shields, and Steven Spielberg as fans). Actor Woody Harrelson invested in a new concept on Sunset Boulevard – an oxygen bar, where for a price you can breathe the real, pure thing – and even get it flavored.

Health and fitness today

The sun still shines on the health and fitness scene; and even though the environment may not be as pristine, and life a lot more hurried, LA muscles continue to flex like never before.

Perhaps it's because life has become more fast-paced and stressful than ever that Los Angelenos are turning more than ever to gyms, bikes, jogs, kayaks, surfboards, in-line skates, aerobics, vitamins, minerals, additives, laxitives, herbal tonics, smoothies, and oxygen bars. Once upon a time, health-food stores drew alternative types interested in purchasing boxes of tigers' milk cookies or bottles of strange elixirs from the mysterious East.

Today, according to a health-store manager, "our shoppers aren't just people with crystals and far-out ideas any more. They are more likely to be parents starting their kids off on good diets, or older people on special diets, and all ages who are into fitness." Edmund Burke, director of exercise science at Colorado University, adds: "Three or four years ago, you'd have to go to specialty stores to find sports supplements. Now they're everywhere."

The challenge to remain stress free, and, even more important to some, to *look* stress free, has become a catalyst for constant new approaches to health and fitness. New innovators, weird, wacky or wonderful, are always arriving to try and stake their claim.

The health and fitness industry has seen many a fad, but the principles of physical and mental vitality through exercise and healthy diet have endured, creating a gold mine that has led many to fame and fortune.

No doubt, new products are being hatched in garages, gyms, and minds all over Los Angeles at this very minute – for muscles, like oranges, are indisputably a cash crop. ❑

LEFT: having a break at Venice.

Spectator sports

L os Angeles has a rich athletic heritage. Both collegiate and professional teams have excellent facilities as well as an extra advantage for spectators – the weather. The toughest ticket to get is for the Lakers, the easiest the Clippers or the Galaxy. The cheapest to watch is volleyball; all you need is a beach chair. For agents, see Travel Tips.

NBA Basketball

Los Angeles Lakers – 11 championships, home to Shaquille O'Neal and Kobe Bryant. Alumni: Magic Johnson, Kareem Abdul Jabbar, Wilt Chamberlain, Jerry West. Late October to mid-April, then playoffs. Home: Staples Center, Downtown. Tickets: (213) 480-3232; www.nba.com/lakers/

Los Angeles Clippers – poor management keeps letting good players get away...rarely in the playoffs....but a good chance to see NBA action with better seats and prices. Late October to mid-April, then playoffs. Home: Staples Center, Downtown. Tickets: (213) 480-3232; www.nba.com/clippers/

WNBA – Womens' Basketball

Los Angeles Sparks – Relatively new (1997) league. Top women basketball professionals, including several international stars. June to August. Home: Great Western Forum, Inglewood. Tickets: (213) 480-3232; www.wnba.com/sparks/

Major League Baseball

Los Angeles Dodgers – 6 championships, legends include Sandy Koufax, Jackie Robinson. Current stars include pitcher Kevin Brown and slugger Gary Sheffield. Stadium just above Downtown. April to September. Home: Dodger Stadium, Downtown. Tickets: (323) 224-1-HIT; www.dodgers.com

NHL Hockey

Los Angeles Kings – greatest days with Wayne Gretzky and Marcel Dionne. October to early April, then playoffs. Home: Staples Center, Downtown. Tickets: (213) 480-3232; www.lakings.com

Major League Soccer

LA Galaxy – many international stars and consistently one of the leagues' best. Mid-March to mid-September. Home: Rose Bowl, Pasadena. Tickets: (877) 3-GALAXY; www.lagalaxy.com

---

RIGHT: volleyball tournaments are held on the beach.

NCAA College Athletics

Several universities compete in top-tier athletics, but the University of Southern California and the University of California at Los Angeles both field strong teams. For USC schedules and tickets call (213) 740-GOSC; www.usctrojans.com; for UCLA call (310) 825-2101; www.uclabruins.com

Horse Racing

Santa Anita – The Breeder's Cup. Late December to late April. Tel: (626) 574-7223.

Hollywood Park – Original shareholders included Bing Crosby and Walt Disney. Late April to late July. Tel: (310) 419-1330; www.hollywoodpark.com

Volleyball

Tournaments almost every summer weekend at the beaches. The largest are the Hermosa Open in June and the Manhattan Open in August. Seating mainly free. Tel: (310) 577-0775; www.avptour.com

Tennis

The Mens ATP and Ladies WTA tours both have their own LA Open – the men play at UCLA in late July, tel: (310) 825-2101. The ladies play early August in Manhattan Beach, tel: (213) 480-3232.

Golf

The LA Open is in mid-February at the Riviera Country Club. Tel: (800) 752-OPEN; www.lajcc.org ❏

AUTOMANIA: CALIFORNIANS AND THEIR CARS

If you don't have a car you'll be regarded as a second-class citizen –

most Angelenos wouldn't be seen dead on a bus

In his 1946 book *Southern California Country*, Carey McWilliams captured a quintessential local attitude: "Driving. Driving everywhere, over great distances with scarcely any thought to the enormous mileages they were logging. A car was the absolutely essential piece of social overhead capital. With it you could get a job, meet a girl, hang around with the boys, go to a drive-in, see football games away from home, take in the beach parties at Laguna or Corona del Mar, or go to the Palladium ballroom in Hollywood. To have a car meant being somebody; to have to borrow a car meant knowing somebody; to have no car at all, owned or borrowed, was to be left out. Way out."

Coming of age in California is marked by the ability to obtain a car, or at least a driver's license, without which one is likely to feel like a second-class citizen. It is not only mobility that is conferred on the driver but a kind of nobility, too — an exalted state from which he surveys the scurrying world around him with a sort of bemused tolerance.

"It's freedom," Skip Weshner, a newly transplanted New Yorker explained back in the 1960s. "The ability to just hop into your car and drive, drive as fast and as far as you like… the radio playing your favorite songs… the interesting architecture and funny billboards… glimpses of the sea…"

But that was a few decades ago and the cloud then seen dimly on the horizon has become an enveloping fog, or smog, and the freedom somewhat constrained by other cars on every side. There are more than 5 million registered in Los Angeles County alone, an area with a high percentage of two- and even three-car families. Recent statistics indicate that Southern Californians drive an average of 117 miles (188 km)

per week. Two-thirds of the urban space is devoted to transportation, and traffic congestion is getting to be the state's biggest environmental problem, pumping 18,000 tons of carbon dioxide into the atmosphere every year

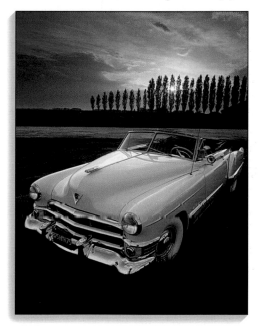

as well as strangling the freeways and producing oil spills, smog, and contamination.

Eschewing the bus

Forty percent of the respondents to a 1990 poll by the *Los Angeles Times* said they believed that cars had ruined the city and yet more than eight out of 10 hadn't ridden a bus for at least a year. Fewer than one out of three said they would not make frequent use of mass transportation, even if it were more available.

"Sometimes it staggers my imagination that people are still so crazy about their cars," says Nissan executive Gerald P. Hirshberg. "You watch them crawling along the freeway; they

PRECEDING PAGES: getting around in style.
LEFT: two-thirds of Los Angeles' land area is devoted to transportation.
RIGHT: a classy 1949 Cadillac.

could walk faster. Then you look at their cars; clean, gleaming, polished objects of love. It's hard to think of Californians without them."

LA's ports employ 200,000 people to unload up to a million cars each year, with the Southern California region accounting for about one-seventh of the entire country's car and truck sales. Even in 1930, the region had more cars per capita than anywhere else in the world.

The benefit that the city derives today from getting 10 percent of its taxable income in one

ELECTRIC FUTURE

Electric cars are seen as the only solution to pollution. In 1998 California ordered 2 percent of all new cars sold to be pollution-free, and the figure will inexorably rise.

ers began to notice that a thick, brown haze was beginning to badly affect their crops.

Sometimes it seems that drivers enjoy sitting in their cars as much as driving them. The 1949 Ford was advertised as "a living room on wheels."

In an article comparing the lifestyles of New York and Los Angeles, Joseph Giovannini wrote: "The car extends the privacy of the single family home into the streets ... generally the windows are up, the doors locked, the music on, the mind set."

way or another from the automobile industry is counter-balanced by the frustration of trying to find more space for cars and yet simultaneously reduce pollution.

While planners talk of double-decking the Harbor Freeway and turning the mostly dry Los Angeles riverbed into a commuter expressway, the regional Air Quality Management District talks of banning drive-through services from banks to burger stands. And this in the state where the drive-in restaurant inspired Ray Kroc to invent the McDonald's chain, and a drive-in movie in Garden Grove evolved into Robert Schuller's Crystal Cathedral. But it's also the place where, as far back as 1940, orange grow-

Homelessness, as familiar a phenomenon here as elsewhere, takes on a special twist in Southern California, where hundreds of people live in their cars. In some parts of Los Angeles, especially at the beach and in the streets bordering Griffith Park, it's become enough of a problem to bring a ban on overnight parking for everyone but residents. Park officials complain of vandalism, and residents say their gardens are filled with trash and are sometimes used as toilets.

Californians' love affair with their cars is reflected in the number of dealers – 17,000 in LA County alone, selling 100,000 vehicles a year out of 3,500 agencies whose average $19 million revenue annually compares with $12 million elsewhere, according to the dealers' national association. With $80 to $500 commission on each car, some salesmen earn as much as $200,000 a year.

Buyers enjoy haggling

According to the *Los Angeles Times*' poll, car dealers are not popular, having been placed last (along with insurance agents) on a list of nine occupations rated for honesty and ethical standards. More than half their customers buy new rather than used cars. Toyotas – whose owners tend to be young, single and more affluent –

making him feel he really needs it." *The Automotive Sales Script*, a comprehensive book owned by most salesmen, lists 722 ways to respond to customers' questions or doubts.

Some amateur analysts choose to identify owners by their cars. Magazine writer David Knudson, while sneering at American sedan owners' preference for patriotism over quality, described the typical female owner of a Honda Prelude as "always late … aggressive in her middle-management job … tailgates, honks and screams her way to and from work." And Tom Crouch referred to a Trans Am driver as "a cross between a live grenade and a peacock."

and Hondas sell best, but Mercedes is the make most people say they would like to own.

Despite their disdain for car salesmen generally, customers seem to regard haggling over prices as part of the game. "Dealers have tried to go other ways," says Bert Boeckmann, who owns three agencies. "They've even put fixed prices on their cars. But those dealers are the ones who have gone broke. Most people want to bargain; this is a horse-trading business." One salesman explained his technique of "trying to find out what a person wants and then

LEFT: California girls love their cars.
ABOVE: size doesn't matter...

PAYING FOR THE PLEASURE

One of California's proudest achievement was having a highway system which was not expensive – roads that were literally freeways.

But now in different parts of the state toll roads have appeared. The first stretch of private road runs for 10 miles between the Riverside County Line and the Costa Mesa Freeway (Route 91) in Orange County. The tolls are electronically controlled.

These toll roads are one of the ways in which the state's transit officials are trying to solve the problem of increasing congestion, which results in pollution, human stress and expense, not to mention fatal accidents.

Crouch wrote an entire book of definitions, *U R What You Drive*, in which he claimed that Mercedes owners were "constantly mistaking themselves for celebrities," that a Nissan 2X driver was "in mid-life crisis, one rejection away from his first anxiety attack," and that longtime nightclub crooners Steve Lawrence and Eydie Gormé tended to be "the favorite singers of the Cadillac Seville driver."

The California car

The automobile industry has its own prototype of "the California car," once the woodpaneled station wagon but currently the Mazda Miata

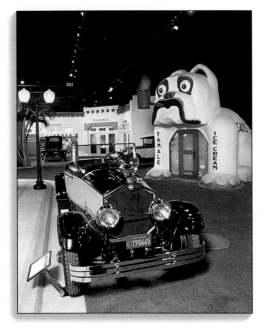

convertible which its designer describes as "the appeal of the open road, the wind in your teeth, tooling along… We wanted it to give a feeling of freedom, you know, letting the top down, getting out on the back roads, opening the throttle and letting go." The flamboyant Miata launch created such demand that dealers were being offered more than double the $14,000 sticker price by customers unwilling to join a lengthy waiting list.

Nissan's $38,000 Infiniti was the result of years of study, including a Japanese researcher's lengthy stay in a California household, noting the family's views, habits, work and leisure before coming to the conclusion that what the

family needed was "an antidote to stress." Another feature that came out of the research was that many coffee-sipping drivers would welcome a plastic cup holder in their car.

Southern California is the section of the country most favored by carmakers to set up their design clinics, of which there are at least a dozen. "This is the place where trends start," says John Schinella, head designer at General Motors' Advanced Concept Center in Thousand Oaks. "We're here to pick up on them before somebody else does." And a few drivers, not content with distinctive models, express their identity by having their cars "customized," a trend that has been popular in California ever since cowboy star Tom Mix had a saddle mounted on the hood of his 1920s automobile. Some of today's drivers have covered their cars with carpeting, running shoes or even grass, but topping a Cadillac hood with a miniature candelabra (for Liberace) and gold-plating Elvis Presley's limousine was the specialty of North Hollywood's George Barris. Barris called himself the "King of the Kustomizers."

Personal license plates

Not everybody is affluent enough to make a gold-plated statement or to pay what a Lotus, Ferrari, Porsche, Lamborghini or some obscure European model must cost. But almost every driver can afford a few bucks for a personal license plate, and this is a state where almost one million drivers have done so. Ranging from the suggestiveness of BUSH DR (owned by a tree surgeon) to the obscurity of EZ4U2LV, the requests pour in at the rate of several hundred a day, keeping a special staff at California's Department of Motor Vehicles busy sifting out the unacceptable ones.

"You wouldn't believe the number of variations on the four-letter word," said one official, admitting ruefully that, despite the help of multilingual interpreters, mirrors, medical dictionaries and a copy of the California Penal Code ("in case they stick the code number for some particularly heinous crime on the back of their Chevy"), the occasional naughty slips through. One such example was 4NIK8 which the DMV later recalled. They also called back COKE DLR – until the recipient sent in a photo of the plate attached to his Coca Cola truck.

"There's an irresistible challenge in trying to condense an entire statement into six or seven characters, perhaps akin to that felt by writers in such rigid poetic forms as haiku or sonnets," wrote University of Arizona professors Margaret Fleming and Duane Roen.

License plates are made by inmates at Folsom Prison who occasionally enclose their own statement ("Help" or "You Bum") with the package. The most-requested plate is for PEACE, and probably the most regretted one is NOPLATE, whose owner became the recipient of parking tickets for every vehicle that was unidentified. Parking has

CAR CULTURE

According to Nissan's Gerald P. Hirshberg, "It's a car-loving culture. Living out here is like living in a permanent international automobile show."

one-third win – usually because the officer doesn't show up. Hundreds of others battle with meter maids ("parking control officers" they call themselves) on the street, after failing to get away with such ruses as putting an old ticket on the windshield, jamming the meter, or leaving the emergency flashers on.

In Newport Beach, which is debating whether to equip its officers with cans of Mace, one meter maid spotted a disgruntled miscreant dropping a smoke bomb in the back of her car.

spawned an industry of its own, in a city whose 6,500 miles (10,500 km) of streets have 143,000 signs prohibiting it for some of the time and 29,000 signs during every part of the day.

Battling over tickets

Los Angeles collects $100 million annually in fines for payment of most of the 4½ million tickets issued each year by an army of 564 gray-uniformed meter maids. Of the 60,000 drivers who contest their tickets in court, about

---

LEFT: an exhibit at the Petersen Automotive Museum.
ABOVE: the "stack," one block from Sunset Boulevard, where several freeways overlap.

Another was so abused that she acquired an ulcer and quit the job on her doctor's orders. "It's not worth being outside and getting beaten up," she said. "People think we (issue tickets) on purpose just because we don't like them."

Valet parking became big business relatively recently, and at virtually all major restaurants it is mandatory. Tips range from zero to half a $20 bill (the rest handed over when the driver gets back his car fast and unharmed). Car valets are mostly young because they're usually expected to *run* to retrieve the car, and about half the customers want their vehicles to be parked "upfront" and will pay extra for this privilege. Good valets know all the legends about people who have "lost" their tickets and drive off with somebody else's Porsche or how some drivers will protest that a dent wasn't there before. Bad valets are likely to search the cars for drugs or money, make copies of the house keys or just treat the vehicle as their own, changing the radio dial or using the stereo to play their own tapes.

"Women tend to take more care of cars," says one veteran valet, which is the rationale behind Valet Girls, a Los Angeles parking service with 40 women employees, which handles private parties. The biggest and longest-established company is Herb Citrin's 44-year-old Valet

DENIS FITZPATRICK 3-20-75

DESIGNER FEATURES

The need for car accessories to aid those who want to guzzle while they drive has become increasingly more important in Los Angeles.

Los Angelenos who pay upwards of $40,000 for a brand new European car are united in their complaint about the lack of cup-holders.

Eating while driving is such a common preoccupation that Jerry Hirschberg, vice-president of Nissan design, speculates that future innovations might include ashtrays replaced by larger cup-holders, a built-in trash container, and an armrest made of double thickness plastic to act as a thermos for hot and cold drinks.

Parking Service, whose business grosses $10 million a year handling parties at the Playboy Club and other such high-profile events as the Academy Awards.

Fighting freeway phobia

Slow drivers and those who turn without signaling registered highest on the list of pet peeves of motorists polled by the *Los Angeles Times*, with about one-third declaring that what worried them most was encountering "bad drivers." Some of these complaints originate out of simple, stark fear, a syndrome widely known as freeway phobia.

"The system overwhelms them so much that they develop an avoidant lifestyle," explains L. Jerome Oziel, USC's associate professor of psychiatry. "They lie to friends about driving the freeways and make excuses to vacationing visitors as to why it's taking them much longer to get somewhere." Fear of freeways is sufficiently common to have prompted Sy Cohn to institute a course at LA's Pierce College, "Overcoming Driving Fears." Beginning with deep breathing, relaxation, listening to subliminal tapes, and conjuring up visions of "a warm protective light around the car," the class eventually takes to the streets.

"I saw the need for this," says Cohn,who was a former driving instructor. "The freeways are more congested and everyone is stressed out. I get people who've held a license for 30 years but have stopped driving because of the fear. People in LA want a quick fix for their driving phobias. The important thing is just to get in the car and drive."

For some people there is no choice. Forced out of town by escalating housing costs, they face daily commutes of 100 miles (160 km) or more each way. Ten percent of commuters say that, even without congestion, accidents or bad weather, their drive to work takes an hour or more. During this trip they munch on snacks, listen to the radio or books on tape, or simply get exasperated. Doctors say long journeys are bad for the health, raising blood pressure and causing memory loss; employers note increasing stress among workers.

A local top-selling book, *LA Shortcuts: A Guidebook for Drivers Who Hate to Wait* by Brian Roberts and Richard Schwadel, investigated the phenomenon. They wrote that "shortcut sharks instinctively know that to move is to live; to stop and lose momentum is to suffocate and die." Indicating alleys, driveways, parking lots and gas stations, the authors declare: "If it's wide enough, drive it" and amplify their credo with such commandments as: "The shortest distance between two points is never a straight line", and the dictatorial admonition: "Accept no uprisings. Passengers are merely baggage and have no vote."

Despite increasing congestion, speeding is hardly obsolete. Some communities have been experimenting with big-screen radar devices that flash the speed of approaching cars in foot-high digits. But even speeding tickets

"Less Stress 4 U"

Usually, however, they deem justice to have been done if the lawbreaker returns with a certificate proving attendance at one of the approved classes. "Lettuce Amuse U Traffic School" or "Some Laffs, Some Laws, Some Learning" or even "Less Stress 4 U; Humor 2" are typical of the genre whose titles tend to stress money (Easy On Wallet, Loco Cheapo) or humor (Wheel Make U Laff) or both (Great Comedians For Less Money).

In actuality, attendance at traffic school is not only a bargain but a ball; a party atmosphere prevails as the mostly young (20s and 30s)

sometimes can be handled differently – by that distinctively Californian invention, the traffic school.

What might seem ludicrous to the visitor – a class where you learn as you laugh or as you eat – makes perfect sense to the Los Angeleno. The average fee for a six-hour class is considerably less than the typical fine, not to mention an annotated driving record which would have been the alternative, although the courts sometimes impose a fine as well.

LEFT: *Chevy* by Denis Fitzpatrick.
ABOVE: even surfers won't be parted from their beloved car.

attendees flirt, watch short videos, and vie with each other to tell the raciest jokes. Michael Jeffreys of the Comedy Magic traffic school says that as long as certain subjects are covered – drunk driving, speeding, safety laws, insurance, etc. – the rest of the time can be filled at the instructor's discretion.

Jeffreys, a magician, usually begins by asking everybody why they are there. This gives him the opportunity to pass out some advice. "Maybe you should have been a bit politer to the officer" usually earns him a laugh. Like other instructors, Jeffreys had to pass a 100-question quiz before being certified to conduct classes, but he enlivens his lesson with a few tricks. Borrowing a coat from one of the pupils, he'll appear to push a lighted cigarette through the sleeve before handing it back with the comment, "Now it's a smoking jacket."

Critics have complained about the absurd names of many of the schools, but the DMV seems satisfied that they serve their purpose. And they offer other hazards: some advertise "fine restaurants" and one Beverly Hills school advertises itself as being "for chocoholics."

Rippling gridlock

Motorists embraced the freeways because of the ease and speed with which they could cover

pollution reaching "unacceptable" levels on 200 days each year, drivers increasingly sit in their cars and fume.

Psychologist Ange Lobue calls it "a metaphor for the powerlessness we experience in our daily lives... we begin to feel the delay threatens our survival. The threat becomes overwhelming and in an attempt to avoid these feelings (of helplessness) we become more aggressive, tailgating the driver in front (who), insulted by our 'territoriality,' responds with an abrupt lane-change and a passive-aggressive slowing or abrupt braking. This is followed by an exchange of insults leading to more danger-

great distances without having to stop for lights, but the rippling gridlock resulting from even a minor accident sometimes brings paralysis to the system. Congestion has added 20 minutes to the average commute and now rush hour lasts all day long.

Aware that every minute a stalled car is on a freeway causes at least four minutes of lingering congestion, some authorities have experimented with co-ordinating helicopter surveillance with tow-truck routes. But the real problem – the 55 percent increase in traffic in the past decade as against 2 percent of new roads – would take at least $8 billion to cure, according to some studies. Meanwhile, with

ous maneuvers." Sometimes this escalates into murder, as in the rash of freeway shootings that occured one hot, sticky summer. The incidents prompted this bumper sticker: IF I CUT YOU OFF DON'T SHOOT.

Perhaps unconfident that they are making a statement with the cars themselves, some owners display bumper stickers to entertain or provoke, with such typical Californianisms as SORRY IF MY KARMA COLLIDES WITH YOUR DOGMA or I BRAKE FOR HALLUCINATIONS.

In a 1970 experiment, researchers asked 15 drivers with no recent traffic violations to put Black Panther bumper stickers on their cars and found that within weeks this group of drivers had collected more than 33 citations from the local police.

More happily productive are the brightly colored and numbered stickers handed out by dating services – Freeway Singles Club, Tail Dating or Drive Me Wild – which enable members to contact each other via a central office. Roadway Romeos are commonplace, as Art Seidenbaum noted when writing about the widespread flirting and concluded that: "only in a culture created by car can love blossom between the lanes."

ing on shoulders, abrupt lane changes and possessing a free-floating hostility (honking the horn, cursing, pounding the steering wheel, obscene gestures); and Type B, whom Martin Brenner defines as "freeway wimps" who "rarely get angry, seeing it as pointless. They don't respond to provocations from other motorists; they drive with a smile on their faces and don't fight traffic."

LA's freeways see an average of 75 accidents a day, or 27,000 every year, of which about a

Vulnerable drivers

Sadly, more drivers prefer to fight than flirt. "In our cars we assume we are in charge. Our feelings of dominance and authority are increased, but they are also made vulnerable" write Peter Marsh and Peter Collett in *Driving Passion: The Psychology of the Car*. Speeding away at the lights is "a kind of gauntlet-throwing" they say. "It presents a challenge to other drivers."

Some psychologists classify drivers: Type A, a need to do more in less time, tailgating, pass-

LEFT: traffic is one of the biggest problems in the city, and it's getting bigger every day.
ABOVE: one solution is the ever-popular car pool.

third cause injuries and one percent are fatal. Driver fatigue and alcohol are reasons why the worst accidents occur at night, with Friday the worst day, and the major cause of pile-ups is cars following each other too closely.

But highway officers watch men shaving, reading newspapers or using car phones, women putting on makeup, drivers doing crossword puzzles, or even engaging in heavy sexual activity at excessive speeds. "The practice of making love on the highways is becoming alarmingly prevalent. In many cases it is flagrantly open," the city's Board of Supervisors was told by Captain Cannon of the LA motorcycle squad. The year of his report was 1921. ❏

MOJAVE
DESERT
Los Angeles Aqueduc
Garlock F.
Mts.
Rosamond
Lake
farms
farms
Wright
Mud
Lancaster
San Andreas Fault
Palmdale
Clearwater
F.
San Gabriel Mts
San Gabriel Fault
Fernando
arthquake
picenter
(1971)
Sierra Madre F.
San
Fernando
Valley
Pasadena
Monica Mts.
?
?
Los
Angeles
Whittier F.
Chino
Santa
Monica
Palos
Verdes
Hills
Long Beach
Santa Ana River

EARTHQUAKES AND OTHER CALAMITIES

Living in paradise can have its drawbacks – although most of the city's residents think the price is worth paying

Architect Frank Lloyd Wright once theorized that the reason all the loose nuts in the United States ended up in Los Angeles was because of the continental tilt. Although he was only joking about the city and its flaky reputation, America's premier architect knew full well about the difficulties of building on such notoriously unstable ground.

LA is earthquake territory. And if the constant rumblings and jolts aren't unsettling enough, ask any informed resident about the 6.7 temblor of January 17, 1994, or – even more frightening – the "8.3" in LA's future, shimmering like a macabre mirage. An 8.3 is the Richter scale magnitude of the shaker which, according to forecasters, will decimate the city some time in the next 30 years. It's the price one pays for living in paradise. Some Los Angeles driver is already sporting the license plate: W8N4BG1.

Actually, it's only a fraction of the price. A host of deadly disasters – drought, brush storms, floods, landslides – snap at the bare, tanned heels of America's most laid-back folk.

A hot time in the old city

To begin with, those postcard skies, pleasant though they are, often mean long periods of drought which time and again turn Los Angeles into a parched, anxious, water-obsessed community. And even worse, drought intensifies Los Angeles' seasonal fire problem.

Typically in the late fall, after long arid summers, the chaparral that carpets vast areas of Southern California becomes extremely flammable. This is the time when hot, desiccating Santa Ana winds sweep westward from the desert, turning sparks into flames which can tear through the land at 90 mph (145 km/h).

PRECEDING PAGES: the result of the epicenter of an earthquake at Northridge Apartments, LA.
LEFT: satellite view of the San Andreas Fault, photographed by NASA.
RIGHT: walk, don't walk ....

Because the most fire-prone areas are in the city's 140 sq. miles (363 sq. km) of crests and canyons, it's the wealthy who really get burned. Malibu, that well-known haven for the rich and famous, has repeatedly taken the heat. Between

1925 and 1956 the area suffered 33 fires which charred 174,680 acres (71,000 hectares) – a recurring reminder that, even in Shangri-la, Mother Nature can have a hot temper.

One of the worst fiery disasters was the Bel Air fire of November 6, 1961, the fifth costliest blaze in the United States' history, which disemboweled Los Angeles' most exclusive neighborhood and, along with everything else, reduced closets of minks and at least one original Van Gogh to ashes.

After strong Santa Ana winds fanned the flames at 13 acres (5 hectares) a minute through the brushy hillsides of Bel Air, firebrands made an incredible leap across the San Diego Freeway into the classy lap of Brentwood. Nearly 500 of the city's priciest homes were devoured, with losses of more than $30 million. Taking that same fire today, and accounting for subsequent development and inflation, you'd be talking about 3,000 houses destroyed and in the region of $600 million in damages.

During a really bad blaze, flames that began in Agoura Hills ripped toward the ocean, cutting across the Pacific Coast Highway and sabotaging Malibu's exclusive Broad Beach community. As 25,000 acres (10,000

> **SAN ANDREAS FAULT**
>
> An 835-mile fault stretching from the Mexican border to Cape Mendocino has averaged a major earthquake every 130 years. The last one was in 1857.

hectares) blackened, many watched a lifetime of work and dreams go up in smoke.

"The wind was strong and hot and… it blew everything in the garage out," said Frank Cornell who arrived home from work to find the Santa Monica Mountains ablaze. "Then it became so hot I could barely breathe, and the sky got dark, and there were flying embers and bits of trash and I knew I was in the middle of a fire storm."

The singer Neil Young's house burned down, actor Nick Nolte's corral was torched. Actress Irish McCalla buried her paintings in the sand before fleeing to the beach, along with such other escapees as actress Katharine Ross (who starred in *Butch Cassidy and the Sundance Kid*) and her horses. "It was so unreal," said McCalla, "like you were in a movie and someone was going to yell, CUT." And it seemed like the same old scenario all over again in the fall of 1993 when wind-whipped wildfires demolished 500 buildings in the Altadena area, killing three people and scorching more than 23,000 acres (9,300 hectares).

When it rains

Not long after the firefighters have shut off their hoses, county flood control officials often start buckling up their boots. In a continually spinning wheel of natural disaster, the fall blazes denude Los Angeles' slopes of vegetation and destroy the root systems that hold the soil in place. As the rains continue, swollen rivers cascade down from the surrounding mountain ranges, filling up the metropolitan bowl like a large swimming pool. Ultimately, after a good watering, the brush grows back, providing potent fuel for the next fire season. And the cycle goes on.

But wait. They say it never rains in Southern California. Ask any native about the drizzle and they'll probably tell you it's "unusual weather." Well, they're wrong. In fact, despite LA's image as a year-round vacation-land, the cooler months have been stormy. Punishing storms dumped 16 inches (40 cm) of rain on the Los Angeles area in February 1992, causing seven deaths and producing dramatic rescues by helicopter of motorists stranded on top of their cars. The following February floods and mudslides came again, this time damaging almost 100 homes and costing the Federal Emergency Management Agency almost $200 million in statewide aid. A further 45,000 Los Angeles County residents applied for aid in January 1995 after 38 counties had been declared disaster areas following a week-long volley of violent storms.

Going back a few years, nobody is likely to forget the spring of 1978 when hurricane-force winds and rain thrashed Los Angeles, sweeping cars off highways like Tonka toys, tearing up actor Burgess Meredith's house in Malibu, and demolishing millions of dollars' worth of property for miles around. Tujunga residents witnessed a Night of the Living Dead as torrents of water flushed out 30 graves from the Verdugo Hills cemetery, sending corpses and coffins tumbling into the streets and backyards below. Three wild lions escaped from their flood-ravaged compound and terrorized Soledad Canyon until deputies hunted them down and shot them.

Poor Burgess Meredith (a long-time actor best known for his role as the Penguin in the *Batman* TV series). In the winter of 1983, his house was reamed again by the rain, along with the houses of Bruce Dern, Steven Spielberg and Dyan Cannon as a series of storms chewed up and spit out Los Angeles' entire coastline. "I knew it was all over when I saw the hot tub sail

kets in the city's history. Venice's beachfront came to resemble its Italian namesake as lifeguards manning boats navigated the flooded streets trying to rescue people who had been marooned in their homes. Buildings collapsed like stage scenery and trees toppled as 821,750 cubic yards of debris accumulated on the sidewalks. Every main road into the city was closed. By the time the rain stopped, LA was looking at $78 million (that's 1938 dollars) in damages and 88 lost lives.

Even more lives were lost to flooding in January 1969. Southern Californians let out a whoop of relief when they saw the sun on

by into the ocean," said a Malibu neighbor as her house literally went down the drain. That was peanuts compared to the horrific sight Santa Monicans saw when the end of the Santa Monica Pier went crashing into the 15-ft (4.6-meter) waves, carrying with it the Porthole Restaurant and harbor master's office.

Water, water, everywhere

When it comes to floods, Angelenos always point to March 1938 as one of the wettest blan-

LEFT: entrance sign to the earthquake experience at Universal Studios.
ABOVE: Universal Studios' idea of an earthquake.

DEALING WITH CALAMITIES

"Leave, why should we leave paradise?" the locals always say to the camera, even when their house has just been destroyed for the seventh time. After spring floods have repeatedly poured down the Malibu hillsides and inundated coastal homes, residents are often seen on TV stoically sweeping up the mess.

Maybe a lighthearted approach is the best way to handle the hazards of living in a state with the potential for so many disasters. After a series of fires, earthquakes and floods in the 1980s and 1990s, Californians even began to joke that their telephone area code should be changed to 911, the same number for emergencies.

January 22 after four straight days of rain. But next day it started pouring for four more days. Mudslides slithered down the Santa Monica Mountains onto the 20th Century-Fox lot and wrecked sets for the movie *Planet of the Apes*.

Meanwhile, sleeping residents of Brentwood, Bel Air and the Hollywood Hills were buried alive in sludge that crushed and suffocated them. All told, 100 people were killed and 9,000 left homeless. Such mudslides, technically called "mud flows," which avalanche at 10, 20 and 100 mph (16, 30, 160 km/h) – speeds no human can outrun – are often the grizzliest signatures of LA's rainy tantrums.

idents knew something was wrong when kitchen counters began pulling out from the walls and holes started gaping between floorboards. It turned out they had built their dream homes on an ancient landslide which had somehow been reactivated – perhaps by landfill dumped when the county started building an extension to Crenshaw Boulevard. Around 150 elegant homes were slowly distorted beyond habitation, while 300 acres (120 hectares) of land beneath slid as fast as a foot a month.

People farther down the coast in Laguna Beach's Bluebird Canyon had the rug swept out from under their well-heeled feet even more

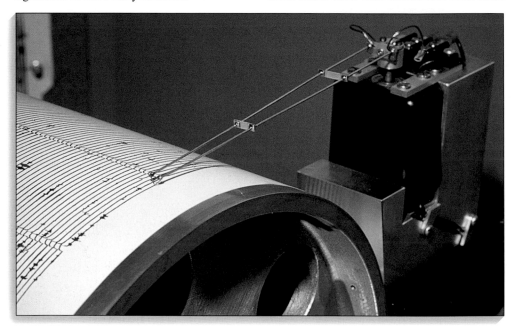

Slip-sliding away

While mudslides destroy life, landslides usually go for property. All over the Los Angeles area are pieces of ground which are always in motion. Most landslides occur because the city is built on uplifted marine rock filled with silt, mud and clay, and riddled with faults. Like a pencil balanced on its eraser until someone knocks the table below, a potential landslide often remains still, yet ready to roll at the slightest provocation.

This is what happened in Portuguese Bend, a gated neighborhood with a spellbinding view of Catalina Island that lies nestled in the very ritzy Palos Verdes Peninsula. Back in 1956, res-

dramatically in the fall of 1978 when the loud crack of power lines snapping along their moving street wrenched many from their beds. One woman remembers her neighbor yelling, "Come out as you are, your house is leaving." As she exited, her entire home, along with 49 others, did in fact disappear into the churning earth.

Through various engineering techniques, these two slides have been halted in their tracks. Since 1952, when Los Angeles instituted the first grading ordinance in the country, tremendous loss has been averted by stabilizing hillsides before building on them. Now home owners have become savvier about preserving their hillside property by planting deep-rooted plants and trees, burying baffles to slow the water's downward course, and cutting drainage channels.

But sometimes not a great deal can be done. The Big Rock landslide in Malibu, which so often closes down the Pacific Coast Highway, is still moving and has caused more than $100 million in property damage. "The slide is fixable by several engineering methods," says Allan Barrows, senior geologist at the Division of Mines and Geology, "but these people insist

ably leave tens of thousands of residents dead and cost survivors many billions of dollars.

Written records of earthquakes in this region have been made since the Spanish explorers felt their boot soles quiver. "Four violent shocks of earthquake frightened the Indians into a kind of prayer to the four winds, and caused the stream to be named also Jesus de los Temblores," wrote General Gaspar de Portolá in July 1769 as he arrived at the Santa Ana River with his Spanish expedition.

on litigation, which is probably more expensive and it doesn't fix anything."

In fact, lawsuits resulting from LA's most renowned landslide tied up the courts for over seven years, and cost more than $50 million in litigation fees.

The "Big One"

Fire, flood and mud aside, what could be more earth-shattering than an 8.3 killer quake? Not much. The next "Big One" to strike will prob-

---

LEFT: a seismograph shows minor tremors.
ABOVE: the modern architecture at Malibu looks like an accident waiting to happen.

Geologists now know that underneath all the palm trees and convertibles lies a network of active faults created by two giant chunks of crust, the Pacific and North American "plates," which inch past each other like two pieces of sandpaper rubbing against each other, causing an earthquake any time they slip. The San Andreas Fault itself runs along the San Gabriel Mountains, about 35 miles (56 km) north from LA's Civic Center; you can see the trough-like scar as you cross on the Antelope Valley Freeway south of Palmdale.

The fault moves no faster than a fingernail grows, producing a major temblor roughly every 145 years. And during the quiet years people easily grow complacent. Throughout the 1960s, for example, LA residents experienced nothing more serious than a 5.0 tremor, which can be upsetting but is hardly devastating.

Although the 6.7 temblor of January 17, 1994 *was* devastating, it had been 133 years since the last really big quake shook the area. This was near Fort Tejon, 100 miles (160 km) north of Los Angeles. The shaker was felt from the Mexican border to Monterey in Northern California, and was estimated to have been 8.3 on the Richter scale.

The numbers on the Richter scale rise logarithmically, an 8.0 being 10,000 times as pow-

destroyed, a further 16,000 homes and apartments made uninhabitable.

Damaging the dam

In another hard knock that struck 25 miles (40 km) north of downtown, many a "Valley Girl" was tossed out of her bed when the earth convulsed at the inconvenient time of 6am on February 9, 1971. In mere seconds, the 6.6 quake took 64 lives, and caused over half a billion (1971) dollars' worth of damage to 21,761 single family homes, 62 apartment houses, and 372 commercial structures. Roofs fell into hospital wards, crushing 46 patients, and a section of the

erful as a 4.0. Since the 1861 quake, the epileptic ground around Los Angeles has thrown some major fits. The most devastating quake in recent history struck at the height of the Great Depression on March 10, 1933, along the Newport-Inglewood Fault. Centered in Long Beach, this registered only a 6.3, but because of substandard building construction – LA now has the toughest building codes this side of Tokyo – it killed 115 people.

The 1994 quake was not as serious as that in magnitude but considering how much the city had grown in the intervening years it did almost as much damage: 57 deaths, almost 9,000 injuries as well as 12,000 buildings damaged or

Golden State Freeway collapsed. Meanwhile, the earthen walls of the Lower Van Norman Dam were seriously damaged by liquefaction and landslides. Had that dam broken instead of just being drained, about 19,000 more people would have died.

Lesser quakes take their toll, too. A visitor can still see vacant lots in Whittier where a 5.9 temblor on October 1, 1987, destroyed buildings, killing six people in the process and chalking up around $358 million in the damages department.

Even a recent 5.5 near Upland – whose biggest disturbance may have been to law students taking the Bar exam – managed to cause

$10 million of damage in the 30 seconds it made the earth do the *cha cha cha*.

What's next? The scenario's grim. The US Geological Survey report estimated that there was a 60 percent chance of a 7.5 or larger earthquake occurring along the San Andreas Fault before 2020. According to a Federal Emergency Management Agency report, if that quake tops 8.3 on a weekday afternoon it could kill over 13,000 people and cause property losses of tens of billions of dollars.

Worse, the report projected that a 7.5 on the Newport-Inglewood Fault, which cuts right through the Los Angeles area, could increase

les has experienced only small *tsunamis*, there's no guarantee that a monster wave won't slam into its peaceful shores.

How do Los Angelenos live with such grim uncertainties? Though some stock their cars and homes with earthquake survival kits and others take first-aid courses at the office, this is a town where even the most gruesome of topics is grist for the entertainment mill.

Go to Universal Studio Tours and experience the real thing (as if you need to) on "Earthquake – The Big One," an attraction where the ground cracks, streets collapse, and a 60,000-gallon (230,000-litre) flood finishes off the catastro-

the death toll to 23,000, causing damages in excess of $70 billion.

Washed away

Someday the whole city could just wash away in one big wave – and not the kind surfers lust after. We're talking about a *tsunami* triggered by an earthquake out at sea. These seismic waves can travel at 450 mph and, once they reach shallow waters, swell up to heights of 100 ft (30 meters) or more. Although Los Ange-

LEFT: the owners of the cars parked here were in for a surprise.
ABOVE: even if you leave LA, you're still not safe.

phe. Or, for a little education, scramble inside the "Shakey Quakey" van with a bunch of schoolchildren and watch Yogi Bear discussing earthquake preparedness on TV as the vehicle vibrates like a temblor.

Natives, however, try to take the unstable earth they live on in their inimitably cool stride. "After more than 30 years living here," writes Beverly Hills author Stephen Longstreet in *All Star Cast – An Anecdotal History of Los Angeles*, "when my windows rattle and cherished objects on shelves begin to dance, I merely count the seconds, three or four, and if the St Vitus shakes don't continue, I go on with whatever I'm doing." ❏

Universal Studios

Hollywood Freeway

GRIFFITH PARK

San Francisco

Hollywood Reservoir

Griffith Observatory

Hollywood Bowl

RUNYON CANYON PARK

Magic Castle

Mann's Chinese Theater

Hollywood/Western

HOLLYWOOD

ta Monica Boulevard

Hollywood/Vine

HOLLYWOOD FOREVER MEMORIAL PARK

Paramount Studios

Wilshire Country Club (Priv.)

PAN PACIFIC PARK

HANCOCK PARK

ounty La Brea seum Tar Pits of Art

Wiltern Theater

Ambassador Hotel

MACARTHUR PARK

KOREATOWN

Westlake/MacArthur Park

DOWNTOWN

Civic Center

MOCA

City Hall

Pershing Sq.

Bradbury Building

Union Station

Convention Center

7th Street/Metro Center

Pico

Santa Monica Freeway

Grand

San Pedro

University of Southern California (USC)

Natural History Museum

EXPOSITION PARK

Science & Industry Mus.

Memorial Coliseum

Washington

Watts Towers

South Los Angeles

MARINA DEL REY

Manchester Av.

Firestone Blvd

LA International

INGLEWOOD

Century

Frwy

EL SEGUNDO

MANHATTAN BEACH

Rosecrans Av.

HERMOSA BEACH

Artesia Blvd

TORRANCE

Rosecrans Av.

Commonwealth Av.

Artesia Frwy

Movieland Wax Museum

Knott's Berry Farm

ANAHEIM

REDONDO BEACH

Carson St

Lincoln Av.

CENTINELA PARK

PACIFIC OCEAN

Palos Verdes Peninsula

Disneyland

Sepulveda Blvd

Pacific Coast Hwy

LEWOOD

Inglewood Park Cemetery

Wayfarers Chapel

Point Vicente

SAN PEDRO

Los Angeles Harbor

LONG BEACH

SEAL BEACH

HUNTINGTON BEACH

Garden Grove Frwy

San Clemente, San Diego

The Forum

Santa Catalina Island

San Pedro Bay

Santa Catalina Island

0   5 miles
0   5 km

DOWNTOWN

*The heart of Los Angeles, and where it all began,
the Downtown area is the key to the city, from
Olvera Street to the latest skyscrapers*

Map
on page
119

Founded by the governor of the Mexican state of California in September 1780, **El Pueblo de Nuestra Señora la Reina de Los Angeles** began as a dusty plaza just west of the Los Angeles River, an inland site selected because the coast lacked a supply of fresh water. It was here that the 11 families who had been enticed by the governor Felipe de Neve ended their six-month trek from Sonora, building their adobe huts around the central square which was used as a meeting place and roped off with rawhide cord for Sunday bullfights and the occasional horse race. The original population of 44 comprised two Spaniards, 26 blacks and 16 Indians and *mestizos*.

Not a trace of the original plaza – moved northwest because of flooding – remains today; it was obliterated along with other sections of Downtown in the postwar demand for more freeways, but its site is marked, perhaps appropriately, by a parking lot. Today, the city's origins are commemorated by **Olvera Street** (once Wine Street), which many Latinos often refer to as La Placita Olvera. It contains 27 historic buildings, a traditional Mexican-style plaza area, where you can wander around, shop for souvenirs and handcrafted Mexican wares typical of old Mexico, and stop for the popular taquitos, tacos, enchiladas, mole and other native dishes at the outdoor cafés. On most weekends you will see strolling bolero musicians, Mariachis music, and perhaps performances by Aztec Indians and folkloric dancing. There are free tours by Las Angelitas (check in at the El Pueblo Visitors' Center; tours are given Wednesday to Saturday each hour from 10am to 12pm).

Situated on Olvera Street is the oldest house in Los Angeles, the **Avila Adobe ❶** (constructed in 1818). Apart from being concrete-reinforced after the 1922 earthquake, the house is as it was left by Francisco Abela's widow, Encarnacion, who died here in 1855. Married at 15, she was his second wife and the family lived in a style befitting the prosperous rancher, a man who had made a fortune by trading cowhides and tallow from his Rancho La Cienegas with the merchant ships plying up and down the California coast. Among the wealthy trappers of that day, wrote his friend Jedediah Smith, a fur trapper who stayed at the house in 1826, "Señor Francisco and his brother Ignacio are perhaps the richest."

Fourteen years after Abela (Avila) died in 1832, the house was briefly occupied during the Mexican-American war by Commodore Robert F. Stockton. Doña Encarnacion eventually moved back in, followed by her youngest daughter Francisca who had married a German settler. After her departure, both the house and the neighborhood steadily deteriorated and by the 1890s it was best known for "Nigger

Alley," a rowdy block of saloons, brothels, gambling houses and cockfighting.

Native Americans were still being exploited for cheap labor, as they had been from the beginning, but now they had been joined by thousands of Chinese, discharged after completion of the transcontinental railroad.

Saved for posterity

Deserted for years, the Avila Adobe was finally condemned by the city as unsafe, but was saved from demolition by a civic-minded group. Since it was acquired by the state in 1953, it has been restored with some of the original furnishings (Doña Encarnacion's black workbox, an early Steinway piano donated by the neighboring Pelanconi family), but mostly with reproductions of the era. In the rear courtyard a section remains of the stone channel, the *zanja madre* or mother ditch, that channeled water from the nearby river.

Across Olvera Street, the **Pelanconi home**, the oldest (*circa* 1853) brick house in the city, is now an attractive sidewalk restaurant, La Golondrina, where diners are serenaded by strolling *mariachis*, as at the nearby El Paseo. The block-long street, open until late in the evening, is always crowded with tourists sampling cactus candy or Mexican cooking from the numerous *puestos* (stands), buying clothing or pottery and watching craftsmen at work making papier-mâché animals, jewelry or wrought-iron gates.

The **Plaza Church ❷**, built in 1818 to replace a smaller earth-floored chapel, always seems crowded, too, being the spiritual center of the Latino community. The church is famous for its annual Easter ceremony, to which children bring their beribboned pets from miles away to be blessed. Open-air concerts take place here on summer Sundays.

Other attractions are less besieged, easier to visit, although weekends are better avoided. They include the 120-year-old **Pico House ❸**, the city's first three-story building and once its finest hotel, with 82 bedrooms, 21 parlors, two interior courtyards and a French restaurant. Named after the last Mexican gov-

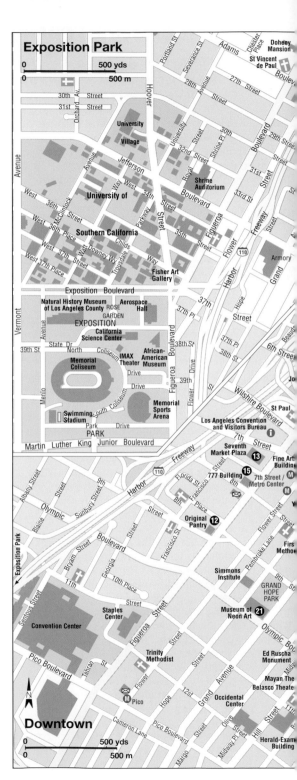

Hollywood, Universal City →

← Dodger Stadium →

NEW CHINATOWN ⑦

Sunset Freeway

Pasadena Boulevard

Hollywood Freeway

110

Board of Education

Fort Moore Pioneer Memorial

Plaza Church ②

EL PUEBLO

Sepulveda House

Avila Adobe ①

LOS ANGELES HISTORIC PARK

Pico House ③

Merced Theater ④

Garnier House ⑤

Union Station ⑥

Union Station Ⓜ

County Health Department

Department of Water and Power

Ahmanson Theater

Mark Taper Forum

Music Center ㉓

Dorothy Chandler Pavilion

Hall of Administration

Hall of Justice

Children's Museum

Walt Disney Concert Hall (under construction)

Civic Center

County Courthouse

Hall of Records

US Courthouse

⑳

Federal Building

World Trade Center

Civic Center Ⓜ

Law Library

Criminal Courts Building

City Hall ㉒

City Hall East

Westin Bonaventure Hotel ㉚

Ketchum YMCA

Wells Fargo History Museum ㉘

Museum of Contemporary Art ⑰

State Offices

City Hall South

City Hall

Parker Center

444 Plaza ㉛

Bunker Hill Steps ㉗

First Interstate World Center (Library Tower)

㉙

California Plaza ⑱

Angels Flight

㉖

Million Dollar Theater

Los Angeles Times Building ㉔

Times Mirror Square

Latino Museum of History, Art & Culture

Japanese American National Museum

Central Library ㉜

Subway Terminal Building

Grand Central Market ㊲

Bradbury Building ㊴

Department of Transport

New Otani Hotel ⑧

Japanese Village Plaza

Geffen Contemporary ⑲

Biltmore Hotel ㉝

Temple Baptist Church

St Vibiana's Cathedral

LITTLE TOKYO

Univ. Club

Oviatt Building

㉟

Pershing Square

BIDDY MASON PARK

Japan America Theater

Jewelry Mart ㊱

International Jewelry Center

Pershing Square Ⓜ

Alexandria Hotel

Arcade Theater

Japanese American Cultural & Community Center ⑨

Yaoban Plaza

Los Angeles Theater ㊷

Los Angeles Theater Center

㉕

Orpheum Theater ㊸

㊶

Pacific Coast Stock Exchange

SKID ROW

Clifton's Cafeteria

Western Columbia Building

Tower Theater

GARMENT DISTRICT

Cooper Building

Flower Market ⑩

California Mart ⑪

⑯

Terminal Annex Post Office ✉

ernor of California, Pio Pico, who lost it after foreclosure proceedings in 1880, it shares a wall with the city's first playhouse, the **Merced Theater** , later converted into a department store, whose ground floor originally sheltered the hotel's bar and billiard saloon.

Both buildings have been undergoing restoration, along with the **Hellman Quon building** (1900), a Chinese store and lodging house that replaced Pico's former home, and the **Garnier House** ❺ (1890). It was on the site of the Garnier House, many years before, that a duel, fought over a desirable prostitute, resulted in the deaths of two Chinese people and sparked a riot which ended with the lynching of 19 others. Lynchings, mostly of Mexicans, were a way of life as late as the 1850s.

Also on this block is the restored **Fire House**, which served the area until 1897, complete with fire-fighting equipment, a horse-drawn engine and photo of Blackie, the city's last fire horse (he died in 1939). Free walking tours of the Fire House leave hourly 10am to 1pm daily except Monday.

Traveling in style

East of Main Street, the spectacularly lavish **Union Station** ❻ – all black marble, mahogany, inlaid tiles and enormous leather seats – should be seen if only as a reminder of how splendid travel once could be.

Built with a 135-ft (41-meter) tower, arched corridors, 52-ft (16-meter) high ceilings and literally acres of space, the station once served almost a million passengers a day. It is maintained by Amtrak, which operates about 20 trains a day. The city's subway system, the **Metro Red Line**, begins here, and the imaginative murals and artwork in the subterranean station are worth going under-

BELOW: elegant Union Station.

ground to see. Behind the station sits the glass-roofed **Gateway Transit Center**, the attractive, fountain-filled transportation hub of the area.

Map on page 119

Originally three railroads served Los Angeles, and it was only after considerable pressure (and a $1 million subsidy) that the city persuaded them to agree on a single terminal, Union Station, which opened on May 7, 1939. The first of the streamlined, all-Pullman trains from New York brought 600 fashion retailers and editors here in 1946 for a swimsuit show on the beach at Catalina Island. For many years afterwards, newspaper readers saw photographs of pouting movie stars poised on the steps of the arriving or departing *Twentieth Century Limited*, and even today Union Station is often used as a backdrop in 1930s-era movies filmed around Hollywood.

The Southern Pacific reached Los Angeles in 1876 following a trail across the Tehachapi Mountains hacked out by thousands of Chinese laborers. When, a decade later, the lines of the Atchison, Topeka and Santa Fe were completed, many of these Chinese filtered down into the city, joining immigrants who had arrived during the 1840s Gold Rush. It was this sizeable colony that had to be evicted when the ground was cleared for Union Station in 1933.

A typical stone embellishment in Chinatown.

Just across Alameda from Union Station, try **Phillipe's** for lunch, a funky, sawdust-on-the-floor landmark that invented the French dip sandwich.

Exotic flavors

The area called **New Chinatown** ❼ opened officially in 1938 in an area between Spring and Hill streets. Here, and on Broadway north of Ord Street, innumerable Chinese banks, vegetable markets, stores filled with squawking poultry or captive fish, and supermarkets with barely an English label to be

BELOW: Chinatown opened in 1938.

THE BEST OF LOS ANGELES

ART AND CULTURE MUSEUMS

SCIENCE AND TECHNOLOGY MUSEUMS

THEME PARKS

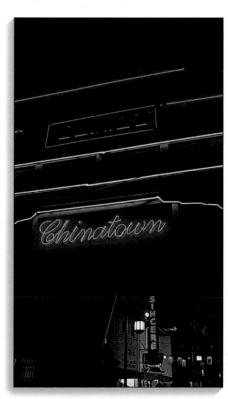

seen manage to absorb endless streams of tourists without ever losing their rural ambience. Even that ubiquitous mid-Western cliché, the shopping mall – here named **Gin Ling Way** – has an Asian flavor. Maybe it's all the images of fire-breathing dragons. The **Food Center** and exotic **Kong Chow Temple** (931 North Broadway) are worth a visit. The concourse between Hill and Broadway, designed to look like Beijing's Forbidden City with ceremonial gates and Oriental curlicue tiled roofs, features a wishing well surrounded by dwarf plants and statues.

For an even deeper look at Chinese heritage and art, dart on over to 423 Los Angeles Street, where the **Chinese-American Museum** recently opened in what was the Old Chinatown's City Hall.

Little Tokyo, an area radiating from the intersection of San Pedro and Second streets, has a more sterile appearance but is unmistakably Japanese. Most of it was rebuilt after World War II, following the return of most of the 110,000 Japanese who had been relocated to internment camps in the hysteria after Pearl Harbor. About 80,000 people – roughly one quarter of all Japanese resident in the US – live in the area. Note the monument on Onizuka Street, named for Ellison S. Onizuka, the first Japanese-American astronaut.

The most visible landmark of Little Tokyo is the lavish **New Otani Hotel ⑧**, topped off by the **Japanese Garden**, a rooftop oasis by famed landscape architect Sentaru Iwaki, who modeled it after a 400-year-old garden in Tokyo. East of the Otani is a pristine mall punctuated with massive boulders and small performance areas. It is more interesting, however, to walk through the gardens of the adjoining high rise, admire the stylish **Higashi Hongwanji Buddhist Temple** with its overhanging tile roof, and then head for the three-story **Yaoban**

Plaza shopping center at the corner of Central Avenue and Third Street. Here is a Japanese bakery, book and magazine store, plus a genuine Japanese supermarket beneath a second-floor department store displaying all the panache (and unfortunately the same high prices) that visitors to Japan have come to expect. The third floor includes a twin-screen cinema, one of whose presentations is always subtitled in English.

The major influx of Japanese into the Los Angeles area came at the beginning of the 20th century when, unable to acquire or afford fertile land, they concentrated on making the deserts bloom as in the now-lush Imperial Valley. A moving tribute to the skills they contributed can be seen in calligraphic tiles on a wall opposite the **Japanese American Cultural and Community Center** at San Pedro and Third (open Monday–Friday 9am–6pm. Art Gallery only open Saturday and Sunday 11am–4pm) as well as at the Japanese American National Museum on First Street (open Tuesday–Thursday 10am–5pm, Friday–Sunday 11am–8pm, closed: Monday).

And, long renowned for their gardening and topographical expertise, many Japanese can be found among the 400 growers at the **Flower Market** ❿ in two white buildings at Seventh and Wall streets, where the action begins before dawn (best days: Monday, Wednesday and Friday) and is all over by noon. The produce market, one block away, keeps similar hours. This is also the garment district, whose centerpiece, the **California Mart** ⓫ at Ninth and Main, houses hundreds of clothing manufacturers as well as a fashion theater and restaurants.

Up the street is the **Seventh Market Plaza** ⓭, a stylish mall whose sunken plaza with its open-air restaurant sits among three-story palm trees shading such stalwart stores as Bullocks, Benetton and the May Company. Among the interesting art work scattered around the plaza is a stooping bronze businessman, on the north side of Citicorp Center.

Cross the street and walk half a block to the **Fine Arts Building** ⓮ at 811 West 7th, its artists' studios long ago converted to offices. Built in 1936, it was lovingly restored a decade ago. A medieval-style lobby, with 15 chandeliers and a tiled fountain, hosts color drawings of some of the ambitious artwork planned for 30 stations of the city's new Metro system. Admire the gaudy, gilded facade of the **Home Savings building** as you head back to Figueroa. The stepped, white tower of the **777 Building** ⓯ ("subtle profiles and strong silhouettes" says one critic) was created by Argentine-born César Pelli, also responsible for the distinctive Pacific Design Center (known locally as "the Blue Whale") in West Hollywood.

A fountain by Eric Orr sits outside the **Sanwa Bank** building in the 80-ft (24-meter) high art-deco lobby in which, among acres of brown marble, sit two of the largest plants ever seen in captivity.

The Downtown area has seen something of a renaissance of the art scene in the last decade, with many artists flocking to live and work in old lofts and such interesting places such as the **Brewery** ⓰, a repository of artists and galleries among the more interesting of the Downtown area. Literally once a Pabst beer brewery, the building is now billed as the world's

Map on page 119

TIP

After a very early morning at the markets, it might be useful to know about the **Original Pantry** ⓬ (877 Figueroa), a 24-hour restaurant that claims never to have closed since first opening its doors in 1924.

BELOW: MONA's neon portraits.

largest artists complex (2100 N. Main Street; tel: 213/694-2911 for exhibition info). Other Downtown museums: the **Museum of Contemporary Art** ⓱ (MOCA), designed by Arata Isozaki as the showpiece of the ambitious **California Plaza** ⓲ on Grand Avenue – "a small village in the valley of skyscrapers" – and its satellite, the **Geffen Contemporary** ⓳ at 152 Central Avenue (both open Tuesday–Sunday 11am–5pm, Thursday 11am–5pm). Both offer a wide range of styles with special concentration on Californian artists. The delightful **Children's Museum** ⓴ (open Saturday and Sunday 10am–5pm, Tuesday–Friday school groups only, except during summer vacations 10am–5pm, closed: Monday) encourages kids to make their own videotapes, drive a (stationary) bus, and generally cut loose.

The **Museum of Neon Art** ㉑ (MONA) (open Wednesday–Saturday 11am–5pm, Sunday noon to 5pm), at 501 West Olympic Boulevard, is the world's only museum devoted to neon.

A new addition to the Downtown scene is the **Latino Museum of History, Art and Culture** at 112 Main Street (open 10–4 daily, closed: Wednesday).

The Children's Museum closes off one end of the sunken **Los Angeles Mall**, bedecked with waterfalls and palm trees around a central area of tables and fast-food restaurants. On its upper level is a 60-ft (18-meter) tower in which are embedded 1,500 triangular glass prisms, the **Triforium**. When this device is operating it provides a light show to coincide with the frequent lunchtime concerts. Its creator, Joseph Young, calls the tower "a kinetic color-music sculpture."

The mall, which sits on the site of what was once among the world's most prolific oil wells, contains a post office and many shops as well as one of those typically enormous California drugstores that sells just about everything and has a

BELOW: Peace on Earth sculpture at the Music Center.
RIGHT: Angels Flight.

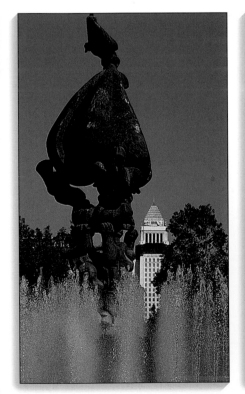

do-it-yourself photo machine. Escalators at the mall's western end lead up to **City Hall ㉒** which, when it replaced the city's second one in 1928, was the tallest building in Los Angeles and remained so until "earthquake-proof" architecture was invented in the 1950s. Built from all-California materials, its mortar included sand from each county and water from each of the state's 21 missions. However, even this divine combination didn't hold back nature's wrath – after damage from the 1992 and 1994 earthquakes, City Hall was recently closed for a period for seismic retrofitting.

Map on page 119

Views all around

Connecting City Hall (the *Daily Planet* of TV's *Superman* series) with its eastern annex is a third-floor bridge which usually houses an art show. The best view, however, is from the 26th-floor balcony at the top of the building (free admission most weekdays). From here you can see **Dodger Stadium** (baseball, April to October) and freeway-framed **Elysian Park** just to the north; the sterile **Convention Center** and modern **Staples Center** (home of the professional basketball teams the Lakers and Clippers, and professional hockey team the Kings) near the Harbor and Santa Monica freeway intersection to the south; and, just a few blocks to the west, the marble and black glass **Music Center ㉓** with its Peace on Earth sculpture. This is the current home of several companies, including the Los Angeles Philharmonic, the Los Angeles Opera, and the Center Theatre Group.

Get your Los Angeles Times *here!*

The Music Center, hub of the cultural establishment, celebrated its 25th Anniversary in 1989 with plans to add an imaginatively designed (by Frank Gehry) **Walt Disney Concert Hall** (gift of Lillian Disney, Walt's widow) to the

BELOW: Dodger Stadium stretch.

existing complex. After a period of financial and political difficulties, this majestic project (and new home for the Philharmonic) is finally taking shape right across the street, just south of the Music Center, and is expected to open its doors in October 2002.

The corner of Spring and Broadway, just below City Hall, houses the block-long complex of the *Los Angeles Times* ㉔, at 202 W 1st Street (entrance on Spring Street). This was where Hollywood's founder H.H. Wilcox had his first office and before that it was the office of Nathan Cole, the paper's unsung founder who went bust in 1880 before the Chandler family took control.

At Spring and Fifth, the eight-story **Alexandria Hotel** ㉕, with its marble-pillared lobby and 28-ft (8.5-meter) ceilings, was the first to have complete fire-proofing when it opened in 1906 and sheltered the visiting elite of the day, including presidents William Taft and Theodore Roosevelt. It was also a second home for Charlie Chaplin. The hotel, sadly, is far from elegant today, but old photographs on its faded, red-velvet walls depict some of its past glories.

Sightseeing around Downtown takes a couple of hours on foot, but making it easier is the city-operated bus which runs every few minutes. Books of tickets are available, or you can pay each time you board; there are frequent stops and passengers can transfer free from Route B (Chinatown to the Arco Plaza via Olvera Street, the Music Center and Library Square) to Route A (Little Tokyo to the TransAmerica building at Hill and 12th).

Understanding the Old West

Buses cover most of the route that follows, and it makes sense to board one outside City Hall for the trip to the **Wells Fargo Plaza** at Grand and Third

There are free tours of the Los Angeles Times *from Monday to Friday, with no reservations required.*

BELOW: post haste at the Wells Fargo Museum.

because there isn't too much to see on the way, although you might want to take a ride up **Bunker Hill** on the recently restored **Angels Flight funicular railway** ㉖ (open daily 6.30am–10pm), originally removed in 1969, when the upscale housing project was built. It was part of the only profitable passenger line in the US at the time, and got a passing reference in *The King in Yellow*, whose author, Raymond Chandler, lived on Bunker Hill. The Hill Street tunnel, built in 1909, was originally the route of the Pacific Electric trolley car and its construction cut 12 minutes off its run from Downtown to the coast. The dramatic **Bunker Hill Steps** ㉗ ascend the hill from 5th Street to Hope Street.

Map on page 119

The engaging **Wells Fargo Museum** ㉘ (open Monday–Friday 9am–5pm) earns a rave review for its attractive layout and interesting contents. Posters for the films *Stagecoach* and *Wells Fargo* line the walls and the atmosphere of Gold-Rush days is evoked by a 19th-century stagecoach, a re-created banking office equipped with codebooks and telegraph key on which visitors can punch out messages, an old carpet bag, early coins and travelers' checks, mining equipment and a tattered volume titled *5,000 Miles by Stage*.

From the 335 S. Hope Building's (formerly Security Pacific Bank) attractive garden behind Wells Fargo you can begin a pedestrian odyssey that will take you four blocks without touching the sidewalk. A sky ramp connects the bank with the antiseptic **World Trade Center**. Nearby, between Hope Street and Grand Avenue, is the 73-story **First Interstate World Center** ㉙, designed by I.M. Pei & Partners. A contender for tallest building in the West, it was nicknamed the Library Tower because it used the library's air rights during construction in exchange for helping to fund the library's renovation. Its tree-lined gardens, with fountains and waterways, sit above a large parking structure.

BELOW:
Los Angeles'
Central Library.

Another architecturally interesting Downtown showpiece is the futuristic **Westin Bonaventure Hotel** ㉚. Designed and built by John Portman & Associates, its interior is both amusing and confusing, with mini-lounges at different levels wedged between columns and clustered around the fountain and pool of a central atrium. A glass elevator speeds up to the revolving lounge, **Top of Five** (open Sunday–Thursday 5.30–10pm, Friday and Saturday to 11pm) for drinks and snacks but from which the view is partially blocked by surrounding skyscrapers like the **Union Bank of California**.

These futuristic skyscrapers actually look better from below as you pause on your way across the skybridge that connects the hotel with the majestic **444 Plaza building** ㉛, a familiar landmark to viewers of various television series (especially *LA Law*). Vast sums of money have been spent on a satisfying collaboration of art and architecture around this building and the adjoining **Arco Plaza**. Dotted amidst the waterfalls, escalators and 30-ft (9-meter) palm trees are enormous sculptures by Mark DiSuvero, Robert Rauschenberg, Frank Stella, Bruce Nauman and Michael Heizer, all of them site-specific. At noon on certain summer days, free concerts are presented in the plaza. Underneath the twin towers of Atlantic Richfield and Bank of America is one of the country's biggest and busiest subterranean shopping centers.

Restoring the library

The very stylish **Los Angeles Central Library** ㉜, 630 West 5th Street, a 1926 creation of architect Bertram Goodhue, has been beautifully restored after being damaged by fire in 1986. Some hints of its former Beaux Arts grandeur can be gleaned from the surviving blue-tiled, pyramid-shaped tower. The fire was

BELOW: Downtown cityscape.

catastrophic, but 2 million volumes survived. The library is open Monday–Thursday 10am–8pm, Friday and Saturday 10am–6pm, Sunday 1–5pm.

The nearby **Biltmore** ㉝, whose 1,000 rooms made it the largest hotel in the West when it opened with a star-studded party in 1923, has a lobby festooned with frescoes, murals, and a remarkable cherub-and-cloud ceiling that evokes 14th-century Italy with a 20th-century sheen.

Featured in many films, the Biltmore has held a special place in history since 1927, when MGM's art director Cedric Gibbons first drew a still-to-be-named Oscar on his hotel napkin. A picture in a sidewalk window depicts attendees at the 1937 Academy Awards.

One block east along Fifth Street, the 1932 statue of Beethoven, erected by musicians from the Philharmonic in garishly remodeled **Pershing Square** ㉞, is a reminder that a century ago the now-sterile plaza became an upscale alternative to the fast-declining Olvera Street neighborhood. Once more there are ambitions plans to bring life back to the square via an extensive redesign.

The **Auditorium Building**, at the northeast corner, used to be where the Philharmonic played. Long before that, it had been the Clunes Theater, largest in town and offering "opulent luxury," according to D.W. Griffith's assistant Karl Brown who attended the 1915 opening of the director's *Birth of a Nation* there. He later wrote: "After that first night at Clunes … anybody could be a millionaire for three hours."

Under the direction of a determined architect named Brenda Levin, many of these once-magnificent Downtown buildings are being restored to their former glory. One is the 13-story **Oviatt Building** ㉟ (617 South Olive) which is listed on the national register of historic places, and whose lobby was decorated by

Broadway is a name familiar all over the world.

BELOW: Grand Central Market on Broadway.

several tons of now almost-priceless Lalique glass when it opened in 1928. The luxurious fittings with which James Oviatt had his architects Walker and Eisen equip his ground-floor store (he also had a penthouse pool with a sandy "beach") were incorporated into what is now among the city's most gorgeous restaurants, **Cicada**, which opens off the lobby and whose bar has a black marble dance floor. In Raymond Chandler's *The Lady in the Lake*, the structure is known as the Treloar building. Today Hollywood still comes calling as the restaurant and the 13th floor penthouse are a favorite for private parties.

At Pershing Square's southeast corner, the **Jewelry Mart** ❸ was once the Pantages building, a theater that combined films with vaudeville shows. Nine years after opening, Alexander Pantages was falsely accused of raping one of his teenage female ushers and served two years in jail before being acquitted in 1931. He died shortly afterwards.

California's first movie

Just behind the Jewelry Mart, off Seventh Street, is a little-noticed alley called **St Vincent's Court**, an unprepossessing dead-end with a faded mural of an old Parisian street covering the wall opposite a small take-out deli with a couple of sidewalk tables. Despite the towaway signs it would seem a tempting spot to park, but it also happens to be a popular place for parking enforcement officers.

Should you wish to park on a landmark, ease on down a couple of blocks to the parking lot at 751 South Olive where in 1909 William N. Selig, a Chicago producer of one-reelers, rented an old mansion to film *In the Sultan's Power,* the very first movie to be completely filmed in California. One star of the film, Francis Boggs, was shot and killed here only a few months later and the other, Hobart Bosworth, died in 1943 after predicting (according to author Ken Schessler) that someday a brass plaque would mark the site. He was optimistic – but incorrect.

BELOW:
fixture at Grand Central Market.

And so we come to the busiest street in town, **Broadway**, which with its predominance of fast-food counters, cheap jewelry shops, amusement arcades, slasher movies, hustlers, impatient shoppers and assorted lowlife is still the nearest Los Angeles gets to the lively, bustling street scene of the more traditionally ambulatory cities. It's intensely Latino in style, as a visit to **Grand Central Market** ❸ (between Third and Fourth) will confirm. Rabbits, hot chilis, Mexican clothing, day-old pastries, $1 sacks of oranges, turtle meat, leather purses, 20 varieties of tea – these and hundreds of other items are stacked under a multiplicity of bilingual neon signs. Open Monday–Saturday 9am–6pm, Sunday 10am–5.30pm, the giant mercado is never uncrowded but always a delight. It offers the cheapest food in town.

Worthy of a paragraph to itself is **Clifton's Cafeteria** (648 South Broadway), which still retains the lofty aims of its humanitarian founder, who used to allow indigents to pay what they could afford. A notice of these aims is posted by the door. Its pseudo-South Sea decor makes it like dining on a stage set, and the cafeteria's prices are probably the most reasonable of any in the Downtown area.

Map on page 119

Sumptuous elegance

The Grand Central Market's owner, Ira Yellin, working with architect Brenda Levin, who designed its stylish neon signs, has been spiffing up both the market and the adjoining **Million Dollar Theater ㊳**, a paragon of elegance when it was opened by showman Sid Grauman in 1916 with the premiere of William S. Hart's *The Silent Man*. Yellin also owns the wonderful **Bradbury Building ㊴** across the street, a beautifully preserved showcase of wrought-iron balconies, old-fashioned hydraulic elevators, and elegant stairways surrounding a spotless atrium illuminated by an overhead skylight. Designed by novice architect George H. Wyman for a mining mogul in 1893, it was once occupied mainly by law firms but in recent years has mostly been rented out for moviemaking, notably as Philip Marlowe's "Hollywood office" in the 1969 adaptation of Raymond Chandler's *The Little Sister*, and in the brooding, futuristic film *Blade Runner*.

Norma Jean Baker is rumored to have appeared as a stripper at the Million Dollar Theater long before she became Marilyn Monroe.

Many Downtown sites are popular with moviemakers, but in the old days most people came down here to see movies and rowdy vaudeville shows. Marilyn Monroe appeared at the **Mayan Theater ㊵** (1044 South Hill) – "somewhere between a pre-Columbian temple and a wedding cake iced by a madman," wrote Richard Alleman – which opened in 1927 with Anita Loos' *Gentlemen Prefer Blondes*.

In the 1930s LA had 1,500 theaters, more than any other city in the country. Many were as ostentatious as the industry itself with elements reminiscent of Europe's castles and cathedrals, influences reputedly on Mary Pickford's mind in 1926 when she commissioned the flagship **United Artists' Theater** at 933 South Broadway. Its walls display the murals of Pickford and her partner Douglas Fairbanks. It is now the headquarters of Dr Gene Scott's ministry.

BELOW: there are plenty of snacks available while you tour around.

The **Orpheum Theater ㊶** at 630 South Broadway, had already stunned moviegoers with an arched lobby whose huge chandeliers had each cost about 10 times the manager's annual salary and bore enough goldleaf to cover a dozen streetcars. Even more splendid is the interior of the **Los Angeles Theater ㊷**, hurriedly completed by designer S. Charles Lee for the 1931 premiere of Charlie Chaplin's *City Lights*. The last of the great Downtown movie palaces, it had an art gallery, mahogany-paneled ballroom, extravagantly baroque ceilings and a fountain, as well as an attended kiddies' playroom at which patrons could drop off their offspring.

The nearby **Tower Theater**, the first to be designed specifically for the new talky films, is an earlier Lee creation, modeled on the lobby of the Paris Opéra.

The **Arcade** (534 South Broadway), its interior resembling an old-time English music hall, was built by Alexander Pantages, fresh from Alaska where he had grown rich producing the kind of show popular with entertainment-starved goldminers. The **Palace** was the Orpheum when it opened as a vaudeville house in 1911, and the tiny **Cameo** had opened the year before as a nickelodeon, the type of place from which many of the early movie moguls had made their fortunes.

Tours of the old Broadway theaters and downtown architectural sites are conducted every Saturday by the Los Angeles Conservancy (tel: 213/623 2489). ❏

DOWNTOWN ENVIRONS

The area around Downtown is no less interesting.
Exposition Park is a huge entertainment area,
and there are many other museums and galleries

Map on page 134

About a mile south of Downtown along Figueroa is **Exposition Park ❶**, which, when it opened as Agricultural Park in 1880, featured a racetrack that attracted both the sporting crowd and the wealthier hookers who came over in their horse-drawn carriages from the red-light district on Alameda Street. The racetrack gave way first to camel racing, and then at the turn of the century to an auto track on which Barney Oldfield set a world speed record of a dizzying 53 mph (85 km/h). Since 1928 the immense **Coliseum** (capacity: 93,000), site of the Olympic Games in 1932 and again in 1984, has dominated the park.

Exposition Park also contains a 14-acre sunken rose garden, the **Natural History Museum**, the **Museum of Science and Industry**, the **Aerospace Hall** (including ultralites and helicopters), the recently added **California ScienCenter,** with a new IMAX Theater, and the fascinating **African-American Museum**, at which a recent exhibit provocatively featured separate entrances for "white" and "colored." You might also want to investigate the **Museum of African-American Art** on nearby Crenshaw Boulevard (open Thursday–Saturday 11am–6pm, Sunday noon–5pm).

Film school

Exposition Boulevard separates the park from the 138-acre (56-hectare) campus of the **University of Southern California** (USC) ❷, which is a pleasantly tree-shaded campus through which to walk (call for a place on the free, one-hour weekday walking tours). The stroll may evoke memories for longtime movie fans*: The Hunchback of Notre Dame* and *The Graduate* were among the many films shot here. John Wayne, George Lucas and Steven Spielberg graduated from USC, as did O. J. Simpson – who is now remembered for more sensational reasons than the trophy collection opposite the football field.

Also of interest is the **Hancock Building** which contains four stately rooms of marble, oak paneling and crystal chandeliers salvaged from the Hancock family home in 1937 and embedded into this structure. Reservations are needed if you wish to look around (tel: 213/ 740-5144).

Also on campus is the **Fisher Art Gallery**, a highly unusual gallery with one foot in the past and one in the future – some of the Fisher's collection dates back five centuries, yet it is also an interactive museum, billed as a testbed for the "virtual museum of the future." (Open during exhibitions Tuesday–Friday noon–5pm, Saturday 11am–3pm; tel: 213/740 4561.)

The northeast corner, where Figueroa meets Jefferson Boulevard, is dominated by the exotically shaped **Shrine Auditorium** in which Darryl Zanuck restaged

LEFT: life in Watts.
BELOW: the easy life.

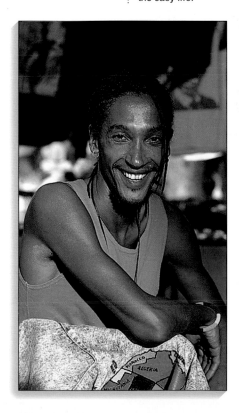

the 1912 Democratic convention for his 1950 flop *Wilson*. The auditorium also played a significant role in the ill-fated romance between Judy Garland and James Mason in the 1954 version of *A Star Is Born*. Its 186-ft (57-meter) stage is where the captured King Kong was put on show, where Michael Jackson caught fire while making a Pepsi Cola commercial, and has been the venue numerous times for the Grammys and Academy Awards.

A few blocks north of Jefferson is West Adams, some of whose early residents were wealthy Mexicans fleeing the revolutionary leaders Emilio Zapata and Pancho Villa. Big Victorian mansions filled out the street, nowhere more than in the private enclave of **Chester Place** ❸ which has been filmed dozens of times by moviemakers seeking the characteristic look of older eastern cities without the necessity of having to go back east and film the real thing.

Among the most impressive homes was that of Edward Doheny, for which the mining prospector-turned oil tycoon paid $120,000 in gold coins in 1901. It now houses the faculty from Mount St Mary's College, which surrounds it. Doheny also built the impressive **St Vincent de Paul Church** ❹ nearby, with its 90-ft (27-meter) dome and ornate belltower. The building that draws the most sightseers, however, is the Tudoresque mansion at **649 West Adams**, which has been the home, at different times, of silent movie stars Theda Bara and Roscoe "Fatty" Arbuckle.

Farther west, at Adams and Cimarron, is what should be one of the city's best-known landmarks, the relatively neglected William Adams **Clark Memorial Library** ❺ (open Monday–Friday 9am–4.45pm), built as a memorial to his father – a Montana rancher, copper tycoon and US senator – by the man who founded the Los Angeles Philharmonic Orchestra.

The Stars and Stripes American flag flies outside many sights.

BELOW:
Simon Rodia's
Watts Towers.

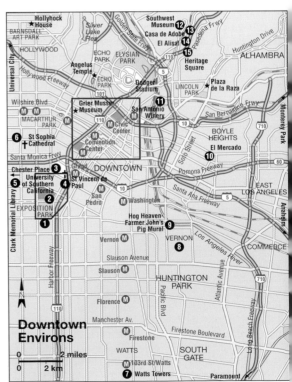

Downtown Environs

It contains, in a 1926 Italian Renaissance building, an impressive collection of early editions of Daniel Defoe's *Robinson Crusoe*, the *Diaries of Samuel Pepys*, Chaucer, Sir Walter Ralegh and Shakespeare, along with 75,000 other volumes, many of which date back to the 16th and 17th centuries. In addition, the library (open to the public) has one of the world's most complete collections of the 17th-century dramatist John Dryden. There is also a 1695 globe depicting California as an island. The library also possesses one of the most complete collections of books by Oscar Wilde – mostly original editions – plus 3,000 original manuscripts, letters and other documents from that late Victorian era (tours of decorated rooms by appointment only; tel: 323/731-8529). And for more Victoriana try the **Grier Musser Museum**, a Queen Anne and antique collection that offers a look into Los Angeles' past (open Wednesday–Friday noon–4pm; Saturday 11am–4pm; tel: 213/413-1814).

With the obvious exception of Hollywood and the beach towns, most of the communities surrounding LA's Downtown core are "suburban" from a tourist point of view and, as in most cities, ethnic groups tend to stay together. Greeks, for example, have clustered in some numbers around **St Sophia Greek Orthodox Cathedral** ❻ on South Normandie, a magnificent edifice financed by the Skouras brothers, among the film colony's earliest moguls. The mix around Wilshire and Western is mainly Korean.

Due south are the predominantly black areas such as Watts, ill-served by transport and for a long time suffering neglect, discrimination and unemployment, a deadly combination that has occasionally provoked riots. Watts, though hardly better off today, is quiet and still home to one of the city's most astonishing masterpieces: the fantastic **Watts Towers** ❼, created between 1921 and

Map on page 134

BELOW:
Watts Towers
are covered with
70,000 seashells.

1954 by Simon Rodia, a penniless Italian tilesetter who patiently constructed the trio of lacy columns as an affectionate tribute to his adopted land.

Composed of broken bottles, pottery shards, tiles, pebbles, and steel rods all stuccoed together and covered with 70,000 seashells, the towers are a set of sculptures so far ahead of their time that they were unappreciated for years; vandals tried to destroy them and the city planned to pull them down. They were reprieved after attempts to dismantle them, using steel cables pulled by a tractor in full view of television cameras, were unsuccessful. In time, the towers started to accumulate the adulation they had long deserved. Rodia died in poverty in 1965 at the age of 86.

The towers can be seen behind the fence even when the adjoining Arts Center is closed (open Tuesday–Sunday 9am–5pm, closed: Monday). The center stages rotating shows by artists in the area. In 1995 the city began a renovation project to strengthen the tower's internal supports, which had become weakened by water seeping through fissures.

Another unlikely attraction can be found in the otherwise unenticing industrial city of **Vernon ❽**. In the era of five-cent trolley rides, when more than 100 million passengers each year rode the Red Cars, and even Santa Monica was only 40 minutes from Downtown, Vernon was a wide-open community with gaming houses, saloons and brothels that operated around the clock.

BELOW: detail of *Hog Heaven* by Les Frimes, one of the largest murals ever painted.

More decorous today, Vernon is known to many as the home of one of the largest murals in California, a huge creation by Les Frimes at 3049 East Vernon Avenue amid miles of factories. The pig mural on Farmer John's Packing Plant, *Hog Heaven* ❾, depicts hundreds of pigs running through fields on the outside walls of a building inside which they are turned into pork chops. A monument to

foodie Americana stands on Lakewood Boulevard in Downey: the **oldest McDonald's** in the world, still dressed (including the staff) in all its 1950s glory.

The Latino population of Los Angeles has risen and fallen ever since they became the city's first residents two centuries ago. Today the sprawling *barrio* of East Los Angeles, centered in **Boyle Heights**, is mainly Latino. Along Whittier Boulevard or Brooklyn Avenue, English tends to be a second language.

El Mercado ⑩ (3425 East First Street) is a lively place to pick up the flavor, and many of the ubiquitous murals of the area have their genesis in art classes held at **Plaza de la Raza**, next to **Lincoln Park**, which sponsors exhibits and concerts. East Los Angeles is, in fact, home to the largest mural in the world: the 2,500-ft (760-meter) **Great Wall of Los Angeles Mural** tells the story of ethnic pride.

There's a state park at **Whittier**, and in attractive **Hollenbeck Park**, just west of the Golden Gate freeway, is Los Angeles' only winery, the **San Antonio Winery ⑪**, on a 3-acre (1.2-hectare) site with tasting rooms and restaurant, at 737 Lamarr Street. It is open for tours daily 10am–4pm, shop and restaurant open 10am–11pm.

An ethnic exibit at the Mission-style Southwest Museum.

Old-time California is preserved in the district of **Highland Park** by several distinctive sites, chief of which is the Mission-style **Southwest Museum ⑫** on Museum Drive, with its absorbing collection of Navaho blankets, moccasins, weapons and Indian artifacts, including baskets woven so tightly that they hold water (open Tuesday–Sunday 10am–5pm, closed: Monday). There is a branch of the Southwest Museum at the LA County Museum of Art *(see page 176).*

BELOW: billboards advertising the music scene.

The Mayan-style entrance to the museum, which also includes an Eskimo collection, is via a 260-ft (79-meter) tunnel lined with dioramas of Indian life and then by elevator to the top of a steep hill. A sound track of drums, rattles and whistles sometimes accompanies visitors as they inspect watercolors and exhibits illustrating the way Indians lived both in the past and today. The collection includes photographs from the end of the 19th century. Nearby, the **Casa de Adobe ⑬** (4605 North Figueroa) is a replica of an 1850s hacienda furnished in appropriate style.

The man responsible for assembling the museum's collection, Harvard-educated Charles Fletcher Lummis, arrived in Los Angeles in the 1890s after hitchhiking from his home in Massachusetts. He built a two-story "castle" in which many of his Indian treasures were stored. Lummis became city editor of the *Los Angeles Times* at 25 and later director of the Los Angeles Central Library.

He built his house, **El Alisal ⑭**, partly from granite and railroad ties as a demonstration of his regard for "primitive" styles. Among the many luminaries he entertained was Will Rogers, who delighted guests with his rope tricks long before becoming famous. The Lummis home is open some afternoons.

Nearby, in a grassy enclosure at the end of a dead-end street, is **Heritage Square ⑮**, a city-sponsored restoration project which has collected together and restored a group of wonderful old Victorian houses. Guided tours are conducted most weekends noon to 4pm; last tour leaves at 3.15pm. ❑

HOLLYWOOD HIGH

CLASS OF **89**

Sheik
TERRITORY

STOP

HOLLYWOOD AND THE WEST SIDE

This area covers Hollywood, the West Side and Sunset, Hollywood and Wilshire boulevards

More than anywhere else in Los Angeles, Hollywood illustrates the curiously ambivalent attitude displayed by its natives towards the subject of history. While few would seem to bemoan the recent demolition of a 150-year-old adobe building, virtually everybody is ready to wax sentimental about the site of long-gone movie sets, or homes once occupied by silent stars, or – unlikely as it may seem – even where the homes once stood.

In the chapters that follow, due attention has been paid to this phenomenon. What Hollywood tends to regard as "history" took place almost entirely in the 20th century, but, transmuted by the special magic that is Hollywood, it already seems to be as timeless as the most ancient of legends.

There's a certain cachet to living on the West Side – or so Westsiders like to think – but the question of where the area actually begins has always been in dispute. For this guide's purposes, the point where Santa Monica Boulevard meets Sunset Boulevard approximately marks the eastern boundary, with the southern border defined by Wilshire Boulevard, which parallels it a few blocks to the south. This is, however, a flexible guideline.

The area between here and the coast – Hollywood, Beverly Hills, Century City, Westwood, Santa Monica and the contiguous communities – is regarded as the West Side. And of the major routes that cross it, our concentration is on Wilshire, Santa Monica and Sunset boulevards, with some attention to Hollywood Boulevard and the hills which it borders.

Of course, if you're in a hurry to go west you will take the freeway, in which case you'll be in the company of the 315,000 other vehicles that traverse all or some part of this east–west route every day. In fact, reports the California Transportation Department (CALTRANS), drivers on this and other freeways in Los Angeles County waste a total of 137,397 frustrating hours daily in traffic congestion.

On second thoughts, why not take the bus? ❑

PRECEDING PAGES: Fred Hayman outside his chic boutique on Rodeo Drive.
LEFT: not all Hollywood's players are in the movies.

Sunset and Western

In 1917, William Fox, who had risen from a lowly cutter in New York's garment district to become the wealthy owner of a string of nickelodeons, bought land at 1417 North Western to construct his own movie studio. He brought with him Theodosia Goodman, a tailor's daughter from Chillicothe, Ohio, whom imaginative publicity had already transformed into the exotic Theda Bara. With Bara and such other performers as Tom Mix and, a decade later, John Wayne, Fox built his studio into a Hollywood giant. Stores cover the original site today.

Sunset Boulevard quickly became the hotbed of Hollywood movies, as a few years later and a bit farther down the road Columbia Pictures Studios was founded just east of the intersection of Sunset and Gower. Built in 1921, Columbia spent 50 years on this studio lot (before moving on to Burbank, and later, Culver City), producing a mixture of B-movies (*The Three Stooges*) and such classics as *It Happened One Night, On The Waterfront, and Oliver!*. Now called the **Sunset-Gower Studios ❶**, recent tenants have been primarily television shows such as *Married with Children* and *Fresh Prince of Bel Air*, starring Will Smith. No public tours, but audiences are invited to the live tapings.

Sunset and Hollywood boulevards; two of the most famous streets in the world.

Also around the area, the low-budget cowboy or Western movie was already established and dozens of small studios had been grinding them out in **Gower Gulch ❷**, the area around Sunset and Gower. On the northwest corner Hollywood's first film studio, the Nestor Film Company, had opened in 1911, paying $40 a month to rent a defunct tavern. CBS now stands on this site (the Burns & Allen and Edgar Bergen radio shows were broadcast from there) and another TV station, Channel 5, has replaced the old Warner Brothers studio across the street where in 1927 Al Jolson emoted on the soundtrack of *The Jazz Singer*.

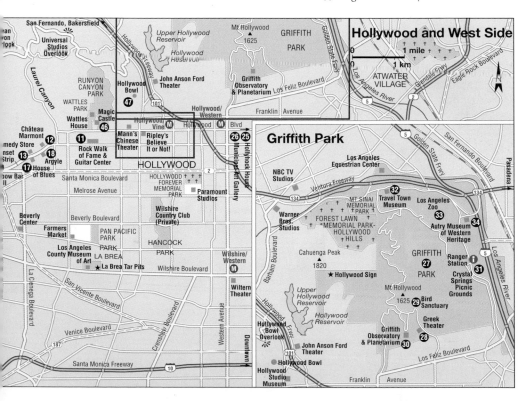

The memory of all those Westerns and the would-be cowboys who hung out on the corner looking for work is retained in the **Gower Gulch shopping center**, with its wooden, frontier-style signs (Lil's Boarding House, Forge & Stables, etc.) above the fast-food places. The walls of **Denny's** (open 24 hours) are lined with movie posters from the era.

In the next block the **Hollywood Palladium ❸**, now a venue for rock groups, opened in 1940 with Tommy Dorsey's band and Frank Sinatra, while the **Aquarius Theater ❹** across the street, which hosted *Hair* in the 1960s, was known to an earlier generation for its famous sign: "Through these portals pass the most beautiful girls in the world," a reference to the 60 lovelies who danced inside the Earl Carroll Theater on what was then the world's biggest revolving stage. Earl died in a plane crash in 1948, after which the club became the Moulin Rouge nightclub, from which *Queen For a Day* was broadcast in the 1950s.

Sunset and Vine

What cinema fan has not heard of that evocative location? And how typical of these times that three of its corners have been claimed by banks and the fourth by a soulless shopping mall. But there is a fountain and beside it a sidewalk plaque (covering a time capsule buried in 1954 and scheduled for retrieval in 2004) placed by the local Chamber of Commerce. "On this corner," reads the inscription, "Hollywood was born with the filming of *The Squaw Man* in 1913."

Well, not exactly. Leaving aside the fact that Hollywood itself had been incorporated as a separate town a decade earlier and that some folk had been making movies in Palo Alto, Chatsworth and Santa Barbara a full decade before that, the location of that famous horse barn in which Cecil B. De Mille and Jesse

TIP

Today, **The Palace** is a very popular dance and concert venue – check it out if you're into alternative, house, and new music; tel: 323/462-3000.

BELOW: a section of Echo Park.

Lasky filmed Hollywood's first full-length feature was at 1521 Vine Street, slightly to the north. Preserved as a museum devoted to the silent movie era, the barn is on a large vacant lot on Highland Avenue near the Hollywood Bowl.

Nothing remains from the Vine Street of the silent movie era except for the **Doolittle Theater ❺**, opened as the Wilkes in 1927, and the old Hollywood Playhouse (since 1964, **The Palace ❻**) from which Fanny Brice did her radio show. The former NBC studio from which the Bob Hope and Jack Benny shows were broadcast is now a bank, and the old Brown Derby at 1628 Vine (the hat-shaped one was on Wilshire) where Clark Gable proposed to Carole Lombard burned down in 1988 and is now a parking lot. The former café opened by Clara Bow and her husband Rex Bell in 1943 is long gone from the lobby of the once-swanky Plaza Hotel, now the Hollywood Plaza retirement home.

South of Sunset at 1411 North Vine, next to the Greyhound bus terminal, is what is probably the most unusual **McDonald's ❼** in the US. A huge blow-up of a scene from *Casablanca* sets the tone along with stills and props from the movie, ceiling fans, Moorish light fixtures, plants, a piano (locked), imitation bamboo seating, and an amusing neon sign reading Rick's Americaine Café.

West Hollywood

Back on Sunset, the dusty pink building with penthouse at No. 6525 was once the Hollywood Athletic Club. John Wayne and John Barrymore got drunk here together and Clark Gable did laps in the Olympic-sized pool. Following its recent $1 million restoration, it now houses a health club, a posh poolroom and an upmarket restaurant and bar and has changed its name to the Sunset Landmark. The whimsical **Crossroads of the World ❽** on Sunset, built in the shape

Map on page 144

BELOW: LA's first shopping mall, the Crossroads of the World.

of an ocean liner, was originally Hollywood's first shopping mall before being converted to offices.

Where else but **Hollywood High School** ❾, at Sunset and Highland, could you find a homegrown celebrity alumni roster such as this: Judy Garland, John Huston, Lana Turner, Mickey Rooney, Carole Lombard, Carole Burnett, Linda Evans, Ricky and David Nelson, Stefanie Powers, Laurence Fishburne, to name just a few. Was it in their blood, or in the shakes at the nearby Top Hat malt shop (where Lana Turner slipped out to – not Schwab's, as the legend insists – and was discovered one famous day)?

Nowadays, stars-in-waiting order their shakes at the nearby **In'N'Out** restaurant ❿, a Southern California burger chain and institution. Burgers, fries, and drinks, that's it – and don't forget to order your Double-Double "Animal-style." Then loosen up your belt and cruise on down to the **Rock Walk of Fame** and **Guitar Center** ⓫ at 7425 Sunset – handprints, signatures, and memorabilia from rock music's greatest musical performers and innovators – and you may very well see one of your favorite rockers pop in to replace that Stratocaster he trashed the night before.

Beyond, Sunset is fairly uninteresting until Sunset Strip begins at Crescent Heights. The castle-like **Chateau Marmont** ⓬, built as luxury apartments in 1927, has always been favored by stars who eschewed the more flamboyant showbiz haunts: Greta Garbo, Howard Hughes, Mick Jagger, Keanu Reeves, Sting and Robert De Niro have all stayed here, as well as the unfortunate John Belushi, who died of a drug overdose in one of the bungalows.

In the 1920s, a particularly lush kind of Spanish architecture seemed to be the prevailing style in West Hollywood. Many of the courtyard apartment com-

Stravinsky stayed at the Chateau Marmont hotel in 1940 while his music was being adapted for Walt Disney's Fantasia.

BELOW: Sunset and Vine, looking north.

plexes that went up then remain incomparable. The blocks between **Fountain and Sunset** west of Crescent Heights are especially rewarding to explore and, although some patios can be glimpsed only through locked gates, others are accessible to the discreet visitor.

Map on page 144

The irresistible **Mi Casa** (1406 North Havenhurst), with its balconied apartments overlooking twin patios, is the real thing, having been imported *in toto* from Ronda, Spain, in 1926 and designated as a national historic place (as was its red-brick neighbor, the British-style **Colonial House**). Even before that, the husband and wife architectural team of Arthur and Nina Zwebell had designed the enchanting **Villa Andalusia** across the street; here Clara Bow, Claire Bloom and Marlon Brando's father all lived at one time or another.

The same architects also created the **Villa Primavera** (1300 North Harper) with the usual plethora of fireplaces and tiled surfaces surrounding a gentle fountain, as well as the elegantly Moorish **Patio del Moro** at 8229 Fountain. Opposite the Andalusia is **Romany Villa**, the beauty of whose apartments, with their 20-ft (6-meter) ceilings, can only be guessed at from the exterior.

But most impressive of all is the **Villa D'Este** (1355 North Laurel), built by the Davis brothers, Pierpont and Walter, in 1928. Pola Negri and other movie greats have lived around its jungly courtyard; Cecil B. De Mille is said to have maintained a romantic hideaway here.

At 1403 North Laurel, F. Scott Fitzgerald was still working on his uncompleted novel, *The Last Tycoon*, when he died of a heart attack in 1940. His lover, columnist Sheila Graham, lived a block away at 1443 North Hayworth and the couple spent much of their time visiting famous friends in the poolside bungalows of Alla Nazimova's Garden of Allah. It is now a shopping center.

Marlene Dietrich stayed at the Romany Villa with her mentor, Josef Sternberg, when she first arrived in Hollywood in 1930, and Zsa Zsa Gabor was a later tenant.

BELOW: a typical patio court in Spanish-Colonial style.

Carney's (open Monday–Thursday 11am–midnight, Friday and Saturday 11am–3am), the railroad car restaurant at 8351 Sunset, is a reminder of the electric tram that once ran out here and from which passengers could transfer to a trackless tram running up Laurel Canyon, once the haunt of outlaws.

Sunset Strip

At the Comedy Store Johnny (Tarzan) Weissmuller once threw a plate of spaghetti at his wife Lupe Velez.

In more recent times gangster Micky Cohen came to a violent end – not in Laurel Canyon where he owned a secret casino and brothel, but in Sherry's restaurant (which became the rock club Gazzari's) on Sunset Strip. In the 1960s, Gazzari's pioneered the idea of filming the dancers one night and projecting the pictures on the dance floor walls the following night.

It's impossible to miss the enormous, imaginative and ever-changing billboards on this stretch of Sunset. Painted meticulously on plywood panels and brought here intact, they are often mandated by ego-gratifying clauses in stars' contracts and are aimed squarely at the attention of influential movie people who are presumed to pass this way.

The ever popular **Comedy Store** ⓭ (tel: 323/650-6268) with its open nights for aspiring comics, was once Ciro's, the supreme "in" spot where a drunken, bare-chested Darryl Zanuck was photographed trying to chin himself on a trapeze. The Trocadero, where Rita Hayworth was discovered and Nat King Cole was the house pianist, survives only as a trio of weed-covered steps. The Villa Nova, where Vincente Minnelli proposed to Judy Garland and in 1953, Marilyn Monroe met Joe DiMaggio on a blind date, is now the **Rainbow Bar & Grill** ⓮.

BELOW: you're no-one without a Beverly Hills nanny.

Opposite the Comedy Store the patio of **Butterfield's** restaurant is as it was when it was linked to John Barrymore's guesthouse. Errol Flynn stayed here.

Where the stars of the 1940s shopped at the West Side Market, music fans line up to attend the **Roxy** , although today's young stars are more likely to be found in the trendy bar of the Chateau Marmont hotel or at **Le Mondrian Hotel's Skybar**, owned by Cindy Crawford's husband. Rod Stewart, Elle McPherson, and Leonardo di Caprio have all been seen here, and Jean Claude van Damme fell in love with pop-star Jewel here. It's tough to get into unless you are staying at the hotel. For years clubbers have flocked to the Strip seeking the city's brightest lights, personifed by the venerable **Whisky A Go Go** (tel: 310/535-0579). In its 1960s heyday, the Whisky was the nerve center of the Strip, before temporarily closing in the early 1980s.

For a more alternative edge, visit the **Viper Room** ⑯ tel: 310/358-1880, actor River Phoenix's sad last stop. He collapsed and died outside from a drug overdose. Owned by actor Johnny Depp, the Viper keeps an eclectic schedule, including impromptu appearances by major acts such as Matchbox 20, Oasis, Green Day, and the Red Hot Chili Peppers; or check out **Club ID** (formerly Club Lingerie) at 6507 Sunset, tel: 323/466-8557, which offers a wildly diverse variety of LA bands, R&B, soul, and oddball one-offs.

Those seeking more mainstream fare, whether rock, blues, or zydeco, check into the cajun-flavored **House of Blues** ⑰ (whose investors include Dan Aykroyd and James Belushi), which features star performers and "international peasant food" at non-peasant prices. For a real treat, check out the Sunday Gospel Brunch (tel. 323/848-5100).

If a night of shaking your booty leaves you hungry, **Mel's Diner** is the spot to fill up and swap stories (you may even recognize a face or two). Or try the previously mentioned **Rainbow** – great pizzas and an amazing sideshow of

TIP

You might catch Johnny Depp's pal Keanu Reeves' band "Dogstar" jamming at the Depp-owned club the Viper Room – if you can get in, that is.

BELOW: clean, healthy living, that's the California girl.

BELOW: the house you probably want to see is behind those railings.

heavy rockers. Of course, if seeing stars is your goal, then you would have started much earlier at **Spago's**, Wolfgang Puck's original fame-claim just above the Strip. Although you'll probably be stuck in the backroom, enough trips to the bathroom should enable you to survey the regulars, such as Jack Nicholson, Whoopi Goldberg, Michael Douglas, and Sharon Stone.

Graceful **Sunset Towers**, with its marble lobby and hand-carved elevator doors, and the chic stores of **Sunset Plaza**, two blocks west, are worth noting. Both retain their 1930s appeal, with the art-deco Towers – after a $40 million restoration – looking even better than when it was a favorite of Jean Harlow, Errol Flynn and other stars of that era. Now renamed the **Argyle** ⓱, its 68 rooms and sites have recently been renovated, and its hip restaurant/bar **Fenix** has become a hangout for young stars such as Leonardo DiCaprio and Winona Ryder. Although Leo has also been spotted at the Whiskey Bar of the Sunset Marquis Hotel, a rock band retreat. Other celebs seen here include U2, UB40, Bruce Springsteen, Drew Barrymore, and Ben Stiller.

North of Sunset

Dominating the hill above Sunset, at 501 North Doheny, the 50-room **Greystone Mansion** ⓲ belongs to the city of Beverly Hills. The house is closed but sightseeing is allowed in the 18-acre (7-hectare) gardens – what remains of a 400-acre (160-hectare) estate (open daily 10am–5pm, in summer 6pm). Edward Doheny who, with partner Charles Canfield, was the first to strike a substantial supply of oil in LA, spent $6 million in 1926 building the mansion whose intricately carved woodwork, marble floors, and specially designed chimneys make it irresistible to film-makers. Movies shot here include *The Bodyguard*

STAR HOMES

Sellers of maps to movie star homes are ubiquitous along the north stretch of Sunset. Although they are reasonably accurate, if not too old, the maps promise more than they can deliver, if only because the bigger mansions offer only tantalizing glimpses through hedges, high walls and locked gates. The best single trip to take may be up **Benedict Canyon**, where even the non-star homes are spectacular. The panorama, especially from the intersection of Seabright and Tower Grove Drive – where Greta Garbo and John Gilbert used to cavort in his stately Spanish-style house (demolished in 1986) – is breathtaking.

The legendary **Pickfair**, at 1143 Summit Drive, was bought for $6.6 million in 1988 by Pia Zadora and her husband Meshulam Riklis. They demolished it in 1990 to build a bigger mansion. Harold Lloyd's stunning 40-room **Green Acres**, with its 26 bathrooms and private golf course, was sold after heavy financial losses in 1933. It was a museum until 1974, but neighbors complained about the crowds. Rudolph Valentino's **Falcon's Lair** (1436 Bella Drive) can be glimpsed behind iron gates. Nearby, misleadingly numbered because it hides behind a blocked driveway, is the former Sharon Tate home at 10050 Cielo Drive, scene of the murders by Charles Manson in 1969.

and *Witches of Eastwick*. Admission is on Loma Vista Street which is about 200 yards above the padlocked gate.

Beverly Glen, the narrow canyon which separates the plushy communities of **Holmby Hills** and **Bel Air**, offers a direct route over the mountains into the San Fernando Valley and should be avoided at rush hour. The narrow roads leading into the hills, north of Crater Street, are quite charming. Look for **Four Oaks**, an elegant California-French restaurant housed in an 1886 landmark building along the west side of the Glen (tel: 310/470-2265). Beverly Glen crosses **Mulholland Drive**, which offers some of the best views in LA.

At Benedict Canyon's lower end, along immaculate North Roxbury Drive, passers-by can stand and stare at the unconcealed former homes of Marlene Dietrich (No. 822), Jimmy Stewart (No. 918), Lucille Ball (No. 1000), Jack Benny (No. 1002) and, at No. 1027 Chevy Chase Drive, Greta Garbo. The house at **1700 Lexington Road**, one of many bought by William Randolph Hearst for Marion Davies, was where Greta Garbo and John Gilbert were scheduled to be married in 1926. When the bride failed to appear, Gilbert got drunk and decked Louis B. Mayer after an argument.

Back on Sunset, past Irving Thalberg's home, in which he married Norma Shearer in 1927, the next landmark is the famously pink, 320-room **Beverly Hills Hotel** ❷⓪, standing in 16 acres (6.5 hectares) of lush gardens at the corner of Beverly Drive. The $1,000-a-night bungalows are as much in demand as when Howard Hughes rented one for an annual fee of $250,000 – for almost 30 years. The shops adjoining the lobby are appropriately expensive and include an art gallery once owned by Elizabeth Taylor's father. The Polo Lounge, favored after-polo respite of Will Rogers and Douglas Fairbanks Sr., is still a power-meeting spot for stars and dealmakers (especially at breakfast). You name them – they've stayed here – from JFK to the Duke of Windsor, John Wayne to John and Yoko. Movies featuring the hotel include *The Way We Were* and *California Suite*.

For a considerable distance above Sunset, huge 50-ft (15-meter) palms line **Beverly Drive**, a street of impressive mansions. One of these was owned by Marion Davies and was big enough to house 1,000 guests at the wedding reception she gave for singer Johnny Ray in 1952. She died in the house in 1962, at the age of 64. The mansion is no longer visible from the street.

Even pinker than the Beverly Hills Hotel is the former home of Jayne Mansfield and her muscle-bound husband, Micky Hargitay. Once owned by Englebert Humperdinck, the startling-looking house pales in comparison with its lavish neighbor on **South Carolwood**, which was owned by 20th-Century-Fox boss Joseph Schenck in 1934. For a while, it's said, he kept the young Marilyn Monroe in a guesthouse on the grounds as an on-call concubine.

Clara Bow's home used to be at 512 North Bedford, in whose bedroom she reportedly once took on the entire USC football team. Bing Crosby and Bogie and Bacall lived respectively at 594 and 232 South Mapleton. Hidden cameras guard the gates of the **Playboy Mansion** at 10236 Charing Cross Road, remodeled by Hugh Hefner, who bought it in 1971. One house that welcomes visitors is the oldest in

Map on page 144

You'll find cocktails at any of the smart hangouts.

BELOW: poolside at the Beverly Hills Hotel.

John Paul Getty, founder of the excellent Getty Villa and Getty Center.

BELOW:
you may have to stand in line for the tram to the Getty Center, but it's worth the wait.

Beverly Hills – the **Virginia Robinson Home ㉑**, with its 6-acre (2.4-hectare) gardens at 1008 Elden Way (open by appointment only Tuesday–Friday).

On a hilltop above where Sunset crosses the San Diego freeway, the state-of-the-art $733 million **J. Paul Getty Center ㉒** is a recent addition to LA's cultural scene. Designed by Richard Meier, the fabulous complex contains most of the Getty collections in a new J. Paul Getty Museum, as well as housing the Conservation Institute, the Art Research Institute, and other educational departments. The center has five pavilions, including a library with a million volumes and five million photographs. The 110-acre (45-hectare) site offers spectacular views of the sea (open Tuesday and Wednesday 11am–7pm, Thursday and Friday 11am–9pm, Saturday and Sunday 10am–6pm).

In the Canyons

Although the Beverly Hills Hotel has been the best-known landmark since it opened in 1911, its setting takes second place to that of the **Hotel Bel Air,** which nestles among large grounds in secluded Stone Canyon. Grace Kelly lived here, and as a romantic hideaway it has few equals. Warren Beatty and Annette Bening stayed here while their earthquake-damaged home was being repaired, and Tony Curtis is often in residence. Oprah Winfrey threw a slumber party for her 40th birthday here. Other celebrities hiding out here have included Diana Ross and Tina Turner, and even Prince Charles. **Stone Canyon** and **Bel Air Road** are the two major routes that ascend through Bel Air, a semi-private community that has a large number of multi-million dollar homes.

Just before crossing the San Diego Freeway, Sunset skirts the top of the University of California at Los Angeles (UCLA) *(see page 179)*.

Map
on page
144

Brentwood

One of novelist Raymond Chandler's many homes in the 1940s was at **12216 Shetland Place**, between Sunset and San Vicente, where he wrote two of his Philip Marlowe books, *High Window* and *The Lady in the Lake*.

Twenty years later, on August 5, 1962, the tormented Marilyn Monroe died a lonely death a stone's-throw away in a bungalow at **12305 Fifth Helena Drive**. In 1982, after an investigation, the LA district attorney specifically ruled out murder, declaring her death to be either accidental or suicide. The bungalow sits at the end of a short, dead-end street but curiosity-seekers will find that it has been screened from view and bears no number on its gate.

Pacific Palisades

A righthand turn at 14235 Sunset leads to the **Will Rogers Ranch ㉓**, a state park since 1944 (open daily 8am–sunset, tours 10.30am–4.30pm). Rogers, who died aged 55 in an air crash in 1935, had been America's top box-office cowboy star and was famed for his witty one-liners. The charming house with its furnishings and Navaho rugs has been left as it was when Rogers occupied it. Tucked away in the foothills adjoining **Topanga State Park**, the secluded ranch is a good starting point for hikes (there is a fee for parking), and a one-mile walk down **Inspiration Point Trail** offers panoramic views over much of the city.

Back on Sunset is the giant lotus archway of the **Self-Realization Fellowship Lake Shrine ㉔**. A sharp left turn into the (free) parking lot, followed by a leisurely walk around the tranquil lake, past the swans, a waterfall, a houseboat, and a windmill has an immensely calming effect – which was the exact intention of its founder, Paramahansa Yogananda, in 1950. ❑

Marilyn Monroe swallowed 40 sleeping pills in what was at first ruled as a probable suicide, but which was followed by years of rumors, including her alleged affairs with John and Robert Kennedy.

BELOW: in the national and state parks, they take the threat of fire very seriously.

HOLLYWOOD BOULEVARD

*The quintessential Hollywood area, with the Walk of Fame,
the Hollywood Bowl, the famous Hollywood sign,
and the venue of the first public Oscars*

Map
on page
144

Hollywood Boulevard begins on the east with **Barnsdall Art Park**, whose genesis was the eccentric oil heiress Aline Barnsdall, a woman who shocked her contemporaries by smoking in public and retaining her maiden name after marriage. She met Frank Lloyd Wright in 1920 while she was directing plays at a little theater in Chicago and had the good sense and taste to hire him to design a theater for her. Moving to Los Angeles, Barnsdall bought 36 acres, a hilltop, just west of what is now the intersection of Sunset and Hollywood boulevards, and ambitiously laid plans for an arts center comprised of theaters, a residence for herself and her daughter and some simple homes for artists and visiting actors.

The Wright stuff

With the assistance of Rudolph Schindler, his Austrian-born pupil, Wright completed the Mayan-style, wood frame tile-and-stucco **Hollyhock House** ㉕ (tours Wednesday–Sunday at noon, 1pm, 2pm and 3pm). But after living here only briefly, Aline Barnsdall moved away, donating the house and land to the city whose Cultural Affairs department organizes conducted tours. Rooftop and semi-interior gardens were obviously intended to relate indoors to outdoors but the result, though attractive, is vaguely claustrophobic. Schindler later extended the experiment to his own house *(see page 192)*.

Hollyhock House shares the hill with the **Municipal Art Gallery** ㉖ (open Tuesday–Sunday 12.30–5pm), designed by architect Arthur Stephens, and a 299-seat outdoor theater. On Sunday in summer there are often outdoor concerts.

Frank Lloyd Wright fans might think it is worth driving up the nearby hillside (turn off Vermont after San Vicente) to **2655 Glendower Avenue**, where they'll encounter the **Ennis-Brown house**, resembling a Mayan temple. It was built in 1924 from patterned-concrete blocks joined by steel rods.

It was the last of the four houses built by Wright in Los Angeles and some think the most beautiful, with its airy, spacious rooms. When the present owner, August O. Brown, bought it (for $119,000) in 1969, Wright's reputation was in temporary decline and the house had sat empty and unwanted for years. Tours are conducted half a dozen times each year *(see Travel Tips)*.

Some of movieland's earliest pioneers chose to live and work in the **Silver Lake** area, just east of here. Walt Disney paid $5 per week for a room at 4406 Kingswell Avenue when he arrived in 1923, drawing cartoons in a garage behind the house and opening his first studio, with Ub Iwerks, up the street shortly

PRECEDING PAGES:
renovating the
famous sign cost
$27,500 for each
letter.
LEFT: cruising
outside Mann's
Chinese Theater.
BELOW:
the Walk of Fame.

HUMPHREY BOGART

thereafter. Mickey Mouse and Snow White and the Seven Dwarfs were born at this first Disney studio (now a Mayfair supermarket). One block away, at 2900 Griffith Park Boulevard, is the cottage whose curious design undoubtedly inspired the home of the dwarfs.

One of the largest city parks in America, the 3,000-acre (1,200-hectare) **Griffith Park** ㉗ (open daily 6am–10pm) has something to offer almost everybody, and on an average weekend more than 50,000 visitors come in search of it. Most of them arrive by car – which is what you'll need to discover most of it. Caution should be exercised. Sections of the park are both lonely and dangerous. During daylight there are usually enough people around to discourage troublemakers, but don't take any chances. The park was gifted to the city by Griffith J. Griffith, a Welsh immigrant who, after making his fortune, took up residence here. He stipulated in his will that his estate should become a place of leisure activity and rest for the whole population.

Because of its size, the park is best described by areas: the entrance from Vermont Avenue leads to the **Greek Theater** ㉘ (open-air concerts in summer), the **Bird Sanctuary** ㉙ (open daily 10am–5pm; walking tours on Sunday), and the **Observatory** ㉚ on top of Mount Hollywood (open summer daily 12.30–10pm, rest of year Tuesday–Friday 2–10pm, Saturday and Sunday 10am–5pm).

The entrance at Los Feliz Boulevard, just off Western Avenue, offers lovely walks past pools and a waterfall through Fern Dell to the **Nature Museum** and also to the Observatory which, incidentally, stages night-time laser shows.

The eastern entrance from the Golden State Freeway leads into the **Crystal Springs picnic grounds** ㉛ and also to the **Ranger Station**, where you can pick up a free map and full information about Griffith Park. The northern entrance, near the freeways' intersection, leads on to **Zoo Drive** at the western end of which both children and adults play trains on Sunday, swapping rides on each other's model railway cars pulled by powerful steam or diesel-powered engines. **Travel Town** ㉜, a free transportation museum, is an elephants' graveyard of hands-on trains plus cable and trolley cars and antique fire engines (open Monday–Friday 10am–4pm, Saturday and Sunday and public holidays 10am–5pm).

At the park's eastern side, adjoining the golf course, is the 113-acre (46-hectare) **Los Angeles Zoo** ㉝, with many endangered species (open daily 10am–5pm). The zoo is in the process of completing a major new habitat for apes. The different sections are far enough apart to make it worthwhile riding the little train. The abandoned and rather eerie cages and subterranean passages of the **old zoo** can still be inspected by going through the tunnel under the road opposite the 65-year-old **Spillman carousel** near the ranger center (runs weekends only).

Unfortunately, no buses run into Griffith Park, but MTA 97 from Downtown runs along Los Feliz Boulevard on its southern border. Bicycles can be rented on Los Feliz and horses can be rented across from Travel Town to ride along a total of 53 miles (85 km) of semi-rural bridle trails.

BELOW: science column at the Griffith Observatory.

A re-creation of a Western town, together with clips from vintage movies, are part of the fare for visitors to the **Autry Museum of Western Heritage** ❸ (open Tuesday–Sunday 10am–5pm) along Zoo Drive, which prides itself on displaying the different contributions made by women and ethnic minorities as well as the white cowboy to our Western traditions. "They were all part of the West then, just as they are now," explains the museum's Cathy Burton.

Artifacts on display include guns, clothing and holsters from the likes of Wyatt Earp, Teddy Roosevelt and Annie Oakley as well as those of the fictional movie cowboys.

Next to Griffith Park's entrance at Riverside and Memorial Drive is the **memorial fountain** commemorating William Mulholland who brought Los Angeles its first reliable water supply from the Owens Valley in 1913.

Hollywood's center

Back on Hollywood Boulevard, the next landmark is the once-impressive **Pantages Theater** ❸, which opened in 1930 with *Floradora* starring Marion Davies and hosted the Oscars from 1949 to 1959. Then comes **Vine Street**, that thoroughfare of renown in Hollywood's golden era when stars would throng Sardi's restaurant (now a porn theater) just past the corner or strut their stuff at the **Hollywood Playhouse** (now a rock music dance club) at 1735 Vine.

The circular **Capitol Records Tower** ❸, topped by a light that blinks out H-O-L-L-Y-W-O-O-D in morse code, was devised by Nat King Cole and Johnny Mercer in 1956 and built by architect Welton Becket, also responsible for the Downtown Music Center *(see page 125)*. Frank Sinatra was the first big star to record in the studio.

Elvis on the Walk of Fame – forever adored.

BELOW:
Marilyn Monroe lookalike on the Walk of Fame.

A visit to **Frederick's of Hollywood**  (open Monday–Friday 10am–9pm, Saturday to 7pm and Sunday 11am–6pm) or even possession of its catalog might have been pretty daring 40 years ago. It's still worth taking a peek at the **Bra Museum**, in which can be admired the underwear of stars both ancient and modern: everything from Judy Garland's nightgown and Zsa Zsa Gabor's panties to Madonna's bustier. Around the corner is the streamline art-deco building renovated by architect S. Charles Lee in 1935 and which until recently housed the Max Factor Museum of Beauty.

The Beauty Museum's photographs, period advertisements and the wigs worn by famous bald leading men like John Wayne and Fred Astaire have been donated to the Hollywood Entertainment Museum. Whatever its future role, the building will always be associated with the diminutive Russian emigré who sold the world on the concept of make-up for the ordinary woman aided by endorsements from the glamorous stars who used his products. Factor, who died in 1938, was the man who re-created Jean Harlow as "the platinum blonde."

Walk of Fame

What the movie industry brought was a world with a new vision, reflected in such architectural innovations as the **Egyptian Theater** ❸, replica of an Egyptian palace at 6912 Hollywood Boulevard, and the even more spectacular **Mann's Chinese Theater** ❸, two blocks west. Both were products of the same architects, Meyer & Holler, as was the neo-Gothic **Hollywood First National Building** at the corner of Highland.

The Egyptian, which in 1922 was the scene of Hollywood's first movie premiere, *Robin Hood*, is owned by the non-profit American Cinematheque, and

BELOW: Al Pacino and Emma Thompson receiving their Oscars in 1993.

completed a major renovation in 1999. It now screens classic films and special events, with room for a live orchestra.

Every day hundreds of tourists throng the forecourt of the Chinese Theater (which opened with Cecil B. De Mille's *King of Kings* in 1926), comparing the length of their nose with that of Jimmy Durante, their legs with those of Betty Grable. "Dreams do come true" was etched into the concrete by Anthony Quinn. Quinn, a few years previously, is said to have fainted from hunger after being turned down for an usher's job at the theater.

About 200 stars have left their imprint and most of them (or their press agents) have also paid up to $3,000 to be immortalized – along with scores of others – by a sidewalk star along the boulevard's **Walk of Fame** ❹.

Many of them are visible too in the garish **Hollywood Wax Museum** ❹ (open Sunday–Thursday 10am to midnight, Friday and Saturday 10am–2am) – the same lustrous stars (Joan Crawford, Bing Crosby, Valentino) who danced in the next-door Montmartre Café (now a boutique) or who ate in the still-unchanged **Musso & Frank's** ❹. The widow of Frank Toulet (known as "Mrs Frank"), who had served as cashier at the restaurant in its early days, died aged 101 in 1995, the Toulets having sold their interest in the restaurant in 1926. This restaurant was especially popular in the 1930s and 1940s with writers Nathanael West, William Faulkner, Robert Benchley, and Raymond Chandler (who first arrived in Los Angeles in 1913, three years before Musso & Frank's opened). Stars such as Charlie Chaplin and Humphrey Bogart used to be regulars. Today frequent visitors include Tom Selleck, Al Pacino, the Rolling Stones, Brad Pitt and Nicolas Cage.

West, whose *Day of the Locust* is still touted as the best-ever book about movieland, lived for a while in the pseudo-Tudor house standing at 1817 North Ivar Avenue. Almost all these books and stars' pictures can be inspected and purchased in the bookstore of historian **Larry Edmunds**, billed as the "World's Largest collection of books and memorabilia on cinema and theater" at 6644 Hollywood Boulevard (open daily 10am–6pm, tel: 323/463-3273). Nearby **Book City** is a great resource as well.

If all of this literature has got you in the mood for culture, stop into the **Los Angeles Contemporary Exhibitions** (LACE) ❹ at 6522 Hollywood Boulevard. Recently relocated from the Downtown area, the LACE is an artist co-op and one of the most interesting galleries in town.

If you start to feel too highbrow just step back out into the t-shirts, mugs, and human oddities that clutter the boulevard – or escape into **Ripley's Believe It or Not** ❹ or the **Guinness Book of World Records Museum** ❹.

Improbable architecture

Architecture may not be the first thing on visitors' minds, but within a score of blocks in this central area is an astonishing assortment of styles. Consider the balustraded mansion at **7425 Franklin** of 1920s megastar Anita Stewart; the charming, upper-middle-class dwelling – "the most televised house in America"

BELOW: tourists will easily find something to buy on Hollywood Boulevard.

– at **1822 Camino Palmero Drive**, which was both the actual Nelson home and the backdrop to TV's *The Ozzie & Harriet Show*.

Other homes include the stylized **Montecito Apartments** (prototype for Raymond Chandler's Chateau Bery) at **6650 Franklin Avenue**, where Ronald Reagan is said to have lived because it was once the home of his idol, James Cagney; and the place where Humphrey Bogart played tennis, the **Chateau Elysee** at 5930 Franklin.

Who wouldn't be impressed by the highly improbable **Magic Castle** ❹ ("members and guests only") at 7001 Franklin; the gorgeously gilded, teak-and-cedar **Yamashiro Restaurant**, a re-created Japanese palace offering tremendous views (open daily 4.30pm–12.30am), on the hill behind; even the splendid **First United Methodist Church** (6817 Franklin) which, like its neighbors, has been in many movies.

On the way to the Hollywood Bowl, stop to admire the secluded Moorish courtyard known as the **Roman Gardens** (200 North Highland); the grandiose **American Legion building** at 2035; the **Italianate tower** at the northern end of Hightower Drive (built to conceal an elevator up the hillside and used by Robert Altman as one of the sites for his 1973 film *The Long Goodbye*); and the yellow barn (badly damaged in a 1996 fire) which houses the **Hollywood Studio Museum** in which Hollywood's first feature was filmed in 1913 (open Saturday 10am–4pm, Sunday noon–4pm).

BELOW: the Capitol Records Tower resembles a stack of records.

The world-famous **Hollywood Bowl** ❹, preceded by two earlier versions designed by Frank Lloyd Wright's son, Lloyd, is the scene of nightly picnic concerts in summer, including the famous Playboy Jazz Festival every June and has a small (free) museum (open Tuesday–Sunday 9.30am–4.30pm).

GUINNESS WORLD RECORDS MUSEUM

In the tradition of Ripley's "Believe it or not" Museum and other such entertainment centers, at the Guinness Book of World Records Museum you can find the worst, the best, and the really funny or unusual, the tallest, the shortest, the fattest, the thinnest, etc., etc.

The presentation can be a bit dull sometimes, but the displays are accompanied by video films. For children there are TV screens where they can search for their favorite animals or other objects of interest.

Some things are indeed out of the ordinary: the parrot that knows 800 words, the man who dived from a height of more than 26 ft (8 meters) into 12 inches (30 cm) of water, the incredible sets of falling dominoes, the most prolonged kiss in the movies (three minutes, five seconds, no doubt every one of them enjoyed by Jane Wyman and Regis Toomey), the 153 roles played by John Wayne, only 11 of them non-starring. Guess which movie star has received the most fan letters? Mickey Mouse, of course: in 1993 he got nearly 800,000 of them. You can see him nestling among the sacks on page 247.

The museum can be found at 6764 Hollywood Boulevard, level with Highland Avenue; tel: 323/463-6433. Open daily 10am–midnight.

Whitley Heights

Behind the barn, Milner Road leads up to **Whitley Heights**, already popular with the film people before Beverly Hills' heyday. Some developers scorned the movie folks but H. J. Whitley had no such scruples. He had sent his architect to Italy to study hilltop villages and designed his community in a similar style. Silent screen actress Barbara La Marr, Hearst's favorite director Robert Vignola and Valentino (whose room became perfumed at the flick of a switch) all bought homes in Whitley Heights, as did Gloria Swanson, Rosalind Russell, Bette Davis, and the writers William Faulkner and James Hilton.

Although many of the original homes are gone, including Francis X. Bushman's rambling estate, Topside, among the palm trees at the peak of the hill, it is well worth a trip to look around. The community recently lost a legal battle in its attempt to become a gated enclave for residents only.

Another hillside community with attractive homes is that of **Hollywoodland**, whose 50-ft (15-meter) sign, now a protected historical monument, was illuminated by thousands of lightbulbs when first erected in 1923. The sign, whose last four letters were dismantled in 1949, can be reached only after an exhausting climb through tangled underbrush from Beachwood Drive.

Back in 1932, the RKO starlet Peg Entwistle, despondent over a lapsed contract, jumped off the "H" and killed herself. Over the years others have made the trek with less tragic results – transforming the sign with various intent to "Hollyweed" (a 1970s tribute), and "Perotwood" for the grassroots presidential candidate in 1992. This may explain why the Hollywood Chamber of Commerce – which raised $27,500 per letter to repair the sign in 1994 – is not anxious to encourage visitors.

Looking cool in Hollywood is part of the culture.

BELOW: Frederick's of Hollywood Bra Museum.

Map
on page
144

A more productive trip into the hills is a visit to the tranquil **Hollywood Reservoir**, where there are rarely more than a handful of romantic couples, joggers and nature lovers. The jog around the reservoir itself is about 3 miles (5 km). It's easy to lose one's way among the myriad streets en route: take Ivar north of Franklin, left on Dix Street, right on Holly Drive under the freeway, then right again on Deep Dell Place to Weidlake Drive, which dead-ends outside the reservoir fence.

First public Oscars

In one of the last blocks before Hollywood Boulevard meanders into the suburbia of the Hollywood Hills is the 400-room **Hollywood Roosevelt Hotel** ❹, where the first Oscars were actually presented in public in 1929. With its Spanish Colonial decor, an art-deco lobby, etched glass panels and charming palm-shaded pool hidden away downstairs, this landmark is a wonderful repository of old Hollywoodiana.

When the hotel first opened in 1927, the newspaper ads promised "the greatest number of stage and screen stars ever assembled" would be in attendance – a promise that co-owners Mary Pickford, Douglas Fairbanks, and Louis B. Mayer found easy to fulfill.

Shirley Temple took her first tap-dancing lesson (from Bojangles Robinson) on the hotel's stairway; Clark Gable and Carole Lombard honeymooned here; and Marilyn Monroe posed on the diving board for her first-ever ad (for suntan lotion). A $35-million renovation has restored the Roosevelt to its former glory.

Many landmarks on Hollywood Boulevard are still standing, like the mirrored **Florentine Gardens** at 5951 Hollywood Boulevard where Sophie Tucker and Sally Rand performed. In 1942, Jim Baker and Norma Jean Dougherty celebrated their wedding in this restaurant, four years before the bride was transformed into Marilyn Monroe.

BELOW: Angelyne, self-promoting star of the billboards.

Not far from the newly refurbished, Disney-owned **El Capitan** ❹, one of the glorious old-time movie palaces from Hollywood's "golden age," is the **Hollywood Entertainment Museum** ❺ (7021 Hollywood Boulevard, tel: 213/469-9151), open Tuesday–Sunday 11am–6pm, recounting the history of the "dream factories" in film and containing many artifacts. Among these is the tower of hot fudge jars from the famous C.C. Brown's Ice Cream Parlour nearby, which closed almost simultaneously with the museum's opening. Long ago, waitress Judy Garland used to serve to customers the hot fudge sundaes that were invented on the premises. There's also a dizzying six-minute retrospective film of clips shown in the central gallery twice every hour.

Continuing west on Hollywood Boulevard, between La Brea and Fairfax, a turn northwards on Curson leads to the entrance of almost-forgotten **Wattles Park**, a steeply rising, 50-acre (20-hectare) canyon hideaway that even on weekends is uncrowded. A few blocks farther west, about a mile up Laurel Canyon on the right, are the abandoned terraces, archways and stairs of the old **Harry Houdini estate**, which long-time canyon dwellers swear is haunted. ❏

Chandler's City

Of all the writers whose work has been identified as quintessentially LA, Raymond Chandler is the one whose name is most often mentioned. Although Billy Wilder once remarked that the only person who accurately caught the Californian atmosphere in prose "was an Englishman," Chandler was actually born in Chicago in 1888 and became a naturalized British subject only in his late teens.

Chandler was 25 when he arrived in LA and in his early 40s before he sold his first magazine story. He had worked in a variety of professions – picking apricots, stringing tennis rackets, and as office manager for an oil company, all the while moving from one address to another with his older wife Cissie.

In one 10-year period he lived in nine different homes, a restlessness reflected in the nature of the cynical but soft-hearted Philip Marlowe. "When Marlowe has a problem," observed Elizabeth Ward and Alain Silver, authors of *Raymond Chandler's Los Angeles*, "he takes a drive around town... to look at the view and to look for answers."

Philip Marlowe was something new in detective fiction – a wisecracking knight errant with a nice turn of phrase and a humanity with which the reader could identify. To him LA was an ambiguous place. But it was a city Chandler understood well from "the violet light at the top of Bullock's green-tinged tower" to "that peculiar tomcat smell that eucalyptus trees give off in warm weather." He was indignant about the lack of appreciation that LA had for Hollywood. "It ought to consider itself damn lucky," he said. "Without Hollywood, it would be a mail-order city. Everything in the catalog you could get better somewhere else."

Marlowe was a favorite with the movies, portrayed by Dick Powell (*Farewell My Lovely*, retitled *Murder My Sweet*, 1944); Bogart (*The Big Sleep*, 1946); Robert Montgomery (*The Lady in the Lake*, 1947); James Garner (*Marlowe*, 1969); Elliot Gould (*The Long Goodbye*, 1973); and Robert Mitchum (*Farewell My Lovely*, 1975, and *The Big Sleep*, 1978).

Cary Grant, who never played the role, was Chandler's vision of the perfect Marlowe, but when he saw Bogart's portrayal he was gratified. "As we say here," he wrote to his British publisher, "Bogart can be tough without a gun. He has a sense of humor that contains that grating undertone of contempt. Bogart is the genuine article."

Chandler's biographer Frank MacShane points out that, despite having some characteristics in common, Marlowe was "not an extension of Chandler. They were both lonely men," he wrote in *The Life of Raymond Chandler*, "isolated in the nonsociety of California, and they held individualistic moral positions that were at odds with the standards of most of the people they associated with."

Long before his death in La Jolla in 1959, Chandler had become disillusioned. "I have lost LA," he wrote to producer John Houseman. "It is no longer the place I knew so well and was almost the first to put on paper. I have the feeling ... that I helped to create the town and was then pushed out of it by the operators." ❏

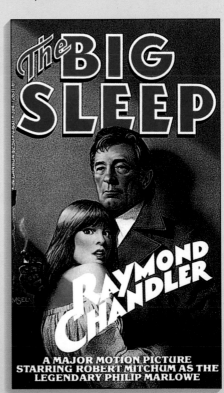

RIGHT: Robert Mitchum in *The Big Sleep*.

HOORAY FOR HOLLYWOOD

For years Hollywood has been more cheese than charm, but as movies do big business around the world, the legendary town is getting a facelift

Movie stars. Handprints in cement. Grauman's Chinese. The Egyptian. The El Capitan. Ciro's. Musso and Frank's. The Hollywood Canteen. The first feature film, *The Squaw Man*, was shot here; the first studios, founded here; the first Academy Awards, at the Hollywood Roosevelt Hotel. For a long time, the glamour went away as Hollywood Boulevard became a rambling collection of tourist shops and fast food. Oscar moved, suburbanization drew customers away, the old studio system died, and Hollywood became a place for wackos and homeless.

But guess who's back?

OSCAR'S COMEBACK

To revive the pulse and glamour of Hollywood, Oscar is scheduled to return in 2001 to his own grand theatre at Hollywood and Highland that will be the permanent site of the Academy Awards, and will mark the comeback of the world's most famous town.

"And now, Mr DeMille, I'm ready for my close-up…"

▷ **YOU BETTER WATCH OUT!**
Santa Claus comes every year in the Hollywood Christmas Parade.

△ **JUST SIGN HERE**
One of LA's most visited attractions, the first star on the Walk of Fame was for Joanne Woodward in 1960.

▷ **PARAMOUNT**
These gates belong to the only major studio still in Hollywood. Its hits include *The Godfather* and *Forrest Gump*.

◁ LOOK AT ME!

In a town that wrote the book on self-promotion, nothing outdoes the town icon itself. The sign originally read HOLLYWOODLAND, promoting real estate in 1923.

▽ FORTUNE COOKIE SAY:

"Having star stick hand in cement very good business." Sid Grauman's Chinese Theatre (now Mann's) was opened in 1927 with its 70-ft (21-meter) jade green roof.

AND THE OSCAR GOES TO...

The Academy of Motion Picture Arts & Sciences was founded in 1927, with 36 original members. Today, it is composed of over 6,000 members. The first Academy Award went to Emil Jannings in 1929, Best Actor for *The Last Command* and *Way of All Flesh*. Most nominees, and even winners, didn't attend. Only the producer of *The Jazz Singer* made a speech. Winners were known ahead of time – the sealed-envelope began in 1941.

So how does one get to become a member of the Academy? The same way you get to the ceremony – by invitation only. The Academy is divided into 13 branches reflecting the different areas of the business. Members make nominations for categories in their own branch (so directors for Best Director, actors for Best Actor and Actress, etc.). The final recipients have to be voted for by the entire member-ship.

◁ SUNSET BOULEVARD

A Paramount classic, the movie starred Gloria Swanson as an aging star who falls for William Holden, a young screenwriter.

▽ ACADEMY WINNERS

Past winners celebrating the 70th Anniversary of the Academy Awards. Walt Disney has 26. Actress Katherine Hepburn has won four.

△ IMMORTALIZED

Al Pacino, Best Actor for *Scent of a Woman*, places his hands into history at Mann's Chinese Theatre.

▷ THE OSCAR

The 8½-pound (4-kg) figure of a knight standing on a reel of film, hands gripping a sword, has been presented over 2,300 times.

WILSHIRE BOULEVARD

Map on page 174

All human life is here: Wilshire is the longest and widest boulevard in North America, intersected by 202 other streets, drives and avenues as it heads down to the ocean

Long before the advent of the **Miracle Mile** in the late 1920s, Wilshire had been a prestige address: the venerable Ambassador Hotel (where Robert Kennedy was shot) had gone up on pastures where Arthur Gilmore had once grazed his cows and was later to be the venue for several Oscar ceremonies. An earlier arrival, Edwin Tobias Earl, who invented the refrigerated railroad car which enabled the state's bumper orange crops to be shipped across country, built a large mansion with some of the money he made in 1900 by selling his business. Earl, who later founded the *Los Angeles Express,* saw his rival, Colonel Harrison Gray Otis of the *Los Angeles Times*, become his neighbor when the latter bought a corner lot at Wilshire and Parkview.

Two of America's first airports were located beside Wilshire (one owned by Charlie Chaplin's brother, Sydney; the other by Jack Frye, who became president of TWA), and for six years in the 1920s the aviation pioneer Donald Douglas built planes on what had been an early movie lot until his business grew too big and he had to move. The MTA 20 bus (express 320) from Downtown runs along Wilshire all the way to the ocean at Santa Monica.

One of the first people to see the future had been the Cincinatti son of an oilman/banker, H. Gaylord Wilshire, who had run unsuccessfully for Congress as a socialist in 1890. After losing most of his inherited fortune publishing socialist newspapers, he filed plans for a subdivision bordered by Parkview, Burton Way, and Sixth and Seventh streets. Before his fatal heart attack in 1927, it was already known as "the Wilshire tract."

PRECEDING PAGES: lighting up for Christmas. **LEFT:** MacArthur Park. **BELOW:** detail from Bullocks.

Inventing the Miracle Mile

What accounted for much of Wilshire's success was the policy of complete obeisance to the motorist. Most retailers who bought frontage for their stores paid equal attention to providing parking spaces at the rear, and some estimated that 85 percent of their business came in through the back door.

The best example is **Bullocks ❶** department store at 3050 Wilshire, built in 1929 as America's first big suburban store and which now houses a law library. Its parking lot is guarded by ornate gates, its glass-walled rear entrance resembles that of a luxury hotel, and shoppers were ushered into a sumptuous world of soft carpets, chandeliers, paneled wood, art-deco design and murals by Herman Sachs.

MacArthur Park ❷, the former Westlake which was renamed in 1942 for General Douglas MacArthur and was once the city's garbage dump, has in recent years been fighting for survival. Run down and rendered virtually unusable by the ubiquity of

drug dealers and other lowlifes, it has undergone something of a revival since it became a stop on the new underground Metro Line. The **Park Plaza Hotel** ❸ at the northwest corner has probably the most impressive lobby in town, used by film and TV producers.

A couple of blocks west are the **Bryson Apartment Hotel** (2701 Wilshire), once owned by actor Fred MacMurray, featured as "a white stucco palace" in Raymond Chandler's novel *The Lady in the Lake,* and the still-chic **Talmadge** (at No. 3278), said to have been built by Fox studio boss Joseph Schenck for his bride Norma Talmadge, whose portrait still hangs in the lobby.

Still standing at 701 South New Hampshire, just west of Vermont, is the unpretentious **Mary Miles Minter mansion**, home of the silent star who was being groomed as a successor to Mary Pickford. Her career virtually evaporated when she was named as a lover of director William Desmond Taylor, whose murder was never solved.

At the corner of Western, the fine art-deco **Wiltern Theater** ❹, opened as a Warner showcase just as the neighborhood began to decline in 1931, has undergone a new lease of life. It now books stage shows.

Wilshire's eastern end, especially between Vermont and Western, contains a lively mix of Korean and Cuban stores, small Japanese businesses, and Chicano auto shops. "If America is a melting pot," a local writer observed, "the flame is at its highest here."

Hotel with history

On 22 hilltop acres the **Ambassador Hotel** ❺ – scene of the June 5, 1968, shooting of Robert Kennedy – still stands, its future uncertain since being bought by a syndicate headed by the New York developer Donald Trump. It has been used in occasional episodes of *Dallas* and *Murder, She Wrote* as well as for such movies as *The Fabulous Baker Boys* and *Forrest Gump.*

Shortly after the hotel's opening in January 1921, a diner was shot in the arm by a bullet from the carelessly aimed gun of a rabbit hunter in the adjoining meadows. From that date to the hotel's closing in 1989, it was a non-stop hive of activity. Almost every big name in Hollywood has had some connection: Marion Davies riding a horse through the lobby to Hearst's party to celebrate Charles Lindbergh's Atlantic flight, Kruschev complaining over drinks at being barred from Disneyland, Barbra Streisand's west coast debut, Alice Cooper swinging from a chandelier while a topless dancer performed at a record company party...

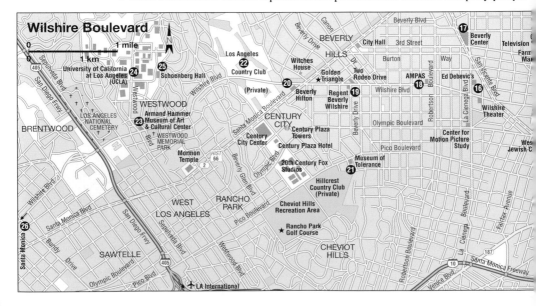

The **Los Altos** apartments **6**, whose early tenants after its 1925 opening included Bette Davis and June Allyson, is still standing at 4121 Wilshire, but a sleek insurance building has replaced the famous old house which stood on the nearby corner of Crenshaw. This was the rambling mansion built (for $250,000 in 1924) by a former consul in Mexico, William Jenkins. In 1950 it was in possession of one of J. Paul Getty's ex-wives when director Billy Wilder decided it was exactly what he needed for *Sunset Boulevard*. Wilder installed a swimming pool, stained-glass windows and a pipe organ, then paid $500 a week for the rented Isotta Fraschini he parked in the driveway. With Gloria Swanson as his Norma Desmond (his fourth choice, after Mae West, Mary Pickford and Pola Negri had declined the role), Wilder went on to make what is probably the most famous movie about Hollywood. The mansion was used once more – to shoot a swimming pool scene in *Rebel Without A Cause* (1955) – and was then demolished in the late 1950s.

Outside the Getty Villa at Malibu are superb sculptures.

Stars at play

The next landmark along Wilshire is the **Wilshire Country Club 7**, flanked by classy **Rossmore Avenue** before it heads north into Vine. The club and adjoining LA Tennis Club were always popular with such stars as Chaplin, Gable, Cooper, Errol Flynn, Jean Harlow, Dietrich and Mae West, who dropped by to watch the tennis pros work out or even swing an occasional racquet themselves.

This is in the heart of **Hancock Park**, site of the old Mayor's mansion, home to some of the most powerful and wealthy in LA, and one of the first wealthy enclaves at the beginning of the 20th century. Residents have traditionally been titans or heirs of industry. While you're on Beverly, jump over to Larchmont and stroll down **Larchmont Village 8**, which has a quaint Disney "Main Street USA" atmosphere, with neighborhood shops and sidewalk cafes.

Just north of the country club, Mae West lived in an all-white sixth-floor apartment at **Ravenswood** (570 Rossmore) for almost 50 years until her death in 1980. Other movie people lived down the block at **El Royale**, both addresses popular because of their proximity to Paramount Studios. During the 1960 Democratic convention, John Kennedy stayed at El Royale.

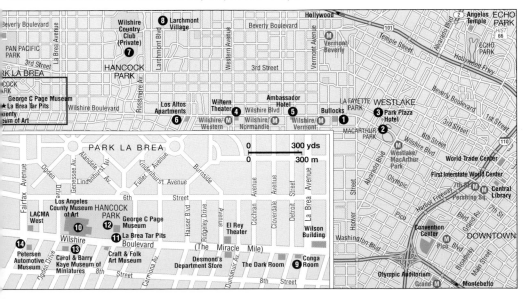

This area of Wilshire has seen renewed growth – with the expansion of **E!Entertainment** headquarters, and an infusion of internet sites, Miracle Mile is more like Media Mile. In addition, the **Conga Room**  at 5370 is providing a Latin spark. Between La Brea and Fairfax, Wilshire offers a lot. The architecturally interesting office complex on the south side, just before the **Craft and Folk Art Museum** (open Tuesday– Sunday 11am–5pm, Thursday to 9pm) contrasts favorably with the forbidding, fortress-like **Los Angeles County Museum of Art** ⓾ (open Tuesday–Thursday 10am–5pm, Friday to 9pm, Saturday and Sunday 11am–6pm). The latter has collections of Impressionists and Old Masters, a Japanese Pavilion and an annex of the Southwest Museum *(see page 137)*.

The museum shares **Hancock Park** with the **La Brea Tar Pits** ⓫ skeletal relics of the Pleicostene era (about 2 million BC). In the **George C. Page Museum** ⓬ (open Tuesday–Sunday 10am– 5pm), fiberglass elephants, tigers and mammoths help tell the story, along with films of the site's excavation.

Across the street from the LA Country Museum of Art is the **Carol & Barry Kaye Museum of Miniatures** ⓭ at 5900 (open Tuesday–Saturday 10am–5pm, Sunday 11am–5pm). Hundreds of palaces, towns and historical figures are reproduced in miniature but in incredible detail.

The **Petersen Automotive Museum** ⓮ (6060 Wilshire; open Tuesday–Sunday 10am–6pm), displays almost everything on wheels, from vintage automobiles to the latest model Mustang. You can don a helmet and sit in a real Indy race car.

The semi-private La Brea housing estate separates Hancock Park from **Pan Pacific Park**, former site of the landmark 1930s Pan Pacific building which was burned down by an arsonist in 1989. The area adjoining the park is shared by CBS **Television City** and the sprawling **Farmers Market** ⓯ (open Monday–Saturday 9am–7pm, Sunday 10am–6pm). This market is one of LA's most popular shopping centers, with fruit and vegetables, kitchens offering baklava and burritos, waffles and wonton, all positioned around an eating area and adjoining a free parking lot. Founded by Earl Gilmore in the Depression era to help an initial group of 17 farmers market their crops, and then popularized by columnist Hedda Hopper (who wrote that the stars ate here), it's a delightful place for a relaxed, lunch but, ominously, has been marked for "renovation." Gilmore died in 1964 and, on the death of his widow 12 years later, the 1852 adobe in which he had been born and died was remodeled and transformed into the Gilmore company headquarters. Sitting in an attractive garden at the market's northeast corner, it also serves as an **information office**.

Grandiose plans for new apartment complexes, hotels and office buildings may endanger the relaxed and distinctly ethnic community along Fairfax. *Los Angeles Times* columnist Sam Hall Kaplan called this area "a microcosm of the Jewish world, a mix as thick and rich as barley soup" and a place he wrote "where people can actually walk around." The district's most famous landmark is **Canter's**, a 24-hour delicatessen whose back room adjoining the bakery is famous for its tasty food and late-night people watching.

La Cienega Boulevard used to be both Restaurant Row and the major art gallery center of LA, and the

Hancock Park is named for Major Henry Hancock, a veteran of the Mexican war who got rich as a gold prospector, and even richer by shipping asphalt from his Rancho La Brea to San Francisco where it paved many of that city's early streets.

BELOW: mammoth at La Brea Tar Pits.

2-mile (3-km) stretch from just below Wilshire and back up to Melrose is a celebration of abundance. From the long-standing excellence of **Lawry's** (nobody does prime rib better), to the exquisite sushi of **Matsuhisa** and showmanship of **Benihana's**, there is something for everybody (including heavy-on-the-garlic **Stinking Rose** and the campy 1950s diner **Ed Debevic's ⑯**).

Opposite one of the best drugstores in town, the Rexall at the corner of Beverly Boulevard, is the **Beverly Center ⑰**, with 100 shops and 14 movie theaters. Don't panic that your car has rolled away and is sticking out of the roof of the restaurant on the northwest side – it's just a prop heralding the **Hard Rock Café**.

As you enter the gleaming city of Beverly Hills, look quickly to catch the **Academy of Motion Picture Arts & Sciences** (AMPAS) ⑱ at 8949 Wilshire. Home of the Oscar, it is mainly an administrative and screening facility, and usually has some interesting photography retrospectives in the lobby.

The structure across from the base of Rodeo Drive is the **Regent Beverly Wilshire ⑲**, a stunning hotel featured in films such as *Pretty Woman* and *Beverly Hills Cop*. Warren Beatty lived in the Penthouse Suite for years, entertaining the likes of Julie Christie and Diane Keaton, and it was Elvis Presley's home while he was making movies.

The attractive **illuminated fountain** at the intersection where Wilshire swings northwest to cut across Santa Monica Boulevard caused traffic jams when it was first placed there in the 1930s. It is more or less the dividing line between the Beverly Hills of the merely comfortable and the luxury of the truly affluent.

Just west of the fountain is the **Beverly Hilton ⑳** – owned by Merv Griffin (who produces *Wheel of Fortune* and *Jeopardy*). It's also home to the Golden Globe awards show and hosted the very first Grammys. The Coconut Room,

Map on page 174

TIP

Beware: the Beverly Center's five floors of parking can be so mind-blowingly confusing that at least one car owner who forgot where he left his car called for a taxi to drive him around the structure looking for it.

BELOW:
Ed Debevic's.

Art-deco details can be found all over the city, adorning gates and buildings.

Merv's ode to the glamorous old Cocoanut Grove where he got his start, has been a hit with the stars – Tom Cruise, Neve Campbell, Jerry Lewis, Michael Jackson and Melanie Griffith have all been spotted there (open Friday and Saturday night only). Out front, the steady **Trader Vic's** restaurant and bar continues its Polynesian traditions – and the dark tables make it a favorite for star affairs.

On the corner of Pico Boulevard and Roxbury Drive, 250,000 the **Museum of Tolerance** ㉑ (open Monday–Thursday 10am–4pm, Friday 10am–1pm, Sunday 11am–5pm) gets 250,000 visitors annually. Its attractions include a video wall about civil rights in America and a Holocaust section which includes a re-creation of a 1930s Berlin cafe scene.

After Beverly Hills, Wilshire Boulevard gets less visually interesting, as it is hedged in for two long stretches where it crosses first the **Los Angeles Country Club** ㉒ and then the grounds of the Veterans Administration. Between them at the edge of Westwood Village is the **Westwood Memorial Park**, where **Marilyn Monroe's crypt** daily draws admirers. When she died in 1962, aged 36, her former husband chose this site because some of her relatives are buried nearby. Richard Conte, who died in 1975, and Natalie Wood, who drowned in 1981, are also buried in this cemetery (open daily 8am–5pm).

The **Armand Hammer Museum and Cultural Center** ㉓ (open Tuesday, Wednesday, Friday and Saturday 11am–7pm, Thursday to 9pm, Sunday to 5pm) has a $450 million collection, amassed over the past 50 years by Hammer.

BELOW: a battle of minds in MacArthur Park.

Westwood

There was a time when Westwood was *the* place to be for young adults on a weekend night – but redevelopments elsewhere and violent incidents led to a

Map on page 174

mass exodus. It's experiencing a rebirth of sorts, led by the patronage of the skyscrapers nearby, and the popularity of the upscale **Eurochow** restaurant. One thing that has remained constant, however, is moviegoing – most major premieres are held at the big theaters here.

Even before William Fox opened his Movietone City here in 1928 as headquarters for his ubiquitous newsreel camera crews, **Westwood Village** was the place to preview movies. Westwood's proximity to the 400-acre campus of the **University of California at Los Angeles** (UCLA) ❷ ensures that large numbers of its 32,000 students are always buzzing around. The "village," with its inexpensive eating places and well-stocked bookstores, is easy to walk around. But UCLA's campus is more interesting, especially the tranquil botanical garden, the outdoor sculpture garden, Japanese garden and bustling student cafeteria with its constant chatter. UCLA has 130 buildings, and its students, 20,000 employees, and more than 2,000 teaching staff mean that the campus is always busy. Visitors are welcome at a variety of sports events, art shows, and musical and theatrical productions. There are concerts in **Schoenberg Hall** ❷, named after the composer who taught here in the 1940s, and free movie showings. **Young Research Library** has rare books and 500,000 maps. Check out the **Frederick S. Wight Art Gallery** (tel: 310/825-9287), the **Fowler Museum of Cultural History**, and the recently renovated **Planetarium** (open Wednesday–Sunday noon–5pm, Thursday to 9pm; tel: 310/825-6847). UCLA's main entrance is on Hilgard Avenue, off which is the **Visitor Center** in Murphy Hall which has maps and information about campus tours.

Once it enters **Santa Monica** ❷, Wilshire Boulevard becomes a rather conventional main thoroughfare lined with service stations, pet groomers, cheap

The Armand Hammer Museum and Cultural Center collection was originally promised to LA's County Museum of Art, but Hammer reneged on the deal when he found he could house his art in a museum with his name on it.

BELOW: fries to go.

Outside entertainers greet you at the J. Paul Getty Villa.

rants, electronics stores and supermarkets. Many of the town's nicer homes are in the blocks to the north through which runs **Montana Avenue**, noted for its trendy shops and the topnotch Il Fornaio bakery with sidewalk tables.

Topanga Canyon

Wilshire ends at the Ocean Avenue bluffs overlooking the ocean. Topanga Canyon Boulevard begins just north of where Sunset meets the Pacific, running through the Santa Monica Mountains to the San Fernando Valley near Chatsworth. It offers access to 35 miles (56 km) of hiking trails, including the scenic, 9-mile (14-km) trail which ends at the Will Rogers Ranch. There are scores of other trails in these mountains, many of them accessible via Mulholland Drive. A complex of shops and cafes can be found around the 100–400 blocks of South Topanga Boulevard and a delightful plant nursery is located at 275 North Topanga Canyon Boulevard. There are no buses up Topanga Canyon,

The **Santa Monica Mountains** and **Topanga State Park** encompass about 150,000 acres (60,000 hectares). Camping is permitted and there are hiking trails through the chaparral and oak forests. Of the many access roads, the easiest are from Mulholland Drive and the Mulholland Highway which follow the crest of the mountains between Cahuenga Boulevard and Malibu. For guided walking excursions call Walk on the Wild Side Hiking Tours (tel: 310/829 2486). Along the Will Rogers State Beach is the **J. Paul Getty Villa** (*see box, page 182*).

Malibu

BELOW:
the Getty Villa is
a sight to behold.

At Santa Monica's northern boundary, Malibu begins, and this famous beach colony stretches for miles along the Pacific Coast Highway all the way to Ven-

tura County. The movie stars responsible for its worldwide fame tend to live in the north sections, and access to their beaches is exclusive. But even in winter the RTD 434 bus runs to Trancas, returning via the **Point Dume** area with its lavish homes, and as an inexpensive sightseeing tour this is hard to beat.

A good place to stop is at the low-key Malibu Country Mart, just north of the Malibu Pier, from which it's a short walk to the lovely Spanish/Moorish Adamson House in landscaped grounds. Adjoining this is the **Malibu Lagoon State Beach** with its wildlife wetlands and beside which the bitchin' surfers play.

The **Adamson House** (open Wednesday–Saturday 11am–3pm), built in 1929 for May Rindge, is richly decorated with attractive tiles from the short-lived Malibu Potteries which she founded. Frederick Rindge, who died in 1905, had bought most of what is now Malibu (for $10 an acre) back in 1887 with the idea of creating an American Riviera. For years the Rindges battled state and railroad interests to keep the area unsullied and virtually inaccessible. But in 1926, May was persuaded to allow the purchase of oceanfront land (at $1 a foot) in what was called the **Malibu Movie Colony**.

Clara Bow and two of her lovers, Gary Cooper and John Gilbert, had cottages here, as did Gloria Swanson, Ronald Colman, and Barbara Stanwyck. "There used to be enormous cachet in looking simpler than you were," recalled Mickey Ziffrin. "We tried to make the outside of our houses look scruffy, in keeping with the beach environment, and kept the comfort inside."

Those early $4,000 shacks got more and more elaborate. Larry Hagman arrived in 1960 and paid $115,000 for his home; now the cost of land alone exceeds $50,000 per oceanfront foot. These prices demand a lot of exclusivity – no wonder so many stars have made it home (or at least their LA home), includ-

One Malibu beach-front home, on just 60 ft (18 meters) of sand, was recently on offer for $3.5 million – and this is considered a bargain.

Map on page 174

BELOW: Malibu Pier.

Map on page 174

TIP

Go up Ramirez Canyon to the **Streisand Center for Conservancy Studies**. Barbra gave this estate to the Santa Monica Mountains Conservancy. It includes 22½ lush acres and five homes. Very exclusive, reservations only.

BELOW:
surfers love Malibu.
RIGHT:
coastal ambiance.

ing Robert Redford, Mel Gibson, Pierce Brosnan, Tom Hanks, Cher, Goldie Hawn and Kurt Russell, Julie Andrews, Nick Nolte, Sting, and Dustin Hoffman.

Malibu Pier, built by Rindge in 1905, collapsed in 1930 and has been rebuilt and restored many times. Until construction of the state highway in 1929, it was the main link with the south. It is currently closed, as is **Alice's Restaurant**, while structural evaluations are made to determine the fate of the pier. Slightly to the north is a countrified shopping mall with cafes and a movie theater.

Trail maps of the area are sometimes available from the Chamber of Commerce; one trail offering both ocean and mountain views begins where Corral Canyon meets the Pacific Coast Highway. PCH is lined for miles with restaurants, shops and motels, but in summer parking is always difficult, even in the gigantic lots which adjoin the state beaches and to which access can be made via stairways in the 24300 to 24700 and 25100 and 27200 blocks. If you are going by bus, it is important to remember these locations to avoid lengthy walks.

The elegant, Spanish-style, modern buildings dominating the coastline past the shopping center belong to **Pepperdine University**, a respected Christian school that stands on land formerly owned by John Wayne. Years ago he offered to donate it to USC for relocation, but the Trustees opted to stay closer to the city center.

The USA's largest beach, **Zuma** is the least picturesque but has the most facilities. **Pirate's Cove**, a secluded nude beach on the Point Dume headland, is accessible via a hike from **Paradise Cove**. The back-country behind Malibu has nature trails, campgrounds, and appealing flora and fauna. The 4,000-acre (1,600-hectare) **Malibu Creek State Park** (dawn to dusk) was formerly a Fox movie lot on whose artificial lake some sequences of *Cleopatra* were shot. ❑

THE GETTY VILLA

Will Rogers State Beach stretches for 2 miles (3 km) along the coast from where Sunset meets the sea. If you are exceptionally lucky, you will find free parking along Temescal Canyon Boulevard, otherwise you'll have to settle for a place in one of the fee-paying beach parking lots which are always crowded in summer. Parking is banned along the highway.

To visit the J. Paul Getty Villa (closed until 2002), you'll need to call ahead for a parking reservation, but admittance and parking are free. Visitors arriving at the foot of the hill via the MTA 434 bus must obtain a pass from the driver. The museum is one of the most interesting in America, centered around a faithfully reconstructed 1st-century Italian villa (with some of the original artifacts) from Herculaneum which was buried by the same eruption of Mount Vesuvius in AD 79 that engulfed Pompeii. Built from 40 different types of marble, this "Pompeii by the Pacific" was bequeathed to the city by the oil billionaire who, astonishingly, never saw it. He died in England in 1976. The museum is currently in a state of flux while much of the Getty collection, including priceless Persian carpets, centuries-old furniture and fabulous paintings, is transferred to the J. Paul Getty Center near Brentwood.

SANTA MONICA BOULEVARD

Map on page 188

*Starting with the late movie stars and their burial ground,
Santa Monica Boulevard heads past Paramount Studios
as far as the bohemian haven of Venice Beach*

It almost goes without saying that what most visitors want to see is stars: to bask in the reflection of their radiance or even to go where they might have been. It matters hardly at all whether the star is alive or dead. Hollywood is surely the only place in the world where dead stars evoke as much interest as those still alive and preening. Pilgrims are always present – searching for the orphanage where Marilyn Monroe once lived *(see page 189)*, where Jean Harlow attempted suicide (1353 Clubview Drive), or for the last resting places of Rudolph Valentino (died 1926), Douglas Fairbanks (1939) or actress Virginia Rappe, whose fatal rape in 1921 ended comic Fatty Arbuckle's career.

The last three, entombed in the **Hollywood Forever Memorial Park ❶** (6000 Santa Monica Boulevard; open daily 8am–5pm) in company with notables such as gangster Bugsy Siegel, irascible Columbia Studios boss Harry Cohn, Hearst's perky mistress Marion Davies and Cecil B. De Mille, would surely be pleased to know they can still effortlessly draw the fans.

The cemetery's largest monument is that of fabulously rich William A. Clark, the copper and railroad heir who founded the Los Angeles Philharmonic and in 1920 built the island tomb in which he now rests, flanked by his two wives.

Rudolph Valentino had a bigger wake, though: 10,000 fans crammed the cemetery for the charismatic hero of *The Sheik* who was only 31 when he died of peritonitis. He is lodged in a corner niche of the cathedral mausoleum beside the crypt of June Mathis, the studio executive who discovered him and who outlived him by only one year. The death, announced in 1989, of the "Lady in Black" who had annually brought flowers, ended an affectionate tribute which had been initiated by the legendary publicity agent Russell Birdwell; the ritual had in fact endured twice as long as Valentino himself had lived.

Weekly flowers

Rappe, whose heartbroken lover, producer Henry Lehrman placed flowers on her grave until his own death in 1946 (his tomb adjoins hers), holds an unshakeable appeal for moralists who like to point to Hollywood's "bad old days." After her death (from a ruptured bladder, according to movie-historian Ken Schessler) following a drunken San Francisco party, Arbuckle faced trial, was acquitted but never regained his former stardom. There is some evidence that he might have been manipulated into the encounter. Rappe's grave, near those of Tyrone Power and Marion Davies, shares the same lakeside section as Cecil B. De Mille, Nelson Eddy and Adolph Menjou.

Douglas Fairbanks Sr, who was 56 when he died in 1939, gets an impressive sunken garden all to himself, along with a huge marble monument, paid for by his former wife. (Mary Pickford is buried in Glendale, at Forest Lawn Cemetery.)

Among others buried here are Bugsy Siegel, the mobster who "invented" Las Vegas and was himself the victim of a mob hit in 1947, Colonel Griffith J. Griffith – who donated to the city the land which became Griffith Park and who died in 1930 a decade after serving two years in San Quentin for shooting his wife – Peter Finch, Eleanor Powell, Jesse Lasky, Clifton Webb, Peter Lorre, and Horace and Daeida Wilcox, the couple who founded Hollywood.

If famous deaths are your thing, try **Grave Line Tours** for the most outrageous tour in town – a classic Cadillac hearse transports guests to scenes of celebrity deaths or last breaths, with the emphasis on murder and intrigue (tel: 323/469-4149).

Charlie Chaplin was one of the first real stars of Hollywood.

Hollywood at work

It seems fitting that the last stop for many of these stars should be so close to where they worked. **Paramount Studios ❷**, formed by Jesse Lasky and Adolph Zukor merging their companies in 1926, adjoins the cemetery. On the 62-acre (25-hectare) lot – where Crosby, Hope and Lamour clowned their way through the *Road* pictures – Cecil B. De Mille produced such epics as *Samson and Delilah* and *Cleopatra*, Captain Kirk and Spock saved the universe in *Star Trek*, and Harrison Ford was victorious in the dramatic boat climax to *Patriot Games*. In more recent years some of America's top TV shows, such as *Cheers* and *Frasier*, have also been made here. Since Paramount now offers a two-hour tour (Monday–Friday 9am–2pm on the hour), you too can sail majestically through the famous gate like Norma Desmond in Billy Wilder's *Sunset Boulevard*.

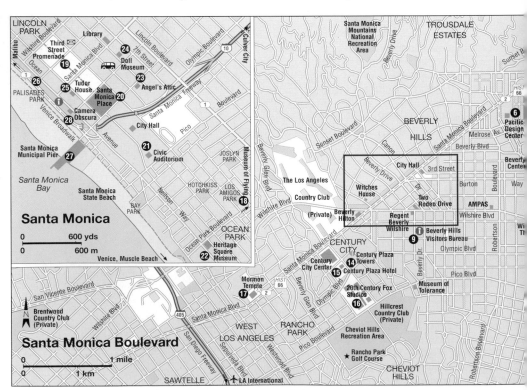

Map on page 188

It's almost 20 years since Paramount absorbed RKO Pictures (then owned by Lucille Ball) but a painted-over RKO globe can still be spotted on top of one of the sound stages, a solitary reminder of the company that gave us *King Kong* and the Astaire/Rogers movies in the heady 1930s.

It was the RKO sign that 10-year-old Norma Baker could see from her window in the Los Angeles Orphans' Home (demolished in 1977) on nearby **El Centro Street**. Twelve years later, as an aspiring starlet, Marilyn Monroe lived only a few blocks away on **Lodi Place** at the Hollywood Studio Club (now a YWCA). Her view was of Columbia Studios, then on Gower Street where the tyrannical Harry Cohn had already "created" Rita Hayworth and was about to repeat the trick with Kim Novak.

Although the famous old names are long gone and most of the bigger studios have moved away, this area is still the working center of the movie industry. The newly renovated, 75-year-old **Producers Studios** beside Paramount, once owned by the man who produced D.W. Griffith's *Birth of a Nation* and which served as the home of Hopalong Cassidy films, has been the site of recent movies by Cher, the late George Burns, Kevin Costner and Peter Bogdanovich.

Burns maintained an office at the **Hollywood Center Studios** (1040 North Las Palmas) where Francis Ford Coppola's Zoetrope went bust in the 1980s. Its stages are now used mainly for television shows. This was also where Howard Hughes launched starlet Jean Harlow in the 1927 *Hell's Angels*, and where Mae West kept a production bungalow (recently torn down, but it was Tim Robbins' office in Robert Altman's movie *The Player*).

There are no traces of the old Metro Studios at Romaine and Cahuenga, where Valentino's first hit, *Four Horsemen of the Apocalypse*, was made in 1921, nor

BELOW: Via Rodeo, Beverly Hills.

Many a star has passed through the gates of Paramount Studios.

of Lone Star Studios across the street where Charles Chaplin and Buster Keaton made their first films. But Chaplin's distinctive-looking 1918 studio at La Brea and De Longpre – where his footprints are still embedded in the cement beside one of the sound stages – is still standing and has become a film studio again. Until recently, it was the headquarters of A&M records; in 2000 it was purchased by the five children of Jim Henson (*The Muppet Show*), who have moved the Jim Henson Company in. The curious **French Village** at 1330 Formosa (built by architects Arthur and Nina Zwebell in 1929) is also said to have been Chaplin's.

The famous **Formosa Café** ❸ (featured in the movie *LA Confidential*) has walls lined with autographed star pictures and sits on the corner of the Santa Monica Boulevard and Formosa Avenue, on which is the old **Warner-Hollywood Studios** ❹, used by Aaron Spelling for his many productions (including *Dynasty* and *Beverly Hills 90210*). It was previously owned by Samuel Goldwyn and before that by Hollywood's regal pair, Mary Pickford and Douglas Fairbanks. "There's nothing but fields around here," said Fairbanks, when he bought the studios in 1922 to make *Robin Hood*, "and we can put up some really big sets." In 1994 Warner's almost leveled the Formosa for a parking lot – however, its legions of patrons and decades of history saved this film industry hangout from the wrecker's ball.

By the end of World War I, four out of five of the world's movies were being made in this area. It's salutary to remember that the industry has always needed the support of hundreds of ancillary businesses and services – recording studios, prop houses, talent agencies, lighting equipment companies, equipment rentals – many of which are also located nearby. Eastman Kodak and Consolidated Film Industries process millions of feet of film each day; Technicolor, which in

BELOW: Paramount Studios gates as they were originally.

1931 developed the three-strip color process that changed movies forever, was for 40 years located in the art-deco building on Romaine; Western Costume, which moved to North Hollywood in 1990, built up an inventory of three million items in the 58 years it occupied premises along Melrose.

Santa Monica Boulevard, traversed in its entirety by MTA 4 (express 304) which starts Downtown, begins at the 4000 block of Sunset, more or less the eastern boundary of Hollywood itself. Because Hollywood is not a legal entity, its boundaries are not specifically defined but are generally accepted as stretching south to Melrose, the site of what is now the last major studio still to be found in this community – Paramount Pictures.

A few blocks west of La Brea, at 7304 Santa Monica Boulevard, is one of the stores most cherished by Westsiders – **Trader Joe's ❺**, an upscale market specializing in everything from scores of cheeses to an enormous variety of wines at all price levels. If you shop at Trader Joe's, then you're very LA.

West Hollywood

There's no reason you'd especially notice the difference, but once you cross Fairfax you're actually in **West Hollywood**, technically a separate city with a relatively large gay population. There's a small, pleasant park down San Vicente just behind the library and the nearby **Pacific Design Center ❻**, an immense 600-ft (180-meter) structure known as the **Blue Whale**, marks the western end of a fascinating stretch of **Melrose Avenue** (mostly between Fairfax and La Brea), which offers some of the best window-shopping in town.

This area has some of the frenetic atmosphere of New York's Greenwich Village, SoHo and the East Village combined: offbeat shops and boutiques with

Map on page 188

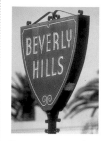

You are now entering the hallowed ground of the rich and famous.

BELOW: Hollywood's earliest "royalty."

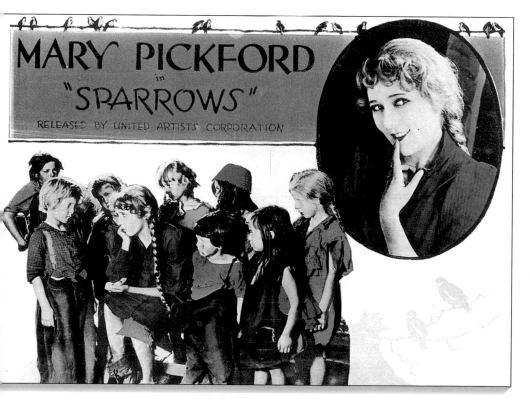

names like Wacko and Fat Chance, avant-garde galleries, old clothes stores, see-and-be-seen eating places and acres of neon.

Much of the style is 1950s, seen clearly at **Johnny Rocket's** ❼, a diner where bikers, artists and fashion victims mingle. Trendies, being what they are of course, claim that Melrose became passé long ago when the *real* action moved around the corner to the boutiques and restaurants of **La Brea Avenue**.

Just before La Cienega it's worth making a detour to 833 Kings Road for a look at the **Rudolph Schindler home** ❽, a concrete and glass house that Frank Lloyd Wright's Viennese-born colleague designed and in which he lived with his wife and fellow architect Richard Neutra and his wife from 1925 to 1930. Oriented to semi-outdoor living, it displays a touching (and slightly misplaced) optimism about the Californian climate, but its modernist style influenced many architects and is echoed in some of Neutra's later works. Back on the boulevard, the pub-like **Barney's Beanery**, with its worldwide roster of 300 beers, has been a popular hangout for almost half a century.

A direct bus, MTA 220, runs down Robertson Boulevard through Culver City to Marina del Rey, but unless you have an appointment at **Sony Picture Studios** (the former MGM Studios), **Culver City** is not very interesting. If **Culver Studios** look familiar, it's because the familiar Tara-like mansion in which it is located became David O. Selznick's movie trademark when he owned them, after the success of *Gone with the Wind*.

Jim Morrison and the Doors were regulars at Barney's Beanery and Janis Joplin partied here the night she took her final fatal overdose.

Beverly Hills

As it enters Beverly Hills, Santa Monica Boulevard is bordered by a grassy strip which is all that remains of the bridlepath that until the 1920s ran from the

BELOW: the Blue Whale dominates the scene.

downtown Biltmore to the Beverly Hills Hotel out here in the countryside. Today the strip hosts a rotating display of sculpture which provokes occasional outrage from many locals who, by contrast, seem surprisingly good-natured about tourists gawking at their homes because of some real or imagined movie star connection. On Palm Drive two such houses, Nos. 508 and 512, are much visited, being the former homes respectively of Marilyn Monroe and her husband Joe DiMaggio, and Jean Harlow.

The **Beverly Hills Visitors Bureau** ❾, 239 S. Beverly Drive (tel: 310/248-1015), offers free information about the community and a two-hour guided tour, but historical information is found more readily in the library on North Rexford Drive.

Beverly Hills came into being when three partners who had drilled 30 wells in an unsuccessful search for oil on the old Rancho Rodeo de las Aguas formed the Rodeo Land and Water Company to develop the land. One-acre lots along what is now Santa Monica Boulevard were offered for $400 with similar plots along Sunset Boulevard at double that figure. One of these model homes, at 515 North Canon Drive, is still standing.

When developer Burton Green built the mission-style Beverly Hills Hotel in 1912 to be the focal point of the new community, he lured Margaret Anderson from the old Hollywood Hotel along with her chef, recipes. and famous clientele. The hotel's bungalows soon became popular lovenests for everybody from Clark Gable to John Kennedy.

In 1918, Douglas Fairbanks bought an old hunting lodge in the desolate hills and, with the help of his studio's art director, created Pickfair. Because of the prejudice against movie people in other upscale neighborhoods, many of them

BELOW:
The Witches House.

Healthy living is a way of life for most Californians.

...ose to live in Beverly Hills, whose population in the decade between 1920 and ...0 jumped from 634 to 17,428. It has doubled again since.

Oddly enough, despite the money lavished on them, many of the homes are not especially imaginative or distinctive, often being merely larger versions of familiar styles. The really interesting houses are aberrations such as the bizarre **Witches House** ⑩ at 516 Walden Drive, which began life as a 1921 movie set before being moved to this site, and the elaborately ornamental **O'Neill House** along North Rodeo Drive. From May to December, try the **Beverly Hills Trolley** "Sights and Scenes" tour, which travels from Downtown to celebrity homes and back daily 11am–5pm.

The short stretch of **Rodeo Drive** between Santa Monica and Wilshire boulevards, with its branches of such world-renowned stores as Gucci, Hermes, Chanel, Fendi and Van Cleef & Arpels – "the most staggering display of luxury in the Western world," says novelist Judith Krantz – sees the kind of customers who pay $800 for a white satin shirt at Giuseppe Battaglia's or $8,500 for a mink-lined denim jacket at Bijan (where it's necessary to have an appointment to get inside the door). Lavish but lesser-known stores line three levels around a central courtyard called the **Rodeo Collection**. The **Café Rodeo** has a tree-shaded terrace overlooking the sidewalk.

The nearby $200-million **Two Rodeo Drive** ⑪ was modeled after some imaginary cobble-stoned European walkway, its classy emporiums featuring granite colonnades and copper-toned roofs. Among its many distinctions is a Japanese restaurant so exclusive it has an unlisted number.

BELOW: Gucci feels right at home on exclusive Rodeo Drive.

Just around the corner from Rodeo Drive is a branch of **The Museum of Television and Radio** ⑫ (there is one in New York, too). An incredible archive of old shows and information, the museum also holds screenings each afternoon in two screening rooms and two theaters. On Saturday mornings, there's a kids radio workshop (open Wednesday–Sunday noon–5pm, Thursday to 9pm; tel: 310/786-1025).

The area's lifestyle and ambiance tend to evoke envy. "If ever there was a Camelot on earth," boasts city councilman Bob Tanenbaum, "in my opinion it is Beverly Hills." Operating out of a grandiose **City Hall** ⑬ capped with a tiled cupola, he and his colleagues oversee a city government that bans billboards, insists that "For Sale" signs be less than 1 foot square, demands that lawns be maintained, and whose 654 employees – only half a dozen of whom can afford to live within the city limits – perfume the city's garbage before disposing of it.

The city spends $2½ million (from a $110 million annual budget) maintaining 30,000 trees, one for almost every resident, and its educational system is the envy of neighboring communities, few of which can boast (as can Beverly Hills High School) of having 17 oil wells on campus.

Century City

From his office high up in **Fox Tower**, actor-cum-US president Ronald Reagan once gazed down on his affluent neighbors, the banks and insurance companies, high-priced lawyers and high-flying corpora-

Map on page 188

tions that inhabit the sleek skyscrapers of **Century City**, the area's most sterile community. Down there, he might have mused, Shirley Temple once played, Jennifer Jones walked to church, and Don Ameche invented the telephone. And before all that it was Tom Mix's ranch.

Four decades of moviemaking were swept into the memory bank when 20th Century-Fox peddled 180 acres (73 hectares) of its lot in 1981 to Alcoa which spent $1 million replanting the studio's trees and then hired architect Minoru Yamasaki to design the twin triangular **Century Plaza Towers** ⑭ and curved **Century Plaza Hotel** ⑮ (a 30th-floor penthouse apartment rents for $7,000 nightly). There is no on-street parking, the expectation being that visitors to the 80 over-priced shops, restaurants, a Shubert theater, and 14 cinemas will either pay the stiff garage fee or buy enough loot to get their parking tickets validated. Most pretentious touch: the Tower's black doormen wearing the costume of Britain's Tudor beefeaters. Although a mite colorless, the Century City shopping center offers a choice of food counters with outdoor tables.

Adjoining Century City to the south is the working lot established by William Fox in 1925 of **20th Century-Fox Studios** ⑯, from whose entrance on Pico Boulevard sightseers can spot the New York City street featured in *Hello Dolly*. There are no tours of the studio.

Between Century City and the San Diego Freeway, the enormous **Mormon Temple** ⑰, completed in 1950, stands on a hill to the north. Tours of the grounds (entrance on Manning Avenue) can be taken daily 9am–9pm, along with a little religious indoctrination, but outsiders are not allowed to view the temple's interior. The well-stocked **Genealogical Library**, however, is open to all (Monday, Friday and Saturday 9am–6pm, Tuesday–Thursday 9am–9pm).

BELOW: letting time go by.

Bundy Drive heads south from Santa Monica Boulevard down to Santa Monica's famous old **airport**, where the workhorse plane, the DC3, was born and from which just about every early American flyer (Charles Lindbergh, Doolittle, Amelia Earhart, Howard Hughes) made some of their first flights.

The McDonnell Douglas plant, employing 40,000 workers, remained here until 1978. Much of this nostalgia is preserved in the **Museum of Flying** ⓲, at the airport's northwest corner (entrance via 28th street, off Ocean Park Boulevard; open Wednesday–Sunday 1–5pm).

Above the museum, the classy **DC3** restaurant offers diners wonderfully engaging views of planes taking off and landing, as does **Typhoon**, an inventive Thai/Southeast Asian restaurant across the runway.

Santa Monica

Santa Monica, where the West Side meets the ocean, is something of an anomaly: an upper middle-class town with rent control and a seaside resort in which the sea sometimes seems hardly relevant. In recent years Santa Monica has undergone something of a renaissance, having been "discovered" as the perfect site by Hollywood types who like to conduct their business beside the seaside: MGM, Sony West, Robert Redford's Sundance Institute, Oliver Stone and Sylvester Stallone currently have offices here.

Additionally, the TV commercial production industry has made a huge migration to Santa Monica – as their out-of-town agency clients have flocked to the surging tide of luxury hotels near the beach, the production companies have found being nearby can mean a difference in getting the job. Office space is getting ridiculously hard to find.

BELOW: the Santa Monica coastline.

Map on page 188

In keeping with the fresher profile, much civic improvement has taken place, on Main Street, on Third Street, on the pier and in Palisades Park. The "Bay City" of Raymond Chandler's novels is a pleasant place, with a wide pedestrian mall at Third Street that is the jewel of the city. As recently as the late 1980s, Third Street was a rundown, grimy retail area filled with discount stores. Today, **Third Street Promenade ⑲** is packed with hip stores and restaurants, and a thriving nightlife with street performers everywhere.

Follow the Promenade down to the sparkling Frank Gehry-designed **Santa Monica Place ⑳** flanked by department stores. This lively eating area, served by a variety of food counters, accommodates 450 people. Upstairs, check out the **Santa Monica Place Neighborhood Gallery** to meet some local artists (open Monday–Saturday 10am–9pm, Sunday 11am–6pm).

In the open-air mall, what is now a four-theater cineplex was first built in 1934 out of reinforced concrete and has been cunningly integrated with a new housing complex. Similarly, in the next block, the city's oldest brick building – formerly the Rapp Saloon built in 1875, which later served as the Town Hall – has been incorporated into the glassy shell of a youth hostel.

A few blocks south, past the freeway and the **Civic Auditorium ㉑**, are the sleek shops of **Main Street**. Nearby is the **Heritage Square Museum ㉒**, a century-old house with rooms representing different eras (open Wednesday–Saturday 11am–4pm, Sunday 10am–4pm).

Other Victorian houses are **Angel's Attic ㉓** at 515 Colorado, which serves tea and cakes, and the **Doll Museum ㉔** at 1437 Sixth Street (open Tuesday–Sunday 12.30–4.30pm), each with an antique doll collection. Some of the most interesting galleries are at the lower end of Main Street between **Pico Boulevard** and **Rose Avenue**, with others clustered along **Colorado**, close to **Lincoln**.

Don't let the fact that the **Santa Monica Museum of Art** is now a bit inland at **Bergamot Station Art Center** stop you from going there. Bergamot's eclectic collection of galleries and creative workspaces (open Wednesday–Sunday 11am–6pm, Friday to 10pm) is worth the trip, and every Friday evening there are free films, discussions, or readings. The museum itself specializes in contemporary work, and considers itself an active laboratory (open Tuesday–Saturday 11am–6pm).

Santa Monica is a haven for homesick Brits who have no difficulty finding fish and chips and all that popular pub grub at such places as the bustling **Ye Olde Kings Head,** with its dart board and draft beer at the corner of 2nd Street and Santa Monica, and **Tudor House ㉕**, an English tea room and shop selling pork pies, crumpets and English candy bars just around the corner on 2nd Street.

The best places to spend time in Santa Monica are at the superlative **library** (an extensive collection of current magazines and a spacious, well-lit reading area) and at clifftop **Palisades Park ㉖**, a eucalyptus-fringed grassy stretch along Ocean Avenue that offers pleasing views of sailing boats and spectacular sunsets. In recent years it has proved to be a popular venue for the homeless. It was given to the city in 1892 for use as a park "forever" by Santa Monica's

BELOW: Third Street Promenade.

Map on page 188

founders, Colonel Robert Baker and his partner Senator John P. Jones, whose house stood at the corner of Wilshire Boulevard now occupied by the **Fairmont Miramar Hotel**. The enormous fig tree outside the lobby was planted by the family in the 1880s.

Among the buildings of note between here across from the tree-lined pathway down to the venerable **Santa Monica Pier** ㉗ are the **Champagne Towers**, named for bandleader Lawrence Welk, whose national TV program used to come from the seaside Aragon Ballroom in nearby Venice. Adjoining the Towers is the **Wilshire Palisades Building**, an eye-catching stepdown design which won an award for architects Daniel, Mann, Johnson and Medenhall in 1960. The **Queen Anne house** at 1333 Ocean Avenue used to be owned by tennis star Gussie Moran.

Beside the park near Santa Monica Boulevard is the **Visitor Information kiosk** and in the Senior Recreation Center is a free **camera obscura** ㉘ (open Monday–Friday 9am–4pm, Saturday and Sunday 11am–4pm). Down the hill is the pier itself, whose wonderful, old **carousel** with its 44 hand-carved horses was featured in the film *The Sting* (open daily in summer 10am–5pm, winter Saturday and Sunday only 10am–5pm). The century-old pier, to which has been added a fun fair and rollercoaster ride, offers an assortment of amusement arcades, souvenir stands, snack bars, and sedentary fishermen.

Visiting Venice

The promenade leading from the pier down to **Venice**, about a mile to the south (buses run down Main Street), gets more and more interesting as it enters that bohemian enclave. Tourists mingle with skimpily-attired rollerbladers, rainbow-haired punks, joggers, magicians, card-players, fortune tellers, itinerant musicians and macho types flexing their biceps at **Muscle Beach**.

BELOW:
a perfect souvenir.

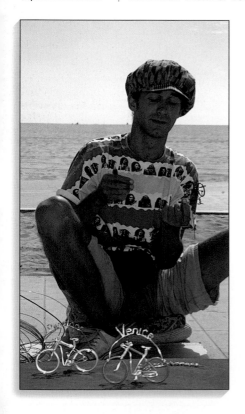

You can rent rollerskates on **Windward Avenue** or a bicycle on **Washington Street** (opposite the abandoned pier from which before World War II water taxis ran out to the gambling ships) or just sit at one of the sidewalk cafes and admire the passing parade. There's plenty to keep you occupied.

Santa Monica's first-rate transport system, the **Big Blue Bus**, costs under a dollar to ride and operates down to Venice (No. 1 and No. 2); Marina del Rey and Los Angeles Airport (No. 3); north to Pacific Palisades; to UCLA; along Pico past Century City and Downtown (via the freeway). It issues transfers to MTA buses. To go up the coast, however, it is necessary to catch the MTA 434 from outside the visitor kiosk. The bus runs south initially to get onto the Pacific Coast Highway.

Lining the beach just north of Santa Monica are what remain of the vast mansions once owned by Peter Lawford and Louis B. Mayer. William Randolph Hearst commissioned Julia Morgan to design a 118-room house into which he fitted an 18th-century bedroom from an English manor house. The house, at 415 Palisades Beach Road, was pulled down in the 1970s but the servants' quarters have been preserved as the members-only **Sand and Beach Club**. ❏

Tranquility Near the Beach

Waves of bright flowers tumble over sagging fences, and ducks nestle under upturned boats on tiny jetties. Only a block away traffic thunders ceaselessly along Pacific Avenue but here, in the wildlife sanctuary formed by the Venice canal system, all is tranquil.

The circulating system for the canals was a disaster, as the 30-inch (80-cm) pipes used to flush sea water through gates on every tide failed. More than 50 years of silt, dirt and refuse have reduced the once 4-ft (1.2-meter) waterways to little more than knee-deep. But you can pick your way along rutted paths, over humpbacked bridges and past well-tended gardens, admiring the architecture, the birds, the flowers. Over 70 years after the death of Abbott Kinney, some of his vision still remains in what is probably the nicest walk in urban Los Angeles.

Venice began when Kinney acquired 160 acres of marshland in 1902. It was the recommendation of his engineers that canals be dredged to reclaim the land that gave him the idea to replicate Italy's Venice. After his workmen had spent three years digging trenches, he installed Japanese lanterns, imported gondolas and encircled the entire area with a miniature railroad.

The opening (July 4, 1905) was attended by 40,000. Entertained by a large orchestra, they strolled in the square, modeled after the Piazza San Marco, and onto the 1,600-ft (490-meter) pier whose showpiece was the Ship Hotel. Wealthy visitors stayed in St Mark's Hotel, modeled on the Doge's Palace; the less affluent slept under canvas roofs in Villa City bordering the lagoon.

Mack Sennett shot Chaplin's second movie (*Kid Auto Races*) in Venice; Mary Pickford was rowed down the Grand Canal; Mabel Normand posed for pictures with a fish on her head; and Carole Lombard hosted a memorable party on the pier. But gradually the resort lost its appeal and deteriorated, as low-grade boardwalk attractions replaced such earlier treats as Sarah Bernhardt and the Chicago Orchestra.

His dream clouded and he died in 1920. In 1925, after residents voted to become part of LA, the main section of the canal was filled in for the benefit of cars, and before the end of the 1920s the Ohio Oil Co. had erected a forest of derricks. By 1931 they had 163 productive oil wells.

The heart of today's Venice is the Windward Circle at Windward and Main streets, where a statue marks the site of the former lagoon. The continuation of Windward Street was once the Lion canal, and Market, Altair and Cabrillo streets follow the track of earlier waterways. The canals can be viewed best today along Dell Street.

Windward, now as then the main drag, had a ticket office at the corner of Pacific for the Pacific Electric railcars. At Ocean Front Walk, what was once the Hotel Stuart and later the St Charles is now the Venice Beach Hotel. The mural outside a skate rental store recognizes Venice's status as capital of the wheelies. ❑

RIGHT: cycling at Venice Beach.

THE VALLEYS AND CANYONS

*Beyond Los Angeles and away from the crowds are
wide open spaces, historical old towns, and Universal Studios,
one of the giants of the entertainment industry*

Map on page 204

A s a rule, there's the Los Angeles the tourists know about, and then there's the Los Angeles only those who live here can understand. The tourists know about the ocean as it stretches from Malibu to the South Bay; they know of Beverly Hills and Bel Air; of Hollywood and Burbank (though all they really know of Burbank is that it's where the hugely popular late-night talk show, the *Tonight Show*, is taped). Beyond that, they've heard rumors of places referred to as the Valley, or as the Canyons. But they don't really know what that means. It all sounds so, you know, rustic – as if Tom Mix were still riding across the landscape, flashing his multitude of teeth, and leaping on and off his noble steed.

Indeed, there are those who have lived in Los Angeles for years who don't really know much about the Valley and the Canyons, except that they're the areas somewhat north of the city itself. When it rains, they flood. When the sun bakes down on Los Angeles, they fry, and fires spread across the landscape, adding to the smog with great billows of jacaranda smoke. Yet in their own distinct ways, the Valley and most canyons are more Los Angelean than Downtown, an area that relates very little to the ethos of the city at all. The Valley and the Canyons are where locals go when they want to find the spirit of Los Angeles. It haunts Ventura and Van Nuys boulevards, and creeps like fog through the hills of Laurel and Coldwater Canyons.

Some definition of terms is clearly in order here. When Los Angelenos refer to the Valley, they're talking about the **San Fernando Valley**, the vast flatness to the north of the Hollywood Hills. There are actually two more valleys of note, the larger of which is the **San Gabriel Valley**, which stretches east from Downtown through Pasadena and Monterey Park, in the general direction of Riverside and San Bernardino.

The other is a smaller, more rural (but nevertheless fast-developing) valley to the north of the San Fernando Valley, called **Santa Clarita**, best known for its many small produce stands, and the looming presence of Six Flags Magic Mountain theme park (*see page 246*).

Passes and canyons

When it comes to the Canyons, things get a bit more complicated, for canyons abound. Some of them are really more passes than canyons – like the **Sepulveda Pass** that connects the San Fernando Valley to West Los Angeles, and the **Cahuenga Pass** through which the Hollywood Freeway travels on its way from Studio City to Hollywood proper.

The canyons that locals refer to when they refer to them at all are **Laurel Canyon**, which connects

PRECEDING PAGES:
Malibu Mountains rancher.
LEFT: a fan of Universal Studios.
BELOW: highway into the valley.

Studio City to West Hollywood, and **Coldwater Canyon**, which connects Sherman Oaks to Beverly Hills.

Farther west, there's **Topanga Canyon** and **Malibu Canyon**, both of which are dramatic routes from the Valley to the ocean, paved strips which have created various territorial wars by giving Valley surfers a direct access to ocean waves annexed for the sole use of Maliboonians. Scattered in between these two are a sundry collection of smaller canyons – **Nichols**, **Rustic**, **Beverly Glen**, **Mandeville**, **Latigo** and several others. Hidden worlds contained within other hidden worlds.

At the hub, the nexus of the valleys and canyons of Los Angeles, the geographic center off which all the others radiate, is the great spreading girth of the San Fernando Valley, the bedroom community to end all bedroom communities. Indeed, a bedroom community that's spawned other communities to house those who serve its needs. Something in the region of 1.8 million people live in the San Fernando Valley, which means that, were it a city unto itself, it would be the fifth largest in the United States, topped only by New York, Los Angeles, Chicago and Houston. In fact, there has recently been a movement afoot by valley activists to secede from Los Angeles and strike out on their own – a lack of influence in the school system and police force being their biggest gripe.

Physically, the Valley is easy enough to define, running from the **Ventura County line** on the west; to the **San Gabriel Mountains** on the east and north; to the **Santa Monica Mountains** and the **Hollywood Hills** on the south. But to define the Valley solely in terms of its geographic boundaries is to miss the point of the lifestyle that's grown out of the Valley. It's a metaphor for, and a symbol of, the direction in which life is heading in the United States in the early years of the 21st century.

America looks to the Valley to say "what's next?" And what America finds is a land filled with pastel-colored boulevards lined with condominiums interspersed with mini-malls and maxi-malls, stretching off into infinity.

It's a land built for the comfort of those adventurers who intersperse driving with shopping and watching rented videos at home. In some ways, the Valley is

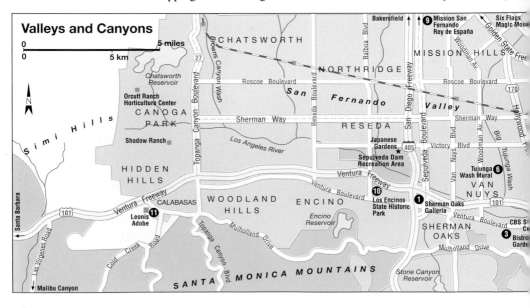

the ultimate triumph of the couch potato; there are probably more branches of Domino's Pizza here than in any other part of the civilized world.

Map on page 204

Image of the future

The Valley that the casual visitor encounters today is, like an archaeological dig, a layering-on of the Valley that was here five years ago. Five years from now, a new layer will have covered over the current one. Like New York City, it's a land that's never finished. But it's a good deal more complex today than it's ever been in the past. It's no coincidence that the music videos for rock hits like Tom Petty's *Free Fallin'* and Randy Newman's *I Love LA* were both largely set in the Valley, for the Valley is everyone's image of what the future is all about, a land of hyperbolic malls, housing developments and freeways that stretch from here until the very edge of infinity.

The dry environment can easily cause forest fires.

You don't hear so many wisecracks about the Valley and Valley girls anymore. No longer is the dominant line a paraphrase of the adage from *Love Story*, something along the lines of "Living in the Valley means always having to say you're sorry." These days, nobody apologizes for living in Studio City, Sherman Oaks, Encino, Woodland Hills, and so forth. Too many people who used to write those jokes now make their homes there.

In truth, the San Fernando Valley is a very good place to live; and it keeps getting better. Shopping is abundant and easy, thanks to a combination of shopping streets like **Ventura Boulevard**, and mega-malls like the **Sherman Oaks Galleria ❶**, the **Topanga Plaza** and the **Glendale Galleria**. Parking is still convenient, in contrast to the rest of Los Angeles, where restrictive neighborhood zoning rules have turned parking into a nightmarish assortment of contradictions. It's one of the last areas in Los Angeles where first houses – starter homes – are still even vaguely affordable. And when its freeways work, they work very well, although as the population of the Valley has soared, they've stopped working nearly as often; traffic jams along the Ventura Freeway are ubiquitous and unarguably among the worst in all of California.

The Valley also maintains an appealing sense of history, with its many orange trees, left over from the days before the arrival of the subdivisions, when this

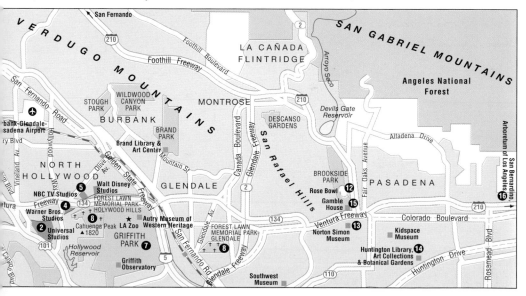

Matt Damon, one of the young movie stars of today.

BELOW: Valley towns as they were 100 years ago.

was one large orange grove. At its northern border, people still ride horses down shaded lanes. In the middle of the Valley, not far from the intersection of the San Diego and Ventura Freeways, corn stalks grow tall basking in the heat of the summer sun.

In a way, there's still much of what Father Juan Crespi called "a very pleasant and spacious valley" when he first climbed over the Sepulveda Pass in 1769. He named the area "Valle de Santa Catalina de Bononia de los Encinos." The only segment of the original name that remains is in the affluent suburb of **Encino**, the Spanish word for "oak," an area noted for being home to the musical Jackson family, along with an impressively large population of Mercedes, BMWs, Jaguars and Rolls-Royces.

The Valley remained essentially rural until the 1870s, when the great *ranchos* were sliced up like pies by men whose names (Isaac Lankershim, I.N. Van Nuys) were later honored in the grand boulevards. With the coming of the railroad in 1874, the land speculation boom swept over the Valley in what would be the first of many waves. It was a period when the towns that dominate the Valley first sprang up, towns with names like **Burbank**, **Glendale**, **Reseda**, **Chatsworth** and **Pacoima**.

Next, the Valley became a major center for the motion picture and television industries. Companies such as Universal, Warner Bros., Disney and Columbia spread across huge plots of exceedingly inexpensive land. It was land that was accessible through the Cahuenga Pass and the Sepulveda Pass, rough cuts through the hills down which cattle and sheep had once been driven to market in Los Angeles. The **Universal Studios** lot ❷, in fact, sits on what had been a 230-acre (93-hectare) chicken ranch. When Carl Laemmle threw a bash to open the

studio in 1915, his guests included Buffalo Bill Cody and Thomas Edison. In more recent years, NBC opened a vast facility in "Beautiful Downtown Burbank," the catchphrase that for late-night American television viewers became a cliché, and in 1963 CBS moved into the old Republic Films lot in **Studio City**.

Around this time, the Valley turned into "LA's bedroom," a community where single-story, ranch-style homes outnumber multiple dwellings by at least two to one. After World War II, the Valley became one of the touchstones of the American Dream, a place where anyone could afford to buy a nice house on a small lot, raise children and put in a good lawn.

Map on page 204

Boring buildings

The American Dream, as it turned out, was not without a few problems. Despite the occasional bit of inspiration, the architecture of the Valley became almost uniformly boring. And the post-war families who settled here, so anxious to separate themselves from the lives their parents had lived in the industrial cities of the East and Midwest, created a breed of gourmet children, excessively spoiled, exceedingly pampered, utterly obsessed with the transitory pleasures of consumerism.

It was an issue dealt with in the mid-1980s by Frank Zappa's daughter Moon Unit, in a hit song called *Valley Girl*. The subtext of her "Val Talk" lyrics were that the children of the Valley aren't so much rebellious as they are parodies of their parents: obsessed with clothing, hair, fingernails, cars, shopping, credit cards, and being at the right place in the right trendy outfit at the right time.

Take a walk through the vast corridors of the Sherman Oaks Galleria or the Encino Town and Country Center any Saturday; the Val Talk may have changed

BELOW: ... and how they are today.

along with the styles, but the *more-is-more* aesthetic underlying it all hasn't changed one bit over the years.

There was a time, not very long ago, when it would have been easy to simply dismiss the Valley as just a suburban community over the hill from the "real world" of Los Angeles. But by the time the new millennium began, the San Fernando Valley had turned into a glittering city all its own, with shops that equal those found along Rodeo Drive (and branches of Beverly Hills' restaurants to match), remarkable mansions spreading through the hills above Encino and farther west in **Woodland Hills**, and an infrastructure of comfort and luxury that would seem to make a journey into Los Angeles redundant. The desert that evolved into a suburb has further evolved into a city – or at least a string of cities – with a distinct and separate personality.

Aside from the appearance of the **Bistro Garden ❸**, which has become the *sine qua non* of Valley restaurants, a population as large as this demands a sizeable number of impressive eateries. The Bistro Garden and many of the small Italian restaurants nearby have become popular watering holes for celebrities from the nearby studios. Intimate Italian restaurants abound in the Sherman Oaks/Encino area, places like **Fab's**, **San Remo** and **La Loggia**.

There's also a lot of ethnic diversity in this area – great Thai dishes at **Jitlada**, great sushi at **Terusushi** and **Sushi Nozawa**, terrific Greek food at the **Great Greek**, wonderful bistro French cooking at the **Barsac Brasserie**, unusual Argentinean cuisine at the **Gaucho Grill**, exceptional Mexican fare at **La Parrilla** and **Marix**, delicious delicatessen fare at **Art's** and **Jerry's**, super ribs at **Village** BBQ and excellent American food at both **Stone Soup** and the **Smokehouse**.

BELOW: don't go in the water at Universal Studios...

Biggest tourist draw

Parts of the southern rim of the Valley have also become a destination for hordes of tourists, thanks in large degree to the high concentration of both the movie and television industry here.

Map on page 204

The **Universal Studio Tour** is unquestionably the single biggest draw in the San Fernando Valley, and the second biggest attraction in the Southland (after Disneyland). Though its films may (and often do) flop, Universal can always count on a steady flow of tourists. The 4½-hour tour is so popular, in fact, that during the summer months full tour groups embark every five minutes from 8am until 6pm, seven days a week.

The tour consists of two parts, beginning with a ride on a "Glamourtrain," taking visitors through a constantly expanding series of cinematic thrills – a monster shark (from *Jaws*) attacks the train which then passes through a reasonably realistic earthquake and is bombarded with laser weapons by Cyclons from *Battlestar Galactica*. The *Jurassic Park* ride is a particular favorite with both young and old. As a bit of cinematic nostalgia, the train has even been known to pass through the Red Sea, parted for the passengers courtesy of Moses (aka Charlton Heston).

The second part of the tour involves moving in and out of a series of stages and arenas, where stuntmen tumble from tall towers, cowpokes get shot and fall off roofs, and clever animals do amusing things. There's even an area where the audience gets to make a movie.

Other attractions include an E.T. ride that twists and turns through the plastic jungles of another planet, and a spacecraft exhibit on the making of *Apollo 13*. It's all much more entertaining than it sounds, even if you have to be in a

BELOW: the American Tail at Universal.

THE UNIVERSAL STORY

Universal Studios was founded in 1912 by Carl Laemmle, a German immigrant. Early stars included Lon Chaney and Rudolph Valentino, and it became noted in the 1930s for its horror movies, such as Boris Karloff's *Frankenstein* and Bela Lugosi's *Dracula*. Although its hits ranged from *The Birds* (1963) to *The Deer Hunter* (1978), it failed to win the consistent critical esteem shown to most other major studios. As television began to win over cinemagoers in the 1950s, Universal became the first movie studio to embrace TV production in a big way. In the 1970s, it signed up the young Steven Spielberg for a made-for-TV movie, *Duel,* and was rewarded with a string of Spielberg hits, ranging from *ET* to *Jurassic Park*, many of which were turned into rides in its burgeoning theme park business.

Universal moved into music, too, and became the world's largest music company when it bought PolyGram in 1998. Then, in 2000, it fell into French ownership when Vivendi bought its parent, the Seagram Company.

The studio tour has been much expanded, but isn't the only attraction in Universal City. The CityWalk promenade premiered in 1993, with restaurants, shops, theaters, and nightclubs, and the Universal Amphitheatre is host to top musical and awards shows. *(See also pages 218–9.)*

tourist mood to get into the spirit of the thing. Wearing a funny duck-billed hat and carrying a camera is *de rigueur*.

"I can't believe how into it the visitors are," says George Silak, a former tour guide who's gone on to work in television production. "There's a tendency at first to make fun of them, because they dress so funny. But when it comes down to knowing the history of Hollywood, they know everything. For a lot of people, going here is somewhere between a studio tour, and a religious pilgrimage." Universal Studios is located on Lankershim Boulevard, off the Hollywood Freeway.

Another pilgrimage is to adjoining **Universal City Walk**, with its movie-souvenir shops, strolling players and plethora of neon. There're many movie screens on which to view the latest releases, but note that parking is pricey.

A short drive away in Burbank is the **Warner Bros. Studios ❹**, home for Clint Eastwood and the television series *ER* and *Friends*, among many others. Warner Bros. offers what is probably the most comprehensive and "real" peek behind the scenes of a studio – a two-hour walk (no children under 10) that takes you to the historic places (see the largest stage in Hollywood, thanks to William Randolph Hearst) and let's you take a look at working sound, music, prop, and wardrobe departments. (Tours take place Monday–Friday 9am–3pm, on the hour.)

Just a little way down Alameda is the NBC **Studio Tour ❺**, a 90-minute excursion that is more serious and has far fewer bells and whistles than the one at Universal. A walk through the largest color studio in America leaves visitors with a good sense of the rigors involved in putting a television show together. It's an odd experience, watching the concept of "hurry up and wait" in action.

BELOW: Forest Lawn Cemetery.

Television looks so glamorous from the outside, less so when you see how a show actually gets made. After the tour, many opt to join the long line for admittance to the *Tonight Show*.

Animal memories

Others head for the Valley to watch the country and western dancers at the **Cowboy Palace,** a funky bar that calls itself "LA's last honky-tonk" on Devonshire just off Topanga Canyon Boulevard, or to admire the history of Los Angeles painted in the **Tujunga Wash** ❻ (near Coldwater Canyon, north of Burbank Boulevard), in what's supposedly one of the longest murals in the world; to drive past the former **Clark Gable Estate** (at 4543 Tara Drive in Encino); and perhaps even to visit the graves of Mae West's monkey, Humphrey Bogart's cocker spaniel, Steven Spielberg's Jack Russell terrier, and Hopalong Cassidy's horse at the SPCA **Pet Memorial Park** (5068 North Old Scandia Lane in Calabasas), a particularly definitive LA attraction.

Farther east is the largest urban park in America, the 4,100-acre (1,660-hectare) **Griffith Park** ❼, which effectively separates Burbank and Glendale from Hollywood and Downtown Los Angeles. As municipal parks go, Griffith isn't exactly awash with charm; indeed, it's basically a large hill, with a **zoo** at its base and an **observatory** at its peak.

Compared with parks like New York's Central and San Francisco's Golden Gate, both of which were apparently designed with strollers in mind, Griffith is a bit of a failure; there's really no place to comfortably perambulate. On the other hand, it's quite an enjoyable experience for drivers – which makes it, of course, the quintessential Los Angeles park.

Abraham Lincoln memorial at Forest Lawn Cemetery.

BELOW: Laurel Canyon Dog Park.

More interesting, perhaps, are the two branches of the **Forest Lawn Cemetery** ❽ (open daily 8am–5pm), which sit at almost opposite ends of Griffith Park, one in Glendale, the other in the Hollywood Hills behind Burbank Studios. They are breathtaking in their strangeness.

Both cemeteries are filled with exact, full-sized replicas of famous churches, like the Wee Kirk o' the Heather and Boston's Old North Church. The Hollywood park also has halls dedicated to the patriotic history of America, which schoolchildren come to visit, one of those only-in-LA oddities that drive cultural observers to distraction. Glendale's park features mammoth murals of the Crucifixion and Resurrection, a stained-glass replica of Leonard da Vinci's *Last Supper* (far more dramatic, actually, than the smog-clouded original in Milan), and a startlingly well-proportioned reproduction of Michelangelo's *David*.

Brochures from Forest Lawn Cemetery, or park – they avoid the term "cemetery" – quote founder Hubert Eaton as wanting to build "the greenest, most enchanting park you ever saw in your life."

More than a fair share of celebrities are buried at Forest Lawn. At the Glendale branch, fans of morbidity will find among others Walt Disney, Errol Flynn, Mary Pickford, Nat King Cole, Spencer Tracy, Casey Stengel, Humphrey Bogart, Tom Mix, Jack Oakie, W.C. Fields, Clark Gable, Hopalong Cassidy, and Lon Chaney. The Hollywood Hills branch is the last resting place for Buster Keaton, Stan Laurel, Charles Laughton, Liberace, Ozzie Nelson, Gabby Hayes, Jack Webb, George Raft, Freddie Prinze, Andy Gibb, and Lucille Ball.

Plenty of history

BELOW: easy riding along Mulholland Drive above the San Fernando Valley.

Those interested in the history of the Valley will find there's actually a good deal of it, even if people who live here seem uninterested in the relics of the past. The **Mission San Fernando Rey de España** ❾ in Mission Hills, at the northern end of the Valley, has had its chapel and monastery carefully restored, and is home

to a wide assortment of crafts and artifacts and a venerable wine press. Just across from the Mission in Brand Park is the original reservoir from which the padres took their water, along with the remnants of an old soap works, and a statue of the Father Junípero Serra. The Mission is open daily 9am– 4.30pm, mass Monday–Saturday at 7.25am, and Sunday at 9am and 10.30am.

Farther south, history buffs will find **Los Encinos State Historic Park ⓾**, home to the 1849 De La Osa Adobe (open Wednesday–Sunday 10am–5pm). The **Leonis Adobe ⓫** at Calabasas is a Monterey-style adobe ranch house dating back to 1844. Strangely enough, the Plummer House, the oldest house in Hollywood, was moved here also. Both are open Wednesday–Sunday 1–4pm. The nearby **Andreas Pico Adobe** goes back to 1834. The surprise is not that these buildings are so old, but that there's anything old to be found in the San Fernando Valley at all.

Due east from the Valley is "the other valley" – the **San Gabriel Valley** – at the heart of which is the burgeoning city of **Pasadena**. A century ago, Pasadena was one large orange grove and idealized pictures of those groves can still be seen on the labels stuck on crates of Californian oranges. One of the main streets in Pasadena is appropriately named Orange Grove. Pasadena rose to prominence as a vacation resort for Midwesterners, who would head here by train every winter to avoid the chill winds blowing off the Great Lakes. At the height of its popularity as a resort in the late 1880s, the town had hotel rooms for 35,000 guests, at grand old piles like the Green Hotel, the Raymond, and the renovated Huntington, now a luxurious Ritz-Carlton.

Back in 1890 the **Rose Parade** on New Year's Day was born, as the "Battle of the Flowers," a ritual that closed with flower-strewn horses and chariots in

Map on page 204

BELOW: Pasadena's Rose Bowl.

a mock Roman chariot race down Colorado Boulevard. Since 1916 the races have been replaced with a football game, the annual **Rose Bowl** ❷ held in the stadium of the same name.

The Tournament of Roses organization is headquartered in the old **William Wrigley Jr Mansion**, an Italian Renaissance home built by the eponymous chewing-gum magnate between 1906 and 1914. The gardens are open daily, and tours of the house are available February–August, Thursday 2–4pm; tel. 626/449-7673. It's a wonderful reminder of early Pasadena's "Millionaire's Row" – as is the **Fenyes House**, filled with 15th- and 16th-century European art and furniture, a couple of blocks away adjacent to the **Pasadena Historical Society** (open Thursday–Sunday 1–4pm).

Pasadena became an independent city in 1886 and mushroomed fast. The town's population was a mere 4,500, but there were 53 real estate agencies selling estates in the surrounding hills. Its growth became genuinely logarithmic in 1942, when Los Angeles' first freeway, the Arroyo Seco Parkway (now the Pasadena Freeway), opened to the public, connecting Pasadena with Downtown Los Angeles.

Art and science

Aside from the Rose Parade, Pasadena is probably best known for being home to two of Southern California's most important scientific institutions – the **California Institute of Technology** (Cal Tech), and the **Jet Propulsion Laboratory** (JPL). It's also home to the **Norton Simon Museum** ❸, and its fine collection of works by Rembrandt, Reubens, Raphael, Breughel, Goya, Cézanne, Renoir, Van Gogh and Picasso (open Thursday–Sunday noon–6pm). The incomparable **Huntington Library** ❹ sits in the middle of the 207-acre (84-hectare) estate of railroad tycoon/ robber baron Henry Huntington (open Memorial Day–Labor Day Tuesday–Sunday 10.30am–4.30pm, rest of year Tuesday–Friday noon–4.30pm, Saturday and Sunday 10am–4.30pm).

The library is the home of Sir Thomas Gainsborough's *Blue Boy* and also the painting *Pinkie*, along with a glorious collection of different gardens seguing into each other. The library sits on what remains of a larger estate that Huntington named San Marino after its Italian namesake, except that Huntington's San Marino covered many more acres than the diminutive European version.

Also in San Marino is **El Molina Viejo**, the first water-powered grist mill in Southern California, built for the San Gabriel Mission (open Tuesday–Sunday 1–4pm). The **Mission** is in nearby San Gabriel – built in 1791, it is the oldest structure of its kind south of Monterey – a museum complements the missio (open daily 9am–4:30pm; tel: 626/457-3048)

There are two more "must-sees" before you leave Pasadena. One is the **Gamble House** ❺, the most complete and preserved work of famed American Arts and Crafts architects Greene and Green (open Thursday–Sunday noon–3pm; tel. 626/793-3334). Called a "symphony of wood," it was built for the Gamble family (of Procter and Gamble) and is now a National

BELOW: Tai Chi in Monterey Park.

Historic Landmark (movie fans may also recognize it as Doc Brown's house in *Back to the Future*).

Take a stroll and relax in **Old Town Pasadena** on the west end of Colorado Boulevard – this restored area of historic buildings has become one of the area's hottest tourist destinations, and offers plenty of shopping, dining and entertainment opportunities.

Also worth noting, just east of Pasadena in Arcadia is the **Arboretum of Los Angeles** ⑯, a 127-acre (51-hectare) park of lush plants from around the world, including waterfalls and a lake where the early Tarzan films and TV's *Fantasy Island* were shot, among many others. It's a relaxing spot, great for birdwatching and plant shows (open daily 9am–5pm).

Pasadena sits in the northwest corner of the **San Gabriel Valley**, cornerstone of the many towns that have sprung from the valley's fertile soil. Much of the San Gabriel Valley is intensely suburban, a land of tract housing and inevitable shopping malls traversed by an arterial system of car-clogged freeways.

Just south of Pasadena, the towns of **Monterey Park**, **Alhambra** and **Rosemead** have turned into the latest incarnation of **Chinatown** – a suburban re-creation of Hong Kong, where the malls are filled with Cantonese seafood restaurants that are among the best of their kind in America. Gone are the clogged alleyways of yesteryear; this is the Chinatown of the future.

Connecting canyons

The canyons of Los Angeles are neatly conceived rustic shortcuts, connecting the city proper with the hinterlands and, for those with the time to spare, they're well worth the time needed for a drive through them.

Map on page 204

Keeping cool in the Valleys.

BELOW: horse, emu and friend at home in the Malibu Mountains.

Map on page 204

The most popular is **Laurel Canyon**, formerly home and hiding place for the 19th-century bandit Tiburcio. It's now a 20th-century haven for musicians and a random assortment of hippies, who settled there in the late 1960s. Several miles to the west, at the very top of **Beverly Glen**, is a shopping center that is home to a restaurant called **Shane on the Glen**, where the cuisine is part Italian and part Southwestern – a perfectly logical combination taken in the context of Los Angeles.

Running along the top of the **Santa Monica Mountains**, between the canyons and beyond, is a wonderfully curving road called **Mulholland Drive**, the spine that separates the Valley from the city. Beginning at the Cahuenga Pass, Mulholland Drive meanders for 50 miles (80 km), occasionally lined with lavish homes and always offering sensational views.

On a clear day, you can see forever in both directions; and after sunset the lights of the Valley sparkle like a string of pearls against the neck of night. Take care up here if you come at night. It's a place where the children of the wealthy tend to show up with their Porsches and Ferraris, testing their driving skills at 100 mph (160 kp/h) on the curves.

The section of Mulholland between the San Diego Freeway and Topanga Canyon is largely unpaved, a gloriously semi-deserted dirt road with a multitude of fire trails that allow weekend hikers access to this semi-wilderness just minutes away from Hollywood. It's an odd feeling to stand in the midst of an unspoiled forest looking out at Santa Monica and the Pacific Ocean only a short freeway drive away.

Topanga is a fine old twisting canyon, filled with New Agers and various relics of the 1960s, many of whom congregate at **The Willows**, a bar/restaurant near the post office about midway through Topanga Canyon.

A few miles farther west along the Ventura Freeway, at the Los Virgenes Road exit, is **Malibu Canyon**, home to a faithful replica of a **Hindu temple** and also an excellent restaurant called **Saddle Peak Lodge**, probably the best spot for wild game in Southern California, served in a setting of half timbers, raging fireplaces and mounted animal heads stuck up on the walls.

In the midst of the canyon is **Malibu Creek State Park** (open sunrise–sunset), carved out of a combination of the Bob Hope Ranch, the Ronald Reagan Ranch, and the 20th Century-Fox Movie Ranch. It's a park filled with movieland tradition – *How Green Was My Valley* and *Planet of the Apes* were shot here and the remnants of television's perennially popular *M*A*S*H* set can be found at Crags Road and Lost Cabin Trail.

It was at **Century Lake** that the cinematic Butch Cassidy and the Sundance Kid (winsomely played by Paul Newman and Robert Redford) leapt into history as they escaped from the Pinkertons.

There are 15 miles (24 km) of trails in the park, making it one of the sweetest spots in Los Angeles, a place filled with hikers and bicyclers on weekends; a fantasy land where things are only as real as you want them to be. ❑

BELOW: climbing in Malibu Creek State Park.

The Man Who Brought the Water

When young William Mulholland rode through the San Joaquin Valley on horseback, arriving in LA in 1877, he "fell in love at first sight," he later recalled. "The country had the same attraction for me that it had for the Indians. It was so attractive to me that it at once became something about which my whole scheme of life was woven, I loved it so much."

Since arriving in the US as a deck-hand in 1872, the 22-year-old Irishman had worked on steamers in the Great Lakes, on side-wheelers on the Colorado River and searched for gold in Arizona. But the service he performed for his newly adopted home – bringing a water supply across 240 miles (390 km) of deserts and mountains – is what enabled Los Angeles to become a major city and why he is memorialized in the spectacular road that bears his name. Beginning at the Cahuenga Pass, Mulholland Drive meanders for 50 miles (80 km) along the Santa Monica Mountains, occasionally lined with lavish homes, more often unpaved and deserted, but at almost every point offering sensational views.

One day soon after his arrival, Mulholland became intrigued by the technique of a well-digger and asked so many questions that he was offered a job as the man's assistant. This post eventually led to his working as a *zanjero* – a man responsible for keeping the water flowing – for the city's water department, which he eventually came to head. He spent his nights reading up in books on mathematics, hydraulics and geology.

By 1900, with the population at 170,000, it was clear that LA's growth would be very limited unless additional water supplies could be found. This problem had also been preoccupying Mulholland's predecessor Fred Eaton. The two men teamed up in a project to siphon off water from the Owens Valley.

Through 1904's blistering summer the pair trekked through the area, devising a plan to bring the valley's water through a concrete-lined aqueduct, 53 miles (85 km) of tunnels and 12 miles (19 km) of "inverted steel syphons." They promised that the project could be completed within 10 years and would cost the city $24.5 million, an estimate that proved to be astonishingly accurate; the water arrived on time and $40,000 under budget. "Here it is, take it," was Mulholland's comment as he pressed the button to start the water flowing.

There was a dark side to the story. Eaton tried to extort $1 million for land in the Owens Valley – land that LA wanted for a reservoir – and the Owens Valley ranchers who had been led to believe that the government was acquiring land rights in order to improve it, suddenly awoke to the realization that the big city 250 miles (400 km) away was about to steal their water and turn the valley into a dustbowl. To his credit, Mulholland seems to have acted only from the purest of motives. He ended his friendship with Eaton over the latter's profiteering.

Before he died in 1935, Mulholland had built the city's water department into the world's largest wholesaler of water, serving more than 8 million people in 100 communities spread over 4,000 sq miles (10,000 sq km). ❑

RIGHT: William Mulholland.

UNIVERSAL STUDIOS

A studio tour, rides, and City Walk – Universal is the most entertaining "behind the scenes" look at Hollywood

Dating back to 1912, Universal Studios has a long history. It opened with a tour of the set of movies in production for 25 cents. The tour shut down in 1930, but that same year Universal won its first "Best Picture" Oscar for *All Quiet on the Western Front*. It became the maestro of monsters, releasing *Dracula* and *Frankenstein*, among others, to great success; but by the late 1930s it took a string of musical hits by teen sensation Deanna Durbin to keep the doors open.

Other mainstays since have included Basil Rathbone in the Sherlock Holmes series; Abbott and Costello; Alfred Hitchcock's *Psycho, The Birds,* and *Topaz.* From the 1970s to mid-1990s, Steven Spielberg made his home here. Other Best Picture Oscars would be won by *The Sting, Out of Africa, Deer Hunter,* and *Schindler's List.*

The studio tour came back in 1961, and has become much grander over the years.

△ **STUDIO KING**
You'll get face-to-face with a 30-ft (9-meter) King Kong as he stalks through New York and sends your tram flying.

▷ **BEWARE!**
Frankenstein and fellow monsters still roam the theme park today.

▷ **CITY WALK**
Expanded recently, there's now a Hard Rock Cafe, the Rumba Room nightclub, a 3-D Imax theatre, a bowling alley, and virtual racing.

△ **WATERWORLD**
The 1995 film *Waterworld* is brought to life as only Universal know how, with jet-skiers, a swooping seaplane and giant fireballs.

▷ **DON'T FEED THE ANIMALS**
Jurassic Park: The Ride is the top thrill. Tour boats speed and there's a 90-ft (27-meter) drop into the Jurassic Jungle.

△ **IS THAT REALLY ...?**
Not all stars roaming the park are monsters. You might see Chaplin and the Marx brothers.

▷ **HITCHCOCK RULED**
Universal was the last studio home for Hitchcock, director of such thrillers as *Vertigo,* starring James Stewart and Kim Novak.

STEVEN SPIELBERG – THE LEGEND

Spielberg films for Universal have included *Jaws, ET, Jurassic Park,* and *Schindler's List.* He directed *Close Encounters of the Third Kind, Raiders of the Lost Ark, The Color Purple,* and *Saving Private Ryan.* His production company produced the *Back to the Future* films, *Twister,* and *Who Framed Roger Rabbit.* Although nominated for Best Director Oscar for *Close Encounters* and *ET,* he was shut out on *The Color Purple,* even though it had 11 nominations. In 1993, he won the Oscar for Best Picture and Best Director with *Schindler's List,* and Best Director in 1998 for *Saving Private Ryan.* His company still operates at Universal, in a hacienda that was a gift from former Universal Chairman Lew Wasserman. When asked why he would spend over a million dollars on such a gift, Wasserman replied "it costs less than the profits of *ET* in Brazil alone!"

△ **THE STING**
The 1973 hit, starring Paul Newman and Robert Redford, brought home seven Oscars for Universal, including Best Picture.

△ **DON'T LOSE YOUR HEAD!**
It's all make-believe as you visit sets and props from Universal films like *Jaws, ET,* and *Back to the Future.* Just don't go in the water...

◁ **MAGNUM P.I.**
This light-hearted detective series was a big hit for Universal, and made an "overnight star" of Tom Selleck.

THE SOUTH BAY

Map
on page
224

The South Bay encompasses much of California's culture: surfing and the ever-present sun, wide sandy beaches, friendly people and individual coastal communities

When Thomas D. Murphy took a coastal ride in 1915 down through the South Bay from Los Angeles to Long Beach for his travel guide, *On Sunset Highway*, he talked about the "prosperous farming lands on both sides." He also referred to the then minuscule communities of Hermosa Beach, Manhattan Beach, and Playa del Rey as "three less frequented resorts… building on expectations rather than any great present popularity."

Health and hedonism

Well, Tom, it just ain't the same. Today, the South Bay is what the Beach Boys (South Bay locals) were talking about when they were singing "Surfin' USA," which was based on their own wave-riding at Manhattan Beach. Average daytime highs reach 60°–80°F (16°–27°C) year around. Bicycling, roller skating, volleyball, swimming, shopping, eating, smiling and friendliness are the name of the game here. The South Bay is simply the best of health and hedonism in one unique package.

Marina del Rey ❶, with berths for 6,000 boats, is the world's largest small-craft harbor, where you can take a trip on everything from an imitation Mississippi riverboat to a Venetian gondola (free champagne and taped music). Dining yachts and restaurants line the dockside in the whimsical Fisherman's Village ❷, its brightly painted shacks clustered around a non-working 60-ft (18-meter) lighthouse. MTA bus 220 runs from Melrose Avenue all the way down Robertson Boulevard to Marina del Rey.

Just below the mouth of the boat haven at Marina del Rey is Playa de Rey ❸. The beaches here are sheltered by breakwaters and offer gentle waves. Behind the beach is Del Rey Lagoon, a quiet little park surrounding a saltwater pond.

The lagoon is part of what was once the last remnants of an extensive marshland where local Chumash Indians used to hunt duck before the Spanish arrived. Some of that marshland still remains in the Ballona Wetlands ❹ east of the community, and both marsh and lagoon attract birds that use the coast as a major flyway on their winter routes from Canada to Mexico. Mallards, coots and Canadian geese swim in the water, while the reeds nearer the shore attract an occasional long-legged heron or egret.

South of Playa del Rey is the Dockweiler State Beach ❺, probably one of the broadest and loneliest sandy stretches in the South Bay: the reason being that it is right under the flight path for departing jets from Los Angeles International Airport. But you can park yourself down by the surf and let the crashing waves drown out the sound of the planes. Dockweiler is a good place to get recharged.

PRECEDING PAGES: Miss Bikini contest at Hermosa Beach. **LEFT:** pedal power. **BELOW:** Point Vicente.

TIP

To complete a surrealistic stay in Playa del Rey, go to the **Prince O' Whales** (on Culver Boulevard) for a beer and a chat with the locals. Ask them how they feel about the development on the marshlands. A lively debate will follow. ▼

The south end of Dockweiler on the bluffs is popular with hang gliders. Aficionados bring their colorful gliders. The hang gliders love to share their suicidal kite flying stories with the tourists as they await their turn on the bluff.

Unfortunately, those same winds are a bane to the residents of **El Segundo**, east of Dockweiler, as the smell from the Chevon refinery and Hyperion Sewage Treatment plant is wafted far and wide. But El Segundans are proud of their small, charming town, with its family-oriented neighborhoods. The most powerful figure to come out of the town is Barbie, the blonde bombshell doll.

East of El Segundo is **Inglewood**, home of the Forum and Hollywood Park. The **Forum ➏**, at Manchester Boulevard and Prairie Avenue, is one of LA's most prestigious sports-entertainment complexes. An 18,000-seat, all-weather arena, it used to be home to the pro basketball Lakers and pro hockey Kings; now it houses the WNBA Sparks, a women's professional basketball team.

The Forum is also one of the top concert arenas: Bowie, Bob Dylan, Clapton, and Springsteen have all appeared here. Most of these concerts, as with the Lakers and Kings, have moved to the Downtown Staples Center (*see page 125*).

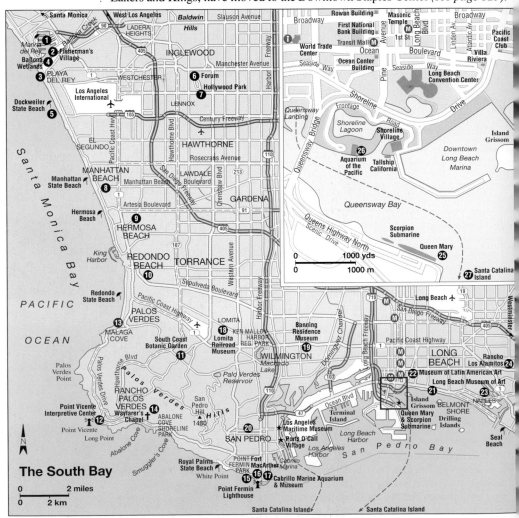

The South Bay

Hollywood Park ❼ on South Prairie Avenue features thoroughbred racing from April to July and November to December, with harness racing from August to October. The park is laid out with palm trees, a lagoon and kids' play area. Post time is 2pm on weekdays and 1.30pm on weekends, but the real armchair jockeys are out there to watch the morning workouts.

Map on page 224

The beach communities

Below El Segundo is **Manhattan Beach** ❽ – together they have formed the bustling corridor of office buildings, retail, restaurants and theaters *(see box, page 227)*. This once sleepy town is now one of the prime residential areas in LA, with wealthy families fleeing the hills and valleys for the South Bay in the late 1990s. The hills are full of million-dollar homes. Crime is low, schools are at the top of ratings, smog is blown inland by the ocean breezes – and the South Bay has been relatively untouched by major earthquakes. Volleyball is king in Manhattan, as the acres of courts show. Visit the quaint **aquarium** on the end of the pier. Among the piers along the South Bay shore are those at Manhattan, Hermosa, and Redondo, and it's worth taking a stroll to the end of any of them (each has been renovated in the last few years).

Fishermen try their luck off Manhattan Beach pier.

Hermosa Beach ❾ is struggling to find a balance between old and new – it sports that early southern California beach-bungalow architecture, and its residents seem a little younger, healthier, and bohemian, perhaps because Hermosa is one of the hot spots for surfers. On most days the adventurous wave-riders sweep across waves at 20–30 mph (30–50 km/h), gliding along for as much as a city block. Revitalizing downtown is the jewel of Hermosa Beach: its new $7 million **Promenade,** where Pier Avenue meets the Strand – an outdoor pedestrian mall

BELOW: Long Beach Marina and Downtown.

with sidewalk cafes, 16 restaurants and bars. This is where young bodies show off their tans. They not only pose, but they rollerskate, skateboard, bicycle or play a few games of volleyball. Bicycles and roller skates can be rented near the **Hermosa Pier**.

The bicycle path here is part of an extensive city bike path that stretches all the way from Santa Monica, through Playa del Rey, Manhattan, Hermosa, and Redondo. A blissful afternoon can be spent by renting a cycle in Hermosa and riding the bike path north to Santa Monica or south to Palos Verdes.

Die-hard fans will find the Beach House from the TV show Beverly Hills 90210 *at the northern end of The Strand at Hermosa Beach.*

Cuisine for stars

As with Manhattan, breakfast is social hour. Favorite meeting spots include **Martha's** on 22nd Street, Hermosa branches of the **Beach Hut** and the **Good Stuff** (outdoor dining with ocean views, along with **Hennesey's** at the pier), and the **Back Burner**, in the Pier area. Again, Italian is popular here – the **Bottle Inn** on 22nd, Italy's **Little Kitchen** and **Il Boccacio** near the pier, and **Buona Vita** on upper Pier. Also up on Pier, **Ragin' Cajun** and **New Orleans** cook up acclaimed, well, ragin' cajun food. If you're thinking vegetarian, **The Spot** on 2nd Street is the South Bay's major vegetarian restaurant. When Paul McCartney was visiting LA, he hired The Spot to cater for his party five nights in a row, undoubtedly sampling the superb "garden burrito" (vegetables, beans, rice and cheese wrapped in a whole-wheat tortilla smothered in a zippy sauce).

Complete a perfect evening with a walk around to browse the stores, especially the eclectic, ethnic mix of beachy clothes and apparel at **Greeko's Sandals**, retro-chic at **ReStyle**, and ultimate surfwear at **Becker's**. For night-time, check the award-winning **Hermosa Playhouse** schedule – they present several

BELOW: national volleyball championships at Hermosa Beach.

top-notch off-Broadway productions a year, often with original cast members. Perhaps pop into the **Comedy and Magic Club**, where *The Tonight Show's* host, Jay Leno, regularly tries out new material, or listen to music at the **Lighthouse**, a landmark jazz institution since the 1940s.

Redondo Beach ⑩ is centered around **King Harbor**, with shops, restaurants and a historic pier popular with strollers and fishermen. Halibut, sea bass, rock cod, yellowtail, and albacore are the specialities.

Harbor cruises and sightseeing boats operate out of Redondo's **Port Royal Marina** from which, between December and March, there are daily whale-watching excursions to admire the playful mammals on their migration from Alaska to the warmer waters of Baja.

Two secret spots to check out are the **Hollywood Riviera** village, with an interesting mix of stores and restaurants, including the unusual **ColletTea** room at 320 South Catalina. Don't worry if you've forgotten your hat, they've got plenty of fun ones to spare while you sip from an incredible array of teas. Don't leave Redondo without exploring the renovated **pier** – eclectic shops, bars, and free concerts on summer evenings. **Kincaid's** is there.

Peninsula and harbor

Mountainous **Palos Verdes Peninsula** is dotted with expensive homes – many with stables in their backyards – whose average price is in the $1 million range. When the area was landscaped, the developers called in the sons of Frederick Law Olmsted (who designed New York's Central Park) to do the job. Remaining traces of their work are the rows of bountiful eucalyptus trees all over the peninsula. **Palos Verdes** used to be home to Marineland, a three-arena specta-

Map on page 224

TIP

The Redondo Beach Performing Arts Center has light opera and the Distinguished Speaker Series (speakers have included Henry Kissinger and Margaret Thatcher), and an eclectic concert schedule. Tel: 310/937-6607.

BELOW: Long Beach Gondola Getaway.

MANHATTAN BEACH FUN

Manhattan Beach has some great eating places: try pizza and ribs at Houston's, gourmet Chinese at P.F. Chang's, and upscale seafood and chops at McCormick & Schmicks (there's also a Wolfgang Pucks.) You might run into a familiar face, as the hit televison show *Ally McBeal* is filmed nearby at the new Raleigh Studios. For Italian food go to Mama D's or the upscale Talia's and Mangiamo. Two of the finest restaurants in the South Bay are the intimate Café Pierre, downtown, and Reed's, in the mall.

To really experience Manhattan, you need to get closer to the water on Highland and Manhattan. At the north end of town, there are nightspots like Baja Sharkeez, Panchos, and the Hole-in-the-Wall; after hours, try El Tarasco for a *carne asada burrito*. On the north end the Hawaiian-style Beach Hut is popular with the local surf crowd, and the Local Yolk is always busy (nearby Sloopy's gets hopping at lunch – great shakes and smoothies.)

Downtown Manhattan is farther south on Highland – the old favorite Uncle Bill's Pancake House is down there, as is the Good Stuff and the 24-hour Kettle Restaurant, the town's social center, where Highland meets Manhattan Beach Boulevard. If you only want coffee there's Starbucks, Peet's, The Coffee Bean & Tea Leaf, and the Coffee Cartel.

Anything goes as far as surfers are concerned.

BELOW: South Coast Botanic Garden.

cle that was closed a decade ago and has been a ghost town ever since. A hotel and golf course are planned for the land.

The peninsula, in prehistoric days an island, is renowned for the delightful **South Coast Botanic Garden** ⓫ (tel: 310/544 6815, open daily 9am–5pm), 26300 Crenshaw Boulevard, whose 87 acres (35 hectares) of paths and trails wind around different sections of flowers, shrubs and bushes, herbs, vegetables, and flowering fruit trees. Birds are drawn to the vegetation and manmade lake.

An easy history lesson on how the peninsula developed through the ages can be absorbed at the **Point Vicente Interpretive Center** ⓬ on Palos Verdes Drive West, south of the Shoreline Preserve. It offers illuminating displays on local geology and is an excellent place to spot whales, sea lions, and dolphins or at least cormorants and pelicans. All it takes is a good pair of binoculars and some patience. The **Point Vicente Lighthouse** is closed to the public.

The Shoreline Preserve begins at **Hagerty's Beach**, another popular surfing strand, above which is **Malaga Cove** ⓭, reputedly a copy of Italy's Sorrento and a desirable place to live, as evidenced by the number of real estate offices. **Rive Gauche**, in the Malaga shopping center, is a longtime favorite French bistro. The attractive library behind the shopping center is set beside a charming English garden and displays historic photos showing Palos Verdes as it appeared a century ago. The nearby **La Venta Inn** is the oldest building on the peninsula, with incredible views of the LA basin. It used to be a retreat for celebrities such as Cary Grant, Charles Lindbergh, and Gloria Swanson.

In the 1920s, two local adherents of the 18th-century scientist-theologian Emanuel Swedenborg, inspired the creation of the glass-walled church known as the **Wayfarer's Chapel** ⓮. It was built by Frank Lloyd Wright's son, Lloyd,

and has been an outstanding landmark on top of the Palos Verdes cliffs for more than 50 years. Open to all and especially popular for weddings, the unique sanctuary is reached via a spectacular winding drive along the rocky coastline.

Around the last bend of our Palos Verdes excursion is **Point Fermin Park** ⓖ with its pretty Victorian **lighthouse** offering a commanding view of **Los Angeles Harbor**. A favorite place for joggers to meet, the park is also popular with amateur pilots who bring their radio-controlled model airplanes to ride the sea breezes. The century-old lighthouse is closed to the public. Another site of interest is **Fort MacArthur** ⓕ, an old army base that defended the Los Angeles Harbor from 1914 to 1974 (open Tuesday–Sunday noon–5pm; museum open Saturday and Sunday noon–5pm).

Going for grunion

The **Cabrillo Marine Aquarium and Museum** ⓗ (Stephen M. Whiter Drive, tel: 310/548-7562) offers guided tours through the tide pool area and also stages group events when the grunion run on Cabrillo Beach. Grunion are small coastal California fish that between March and August come onshore at night in large schools to deposit their eggs. They are the only fish that lay their eggs on land, the females burying them in the sand, which protects them for the nine days they need to hatch. The only legal way to take these fish is with bare hands and during the three-hour spawning runs on the nights following high tides, there are always crowds scurrying around the beach picking up the slippery fish.

For those with time to spare, it's worth making an excursion inland for a trio of tourist attractions: the somewhat kitschy **Alpine Village** of Torrance (open at 11am daily); **Lomita's Railroad Museum** ⓘ, with its memorabilia from the

Map on page 224

Below Point Fermin and along much of the Palos Verdes shore are tidepools. At low tide there are colorful starfish; sea anemones in shades of pink, yellow and red; periwinkles, crabs; sea urchins that look like purple pincushions; even the occasional octopus.

BELOW: wedding at the Wayfarer's Chapel.

age of steam trains (open Wednesday–Sunday 10am–5pm); and the **General Phineas Banning Residence Museum** ⑲ at Wilmington, home of the Delaware-born pioneer who set up some of the earliest Western stagecoach routes (tours Tuesday–Thursday at 12.30, 1.30 and 2.30pm, Saturday and Sunday 3.30pm too).

Back to the coast and **San Pedro** ⑳, once world-famous among sailors for its bars and brothels but currently in the midst of a building boom that includes two $20 million-plus hotels and **Cabrillo Marina Center**. Its ethnic mix of Italians, Yugoslavs, Norwegians, and Mexicans keeps it interesting, besides providing a wide variety of cuisine: the Papadakis Taverna (Greek); Wallaby Damned! (Australian); the Whale and the Ale (British); Ante's (Yugoslav); Babbouch (Moroccan); and Franco's (Italian), which features an organ grinder.

One of the town's main attractions is the **Ports O' Call Village**, a Disney-style attempt to re-create a 19th-century port. There are a few interesting shops here but perhaps Port O' Call's biggest attraction is that it lies across the harbor from the enormous cranes that unload at least 4,000 container ships each year. From **Skipper's 22nd Street Landing** boats set off on whale-watching excursions between December and April.

Long Beach

An impressive bridge, 6,500 ft (1,980 meters) long and 185 ft (56 metres) high, called the **Vincent Thomas Bridge**, connects San Pedro with the city of Long Beach, the official port of LA and currently undergoing a facelift. Long Beach can also be reached from Downtown by the Blue Line. The Long Beach Convention Center on East Ocean Boulevard, with its enormous **Long Beach Arena**, **Terrace Theater**, and smaller, elegant **Center Theater**, have been re-

furbished. The Long Beach Symphony Orchestra, the Long Beach Opera and the Civic Light Opera play at one or another of these different venues.

More and more, Long Beach is becoming an artistic community. Artists who used to be able to rent loft and studio space in Venice are moving to Long Beach because Venice is now too expensive for them. The **Long Beach Museum of Art** ㉑, also on East Ocean Boulevard, deserves credit for promoting art in this city (open Wednesday–Sunday 10am–5pm, Friday to 8pm). It features a variety of contemporary art exhibitions in its stately 1912 mansion and has an active annex, the LBDA **Media Arts Center**, which specializes in showing videos by various local artists. Long Beach has become a major center for video art. It's also home to the **Museum of Latino American Art** ㉒, the first of its kind in the US, featuring contemporary art of the Americas (tel: 562/437-1689; open Tuesday–Saturday 11.30am–7.30pm, Sunday noon–6pm).

There's an interesting contrast to be made between the attractive **Shoreline Village**, a contemporary shopping center built in imitation of a century-old fishing port, and nearby **Seal Beach**, which is a slightly dated, seaside community, albeit the real thing. Most interesting of all, to many people, is the picturesque island of **Naples** ㉓, an affluent village with canals on which tourists can ride in 25-ft (7.6-meter) gondolas. Next best thing to being in Venice: call **Gondola Getaway**, tel: 562/433-9595 for a romantic cruise, then take their 1962 limo over to the delicious Italian restaurant **Ragazzi**, on the waterfront.

Other Long Beach attractions are the sprawling **Rancho Los Alamitos** ㉔, dating from Colonial times, whose 5 acres (2 hectares) of gardens abut the San Diego Freeway (open Wednesday–Sunday 1–5pm); and funky old **Queen's Wharf**, from which the fishing boats and harbor excursions set forth.

Map on page 224

BELOW: industry at Long Beach.

Even the Queen
Mary's *propeller
is enormous.*

BELOW: the
magnificent
Queen Mary.

Long Beach's biggest attraction is still the *Queen Mary* , moored beside the waterfront at the south end of the 710 Freeway (tours daily 10am–4.30pm). The famous Cunard Lines' Scottish-built ship made its maiden voyage across the Atlantic in May 1936 and carried many of Hollywood's elite and other famous people until the outbreak of war, when it was commissioned as a troopship. By the 1950s, air travel was luring most of the travelers away and the *Queen Mary* was bought by the city of Long Beach for $3.5 million in 1967. During restoration the original funnels collapsed and were replaced. (They had been held together only by 110 coats of paint.) The 81,000 ton ship has become a major tourist attraction, with 365 of its lower deck cabins now used as a hotel and the remaining decks open to visitors every day of the year.

The art-deco halls, restaurants and lounges have been beautifully maintained, the teak decks restored, and a schedule of hourly tours instituted (10am–4.30pm) visiting the bridge and the engine room, with its 40,000 horsepower turbines, pipes, pumps and ship's paraphernalia. Various displays recall the period when the ship ferried 800,000 servicemen across the Atlantic. In addition to three fine restaurants, there are fast-food stands and an elegant bar with outside terrace from which to watch adventurers at the adjoining Mega Bungee jump. In winter there is dancing to live music in the Observation Bar.

Nearby is Long Beach's newest and most popular attraction, the **Aquarium of the Pacific** ㉖. It takes you through three Pacific aquatic regions – Southern California/Baja, Tropical Pacific, and Northern Pacific. Walk through a tunnel of sharks and see the world's largest coral reef exhibit at **Queensway Bay**, a Long Beach waterfront development (tel. 562/590-3100; open daily 9am–6pm). Take the **Aquabus**, a 40-ft (13-meter) water taxi, from the *Queen Mary* to the aquarium, or other destinations around the harbor.

Long Beach isn't the best place for good restaurants, except for a couple of classy places such as L'Opera Ristorante on Pine Avenue and 555, on East Ocean Boulevard. Many locals admit they go to San Pedro in search of dinner. Pine Avenue is developing into a nightlife area with restaurants and movie theaters. An amusing attraction is **The Skinny House**, 708 Gladys Avenue, built in 1932 on a lot 10 x 50 ft (3 x 15 meters), three storys, 860 sq. ft (80 sq. meters) in Tudor style – it's in the *Guinness Book of Records*, of course. There is also a big mural program, mostly in the area between PCH, 710 Freeway and Ocean Boulevard.

For a beachtown night out, try **Second Street**, which runs from Livingston to Alamitos Bay. You can get beer, fresh fish, yogurt, croissants, Szechuan food, antiques, new wave gifts, CDs, lambskin jackets, hardware, bank loans and Lebanese cuisine.

Santa Catalina Island

Santa Catalina ㉗ sits 22 miles (35 km) offshore and on clear days is part of LA's ocean vista. There are many ways to get there: try the ferry – **Catalina Express** (tel: 800/ 305-9201) from Long Beach and San Pedro; **Catalina Cruises** (tel: 800/CATALINA) from Long Beach, or other options from Newport Beach and Dana Point as well. A bit more expensive but faster is the **Island Express Helicopter** (tel: 310/510-2525).

Avalon was one of early Hollywood's most popular sets. A day there gives you the feeling of being transported back into the 1920s. There are few cars, and they aren't needed because it's an easy walk from one end of Avalon to the other. **Crescent Street** along the beach front is bounded by the Victorian turrets of **Holly Hill House** at one end and the 12-story rotunda of the **Casino Ballroom** at the other end. The Casino, home of the big bands in the 1930s and 1940s, was once used for special Hollywood screenings and remains an art-deco masterpiece. It's also home to the **Catalina Island Museum**, covering 7,000 years of island history (open Wednesday–Sunday noon–4pm).

Outside the small city of Avalon (population: 2,500) it is almost as undeveloped as when the first Spanish conquistador set foot there 300 years ago. Bicycles can be rented and there are also bus tours of the island's interior on which one invariably catches a glimpse of the island's herd of wild buffalo. About 1½ miles (2.5 km) west of town is the **Botanical Gardens** (open daily 8am–5pm), where access to the hills is through an unlocked gate below to the right of the 150-ft (48-meter) high **Wrigley Memorial.** Wrigley, the chewing-gum giant, used to own the island. His mansion is still intact and is now the **Inn at Mount Ada**, an expensive and beautiful bed and breakfast with grand views from most of the rooms (available for viewing only Sunday noon–1pm; tel: 800/608-7669). There are other hotels in Avalon, including villas at Hamilton Cove (tel: 310/510-0190).

The historic **Banning House Lodge** at Two Harbors was built by William Banning, son of Phineas, who arrived in Los Angeles in 1851 to become reinsman (driver) on the first Southern California stage line, driving 22 miles (35 km) across the prairies from the newly incorporated town of LA to the seaport village of Wilmington on San Pedro Bay. ❏

Map on page 224

On Catalina Island, Clark Gable mutinied on the Bounty, *Benny Goodman swung at the Casino Ballroom, and John Wayne sailed the* Wild Goose.

BELOW:
Avalon Harbor
on Catalina Island.

THEME PARKS

Sunshine is the key to the theme park industry, which thrives in California with Disneyland, Knott's Berry Farm and Six Flags Magic Mountain

Map on page 254

It's no coincidence that LA is both center of the filmmaking universe and spawning ground for theme parks – each uses similar talents to create fake environments that draw feelings of laughter, fantasy or fear. Walt Disney not only capitalized on this symbiotic relationship, he invented it, and as a result, Disneyland has become the "holy land of theme parks."

Anaheim

London, Paris, New York – Anaheim? Ask 99.9 percent of the world pre-1955 where Anaheim was, and few would even be able to tell you it was in California – let alone predict that soon it would be one of the world's premier tourist destinations and home to a cultural revolution.

Anaheim was, in fact, barren land that was cultivated in the late 1800s by 50 German families, who came via San Francisco to form the Los Angeles Vineyard Society. Pitching in $750 each, they bought the land from a local Spanish landholder, and began this small farming community, named "Ana" for the local Santa Ana River, and 'heim' for the German word for "home."

Disneyland

As Walt Disney once said, "it all began with a mouse." Mickey Mouse that is, born in 1928, the offspring of the imaginations of Walt and his longtime creative co-conspirator Ub Iwerks. Walt came to California in 1923, and set up shop in the back of a Hollywood realty office with his brother Roy, with old Kansas City friend Iwerks soon to follow. Based on the success of their short animated films, Walt, ever the entrepreneur, led the company into riskier ventures – feature films, and eventually, TV. By the 1950s, the company had a large Burbank studio and a collection of awards (including Oscars) and characters, and Walt envisioned a little 8-acre (3-hectare) park next to their studio lot where employees could relax, and tourists could take pictures with sculptures of Mickey and Minnie Mouse, Donald Duck, Pluto, Goofy and the whole gang.

The dream began to grow: as Walt's were prone to do – soon he was pitching financiers to back his plans for a much larger theme park, built in the farmland of Anaheim. There were no takers. So Walt turned to Leonard Goldenson, head of ABC TV, who backed the fantastical notion. In 1955, after several years of design and months of construction, the transformation of 80 acres of orange groves into a truly Magical Kingdom was finished – **Disneyland** opened its gates, and in poured 3.8 million visitors in the first year alone. Anaheim, 1955 population 14,000, was now a household word – and never the same again.

PRECEDING PAGES: colorful comic strips. **LEFT:** Knott's Berry Farm. **BELOW:** eager listener.

Walt was not overly concerned about the profitability of Disneyland – he often stated that he was more concerned about the quality of the experience, and would be happy if the park broke even. Little did he know that the Magic Kingdom, and its cousins in Florida, Paris, and Japan, would become the most important and profitable pieces in the corporate kingdom.

Why is Disneyland so special? Two things spring forth: first, obviously, the cute characters that have been woven into the fabric of many cultures; and second, the Disney attention to detail. The entire fantasy is sustained through painstaking attention to minutiae – whether in the lavish and sophisticated animation in Walt's films, or the sumptuousness evident in Disneyland (which was the only Disney park he lived to see completed). The original Magic Kingdom is smaller and more intimate than Florida's Walt Disney World. At Disneyland you'll be rewarded with small, unexpected pleasures, such as throwing pennics in the wishing well at the Snow White Grotto or pulling the sword from the stone and being declared ruler of all England; seeing doves circle the Sleeping Beauty Castle or climbers scaling the Matterhorn at sunset.

The New Disneyland Resort

There's no sign stating "the original," but Walt's first-born is the official home of his characters. Over the years, the influence of these characters has spread around the globe, and while the world has changed dramatically, they have continued to bring joy and familiarity. But that doesn't mean the park has stagnated – Disneyland has been careful not only to maintain its pristine operation, but also to introduce new major attractions every five years. Now, they are expanding with the most ambitious program since the original in 1955.

BELOW: enthralled crowds are at every turn.

The culmination of this $1.4 billion program is the creation of the **Disney-land Resort**, which includes improvements to Magic Kindom and the two Disneyland hotels, plus the new **Disney's California Adventureland**, a 55-acre (22-hectare) theme park with the 750-room **Grand Californian** luxury hotel and a huge shopping, dining and entertainment center called **Downtown Disney**.

The linchpin of the entire addition is **California Adventure**, which is divided into separate themes and lands saluting the Golden State. The Hollywood section is be celebrated with **Muppet Vision 3D**, which has been a hit at Disney/MGM Studios in Florida; also featured is the wild ride **Superstar Limo**, plus an interactive animation studio, and a major theater that will host Broadway-sized shows.

Paradise Pier, representing California beach culture, has a Disney twist. A giant orange peels away to reveal a thrill ride, while the giant rollercoaster (which will be the fastest in either park) races around a silhouette of Mickey Mouse's head. **Condor Flats** celebrates the early jet test pilot days, and includes a simulation thrill ride that takes you gliding over California landmarks. **Pacific Wharf** is where to find the shops and restaurants.

Downtown Disney sits between the two parks (there will be a separate admission for each park, but no charge to visit Downtown Disney), and features plenty of dining, shopping, and entertainment options, including a House of Blues, Rainforest Cafe, and Wolfgang Puck's, an ESPN Zone Bar & Grill, and a 16-screen AMC cinema.

The **Grand Californian** has been built in the Craftsman style, and touted as a rival to the most luxurious Orange County hotels, including the Four Sea-

Map on page 254

Standing in line and getting wet are both part of the theme park experience. You have been warned!

BELOW: the ride of your life.

BELOW: Toon Town, Disneyland.

sons and the Ritz-Carlton. Among its amenities are a 4,000-sq. ft (370-sq. meter) health club and two large outdoor pools (one just for kids), and its own gate entrance to California Adventure.

Disneyland has also reaped some of the new investment, particularly in the **Tomorrowland** area, and the **Haunted Mansion** will be revamped at the beginning of 2002. This brings up the first point in planning a visit to Disneyland: how long do you need?

It takes two full days to really experience and enjoy Disneyland, at a moderate pace, mainly because major attractions like Splash Mountain, Space Mountain, Indiana Jones, Rocket Rods, and the Matterhorn must be seen early in the morning or late at night if you wish to avoid long lines. The park really begins to fill from 11am. It's better to do it in two mornings; this allows you to visit all the major attractions with relatively short waits and prevents you from trying to cram too much into a single day.

Tickets, or "Passports" as they are called here, come in several standard forms, including 1-day, 2-day, 3-day, all available at the gate, or 3- or 5-day Flex Passports, which must be arranged ahead of time.

Tactical strategy – avoiding the herd mentality

There are as many ways to "do Disneyland," as there are visitors, or "guests" in Disney parlance. But whatever your tastes or desired pace, here are a few helpful ideas to get you organized and ahead of, or away from, the crowds.

● **Be early**: Try to be at the gate early, even as much as 45 minutes – sometimes the gates open early without explanation. You can cover a lot of ground with a head start, and even if the park doesn't open ahead of time, guests are frequently ushered into the Main Street section of the park early. This means you get maps, strollers and entertainment schedules; window-shop; visit with the characters who frequently hang around Town Square in the morning; have a bite at the Blue Ribbon Bakery; and still be at the ropes blocking the end of Main Street far ahead of the crowd.

● **Be selective**: Don't try to see all the rides, special performances, and numerous musical acts if you only have one day. Use a map and plan your route. For a park-orientation ride, hop on the **19th-century train** at the entrance which goes round the perimeter of the park – it usually starts operating 15 minutes before the park opens. The **Monorail** also serves the same purpose, with a bird's eye view.

● **Avoid the crowds**: Not always possible, but these tips should help:

1. Plan to see big or new attractions like Space Mountain, Splash Mountain, and the Indiana Jones Adventure either early in the day, late at night, or when a special event, like one of the parades, draws away other potential riders.

2. Adventureland, Frontierland, New Orleans Square and Critter Country are more popular in daylight hours because of their scenic rides and serene settings. At night, the dazzle and excitement of Tomorrowland, Fantasyland, Videopolis, and the fabulous Fantasmic! laser show always draw large audiences under the light of the moon. If you reverse this order you will miss a lot of congestion, although of course you will also miss some of the intrinsic charm of the park. If you have the time, it's great to see the whole park at day and night – but if time is limited, consider visiting Fantasyland during daytime, Tomorrowland during daylight, and hold New Orleans Square for night-time, when the mystique and atmosphere of Pirates of the Caribbean and the Haunted Mansion are steepened.

3. Use FASTPASS, the unique system that gives you a one-hour window of faster access on certain rides, currently Space Mountain, Splash Mountain, Roger Rabbit Car Toon Spin, and the Indiana Jones Adventure. Head first to one of these; get your timed pass by inserting your passport (remember to keep this after you get in the main gate); then head to whatever popular ride does not have the pass, keeping in mind the entry time on your FASTPASS (which is good during a one-hour window of time, usually starting a couple of hours from the time you obtain it).

4. Disneyland hotel patrons are sometimes allowed in an hour earlier than anyone else, delivered by tram.

5. Plan to eat when everyone else isn't. As a bonus, while others dine, you have shorter lines on the rides.

6. During the summer and holidays, Disneyland is open late. Consider making three laps of the park: in the morning, hit as many major attractions as you can before the park fills up; in the afternoon, look for more passive and less crowded attractions that let you rest and sit a bit, like Country Bear, Jamboree or the Mark Twain. You might want to shop and eat on Main Street after noon, which is least crowded at this time, and the stores are air-conditioned (don't waste

Map on page 254

Well everyone needs to use the phone sometimes...

BELOW: Tweedle Dum and Tweedle Dee find a friend.

DISNEYLAND – WHEN TO ATTACK

Three elements are primary when considering your visit – vacation time flexibility, crowd expectations, and the elements. It does rain in California sometimes!

September to mid-December is the best time for families with young children to visit, but there can be disadvantages – some special parades and shows run only in summer. Disneyland closes earlier in the fall (6pm). But you can still pack as many rides in. Thanksgiving, like all holidays, is crowded, but between Thanksgiving and Christmas is a great time to visit. It looks spectacular at Christmas, with a gigantic tree on Main Street. From late November to mid-December the crowds are light.

January to May is also a good time (except President's Day, Easter, and Memorial Day, which are crowded). Note that January and February have the highest average rainfall in Southern California, and can be quite chilly.

If summer is your only option, the first two weeks of June are the best bet. The park is open to midnight, and crowds are not at their peak. Temperatures have also not peaked; in July and August they can reach 85°–90°F (29°–32°C).

The worst times are public holidays. Christmas and spring breaks, Easter and 4 July pull in as many as 75,000 people a day. Prepare to wait in line for up to two hours.

TIP

The best dining spot at Disneyland is the **Blue Bayou** (New Orleans Square). Great food, fairly expensive, and incredible atmosphere under a night-time Louisiana swamp sky. Try to get a table by the water (same day reservations only). Also good for sit-down lunch and dinner: the **Plaza Inn**, on Main Street.

BELOW: colorful marching bands are part of the scenery.

time there in the morning, and it will be crowded at the end of the day!). Visit any of the big attractions you may have missed in the evening, especially the Haunted Mansion or Dumbo, which feel extra special at night.

More tips

● The most usual first-timers' mistake is to try and see things in geographic sequence. Don't – unless you have three days to spare.
● Sunburn is the number one complaint at the first-aid office. Don't let a cool or cloudy day fool you. Wear comfortable shoes and dress in layers – warm days can lead to cool nights.
● Many of the thrill rides, like Space Mountain, have faster speeds at night.
● Adventureland is generally deserted at night.
● The best way to view Fantasmic! is in the Disney Gallery patio, over-looking the Rivers of America. Tickets are not cheap ($39 separately; free everywhere else), but there is a buffet and you won't have to battle the huge crowds. Space is very limited – buy tickets at Main Gate – they often sell out in the first half-hour.
● Favorite recommended snacks include: Really Big Cinnamon Roll from the Blue Ribbon Bakery on Main Street; Dole pineapple whip from the Tiki Juice Bar in Adventureland; clam chowder and mint juleps at Cafe Orleans, and fritters from the Royal Street Veranda, in New Orleans Square; and Mickey Mouse pretzels at the Coca Cola Refreshment on Main Street.
● If you stay to watch Fantasmic! or the fireworks, stop for a snack or browse in the shops after the show is over. It can take about 30 minutes or more for the crowds to disperse.

DISNEYLAND TIPS AND TRICKS

These are some tips from Disneyland fans and former employees to help make your visit a little more special.
● Many attractions have lines that split into two. As a general rule, the left side moves faster.
● The Monorail operator can let a handful of people ride with him in the front cabin – ask when you board – it's a fun view.
● Sometimes the Mark Twain operator will let you up into the wheelhouse and "steer" the Twain. You even get an official certificate.
● Always check the board southwest of the castle for ride closures and other info – it could save you a long walk for nothing.
● If it's your birthday, go to City Hall and you'll get a sticker and sometimes special treatment (front of line status).
● Don't carry those shopping bags all day – ask the clerk to send them Package Express, and take your claim ticket to the Main Gate Newstand on your way out (they'll also send them to any Disney hotel). This service is free.
● If your child doesn't meet the height requirement and you and your spouse want to ride an attraction, ask an attendant for a Switch Pass, which allows one of you to ride while the other stays with the child.

Knott's Berry Farm

About 6 miles (10 km) from Disney in next door Buena Park, Knott's Berry Farm (tel: 714/220 5200) can claim to have been the first theme park in the US. It really did begin as a berry farm in 1920, as Walter and Cordelia Knott began selling fresh berries and homemade perserves from a roadside stand. Several years later Cordelia added fried chicken dinners to the menu, and soon Knott's was such a popular destination that Walter decided to build an authentic Ghost Town and offer pony rides to entertain the waiting patrons.

Even though Knott's Berry Farm has grown tremendously, and was recently sold by the Knott's family to the Cedar Fair amusement group, it still revolves around an Old West California theme and still serves delicious fried chicken and boysenberry pie. The park currently consists of six themed areas beyond the gates – just before the gates is the **California Marketplace**, which does not have an entry fee, and features a wide range of clothing, gifts, and food, including Mrs Knott's Chicken Dinner Restaurant.

What sets this theme park apart from the others is its charm – you can sense its roots, from the berry business that still thrives today, to the buildings in Ghost Town that aren't just movie facades; in fact, they have historic significance, having been brought in from Kansas, Arizona, and other states. There's a handcrafted carousel dating to the late 1800s, and you can ride a real narrow-gauge train that was once part of the Denver and Rio Grande Line. Blacksmiths and other craftsmen hammer out souvenirs all day, and also participate in programs about the history of the Wild West.

Along with its charm, Knott's has some great thrill rides, including **Ghost Rider**, the longest wooden roller coaster in the West (recently rated in the top

Map on page 254

If you want to mingle with Disney characters and get plenty of photos, a Character Breakfast is a must. They are at the Disneyland Hotel daily, and at the Plaza Inn on Main Street from opening to 11am daily – no reservations, and it fills up fast.

BELOW:
the Cup and Saucer ride at Disneyland.

10 in the world). An adjacent waterpark, **Soak City USA**, has recently opened, with 21 rides and attractions on a 1960s Southern California surfer theme. It's geared toward families and preteens, with the exception of a few ultra high-speed slides, and is open from late May to September (separate admission fee, but multi-day passes are available to cover both parks).

If you are going to see both Disneyland and Knott's, visit Knott's first. While an outstanding park in itself, you will appreciate it more if you haven't been overwhelmed by the breadth, magnitude, and characters of Disney first.

The park is split into six themed areas: **Ghost Town** is in the center, and gives the opportunity to peek through windows and see what a jail or a Gold Rush-era laundry looked like. There's also a replicated gold mine and working sluice staffed by knowledgeable helpers, where you can pan for gold. **Indian Trails** has Native American arts and crafts. An 1800s river wilderness area is the setting for **Wild Water Wilderness**, which features the fun (and wet) **Bigfoot Rapids** ride, as well as the **Mystery Lodge** history and special effects show.

Fiesta Village is home to the wicked **Montezooma's Revenge** and **Jaguar!** rollercoasters, as well as the 19th-century **Dentzel carousel. Boardwalk** is the teen hangout, celebrating the Southern California beach lifestyle with the wild **Supreme Scream** (where you fall from the tallest structure in Orange County), **Boomerang, Hammerhead**, and **Log Ride** rides, and the new **Perilous Plunge**, featuring the tallest and steepest water ride anywhere. Last, but certainly not least to anyone with children, **Camp Snoopy** is kiddie headquarters with more than 30 rides, climbing forts, and a petting zoo. Check out the animal shows at Camp Snoopy Theater, where they can even pet tame coyotes, raccoons, and other creatures.

TIP

● The least crowded days at Knott's Berry Farm are Tuesday, Wednesday, Thursday, and Sunday mornings.
● Get there early. This cannot be repeated enough.

BELOW:
Pluto and friends.

How long do you need?

You can cover Knott's in a single day. The same general rules apply to Knott's as to Disneyland. Come early, before the park fills up. It does get hot in the peak summer period, so you'll want to save the afternoon for cooler attractions, such as those indoors or splashing through water. Summer hours are 9am–midnight; the rest of the year, Monday–Friday 10am–6pm, longer on weekends. Closed Christmas Day.

Tactical strategy

● Come a few minutes before opening – you can grab a bite to eat at the Grand Deli, which opens an hour before the park. Once inside, hang on to your program, as it gives the schedule of shows for the day.
● If your gang is up for the wild coasters, head for GhostRider or Boomerang or Supreme Scream right away, before the crowds build. For those with young children, peruse the Ghost Town and then head into Camp Snoopy, which will be your headquarters until lunch, whether you like it or not.
● If it's time for a stunt show, proceed to the Wagon Camp. If you still have some time, consider cutting through Ghost Town and riding the mellow Calico Mine Train or Stagecoach – the view is best from the top of the coach.
● Mid-afternoon, consider the theater-style attractions, like Mystery Lodge or Kingdom of the Dinosaurs, and for refreshment stop and whet your whistle at the Silver Dollar Saloon. Check out Calico Square for outdoor entertainment.
● In the summer, large groups of kids from summer camps often leave the park by late afternoon, so if you're not particularly hungry 5–7pm is often a good time to see leaner crowds on the medium-scare rides.

Map on page 254

You're never too old for a cuddle.

BELOW: riding high at Knott's.

KNOTT'S BERRY TIPS

Here are a few tips to help get you the best visit to Knott's Berry Farm.
● During summer, when the park stays open late, ticket prices after 4pm are slightly less than half, and since it is a relatively small park, it's possible to see the major attractions in five to six hours.
● Have lunch before the crowds, say by 11am – you might try the Grizzly Creek Lodge, where the Peanuts gang likes to hang out for pictures and autographs.
● Many parts of the Ghost Town are shaded – consider cruising the afternoon sights there, including the 1876-built church at Reflection Lake, which still holds services.
● Consider Mrs. Knott's Chicken Dinner Restaurant for an awesome home-cooked style dinner (or late lunch).
● Things to think about on your way out of the park:
1) Munching on delicious and totally non-nutritious funnel cake – a cross between a waffle and a donut – topped with strawberry flavoring.
2) Need a late snack? Mrs Knott's has a special take-out counter (just south of the restaurant) just for bakery items and chicken-to-go (the perfect way to beat the line)
3) Knott's jams, preserves, and syrups make great gifts to take or send home.

Six Flags Magic Mountain

If you had to find just one word that captured each major theme park in the LA area, it might be Fantasy for Disneyland... History for Knott's... and Screams for Magic Mountain.

Once a small amusement park out in the middle of almost nowhere, Magic Mountain has developed fast. It is is about 30 to 40 minutes from Hollywood and West LA, and about 90 minutes from Disneyland. It appeals most to hard-core rollercoaster enthusiasts, as well as teens in general. Although it is not as family-targeted as Disneyland or Knott's, it still offers attractions for all ages.

The park is open daily from 10am end March to September, but only on weekends and holidays the rest of the year (tel: 661/255-4100 or 4111).

Monster coasters

Magic Mountain means BIG, SCARY rides. The latest addition is the monster rollercoaster **Goliath**, a three-minute, 85-mph (140-km/h) journey of spiral curves, banked turns, and underground tunnels. Six Flags loves building the biggest, the fastest, and the scariest. The main reason people come is to scream through the thrills. Check out **Riddler's Revenge** ("The World's Tallest and Fastest Stand-Up Coaster!") or **Superman** ("The Tallest and Fastest Ride on the Planet!").

When evening rolls around, try **Colossus**, the giant wooden coaster that is extra fun at night. Also check out **Gotham City Backlot** at night – the most visually interesting of all the areas, it gains added mystery in the dark. This is the home of **Batman the Ride**, where you are suspended from below the track, your feet dangling underneath you, whipping through hairpin turns, corkscrew bends, vertical loops, and a couple of head-over-heels moves.

Six Flags Magic Mountain is "Home to 13 world-class rides, including four listed in the Guinness Book of World Records."

BELOW: getting wet at Magic Mountain.

Also at night, during the summer, **Batman Nights** is a spectacular laser, fireworks, and special effects show that closes the park.

For those with children aged eight and under, there is **Bugs Bunny World**, as well as milder coasters and water rides. Although you can get those at the other parks, they are especially big on Looney Tune characters here – Bugs, Daffy Duck, Sylvester, Tweety Bird, etc. There's also a petting zoo for children (and exhausted or terrified adults seeking respite).

Next door is **Hurricane Harbor**, a water park whose thrills are definitely at the very top of the scale. But again, there's places for all ages to find fun. On a hot day (which is often – remember this is almost desert) the Harbor offers great afternoon relief. Combination tickets are available for entrance to both Magic Mountain and Hurricane Harbor at the main gate.

Among the 20 water rides at Hurricane Harbor is **Black Snake Summit**, a 75-ft (23-meter) tower connecting five waterslides. All the slides have height requirements of 48 inches (1.2 meters), except one at 42 inches (1.1 meters). **Castaway Cove** is for children under 54 inches (1.4 meters), with small waterslides and waterfalls, squirting objects, and a fortress with swings and slides. At **Shipwreck Shores** the whole family can float lazily down a winding river.

Map on page 254

Mickey has sackloads of fan mail every year.

How long do you need?

Count on one day – although at peak season it is common for the most popular rides to have from one- to two-hour waits, so it may be one very full day if you try to ride all of the big coasters (not recommended!). If you want to spend more than an hour or two at Hurricane Harbor, you may want to consider an overnight stay locally. ❑

BELOW: the end of a busy day.

MAGIC TIPS

Six Flags Magic Mountain is the place for thrills, so here are some thrilling tips.

● As ever, get there early, as you will have shorter lines and it'll be cooler.

● You need to be above 48 or 52 inches (1.2–1.3 meters) for the major rollercoasters.

● Goliath and Superman are the most intense rides, followed by Riddler's Revenge, Viper, and Batman. They are only for the strong of heart. The mildest coasters are Gold Rusher and Ninja.

● Bugs Bunny World is rarely too crowded, so save it for the afternoon, as well as any indoor shows that can shield you from the afternoon sun.

● On Halloween and during spring break, Colossus is run backwards.

● There is some hilly terrain around the park – think about getting a stroller if you have a young child.

● Because it gets so hot, drinking fluids is vital – buy a refillable drinks bottle; the refills are cheaper.

● Dress in layers – hot days can often lead to cool nights, especially in spring and fall.

● Men's and women's changing rooms, as well as showers and lockers, are available at Hurricane Harbor.

DAY TRIPS

Easily reached from Los Angeles via one or other of the freeways are beaches, coastal resorts, mountains, deserts and the Mexican border

Map on page 254

For the visitor who craves variety, LA is blessed. The wide range of attractions includes three cities – San Diego to the south, Santa Barbara in the north, and Palm Springs to the east – which pinpoint the outer perimeter of our one-day trips, and a visit to each offers other attractions along the way.

Heading south

The Pacific Coast Highway from Seal Beach south is lined by glittering beach communities – the most notable are **Balboa Island** and **Newport Beach ❶**. This is a boat-owners' heaven and, whether for fishing, sailing or swimming, the ocean is the major attraction. The Balboa peninsula encloses Newport's harbor, and from the stately **Balboa Pavilion** (*circa* 1902) boats set out on harbor trips, whale-watching expeditions and visits to Catalina Island.

The homes in Newport Bay are stunning – take a boat tour or charter. Check out the harbor entrance, **John Wayne's estate**, the beautiful homes of **Lido Island**. Balboa Boat Rentals (tel: 949/673-7200) offers power, sail, and kayak boats for rent; Adventures at Sea offers luxury boat charters, including not only fancy yachts but historic schooners and cutters (tel: 800/BAY-2412). For the romantics, there's gondolas too – Gondolas of Newport (tel: 949/675-1212).

Balboa Island ❷ is a delightful place to stroll, eat and shop – and shopping is a major pastime of ritzy Newport Beach, the Beverly Hills of Orange County. Too much sun and sand? Try the upscale **Fashion Island** and the **South Coast Plaza**, where there's an annex of the **Orange County Museum of Art**. It's worth a trip to the main branch a short hop away on San Clemente Drive. The museum specializes in mid-19th-century to contemporary California art and there's a varied collection (tel: 949/759-1122; open Tuesday–Sunday 11am–5pm).

For local culture, visit **Newport Harbor Nautical Museum**, 151 Pacific Coast Highway, in the old paddleship the *Pride of Newport*. This former restaurant has become an ode to the maritime heritage of Southern California, with one gallery devoted to the history of Newport Beach, another to ships of the Pacific, and a third gallery with changing exhibits (open Tuesday–Sunday 10am–5pm; tel: 949/675-8915).

You'll find plenty of surf and sandy beaches, or slide down to wide **Big Corona** beach in Corona Del Mar. The world's most famous, and ferocious, body-surfing spot, **The Wedge**, is at the end of the peninsula – an unbelievable sight when a swell hits.

About 30 minutes south is **Laguna Beach ❸**, noted for artists, galleries and antique shops, but most of all for the annual **Pageant of the Masters**, a nightly midsummer show in the outdoor **Irvine Bowl** where res-

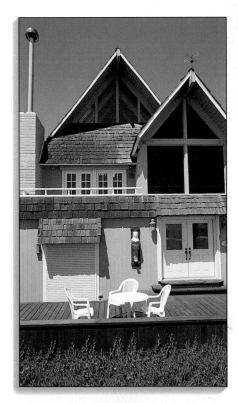

PRECEDING PAGES: waiting for the perfect wave; Orange County's elaborate Crystal Cathedral. **LEFT:** surfers at Newport Beach. **BELOW:** Newport Beach home.

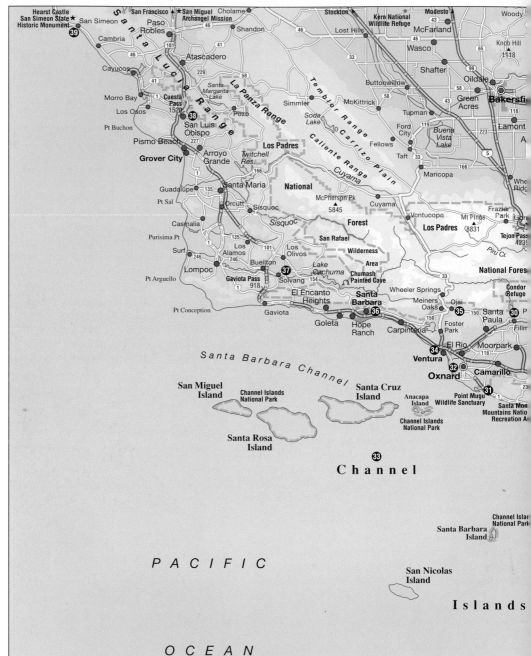

Hearst Castle
San Simeon State ★
Historic Monument
39
San Simeon
★San Miguel
San Francisco Archangel Mission
Cholame
Stockton
Kern National
Wildlife Refuge
Modesto
43
Woody

Cambria
Paso
Robles
Shandon
46
Lost Hills
McFarland
46

Cayucos
46
Atascadero
41
33
Wasco
Knob Hill
1118
65

101
229
Santa
Margarita
Lake
58
Buttonwillow
58
Shafter
99
Oildale

Morro Bay
41
1
Cuesta
Pass
1520
La Panza Range
Simmler
McKittrick
Tupman
58
43
Green
Acres
Bakersfi
118

Los Osos
Pozo
Soda
Lake
Ford
City
119
Buena
Vista
Lake
223
Lamont

Pt Buchon
38
San Luis
Obispo
Caliente Range
Fellows
Taft
33
5

Pismo Beach
227
Los Padres
Cuyama
Maricopa
166
Whe
Ridg

Grover City
1
Arroyo
Grande
166
Twitchell
Res.
National
McPherson Pk
5845
Cuyama
Ventucopa
Mt Pinos
(8831
Frazier
Park

Guadalupe
135
Santa Maria
Los Padres
Tejon
423

Pt Sal
Orcutt
Sisquoc
Sisquoc
Forest
San Rafael
Piru Ct.
National Fores

Casmalia
135
Los
Alamos
101
Los
Olivos
Wilderness
Condor
Refuge

Purisima Pt
Surf
246
246
Buellton
Lake
Cachuma
Area
Chumash
Painted Cave
Wheeler Springs
33

Lompoc
Gaviota Pass
1 918
37
Solvang
154
Meiners
Oaks
Ojai
35
150
Santa
Paula
30

Pt Arguello
El Encanto
Heights
**Santa
Barbara**
Foster
Park
Fillm

Pt Conception
Gaviota
36
Hope
Ranch
Carpinteria
118
Moorpark

Goleta
El Rio
34
Ventura
32
Camarillo
23

Santa Barbara Channel
Oxnard
31
Point Mugu
Wildlife Sanctuary
Santa Mon
Mountains Natio
Recreation A

San Miguel
Island
Channel Islands
National Park
Santa Cruz
Island
Anacapa
Island
Channel Islands
National Park

Santa Rosa
Island

33
C h a n n e l

Channel Islan
National Park
Santa Barbara
Island

P A C I F I C
San Nicolas
Island

I s l a n d s

O C E A N

↑N

Around Los Angeles

0 _____ 20 miles
0 _____ 20 km

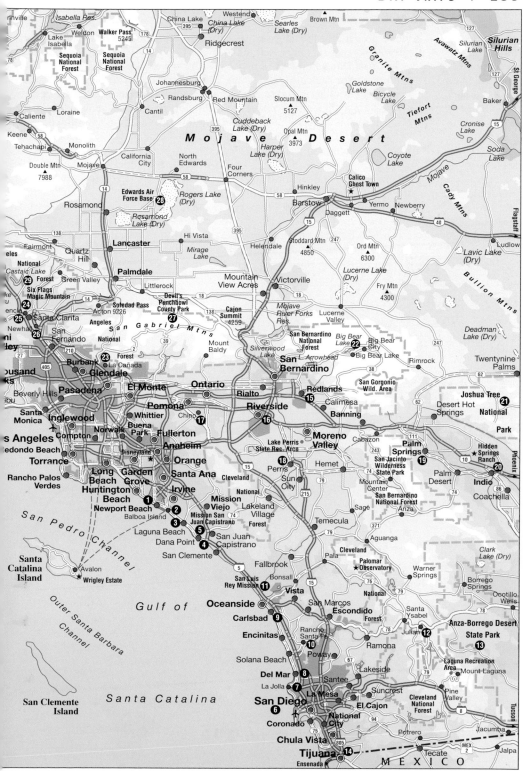

The Laguna Art Museum was founded in 1918 and focuses on Californian, historical and contemporary art (open Tuesday–Sunday 11–5pm). The Laguna Playhouse was where a young Harry (Harrison) Ford debuted in 1965 (tel: 800/946-5556).

idents pose in real-life tableaux, such as *The Last Supper*, accompanied by narrator and orchestral music (tel: 800/487-3378).

Just past **Dana Point ❹**, a major port for the square-rigged ships of 19th-century author Richard Henry Dana, the turn-off comes to **San Juan Capistrano** – a few miles inland from the coast – whose famous swallows hopefully arrive to take up summer residence on St Joseph's Day. The festival for the birds' arrival is around March 19 (the swallows leave for Argentina on the Day of San Juan, October 23) and the **Mission ❺**, considered the jewel of the California missions, is always a pleasure to visit, with its courtyards, fountains, and relics. The original chapel, built by Father Serra in 1776, is California's oldest building, miraculously undamaged by the 1812 earthquake which left the Great Stone Church in the ruins that still stand today.

Interstate 5 (Santa Ana Freeway), is the main southbound route out of Los Angeles if you plan to visit **Disneyland** and its nearby attractions, Knott's Berry Farm, Movieland Wax Museum, and Medieval Times, which are all within a few minutes' drive of one another (*see Theme Parks and box on page 258*).

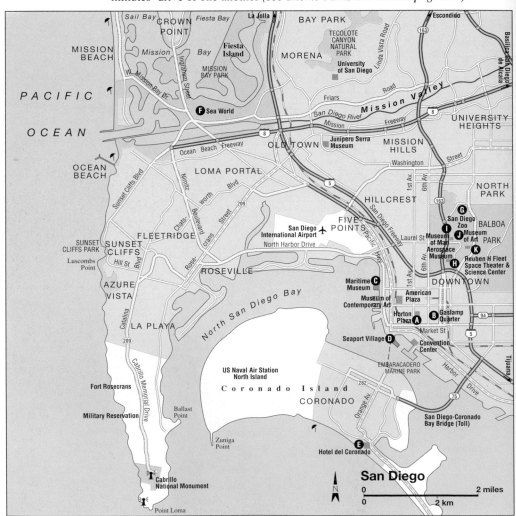

Also of note in Orange County is Robert Schuller's mirrored **Crystal Cathedral** in Garden Grove (tel: 714/971-4000), which was dedicated in 1983 and is the world's first drive-in church, with four Sunday services and free daily tours of the church and grounds (Monday–Saturday 9.30 and 11am; grounds close at 4pm); and the **Richard Nixon Library and Birthplace**, in Yorba Linda, which honors and explores the legendary former US president through film, interactive displays, memorabilia, and never-before-seen photographs (open Monday–Saturday 10am–5pm, Sunday 11am–5pm; tel: 714/993-3393).

Maps:
Area 254
City 256

San Diego

San Diego ❻ is the second largest city in California, and the oldest. First discovered by Portuguese explorer Juan Rodriguez Cabrillo in 1542, it is the site of Father Junípero Serra's first mission, built in 1769. The **old mission** sits in the six-and-a-half-block **State Historical Park**, which also contains the 1927 **Casa de Estudillo**, now a museum (open daily 10am–5pm), and **Casa de Bandini**, an 1829 hacienda which is now a Mexican restaurant. *Mariachis* and dancers perform in the area during the weekend.

The area is called **Old Town** because of its history and village flavor. Old Town's original adobe house restaurants and art galleries, contrasting nicely with modern San Diego, which sprang up around the harbor in 1867. The downtown area wraps around the bay. It is dominated by **Horton Plaza ❹**, a mall noted for its vibrant color scheme as well as its shops. Nearby are luxury hotels, a convention center, the historic **Gaslamp Quarter ❺**, the **Broadway Pier** and adjacent cruise-ship terminal, the Embarcadero, the **Maritime Museum ❻** (where the 135-year-old British *Star of India* is moored), and Seaport Village.

BELOW: Cabrillo National Monument, Port Loma, San Diego.

The restored and rejuvenated Victorian buildings of the Gaslamp Quarter are occupied by businesses, restaurants, art galleries, and specialty stores. **Seaport Village D**, opened in 1980, also has boutiques, restaurants, and shopping plazas built in an interestingly varied architectural mix of Victorian San Francisco, traditional Mexico, and old Monterey. A waterfront boardwalk and 4 miles (7 km) of winding walkways connect its carousel, shops and bars and restaurants.

From Seaport Village a ferry runs across the bay to Coronado, site of one of California's oldest and most renowned landmarks, the red-roofed **Hotel del Coronado E**, which was featured in the 1959 movie *Some Like It Hot*. The ferry leaves every 30 minutes; the ride takes about five minutes.

Adjacent to Seaport Village is the 8-acre **Embarcadero Marine Park**, home to artists, clowns, kite flyers, and picnickers. Along the Embarcadero is the place to sign up for harbor excursions and dinner cruises.

Just north of downtown is **Mission Bay**, which has evolved into one of the world's largest water-oriented playgrounds. It comprises 27 miles (44 km) of beaches and acres of parkland for picnicking, tennis, golf, boating, fishing, and watersports. Here, too, is **Sea World F**, with its lovable killer whales. The whale stadium seats 5,000 and features the entertaining antics of Shamu and Baby Shamu. Also at Sea World's are seals, dolphins, sea lions, otters and penguins (open daily 9am–5pm in winter, 9am–11pm in summer).

The **San Diego Zoo G** (open summer 7.30am–9pm, winter 9am–4pm) uses moats and canyons to separate visitors from residents. They are like a tropical garden, with orchids, palms, and ferns. In the **Children's Zoo**, kids can race tortoises – the tortoises don't know they're racing – and watch baby animals being cared for by their substitute human mothers in the fascinating animal nursery.

BELOW: Horton Plaza, San Diego.

ATTRACTIONS NEAR DISNEYLAND

Near Knott's Berry Farm at Buena Park is **Movieland Wax Museum** (7711 Beach Boulevard, off Freeway 91; tel: 714/522-1154). Exhibits show memorable moments in film and video. The collection includes 250 sets, many using original props and costumes. The wax figures are very lifelike. You can simulate stardom by having your picture printed on money, calendars, and a superstar's body.

Across from the Wax Museum is **Medieval Times** (tel: 714/521-4740), a dinner and jousting theater inside a fabricated 11th-century castle. Reservations required. You are assigned a color which indicates which knight to support. The brave knights on dressed horses challenge each other in an vivid show of sportsmanship and battle.

In the area are also: **Wild Bill's Wild West Dinner Extravaganza**, with vaudeville acts, rope tricks, and Native American dances (open Sunday-Friday 7pm, Saturday 5 and 8pm; tel. 800/883-1547); **Ripley's Believe It or Not** (open weekdays 11am–5pm, weekends 10am–6pm; tel: 714/522-7045); the **Hobby City Doll and Toy Museum**, with 50-year-old dolls of early Hollywood stars exhibited in a miniature White House; and **Adventure City**, a fun "mini-theme park (open Friday 10am–5pm, Saturday and Sunday 11am–7pm, tel: 714/236-9300).

San Diego Zoo is in **Balboa Park**. This 1,400-acre (560-hectare) park also houses a **carousel**, the **Marie Hitchcock Puppet Theater**, as well as the **Natural History Museum, Aerospace Museum** ①, **Hall of Champions, Museum of Man** ①, **San Diego Museum of Art** ①, **Timkin Art Gallery, Museum of San Diego History, Old Globe Theater, Cassius Carter Center Stage**, and **Reubin H. Fleet Space Theater and Science Center** ⑥, with multimedia productions on a mammoth screen. (Most attractions open daily 10am–4.30 except the Fleet Center open Monday and Tuesday 9.30am–6pm, Wednesday–Sunday 9.30am– 9pm. Hours change seasonally, tel: 619/238-1233).

In the park, too, is the **California Tower**, whose architectural features and tile-crowned dome – it was the highest structure of the California-Pacific Exposition of 1935 – have become the city's logo.

North County San Diego

The charming and wealthy coastal community of **La Jolla** ⑦ is 14 miles (22 km) north of San Diego and reminiscent of the towns of the French Riviera, with its clifftop location and access via a winding road. First-class shopping, museums, art galleries, pristine beaches (**Black's Beach** was for a short time legally clothes-optional) attract visitors. The **Steven Birch Aquarium** hosts the largest oceanographic exhibit in the US (open daily 9am–5pm). **Torrey Pines Golf Course** is world famous and an annual stop on the PGA Tour; and the nearby **Torrey Pines Hang Glider Port** is a good place to take lessons or just to watch.

Farther up the coast are the beach cities of **Del Mar** ⑧, **Solana Beach**, **Encinitas**, and **Carlsbad**. Del Mar is famous for its **racetrack** (late July to mid-September), founded by Bing Crosby and Pat O'Brien in the 1930s; its

San Diego's Old Town conjures up memories of the past.

BELOW: Palos Verdes coastline.

stretch of million-dollar homes on the beach, where stars such as Desi Arnaz, Jimmy Durante, Burt Bacharach, and Angie Dickinson have made their homes; and its quaint, English-accented downtown area of galleries and shops. Some of the finest beaches and surf spots in the world are here.

Remember the Beach Boys Surfin' USA? *"you'll catch 'em surfin' at Del Mar....on your knees at Swami's (Encinitas)....all over La Jolla....."*

Carlsbad ❾ began when its first settler dug his well, and noticed the water alleviated his rheumatism – soon people were coming for the "miracle water." Now, people flock to Carlsbad to visit **Legoland**, where attractions are built from 30 million Lego pieces. Opened in 1999, it is set against the backdrop of the **Flower Fields of Carlsbad** and is extremely popular with 2- to 12-year-olds (open daily 10am–6pm, during summer 10am–8pm; tel: 760/918-5346).

Just inland is the pretty **Rancho Santa Fe** ❿ – several decades ago the Santa Fe Railroad company planted thousands of eucalyptus trees imported from Australia, for use as railroad ties. Later abandoned when the wood was discovered to crack, it became a wealthy enclave for retired industrialists and movie stars, settled among rolling hills of citrus and the towering eucalyptus (past and recent stars have included Bing Crosby, Victor Mature, and pop star Jewel). The small and elegant downtown village is home to the definitive California country retreat, the **Rancho Santa Fe Inn**, where staying earns you the privilege of playing the **Rancho Santa Fe Golf Club**. Also downtown is the French **Mille Fleurs** restaurant, considered one of the best restaurants in San Diego.

At the northern end of San Diego County is **Oceanside**, home to a busy **harbor**, and out on Highway 76, the **San Luis Rey Mission** ⓫, called the "King of the Missions" due to its size. Built in 1798, it was the 18th of the 21 California missions, and named for Louis IX, King of France. Today it is operated by Franciscan Friars and is a busy retreat center (open with museum daily 10am–4pm, Saturday Mass 5.30pm).

BELOW:
Legoland suprises.

Taking Highway 76 two hours east leads to two of San Diegans' favorite getaways (and past the **Palomar Observatory**, daily 9am–4pm). **Julian** ⓬ is a quaint mountain community that was the center of an 1870s gold rush, now filled with bed and breakfasts and famous Julian Apple Pie. And the stark and striking **Anza-Borrego Desert State Park** ⓭ combines awesome topography and some surprising flora and fauna (the wildflower season, late February–April, is a very popular time to pay a visit).

Down Mexico way

San Diego's ever-present red trolley cars, in addition to providing transport around town, also take passengers to the Mexican border at San Ysidro. In the daytime, they run to **Mexico** about every 15 minutes. It is a 20-mile ride (32-km) which takes about 30 minutes. After being dropped off, there's a zig-zag walk into Mexico, where taxis and buses transport visitors to downtown **Tijuana** ⓮, about a 10-minute drive.

Drivers can take their own cars to **San Ysidro**, park, and walk into Mexico or drive into Mexico themselves. But the trolley saves visitors from parking hassles at the border, waiting in the long line of autos coming back to the US, and from paying for extra auto insurance, which it is advisable to take out before driving in Mexico.

Among Tijuana's attractions are the horse and greyhound racing at **Agua Caliente Racetrack**, the super-fast *jai alai* at **Fronton Palacio** (closed Wednesday); and Tijuana's **Cultural Center**, which has shops, arts and crafts, a museum of Mexican history and art, and an Omnimax Theater. **Mexititian**, across from the Arts and Crafts market, should be your first stop. Created by the country's most famous architect, Pedro Ramirez Vasquez, it contains enormous relief maps of Mexico with most of its major landmarks reproduced on a scale of 20-ft (6-meter) square platforms.

Statue of St Francis at the San Luis Rey Mission.

Heading east

Just over 100 miles (160 km) southeast of LA is **Palm Springs,** the playground in the desert. Head straight there and it's a two-hour drive, but the main route, Interstate 10, meanders past, or near, various other sightseeing options. **Redlands ⓯**, for instance, is known for some Victorian buildings left over from the town's late 1800s heyday. The turrets, gables, and 5-acre (2-hectare) Italian gardens of the hilltop Kimberly Crest mansion alone are worth a side trip.

Redlands is also home to the **San Bernardino County Museum** (open Tuesday–Sunday 9am–5pm), with exhibits and collections on cultural and natural history, and the **Historical Glass Museum**, which exhibits American glassware from the early 1800s to the present, including several pieces from Liberace (open Saturday and Sunday noon–4pm).

Some landmarks in the city of **Riverside ⓰** also worth a look are the **Riverside Art Museum** (open Monday–Saturday 10am–4pm) in a Mediterranean-style building designated a National Historic Place and designed by Hearst Castle architect Julia Morgan in 1929, and nearby the famous **Mission Inn**, built in 1876. This sprawling, modern-day palace, an eclectic mixture of styles, began as a two-story adobe boarding house run by the C.C. Miller family, whose son Frank kept expanding it. Eight presidents and innumerable movie stars have stayed at the Mission Inn, which is full of bizarre antiques, arts and crafts, furniture, and Spanish and Mexican terracotta.

BELOW: the San Luis Rey Mission.

Its turrets, terraces, patios, and alcoves can best be admired from outside in a "Sidewalk Stroll," sponsored by the Mission Inn Foundation on Friday and Saturday mornings. The adjoining shady pedestrian-only street is lined with unusual stores selling a variety of curiosities and antiques.

One of Riverside's most popular attractions is the **California Museum of Photography**, on the mall, whose $15-million collection of photographic equipment, prints, and negatives is one of the most comprehensive in the country. It also incorporates a new digital studio. The museum is open to visitors six days a week (11–5pm; closed Mondays).

Nature and agricultural enthusiasts will love two other spots of interest in Riverside – the **Botanical Gardens** (open daily 8–5pm) at UC Riverside, which features 39 acres (16 hectares) and 4 miles (7 km) of trails with over 3,500 plants and several microclimates, and the **California Citrus State Historic Park,** which recaptures the time when citrus was "king" in California, with demonstration groves, an interpretive center, and a picnic area, exposing the facts behind California's second "gold rush" in the early 1900s, that of growing citrus. Call for opening hours on 909/780-6222.

Nearby **Chino** ⑰ is home to **Planes of Fame** (open daily 9am–5pm), a fabulous museum and repository to over 140 historical planes, especially World War II fighters – American, Japanese, and German. For a fee you can join the museum and take a flight on a B-25, a P-40 Warhawk, or a P-51 Mustang, among others.

At **Perris** ⑱ is the **Orange Empire Railway Museum** (open daily 9am–5pm). Among the museum's 140-year-old railway cars are an old street car from New Orleans whose signboard reads "Desire Street," and several of the Pacific Electric Big Red Cars which operated on the streets of Los Angeles until the 1950s. Perris is also the skydiving capital of southern California.

Back on Interstate 10, the highway passes **Cabazon**; there's a startling view of gigantic dinosaurs beside a truck stop called the Wheel Inn, which used to house exhibits of various sorts, but is now closed. The dinosaurs are still popular photographic attractions.

Palm Springs

The name **Palm Springs** ⑲ sounds refreshing and the city is, but it is also hot. It is cradled by the **Santa Rosa** and **San Jacinto** mountains. The heat crawls up from 90°F (32°C) in early May to the low 100s°F (over 38°C)by late June. By October, it cools down to about 80°F (27°C) again. The climate is most attractive from the months of November to March.

Palm Springs, by the way, is the name of just one city in the desert area, but the name has come to refer to other nearby resort communities **Rancho Mirage**, **Palm Desert**, **Indian Wells**, **La Quinta**, and **Desert Hot Springs**. The local Agua Caliente Indians utilized the therapeutic qualities of the hot springs by building the first bath house in 1871 on land that presently accommodates the Palm Springs Spa Hotel. Today a variety of similar resorts have sprung up.

More than 7,000 swimming pools can be found within the Palm Springs city limits, and the city also has an **Oasis Water Park** ❹ with a mini "ocean." This makes Palm Springs the only desert resort in the world where people can surf. In addition to 4-ft (1.2-meter) waves, the Oasis Water Park has a Whitewater River innertube ride, a series of water slides and a sandy stretch of beach (open daily at 11am, March–Labor Day, then weekends only).

With about 80 golf courses, Palm Springs and its environs are sometimes thought of as the "Golf Capital of the World." There are two major tournaments held here each year: the Bob Hope Chrysler Classic and the Nabisco Dinah Shore Invitational.

Palm Springs also has 300 tennis courts. When, back in 1933, tennis buffs Charlie Farrell and Ralph Bellamy first opened their Racquet Club, celebrities began rushing to the then tiny resort town. Today stars still live and relax in Palm Springs. In fact the city has been seeing something of a renaissance since the late 1990s. The stars most associated with the city have been Bob Hope, Dinah Shore, Frank Sinatra,

BELOW:
life in Mexico
sounds good.

Sylvester Stallone, and the late Sonny Bono, of the Sonny and Cher pop duo, who was elected. mayor in the 1980s. There are bus tours of the stars' homes. But a bicycle is an even better way to get around.

There are more than 35 miles (66 km) of generally flat, well-marked trails for cyclists, and a map is usually included in the bike rental fee. You can tour downtown in horse-drawn carriages, trolleys and city buses. Three companies even offer elevated sightseeing from hot-air balloons.

To see the rough desert/mountain landscape up close, try Desert Off Road Adventures' three-hour **jeep safari tours** into the mountains, which leave from local hotels twice daily. For a more "man-made" look at the desert terrain, try the **Desert Museum ⓑ** on Museum Drive (open Tuesday–Sunday 10am–5pm), with its dioramas of the desert by night and day and its Indian artifacts.

Or try the **Living Desert Reserve** in nearby Palm Desert (open mid-January–mid-July daily 9am–4pm, otherwise daily 8am–1pm), with such native flora and fauna as cacti, rattlesnakes, lizards, and bighorn sheep. **Moorten Botanical Gardens ⓒ** on Palm Canyon Drive also has desert plants with nature trails winding past prickly pears, chollas and agaves (open Monday–Saturday 9am–4.30pm, Sunday 10am–4pm).

Palm Canyon Drive, a palm-lined, one-way street running south, is the city's main thoroughfare. It has no large signboards, highrise buildings, nor street lamps; at dusk its 2,000 palm trees are illuminated. Here, the city's main shopping district includes the **Desert Fashion Plaza ⓓ**, an upscale complex anchored by renowned stores such as Saks Fifth Avenue and I. Magnin. Nearby is the historic **Plaza Theatre ⓔ**, where the **Palm Springs Follies** has resurrected vaudeville and has been playing to packed houses since 1992.

Maps:
Area 254
City 263

Weird and wonderful shapes in Joshua Tree National Park.

BELOW: wind power in Palm Springs.

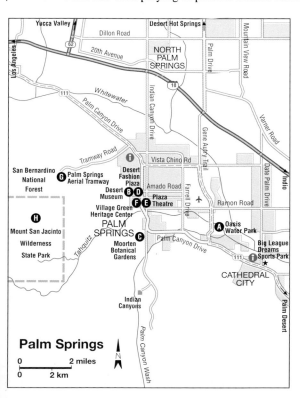

In the center of downtown, on Palm Canyon Drive, the **Village Green Heritage Center ⓕ** is composed of an old adobe, a building made of railroad ties, and a re-created general store of the 1930s, complete with packaged goods (open Thursday–Sunday 10am–4pm). **Indian Canyon Drive**, one block east, parallels Palm Canyon Drive and runs one-way north. Highway 111 connects Palm Springs with other cities in the area.

In nearby Cathedral City, there's a new attraction for sports fans, the **Big League Dreams Sports Park** (tel: 760/324-5600), a 28-acre (11-hectare) sports and entertainment complex with fields for softball, soccer, basketball, volleyball, roller-hockey, batting cages and a sports academy. For local use during the week, the sports park hosts national and international tournaments as well as boxing and concerts, on weekends.

Palm Desert, a 15-minute drive to the southeast, is lined with boutiques and art galleries and features Palm Desert **Town Center** with five major department stores, 180 shops and an indoor ice-skating rink. The fastest way to cool down is to take the Palm Springs **Aerial Tramway ⓖ** (open Monday–Friday 10am–8pm, Saturday and Sunday and public holidays 8am–8pm), which rises 8,000 ft (2,400 meters) from the desert floor to pine-covered **Mount San Jacinto Wilderness State Park ⓗ**. At the top, there are walks and mule trails through 1½ miles (2.5 km) of mountain wilderness which attracts cross-country skiers in the winter. Even in summer a sweater is needed up here. The tramway's upper terminal has a buffet restaurant, cocktail lounge, and gift shop.

Other spots you might want to check on the east side of the valley include **The MacCullum Theatre/Bob Hope Cultural Center** (tel: 760/340-ARTS), which hosts an eclectic schedule including Broadway plays, comedians,

BELOW: the California desert is unrelenting.

jazz, children's theater, international symphonies and musical stars; the **La Quinta Hotel**, an old Spanish beauty where celebrities like to hide out in the bungalows; and the town of **Indio ㉓**, "Date Capital of the World" – take home some tasty date or citrus souvenirs from the desert.

The adventurous might want to hike or camp at **Joshua Tree National Park ㉑** (made famous by the U2 album), north of Palm Springs where the Colorado and Mojave Deserts meet. There are 1,200 sq. miles (3,100 sq. km) of flora, wildlife, hiking trails, campgrounds and of course, Joshua trees.

North and northeast

The grandeur of the **San Bernardino** and **San Gabriel** mountains offers a welcome respite from the often smog-laden, congested valleys. From the romantically named **Rim of the World Highway** (take Route 18 out of San Bernardino) there are phenomenal views of orange groves to one side and the **Mojave Desert** at the other. **Lake Arrowhead** and **Big Bear ㉒** are both popular destinations for summer and winter recreational sports, or just relaxing.

North of Pasadena (take Interstate 210 and then Route 2 north of La Cañada-Flintridge), the magnificent Angeles Crest Highway, way above **Mount Wilson Observatory** (open Saturday and Sunday 10am–4pm), offers awesome views of 10,000-foot Mount Baldy and other impressive snow-capped peaks.

La Cañada ㉓ is home of the celebrated **Descanso Gardens**, a 165-acre collection of flowers and shrubs – camellias, roses, lilacs, azaleas, orchids, blooming on different schedules throughout the year – which can be crossed by tram or by foot along petal-strewn paths (open daily 9am–4.30pm except Christmas). There's also a **Japanese Tea House**, **bird sanctuary**, and **art gallery**.

Maps:
Area 254
City 263

The Joshua Tree National Park is very popular with rock climbers. There are many ranger-led activities; tel: 760/367-5500.

BELOW: Joshua Tree National Park.

Interstate 210 continues northwest through Sylmar to intersect with Interstate 5 a few miles before Valencia, site of **Six Flags Magic Mountain**  *(see page 246).*

The name **Valencia** has for a long time been associated with oranges, and the region does indeed still harvest the juicy fruit from more than 10 million trees. Those in the coastal valleys give off their crop in summer, with the navel oranges of the warmer interior region ripening in winter.

For a bit of western history, see the 264-acre (107-hectare) **William S. Hart Park** in nearby **Newhall**, whose Spanish-style castle, Horseshoe Ranch, was formerly the silent-movie star's home. Before he died at the age of 81 in 1946, Hart stipulated in his will that no admission be charged. Visitors can view the furnishings and Wild West artifacts, roam the nature trails, and admire the collection of animals, including a herd of rare buffalo donated by Walt Disney (open daily 10am–sunset; conducted tours most days).

Before visiting Magic Mountain, if you're in a car, an educational side trip can be north to the **Edmonston pumping plant** (take the Grapevine offramp from Interstate 5) of the California State Water Project. This is where all that water from the San Joaquin River gets its boost over the Tehachapi Mountains. The plant is open weekdays to all comers; but to see the immense, 30-ft (9-meter) pumps in action, you must call in advance to book a tour (tel: 661/858 5509).

The great **California Aqueduct**, in which the water is carried, stretches the entire length of **Antelope Valley** to cross the highway at the foot of **Cajon Pass**.

At the top of the Pass, seismologists have been drilling into the earth's core in the hope of improving their predictions about future earthquakes. The best-

BELOW: *the* way to get around – rollerblading in Santa Barbara.

known (but by no means the only) earthquake threat in California comes from the **San Andreas Fault**, a meeting place for the American and Pacific "plates", 60 miles (100 km) thick, which grind past each other at a rate of 2 inches (5 cm) a year, enough to cause the kind of cataclysmic disturbance that can demolish anything man-made.

Northbound on Interstate 5 and then Highway 14 will bring you to **Devil's Punchbowl County Park** ❷ (open sunrise–sunset) where evidence of this power can be seen in the gigantic rocks and tumbled sandstone slabs resulting from 13 million years of convulsions.

From the pine-shaded park at an elevation of 4,700 ft (1,430 meters) there's a view of the centuries-old trees fringing Mount Baden Powell, which towers another 5,000 ft (1,520 meters) above. Farther to the east, at **San Juan Bautista State Historic Park**, there's a 400-yard Earthquake Walk at the seismographic station set up by the US Geological Survey.

For other points of interest head out on Highway 14 to what is known as the High Desert, site of **Edwards Air Force Base** ❷, the premier flight-testing facility for over 50 years and the place where Chuck Yeager first broke Mach 1 in 1947. Since then pilots at Edwards have broken Mach 2, 3, 4, 5, and 6, and flown as high as 300,000 ft (90,000 meters) – almost into space. Base tours are available Tuesday–Saturday 9am–5pm; tours are also available at nearby Blackbird Park, home to the fastest plane ever built, the SR-71; tel: 601/277-8050.

Santa Barbara pelicans are a common sight.

Not far away in Victorville is the **Roy Rogers Museum**, highlighting moments in the career of Hollywood's famous singing cowboy, his wife Dale Evans, and, of course, his trusty horse, Trigger.

BELOW: sax player on El Paseo, Santa Barbara.

Interstate 5 is the major northbound route for those heading up to San Francisco and beyond. For most of the way it traverses blessedly undeveloped, yet boring countryside. Just outside the LA county line, it passes **Castaic Lake** ❷, the major reservoir to store water brought from the north and from where the water heads through 20-ft (6-meter) concrete pipes down into the city. The enormous **Castaic Dam** creates a popular recreational area for fishing, water-skiing, boating, and other relaxations.

The dam is the last interesting view before the highway heads up into the narrow pass through the mountains and down into a barren valley known as the **Grapevine**. In an international event which he echoed in Japan, the artist Christo lined this valley with yellow umbrellas.

Between Interstate 5 and the coast is **Los Padres National Forest**, at the western side of which is **Santa Barbara**. To get there you can take scenic Highway 126, just north of Valencia, which travels through the valley (the same one the disastrous 1928 dam break flooded) and citrus orchards of the quaint farming towns **Fillmore** ❸ and **Santa Paula** and ends up in Ventura; or you can retrace your steps and take Highway 101, which veers off the Hollywood Freeway in North Hollywood.

The Pacific Coast Highway joins up with Highway 101 at Oxnard, a city about 40 miles (64 km) north of Malibu. A bit east of where they join are two interesting diversions – located in Simi Valley, the **Ronald**

Reagan Library (open daily 10am–5pm) is located on 100 acres (40 hectares), with a view of the Pacific. The largest of the Presidential Libraries, it houses millions of documents and photos from the Reagan years, and more than 100,000 gifts to the Reagans (including 2,000 from foreign heads of state), including a de-activated nuclear missile and a piece of the Berlin Wall.

Nearby in Newbury Park is the **Stagecoach Inn Museum** (open Wednesday–Sunday 1pm–4pm), a re-creation of an 1876 inn along the Butterfield Stage route after the original burned down in 1970.

Just before Oxnard is **Point Mugu** ㉛, a wetlands **Wildlife Sanctuary** adjoining the Navy's Pacific Missile Test Center which is used as a winter home by as many as 10,000 birds comprising scores of different species. There's a vista point beside the highway near **Point Mugu Rock**. Every April the Point Mugu Naval Air Station hosts one of California's largest air shows.

Oxnard ㉜ is chiefly renowned for its annual **Strawberry Festival** in May, although the crop can be sampled from numerous roadside stands throughout the growing season. There's a convenient stand at Las Posas Road, a bypass from and back to the main highway which offers a chance to avoid the downtown traffic congestion.

In addition to some lovely Victorian houses, Oxnard is home to the **Carnegie Art Museum** (open Thursday–Saturday 10am–5pm, Sunday 1–5pm) and has a **Fisherman's Wharf** shipping and dining area which has been modeled after a New England trading port.

The wharf is also a jump-off point for the offshore **Channel Islands** ㉝ – individually known as San Miguel, Santa Rosa, Santa Cruz, and Anacapa – which can also be visited from Ventura.

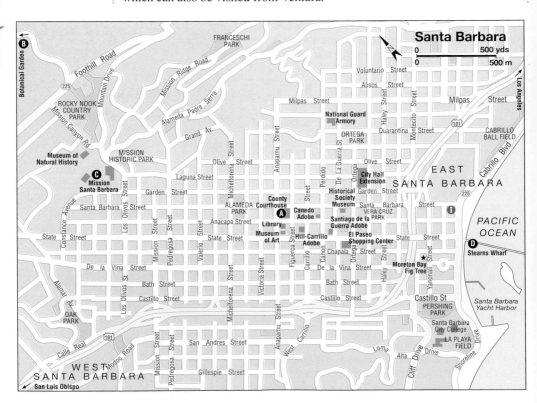

Ventura and the Channel Islands

Ventura **③④** is the site of the restored **San Buenaventura Mission**, ninth and last of the group to be built (in 1782) under the supervision of Father Junípero Serra (museum and store open Monday–Friday 10am–5pm, Saturday 9am–5pm, Sunday 10am–4pm; church open daily dawn–dusk).

 Map on page 254

Much of the area's fascinating history is recorded in the nearby **County Museum of Art**. The museum (open Tuesday–Sunday 10am–5pm) also displays an unusual collection of one-quarter lifesize and astonishingly lifelike characters known as George Stuart Historical Figures.

In addition to what remains of the century-old Chinese community centered around the Chinatown-Figueroa Mall, the 1856 **Ortega Adobe**, the even more beautiful 1841 **Olivas Adobe**, and **Main Street**'s plethora of antique shops, the city has a bustling waterfront area around the pier from which sightseeing excursions are offered all year round by Channel Island Adventures and Island Packers. Most of the trips are to the largely uninhabited islands across the **Santa Barbara Channel**.

A mural evokes the beauty of the ocean in Santa Barbara.

Santa Rosa and Santa Cruz islands are privately owned, although they can be visited with permission. **San Miguel** and tiny **Anacapa** islands are operated by the National Park Service, whose dedicated rangers work hard to preserve their fragile ecosystem. Sea lions, seals, dolphins, and varied birdlife are the rewards of a visit to the islands (one to three hours for the crossing), and overnight camping is permitted on tiny Anacapa. However, visitors must bring everything needed, including an ample supply of water.

North of Ventura, Routes 33 and then 150 lead through "Shangri La" valley (it was featured as such in the 1937 movie *Lost Horizon*) to the charming town of **Ojai ③⑤**, whose year-round temperatures have been attracting residents since the valley was first settled centuries ago by Chumash Indians. The Chumash were responsible for the name, which means "the valley of the nesting moon."

BELOW: statue of Father Junípero Serra at the Old Mission in Santa Barbara.

Today's Ojai (population: 7,000), with its charming Spanish-style buildings, owes most of its origins to millionaire industrialist Edward Drummond Libby (of the Libby Owens glass firm) who commissioned the award-winning Pasadena architect Wallace Neff to design a rambling adobe hacienda clubhouse for the town's golf course.

This commission eventually became the **Ojai Valley Inn**, a historic, self-contained resort complex, whose luxurious attractions now include tennis, lawn croquet, swimming, and horseback riding. The town itself is centered around a solitary main street lined with shops, a handful of restaurants, and the spectacular tower on top of the post office (another Libby creation). Local history is documented at the **Ojai Valley Historical Society and Museum**, open Wednesday–Monday 1–4pm.

Residents fight fiercely against potential changes – on some streets cars must circle around trees – and maintain a sophisticated cool about the famous faces in their midst. Paul Newman, Larry Hagman, and Chris Evert are no different than the boy (or girl) next door in the picturesque Ojai community.

Maps:
Area 254
City 268

Santa Barbara and beyond

Santa Barbara ❸ is probably the most harmonious-looking city in California, largely because an earthquake destroyed much of the previous community in the 20th century. The city was reconstructed under a code that strictly mandated what was acceptable. The predominant style is Colonial Spanish. The graceful look of earlier centuries combined with the comfort and convenience of more recent times make Santa Barbara a beautiful town.

From the roof of the **Courthouse** Ⓐ (whose interior features hand-painted ceilings, giant murals, and imported tiles) the view includes gently sloping red-tile roofs interspersed with white facades and towering palm trees. The grassy lawn below has a sunken area which serves for gatherings, performances, and the occasional wedding; opposite is the magnificent library and art museum.

A short walk away are flawlessly restored adobes, the military buildings from the Colonial era, and an enticingly picturesque shopping center called **El Paseo**; at the northern end of town are the tranquil paths and trails of the **Botanical Garden** Ⓑ.

In the distance is **Mission Santa Barbara** Ⓒ, generally regarded as the most beautiful of all the 21 missions that lined El Camino Real between San Diego and San Francisco. Heavily damaged by earthquakes in 1812 and 1925, it was lovingly rebuilt in the 1950s and now serves as a parish church as well as welcoming visitors every day.

Santa Barbara's main thoroughfare, **State Street**, leads down to century-old **Stearns Wharf** Ⓓ, with its seafood stands, marine displays, wine-tasting rooms, souvenir shops, and fishing.

Whale-watching boat trips set off daily from February to April and sightings of the enormous 45-ton mammals, often accompanied by their newborn calves, are expected, but not guaranteed. To the west and east of the pier, public beaches line the coast for miles. There is an airport 8 miles (13 km) north of town. Santa Barbara is also served by Greyhound buses and Amtrak. The drive from Los Angeles takes less than three hours.

Within easy range of Santa Barbara are a vast number of other possibilities. Just south of town are the luxurious **Four Seasons Biltmore Hotel** (favored as a press HQ when President Reagan was at his ranch in the mountains), the **Mondaytecito Inn** (built by Charlie Chaplin as a refuge for Hollywood stars), and the charming seaside village of **Summerland** with its hilltop Inn on Summer Hill.

To the east are the lovely **Santa Ynez Valley**, which offers scores of wineries to visit, plus the touristy cute town of **Solvang** ❸, with its Danish architecture, windmills, and bakeries.

To the north, US 101 follows the coast before turning inland to bypass numerous seaside resorts. (Check out the quaint but growing **San Luis Obispo** ❸ and its Thursday night street markets.)

The most famous of these resorts is undoubtedly **San Simeon** ❸, with its grandiose **Hearst Castle** owned by William Hearst (open daily except Thanksgiving, Christmas and New Year; tours begin at 8.20am, last tour varies with sunset). ❏

BELOW: keeping the peace.
RIGHT: one of the swimming pools at San Simeon.

INSIGHT GUIDES

Travel Tips

Insight Guides Website
www.insightguides.com

Don't travel the planet alone. Keep in step with Insight Guides' walking eye, just a click away

New Insight Maps

Maps in Insight Guides are tailored to complement the text. But when you're on the road you sometimes need the big picture that only a large-scale map can provide. This new range of durable Insight Fleximaps has been designed to meet just that need.

Detailed, clear cartography
makes the comprehensive route and city maps easy to follow, highlights all the major tourist sites and provides valuable motoring information plus a full index.

Informative and easy to use
with additional text and photographs covering a destination's top 10 essential sites, plus useful addresses, facts about the destination and handy tips on getting around.

Laminated finish
allows you to mark your route on the map using a non-permanent marker pen, and wipe it off. It makes the maps more durable and easier to fold than traditional maps.

The first titles
cover many popular destinations. They include Algarve, Amsterdam, Bangkok, California, Cyprus, Dominican Republic, Florence, Hong Kong, Ireland, London, Mallorca, Paris, Prague, Rome, San Francisco, Sydney, Thailand, Tuscany, USA Southwest, Venice, and Vienna.

🁢 INSIGHT GUIDES
The world's largest collection of visual travel guides

CONTENTS

Getting Acquainted

Monthly average temperatures

January	18.3°C	65°F	July	27.7°C	82°F
Febuary	19.4°C	67°F	August	28.8°C	84°F
March	20°C	68°F	September	28.3°C	83°F
April	20.5°C	69°F	October	25.6°C	78°F
May	22.2°C	72°F	November	22.8°C	73°F
June	23.8°C	75°F	December	20.6°C	69°F

The Place

Area: City, 467 sq. miles; LA County, 4,083 sq. miles. Situated 120 miles north of San Diego, 450 miles south of San Francisco, and 270 miles west of Las Vegas.
Highest point: Mount San Antonio (10,000 ft above sea level)
Population: City, 3.7 million; LA County, 9.7 million; LA Five County Area (LA, Riverside, Ventura, Orange, San Bernardino), 16.3 million
Language: The native language is English but as more than one third of Los Angeles' population is Hispanic, Spanish is spoken in many parts of town. The culture and customs of LA are influenced by its Mexican heritage.
Currency: US dollars
Weights and measures: imperial
1 inch = 2.54 centimeters
1 foot = 30.48 centimeters
1 mile = 1.609 kilometers
1 quart = 1.136 liters
1 ounce = 28.4 grams
1 pound = 0.453 kilograms
1 yard = 0.9144 meters
Electricity: 110 volts. European appliances will require a voltage adaptor. Some hotel bathrooms have electrical outlets suitable for European appliances but an adaptor is useful.
State Bird: The California quail, "noted for its strength and adaptability"
Country dialing code: 1

Climate

The urban area has a pleasantly sunny climate with low humidity throughout the year and an average of 329 days of sunshine.

It is one of the few places in the world where you can ski in the morning and surf in the afternoon. It is not uncommon for the temperature to vary 30–40°F (17–20°C) as you travel from mountains to deserts to the beach.

There is no drastic change of seasons, each one seguing almost imperceptibly into the next, wth the main difference being that rain can be expected for the first three or four months of the year and very little again until winter.

Los Angeles is very pleasant May through October when the temperature rarely drops below 72°F (22°C) during the day. November through April, the "winter" months, the daytime temperatures usually stay above 65°F (18°C). In the summer months the humidity is usually low, so discomfort is rare. The famous LA smog is at its worst in August and September.

Time Zone

California is entirely in the Pacific Time Zone, which is two hours behind Chicago, three hours behind New York and eight hours behind London (nine hours during Daylight Savings Time). On the first Sunday in April, the clock is moved ahead one hour for Daylight Savings Time. On the last Sunday in October the clock is moved back one hour to return to Standard Time.

Local dialing codes

As computer modems, fax machines and mobile phones proliferate in gizmo-happy Los Angeles, the state keeps adding codes at a dizzy rate: as we go to press these are correct, but if in doubt, call the operator.

213 is Downtown Los Angeles
323 surrounds Downtown and includes Hollywood, West Hollywood, and Eagle Rock
310 is the western section, including Beverly Hills, West LA, and the coastal area stretching from Malibu south through Santa Monica,Venice, Manhattan Beach, Hermosa Beach, Redondo Beach, Torrance and Palos Verdes
562 is Long Beach, Downey, and Whittier
818 is the San Fernando Valley, including Glendale, Burbank, Sherman Oaks, Encino, and Calabasas
626 is the San Gabriel Valley including Pasadena
909 includes the San Bernardino and Riverside areas
661 is the Santa Clarita and Valencia area
805 is Thousand Oaks north to Ventura and Santa Barbara
714 is North Orange County including Anaheim, Santa Ana, and Huntington Beach
949 is South Orange County including Newport Beach, Irvine, Laguna Beach, San Juan Capistrano, and Dana Point
760 is North San Diego County including Carlsbad and stretching east and north including Palm Springs
858 is North Central San Diego County including Del Mar and La Jolla
619 is the San Diego city area

Economy

Business and management services (advertising, computer programming, legal services, engineering) are in top place with tourism a close second.

More than 4,000 businesses are associated with the motion picture and television industries and comprise a $20 billion annual business, employing over 150,000 people. The city's ports together are responsible for more import/export business than any other in the United States.

California's economy is the world's sixth largest, its agricultural crops and livestock bringing in around $17.5 billion each year.

Local Government

The Mayor and 15 elected Council members handle the city's day-to-day business. The council elect a President at their first meeting in July of alternate years.
The City Council's work is handled by 15 committees with each member of the Council heading one committee and serving on two others. Councilors serve four-year staggered terms and their ordinances are subject to the mayor's final approval or veto. The veto can be overruled by mustering a larger vote than was necessary to pass the ordinance.

10 Facts About LA

1. Although Los Angeles itself is the biggest by far, there are 87 other incorporated cities in Los Angeles County, of which Vernon (population 85) is the smallest.

2. The Five Counties (LA, Riverside, Ventura, Orange, San Bernardino) would be the 11th largest world economy if they formed a separate country.

3. The LA County coastline from Malibu to Long Beach is 72 miles (116 km) long, and averages beach attendance of 53.8 million people a year.

4. LA, whose inhabitants between them speak nearly 100 languages, has the highest concentration of Mexicans outside Mexico, the most Thais outside Thailand and more Koreans than any city outside Seoul.

5. Los Angeles is the No.1 import/export port in the US.

6. The world's longest mural, the 2,500-ft *Great Wall of Los Angeles*, beside the Los Angeles River in East LA, tells the story of ethnic pride; and the world's largest mural is an ocean landscape on the exterior of the Long Beach Arena.

7. All palm trees are not alike: 25 different varieties line LA streets.

8. The LA area is the headquarters of auto design with General Motors, Ford, Chrysler, Honda, Mazda, Nissan, Toyota, Volkswagen and Volvo all locating their design centers here.

9. Fourteen Rembrandt masterpieces can be found in four LA museums – more than any other US city outside New York.

10. Sprawling Los Angeles has the largest street system in the US, requiring 1,500 workers and $75 million per year to maintain.

Planning the Trip

What to Wear

Los Angeles attire is casual, especially near the beaches. So if you opt for skimpy clothing in the daytime, bring along sun screen. A few restaurants require jackets and ties for men, but most don't. Unless you are visiting the mountain areas, the moderate climate makes heavy clothing unnecessary. Light jackets are needed for summer evenings and bring wool coats during the winter. Expect rain in winter and springtime.

Entry Regulations

Most foreign travelers to the US must have a passport and a visa and, depending on where you are coming from, a health record. In addition, you must make prior arrangements to leave the country. Those exempt from these rules are:
● British and Canadian citizens
● British subjects from Bermuda or Canada entering from the western hemisphere
● Certain government officials
Any person who enters the United States can visit Mexico or Canada for a period of less than 30 days and still be re-admitted to the US without a new visa. Visas can be obtained from any US embassy. If a visitor loses his or her visa while in the US, a new one may be obtained from the embassy of the visitor's home country. Extensions are granted by the US Immigration and Naturalization Service, 425 I Street, Washington, DC 20536, tel: 202/ 514-2000.
Extension to Stay: Most visitors are given a six-month visa. If after

six months you wish to stay longer, contact the immigration office. Obtaining a six-month extension is usually not a problem.

Customs

Whether or not they have anything to declare, all people entering the country must go through US Customs. It can prove to be a time-consuming process, but to speed things up, be prepared to open your luggage for inspection and keep the following restrictions in mind:

● There is no limit to the amount of money you can bring in with you. If the amount exceeds $10,000, however, you must fill out a report.

● Anything you have for your own personal use may be brought in duty- and tax-free.

● Adults are allowed to bring in 1 liter (or quart) of alcohol for personal use. You are also allowed to bring in 200 cigarettes, 50 cigars (Cuban prohibited) or 2kg (4.4lbs) of tobacco. An additional 100 cigars may be brought under your gift exemption, but no additional alcohol.

● You can bring in gifts valued at less than $4,100 duty- and tax-free. Anything over $4,100 is subject to duty charges and taxes. Families cannot group their individual exemptions into one single gift.

● Dogs, cats and other animals may be brought into the country with certain restrictions. The US has no quarantine for pets, but does require a **rabies certificate** which shows that the shot was administered either 30 days to one year prior to arrival, or 30 days to three years before disembarking. Some airlines require health certificates. California has its own regulations, and certain animals are prohibited. Check first with the California Department of Fish and Game, tel: 916/653-7664, www.dfg.ca.gov

For national details, contact the US consulate nearest you or write to the US Department of Agriculture, www.usda.gov

● You are not allowed to bring in food items, seeds, plants,

narcotics, fireworks or hazardous items. Customs officials are strict, particularly about food and narcotics.

● Automobiles may be driven into the States if they are for the personal use of the visitor, family and guests only.

US Customs, 1301 Constitution Avenue NW, Washington, DC, tel: 202/566-8195; www.customs. ustreas.gov

Health and Medical Services

If you need medical assistance, consult the local *Yellow Pages* for the physician or pharmacist nearest you. In large cities, there is usually a physician referral service number listed. If you need immediate attention, go directly to a hospital emergency room. Most emergency rooms are open 24 hours a day.

There is nothing cheap about being ill in the United States. It is essential to be armed with adequate medical insurance and to carry an identification card or policy number at all times. If expense is a concern, turn first to county hospitals, which offer good service and do not charge indigent patients.

In the case of an emergency dial **911** from any telephone for the police, fire department or ambulance service.

Here are some of the larger hospitals in the LA area:

Cedars-Sinai Medical Center, 8700 Beverly Boulevard, LA (Beverly Hills area) tel: 310/855-5000.

City of Hope, 1500 E Duate Boulevard, Duarte (Pasadena area) tel: 818/359-8111.

Daniel Freeman Marina, 4650 Lincoln Boulevard (Marina Del Rey area), tel: 310/823-8911.

Hollywood Presbyterian Medical Center, 1300 N Vermont Avenue, tel: 213/413-3000.

Little Company of Mary, 4101 Torrance Boulevard (South Bay), tel: 310/540-7676.

St John's, 1328 22nd Street, Santa Monica, tel: 310/829-5511.

UCLA, 10833 Le Conte Avenue,

(West LA) tel: 310/825-9111.
USC/LA County, 1200 N State Street, (East LA) tel: 213/226-2622.

Public Holidays

Most federal, state and municipal offices as well as banks are closed on the following holidays:

• **January:** New Year's Day. Martin Luther King Day.

• **February:** President's Day. March or April: Easter Sunday.

• **May:** Memorial Day.

• **July:** Independence Day (July 4).

• **September:** Labor Day.

• **October:** Columbus Day.

• **November:** Veterans' Day. Thanksgiving and following day.

• **December:** Christmas Day.

Some businesses and banks close on: **Lincoln's Birthday** (February 12) and **Good Friday** (Friday before Easter Sunday).

Money Matters

TRAVELERS' CHECKS

Since visitors may face problems changing foreign currency, it is better to use American-dollar travelers' checks. When lost or stolen, most travelers' checks can be replaced and they are accepted in most stores, restaurants, and hotels. Banks readily cash large travelers' checks, although be sure to take along your passport. Smaller denomination travelers' checks (provided you have adequate identification) are usually accepted for purchases in large stores and supermarkets.

EXCHANGE

Changing money in Los Angeles is not as easy as it is in many other parts of the world. **American Express** has locations at 327 N Beverly Drive, Beverly Hills, tel: 310/274-8277 and 8493 W 3rd Street near La Cienega, tel: 310/659-1682.

Also in Beverly Hills at 433 N Beverly Drive, tel: 310/274-7610, is **Associated Foreign Exchange**.

Foreign currency can be exchanged in the departure halls of every terminal at **Los Angeles International Airport**, tel: 310/568-8066, and at the Los Angeles Currency Exchange, tel: 310/646-9346, in the arrival hall of Tom Bradley International Terminal, as well as Terminals 2,5 and 6 (hours vary with terminal). Tel: 310/649-2801 for exchange rates. Also, Bank of America operates Automated Teller Machines (ATMs) on Arrival and Departure floors of every terminal.

Downtown, currency can be exchanged at **American Express**, 901 W 7th Street, tel: 213/627-4800, and at **Bank of America Foreign Currency**, 525 S Flower Street, tel: 213/312-9000. Most banks will change currency only for regular customers but there are exceptions.

CASH

Most banks belong to a network of ATMs which dispense cash 24 hours a day.

CREDIT CARDS

Not all credit cards are accepted at all places, but most places accept either Visa, American Express, or MasterCard. Major credit cards can also be used to withdraw cash from ATMs. (Look for an ATM that uses one of the banking networks indicated on the back of your credit card, such as Plus, Cirrus, and Interlink.) There will be a charge for this transaction.

TAX

The Los Angeles County sales tax is currently 8.25 percent. Sales tax applies primarily to non-food purchases (except meals eaten in a restaurant).

Getting There

BY AIR

The area's largest airport **Los Angeles International Airport** (LAX), is on LA's westside, practically on the beach, approximately 20 minutes from Downtown LA. LAX serves more than 60 major airlines and is the third busiest in the world in passenger traffic. (The airport website, **not** airline information, is www.lawa.org).

Business Services at LAX include notary, travel insurance, postage, hotel reservations, fax, photocopy, computers, and meeting rooms. There are business centers in Terminals 1, 3, 4, 7, and Tom Bradley International, open from 6am-midnight. Call 310/646-7934 for more information.

There are lockers for storage in every terminal, with charges for every 30-minute increment (24-hour limit in the Bradley Terminal). The lockers are in various sizes, the largest being 20in wide x 36in high x 32in deep (51cm x 92 x 82). Large items such as golf bags, surfboards and bikes can be stored at Bag Storage at the upper/departure level of the Bradley Terminal. They also offer packing and wrapping services, and baggage repair. Tel: 310/640-0222 or 640-0223; open 6am–11pm daily. For LAX Airport Police Lost and Found, tel: 310/417-0440.

For airline information, all the numbers bellow are free. Call 1-800 and then the number listed, or check their website:
Aero California: 237-6225
Air France: 237-2747; www.airfrance.fr
Air New Zealand: 262-1234; www.airnz.com
Alitalia: 223-5730; www.alitalia.it
All Nippon: 235-9262; www.ana.co.jp
Asiana: 227-4262; www.flyasiana.com
Aeromexico: 237-6639; www.aeromexico.com
Alaska Airlines: 252-7522; www.alaska-air.com
America West: 235-9292; www.americawest.com

American Airlines: 433-7300; www.aa.com
British Airways: 247-9297; www.british-airways.com
Canadian Airlines: 426-7000; www.cdnair.ca
Cathay Pacific: 233-2742; www.cathaypacific-air.com
Continental Air: 523-3273; www.flycontinental.com
Delta Airlines: 325-1999; www.delta-air.com
Finnair: 950-5000; www.finnair.fi
Hawaiian Airlines: 367-5320; www.hawaiianair.com
Iberia: 772-4642; www.iberia.dk
Japan Airlines: 525-3663; www.japanair.com
KLM Royal Dutch: 374-7747; www.klm.nl
Korean Air: 438-5000; www.koreanair.com
LanChile Airlines; 735-5526; www.lanchile.com
Lufthansa: 645-3880; www.lufthansa-usa.com
Malaysia: 228-0585; www.malaysianairlines.com.my
Mexicana: 531-7921; www.mexicana.com
Midwest Express: 452-2022; www.midwestexpress.com
Northwest: 225 2525; www.nwa.com
Qantas: 227-4500; www.qantas.com
Reno Air: 736-6247
Sabena: 955-2000; www.sabena-usa.com
SAS Scandinavian: 221-2350; www.flysas.com
Singapore: 742-3333; www.singaporeair.com
Southwest: 435-9792; www.southwest.com
Swissair: 221-4750; www.swissair.com
Tahoe Air: 824-6324
Thai International: 426-5204; www.thaiair.com
Tower Air: 34-Tower; www.towerair.com
TWA: 221-2000; www.twa.com
United: 241-6522; www.ual.com
US Airways: 428-4322; www.usairways.com
VASP Brazilian: 732-8277; www.vasp.com.br

Virgin Atlantic: 862-2746; www.fly.virgin.com
Approximately 20 minutes north of Downtown LA is the **Burbank/ Glendale/Pasadena Airport**, tel: 818/840-8840, www.bur.com, which is served by six carriers: Alaska, American, America West, Skywest, Southwest, and United. There are some international flights to Canada, Mexico, and Taiwan. An Amtrak train station is next door, and there are bus, shuttle, and taxi services available.

An hour east of of the city is **Ontario International Airport**, tel: 909/937-1256; www.lawa.org, served by nine carriers: Alaska, American, America West, Continental, Delta, Northwest, Southwest, TWA, and United/United Express. Bus, shuttle, and taxi services are available.

Approximately 30 minutes south of Downtown LA is the tiny **Long Beach Airport**, tel: 562/570-2600; www.lgb.org, which is great for getting quickly in and out of but is only served by three airlines: American, America West, and Allegiant Air.

An hour south of LA is the **Orange County John Wayne Airport**, tel: 949/252-5200; www.ocair.com. It is served by the same airlines as Ontario listed above, plus US Airways. Located on the border of Newport Beach/Santa Ana, it is convenient to all Orange County attractions (although only about 20 minutes closer to Disneyland and Knott's than LAX).

BY SHIP

San Pedro is Los Angeles' official port, where 400 cruise ships dock annually, making it the busiest US harbor for passenger ships outside Florida. The *Queen Elizabeth II* is the most illustrious visitor, but several cruise lines – including Carnival and Royal Caribbean – operate roundtrip excursions from the port. Check out www.sanpedro.com/spcom/harbor.htm for more information.

BY TRAIN

The city's 50-year-old Downtown train station, **Union Station**, still has its original woodwork and lavish furnishings. **Amtrak** provides transportation throughout Southern California. The *Sunset Limited* from New Orleans, stops at Indio, Ontario and Pomona before reaching Los Angeles. The *San Diegan* runs between Los Angeles and San Diego, with stops at Santa Ana, San Juan Capistrano, Oceanside. and Delmar.

The state is tied together by the *Coast Starlight*, which travels north from Los Angeles all the way to Seattle, stopping at Glendale, Simi Valley, Oxnard, Santa Barbara, San Luis Obispo, San Jose, Oakland (from where there's a bus transfer to San Francisco before the route continues), Martinez, Davis, Sacramento, Marysville, Richmond, Chico, Reading, and on across the Oregon border. The Coast Starlight offers bedrooms for couples and families and has a special bedroom available for people with disabilities. For more information, tel: 800/872-7245 or www.amtrak. com

BY BUS

Greyhound Trailways bus company brings visitors to Southern California from all over the country. Unlimited mileage bus passes can be purchased, either a 7-day pass, a 15-day pass, or a 30-day pass. Children travel at reduced fares. For more information tel: Greyhound Trailways: 800/229-9424; www.greyhound.com

Green Tortoise is a "hippie bus" which aids and abets young travelers bound for San Francisco or the east coast, and also does excursions to Alaska, Mexico, and Costa Rica. LA's terminal is at TV Cafe, 1777 E Olympic at Alameda in Downtown LA, with scheduled pickups in Santa Monica at the AYH Youth Hostel, 1434 2nd Street. Information about schedules is available on 800/867-8647 or www.greentortoise.com

BY CAR

Southern California has a massive, intertwining freeway system that can be great if you understand maps and have ample patience. The following guide should be helpful. If you require additional information, call the Automobile Club of Southern California, tel: 213/741-3686, or check out www. aaa-calif.com
The principal north–south byways are:

Interstate 5 (the Golden State and Santa Ana freeways), which covers the distance from Canada to Mexico via Seattle, Sacramento, Los Angeles and San Diego.

Interstate 15, which transits San Bernardino and San Diego after a long passage from Montana's Canadian border, via Salt Lake City and Las Vegas.

US Highway 101 (the Ventura and Hollywood freeways), which proceeds south down the Pacific Coast from Washington State, crosses San Francisco's Golden Gate Bridge, and ends in Downtown Los Angeles.

State Highway 1 (the Pacific Coast Highway), which hugs the coast from San Diego to San Francisco and further north.
The principal east–west byways are:

Interstate 8, which departs from I-10 at Casa Grande, Arizona and ends in San Diego.

Interstate 10 (the San Bernardino and Santa Monica freeways), which begins on the east coast in Jacksonville, Florida and continues through New Orleans, Houston, El Paso, Tucson and Phoenix before cutting through LA and ending at the coast in Santa Monica.

Interstate 40 which connects Knoxville, Tennessee, with Barstow, California, via Memphis, Oklahoma City, Oklahoma, Albuquerque, and New Mexico.

Other important LA freeways are: **Interstate 210** (the Foothill Freeway), from San Fernando, through the San Fernando and San Gabriel valleys to Pomona. (It continues to San Bernardino from San Dimas as **State 66**.)

Interstate 405 (the San Diego freeway) which covers LA and Orange counties from San Fernando to Santa Ana via Westwood and Long Beach.
Interstate 605 (the San Gabriel River Parkway), Monrovia to Long Beach via Whittier.
State Highway 110 (the Harbor freeway) connects Pasadena with Long Beach via Downtown LA.
State Highway 55 (the Newport Freeway), connects east Anaheim with Newport Beach.
State Highway 57 (the Orange Freeway), connects Pomona with Santa Ana.
State Highway 60 (the Pomona Freeway), connects Downtown LA with Beaumont via Pomona and Riverside.
State Highway 91 (the Artesia freeway), connects Torrance with San Bernardino via Anaheim and Riverside.
State Highway 710 (the Long Beach Freeway), connects East Los Angeles with Long Beach.
State Highway 105 (the Century Freeway), which connects LAX to the 405, 110, and east to Norwalk.

Maps

Insight Map: Los Angeles combines clear and detailed cartography with essential information about the city, making it the ideal map to carry. Its laminated finish makes it durable and easy to fold, and you can easily scribble directions on it with a non-permanent marker pen.
The serious urban explorer should also acquire the *Thomas Guide*. This "map" is really a book which charts every street in Los Angeles. The Thomas Guide can be found in any library or bookstore or from Thomas Brothers at 521 West 6th Street, tel: 213/ 627-4018.
The **Automobile Association of Southern California**, with various branches in the area (consult your phone book or www.aaa-calif.com), has many different street maps of the area as well as maps of California, Mexico and other states. It is well worth joining if you are going to be driving here

because the cost of being towed after a single breakdown might well be less than the annual membership fee. Other good sources for maps are the **California Map & Travel Center**, a well-stocked bookstore at 3312 Pico Boulevard, tel: 310/829-6277; and the **Hosteling International Travel Center** which sells travel accessories and Eurail passes. Both are well stocked with travel books.

Motoring Advice

Keep in mind that the national speed limit on all interstate highways in now 65 miles per hour (105 km/h), and 55 miles per hour (88 km/h) on most other local highways. California law requires that every passenger wears a seat belt, that small children and babies be secured in youth or infant seats and that drivers carry a valid license. There is also a state law that requires all motorcycle riders to wear helmets.
A recent innovation in the LA area is the provision of 36 tow trucks patroling the county's 200 miles of freeway from 6–10am and 3–7pm in search of stalled automobiles. Called the Freeway Service Patrol, its operators provide emergency gasoline or offer help in changing tires or towing disabled cars to some public place with a telephone.
If you plan on driving any distance, it's a good idea to join the American Automobile Association ("Triple A," it's often referred to, based at 811 Gatehouse Road, Falls Church, VA 22047, tel: 703/222-6334) or a similar organization (Automobile Association of Southern California is a branch of AAA). In addition to emergency road service, AAA offers maps, guidebooks, insurance, bail bond protection and a $200 arrest certificate to its members.
Travelers should check local listings for the AAA office closest to them. There are reciprocal

arrangements with many international AAA organizations, such as the AA in Great Britain, and those in Australia, Germany, etc.

DESERT AND MOUNTAIN TRAVEL

A word of caution for desert travelers: the single most important precaution you can take is to tell someone your destination, route and expected time of arrival. Check tires carefully before long stretches of desert driving. Heat builds pressure, so have them at slightly below normal air pressure. The desert's arid climate makes carrying extra water – both for passengers and vehicles – one of the essentials. Carry at least one gallon per person. Keep an eye on the gas gauge. It's a good idea to have more gasoline than you think you need. Remember, if you should have car trouble or become lost, do not strike out on foot. A car, visible from the air and presumably on a road, is easier to spot than a person, and it affords shelter from the weather. Wait to be found rather than pursue your rescuers.
Mountain drivers are advised to be equally vigilant about weather conditions. Winter storms in the Sierras occasionally close major roads, and at times chains are required on tires. Phone ahead for road conditions before you depart.

Practical Tips

Business Hours

Most businesses are open 9am–5pm, with many of the city's ubiquitous shopping malls open as late as 9pm. Many large supermarkets and numerous restaurants now stay open 24 hours. Banks usually remain open until at least 3pm from Monday–Thursday, and until 6pm on Friday. Some banks are open for a short time on Saturday, and all are closed on Sunday.

Tipping

It is courteous to show your gratitude for assistance given in the form of a tip. The accepted rate for porters at the airports is $1 or so per bag. Hotel bellboys and porters usually expect the same. A doorman should be tipped if he unloads or parks your car, usually $1 or so. Tip your chambermaids if you stay several days in a small hotel.

Depending upon the quantity and quality of service rendered, 15 to 20 percent of the bill before tax is the going rate for most other help such as taxi drivers, barbers, hairdressers, waiters, waitresses, and bar persons. In some restaurants, the tip or a service charge is included in the bill if it is for a large group.

Religious Services

A religious directory, listing addresses, phone numbers and services for dozens of different denominations, appears in the *Los Angeles Times* every Saturday.

Media

RADIO

There are more than 60 radio stations serving Los Angeles listeners. Formats are often subject to change, but the most popular stations are listed below:

Radio Stations

News: KNX (1070 AM); KMPC (710 AM)
Spanish: KALI (1430 AM); KSKQ (1540 AM); KTNQ (1020 AM)
Urban Contemporary:KACE (103.9 FM); KDAY (1580 FM); KJLH (102.3 FM)
Talk Radio: KFI (640 AM); KABC (790 AM)
Rock: KLOS (95.5 FM); KQLZ (100.3 FM); KROQ (106.7 FM)
Top 40 Pop: KIIS (1150 AM/ 102.7 FM)
Oldies: KGFJ (1230 AM); KODJ (93.1 FM); KRTH (930 AM/ 101.1 FM)

TELEVISION

Including cable TV, there are more than 30 television stations serving the LA area allowing around-the-clock TV viewing. The three major television networks are ABC, CBS and NBC. The Public Television service, PBS, has no commercials and supports itself with grants and donations. Television and radio listings are published in local newspapers. Sunday papers usually have a detailed weekly guide.

NEWSPAPERS AND MAGAZINES

The *Los Angeles Times* became the only daily in town when the Hearst's *Herald Examiner* closed in 1989.

Smaller, daily newspapers serving particular regions include: the *Daily News* in the San Fernando Valley; the *Evening Outlook* in Santa Monica; the *News Pilot* in San Pedro; the *Press Telegram* in Long Beach; and the *Daily Breeze* in the South Bay.

Los Angeles Magazine purchased and incorporated its younger, livelier rival *Buzz* and is the only monthly with service-oriented features and departments. Their monthly listings feature all the local music, art and theater happenings as well as restaurant listings.

Two free weeklies, *LA Weekly* and *New Times,* review plays, movies, art openings, fashions and musical concerts, and compile complete listings of any and all cultural activities – from reggae to ballet to soccer – for that particular week. They are available at most cafes, record stores, or sidewalk boxes.

Municipal libraries offer an abundance of books, including foreign-language, as well as magazines and newspapers. Santa Monica and West Hollywood libraries are especially well supplied. Four newsstands with a vast selection of foreign-language publications are: **World Books and News**, 1652 Cahuenga Boulevard, tel: 323/465-4352; **Westwood International News and Magazine**, 11737 San Vicente Boulevard, tel: 310/447-2080; **Al's Newstand**, 1257 3rd Street Promenade, Santa Monica, tel: 310/ 393-2690; and **LA International News**, 320 S. Pacific Coast Highway, Redondo Beach, tel: 310/374-7530.

Mail

Post offices open between 7 and 9am and usually close at 5pm Monday–Friday. Many of them are also open for a few hours on Saturday morning. All post offices are closed on Sunday. For general and rate information, tel: 800/275-8777 or check www.usps.gov

If you don't know where you will be staying in any particular town, you can receive mail by having it addressed to General Delivery at the main post office in that town. You have to pick up General Delivery mail in person and show proper identification. Near LAX, the **Worldway Postal Center**, 800 W Century Boulevard, tel: 310/337-8841 is open 24 hours a day.

Telephone and Fax

Coin-operated phones can be found anywhere in LA: from public restrooms and gas stations to virtually any street corner. To operate, deposit 20¢, listen for the dial tone, then dial your desired number.
Information assistance can provide telephone listings if no phone book is handy. For either local or long distance information dial 411. For a toll-free number directory dial 1-800-555-1212. For personal calls, take advantage of lower long-distance rates after 5pm on weekdays and during weekends.

 Western Union (tel: 1-800-325-6000) and **International Telephone and Telegraph** (ITT) will take telegram and telex messages as well as money orders over the phone. Check local phone directory, or **411** for local offices.

 Fax machines can be found at most hotels. Public fax companies are located throughout the city, so check the phone directory under "Facsimile" for the fax service nearest you.

Tourist Offices

LOS ANGELES

The main office of the **Los Angeles Convention and Visitors Bureau** is Downtown at 633 W Fifth Street, tel: 213/624-7300 or fax: 213/ 624-9746, and free maps, brochures and information are available both here and at the **Hollywood Visitor Information Center** in the historic Janes House, behind 6541 Hollywood Boulevard, tel: 213/236-2331. Both offices are open daily except Sunday to 5pm. **Beverly Hills Visitors Bureau**, 239 S Beverly Drive, tel: 800/345-2210, is open 8.30am–5pm weekdays. Hotel and restaurant guides are available 9am–5.30pm weekdays at **West Hollywood Convention and Visitors Bureau**, 8687 Melrose Avenue, M-25, tel: 310/289-2525.

REGIONAL OFFICES

Anaheim/Orange County Visitor and Convention Bureau, 800 W Katella Avenue, Anaheim, CA 92802, tel: 714/765-8888, fax: 714/765-8864. Mail: PO Box 4270, Anaheim, CA 92803. E-mail: mail@anaheimoc.org

Value for Money

For a **Family Values Coupon Book** – free – savings on over 50 Orange County attractions, hotels, restaurants, and shops, write to: Department C, 800 W. Katella Avenue. P.O. Box 4270, Anaheim, CA 92803 (include a self-addressed, stamped envelope).

Buena Park Convention and Visitors' Office, 6280 Manchester Boulevard, Suite 103, Buena Park, CA 90621, tel: 714/562-3560; fax: 714/562-3569; 800/541-3953. E-mail: tourbp@buenapark.com
Laguna Beach Visitors Bureau, 252 Broadway, Laguna Beach, CA 92651, tel: 949/497-9229 or 800/877-1115, fax: 949/376-0558; www.lagunabeachinfo.org
Long Beach Area Convention and Visitors' Council, 1 World Trade Center, Suite 300, Long Beach, CA 90831, tel: 562/436-3645 or 800/4LB-STAY, fax: 562/435-5653; golongbeach.org
Newport Beach Conference and Visitors Bureau, 3300 W. Coast Highway, Newport Beach, CA 92663; tel: 949/722-1611 or 800/94-COAST, fax: 949/722-1612; E-mail: info@newportbeach-cvb.com
Palm Springs Desert Resorts Convention and Visitors' Bureau, 69-930 Highway 111, STE 201, Rancho Mirage, CA 92270, tel: 760/770-9000, 800/967-3767, fax: 310/770-9001. E-mail: admin@desert-resorts.com
Santa Barbara Conference and Visitors Bureau, 510 State Street, Santa Barbara, CA 93101, tel: 805/966-9222 or 1-800-927-4688.
San Diego Convention and Visitors Bureau, International Visitors Center, 11 Horton Plaza, San Diego, CA 92101; tel: 619/236-1212, fax: 619/230-7084; E-mail: sdinfo@sandiego.org
San Diego North County Convention and Visitors' Bureau, 720 N Broadway, Escondido, CA 92025, tel: 760/745-4741 or freephone 800/848-3336; www.sandiegonorth.com
Ventura Visitors' and Convention Bureau, 89C South California Street, Ventura, CA 93001, tel: 805/648-2075; www.ventura-usa.com

OTHER TOURIST OFFICES

Australian: 2121 Avenue of the Stars, tel: (310) 552-1988; e-mail: dima-los.angeles@dfat.gov.au
Canada: 550 Hope Street, tel: 213/346-2700, fax: 213/620-8827; www.cdnconsulat-la.com
New Zealand: 501 Santa Monica Boulevard, tel: 310/395-7480; fax: 310/395-5453; www.purenz.com
South Africa: 9841 Airport Boulevard, tel: 310/641-8444.

Consulates

Foreign visitors looking for home country representatives can find listings for consulates in Los Angeles in the *Yellow Pages* of local telephone books, available in libraries and post offices. Alternatively, call "Information" (**411** if calling within town; 1-area code of city-555-1212 if calling from out of town).
Australia: 2049 Century Park E, tel: 310/229-4800
Britain: 11766 Wilshire Boulevard, tel: 310/477-3322; fax: 310/575-1450; www.britainusa.com
Canada: 550 S Hope Street, tel: 213/346-2700; www.cdnconsulat-la.com
Netherlands: 11766 Wilshire Boulevard, tel: 323/268-1598
New Zealand: 12400 Wilshire Boulevard, tel: 310/207-1605
South Africa: 6300 Wilshire Bouevard, tel: 323/651-0902; www.link2southafrica.com

Crime

Los Angeles, like most big cities, has its share of crime. Common sense is your most effective weapon.
• Don't walk alone at night
• Keep an eye on your belongings
• Never leave your car unlocked
• Never leave small children by themselves

Hotels usually warn that they do not guarantee the safety of belongings left in the room. If you have any valuables, you may want to lock them in the hotel safe.

If you are driving, never pick up anyone you don't know, especially if you are alone. Get directions to where you are going ahead of time. Always be wary of who is around you. If you have trouble on the road, stay in the car and lock the doors, turn on your hazard lights and leave the hood (bonnet) up in order to increase your visibility and alert passing police.

If you do happen to run into trouble, dial **911**. The operator will connect you with the emergency service you require: police, ambulance or fire.

Loss of Belongings

If you happen to lose anything valuable while vacationing, report it to the local police department. The officers will have you file a report, and if your lost goods are turned in, they will return them to you as soon as possible.

Most of the airlines and other transportation companies have insurance for lost customer luggage. Ask the company when purchasing your ticket about its insurance policy. Make sure all of your luggage has identification tags. If you leave your luggage at the airport and it is turned in to LAX's lost and found department, someone from that department will usually bring it to you if you are unable to pick it up.

Getting Around

On Arrival

Public transportation is found on LAX's lower level, which is where arriving passengers claim baggage. At this level, there are stops for taxis, LAX shuttles, buses, courtesy trams, and vans in front of each airline terminal. Information boards about ground transport are located in all the baggage claim areas and they are very easy to understand. QuickAID kiosks are in every terminal also, and are operated by touching the symbol or category on the screen that pertains to your interest. Costs and computer printouts are available (although not always in working order). There are also information booths just outside the terminal building.

Shuttles from the airport are reasonably priced, the fare depending on your destination. Among the companies operating 24 hours a day are **Prime Time Shuttle**, tel: 310/641-5039; **LA Xpress**, tel: 310/641-8000; **Best Shuttle**, tel: 310/783-4500, **The Super Shuttle**, tel: 310/782-6600 or 800/554-3146, and **Metropolitan Express**, tel: 310/417-5050. Call them from the terminal *after* you have your bags to let them know you are waiting.

A free shuttle runs to the parking lots, one of which (take bus C to Lot C) is also a terminal for Santa Monica's Big Blue Buses and also those of the Southern California Rapid Transit District (MTA), tel: 213/626-4455 for bus schedules and information. Another line, Oskar J's Red Car Trolleys, tel: 818/501-2217 or 800/458-2388 is now operating between LAX and Downtown, stopping at major tourist attractions. Tickets can be obtained on the trolleys and are valid all day.

Hopping in a taxi at LAX should be avoided if at all possible. Los Angeles' cabs are very expensive – more so than most US cities – and are almost never found driving the streets looking for customers. Taxis can be ordered or found at airports, train stations, bus terminals, and at major hotels. Call **Yellow Cab Co**, tel: 213/808-1000 or **UITD**, tel: 213/462-1088. The **LA Checker Cab Co**, tel: 310/330-3720 also offers vans with wheelchair lifts. An average fare from Los Angeles Airport to Downtown Los Angeles is around $30. At LAX, there is an official line and greeter for licensed taxis outside each terminal baggage claim area. Passengers will be presented with a ticket stating typical fares to major destinations. Only authorized taxis with an official seal on each vehicle are permitted in the airport. Be sure to ignore hotels suggested by the drivers, and accept offers from unlicensed taxis or limos at your own risk.

Free shuttle service is now provided to the Metropolitan Transit Authority – Metro Green Line Light Rail's Aviation Station. Pick up is on the Lower/Arrival level under the LAX Shuttle sign. Check out the MTA bus and Metro Rail routes and schedules at www.mta.net

If you need to shuttle between terminals, step to the island outside any baggage claim area and catch the "A" bus.

Burbank/Glendale/Pasadena Airport is served by City Cab, tel: 818/848-1000.

Public Transportation

LA is notorious for its lack of public transportation, although the new Metro Rail system is slowly nearing completion. The primary public transportation available is the **Southern California Metropolitan Transit Agency bus company (MTA)** offers a discount of 10 percent if you buy booklets of 10 tickets or more. For information and schedules, tel: 213/626-4455 or www.mta.net

Southern California is still in the early stages of implementing its most ambitious public transit plans for half a century which, when completed, will link areas as far apart as Long Beach and Palmdale, 50 miles (80 km) north of the city.

The 400-mile (640-km) system of light rail, subway and other transportation facilities will not be fully in place until 2010, although Metro's Blue Line between Long Beach and Pasadena is already in operation as is part of the Metro Red Line from Downtown heading towards Hollywood, North Hollywood and Canoga Park, and the Metro Green Line to El Segundo. Passengers for Long Beach board at Pico and Flower streets for the one-hour trip, with the last train from LA at 9pm and the last train from Long Beach at 7.50pm. Check the phone number or website above for up-to-date bus and rail schedules.

Taxis

Taxis are reasonable if traveling short- to medium-length distances. They are not advisable for lengthy trips – and LA is really spread out – because of the prohibitive fares. Taxis should be reserved at least an hour in advance. See *On Arrival* for taxi numbers.

Taxi cabs are all the same price. If you are going a long distance, you can usually get the cab driver to give you a fixed rate.

Limousine Services

For a more comfortable, luxurious form of transportation, try limousines. The price does not vary much from company to company:
Carey: tel: 310/670-1166 or 800/336-4646.
Celebrity Car: tel: 323/850-8000.
Commonwealth Limousine Service: tel: 310/399-6666.
Diva Limousines: tel: 310/278-3482 or 800/427-3482.
Fox Limousine: tel: 310/641-9626 or 800/274-4369.
Palos Verdes Limo: tel: 310/544-2777.

Car Rental

The most efficient way to get around LA is to rent a car. You can rent one at the airport, your hotel, or any car rental agency (check the *Yellow Pages* under "Automobile Renting"). Cars often can be delivered to you. Car rental companies all charge basically the same price.

Some of the bigger companies have numerous offices around the city, so consult the phone directory for the one nearest to you. Most require that you be at least 21 years old and possess a valid driver's license and credit card. Foreign travelers may need to produce an international driver's license. If you are insured in the US, you usually do not have to purchase insurance from the rental company. If not, read the rental agency's insurance policy carefully before purchasing the car insurance. Some of the following numbers are free in the US (by dialing 1-800)l:
Alamo: 800/327-9633; www.alamo.com
Avis: 800/831-2847; www.avis.com
Budget: 800/221-1203; www.budgetrentacar.com
Dollar: 800/800-4000; www.dollar.com
Enterprise: 800/736-8222; www.enterprise.com
Hertz: 800/654-3131; www.hertz.com
National: 800/227-7368; www.nationalcar.com
Thrifty: 877/465-3383; www.thrifty.com

Water Transportation

LA has many boat excursions leaving from San Pedro and Long Beach. It is a unique way to see the Pacific coast. **Catalina Express,** Berth 95, PO Box 1391, San Pedro, tel: 310/519-1212, offers daily trips to Catalina, as does **Catalina Cruises,** 320 Golden Shores Road, Long Beach, tel: 800/228-2546 or 562/436-5006. Contact a travel agent for other companies, schedules and prices.

Where to Stay

Reservations

Call in advance and reserve rooms no matter when you are coming. Many establishments require a down-payment or credit card number to guarantee your reservations. When you make your reservation, ask about the hotel's or motel's refund policy on deposits.

Most hotels have toll-free numbers for hotel reservations, which means you do not pay for the long-distance call. The toll-free numbers (numbers that begin with 1-800) listed here apply to the US only, although in many countries you can dial them and pay the cost of the call.

The hotels listed here are grouped according to location: Downtown, Hollywood and Westside, The Coast, the Valleys, and Out of Town.

Price Guide

The price guide indicates rates for a standard double room:
$$$ = (luxury) over $200
$$ = (moderate) $100–200
$ = (inexpensive) under $100

Hotel Listings

Every type of accommodation is available in Los Angeles – from elegant European-style hotels to inexpensive motels rented by the week. The most expensive hotels are situated Downtown and in Beverly Hills, and have the best access to shopping and public transportation. The grander hotels, many of them attractive landmarks in their own right, have concierges who will arrange theater tickets, tours, telexes, limousines with bilingual drivers and airline reservations. Of course, there is no shortage of smaller, cheaper places, too.

LOS ANGELES AIRPORT

Airport Hilton and Towers
5711 W Century Boulevard
Tel: 310/410-4000; fax: 410-6250
www.hilton.com
1200 rooms, with restaurants, pool, jacuzzis, fitness center. **$$$**
Days Inn Airport Center
901 W Manchester Boulevard, Inglewood
Tel: 310/649-0800 or 800/544-8313; fax: 310/649-3837
www.daysinn.com
47 rooms. Near beaches, free LAX shuttle. Restaurant, pool, car rental. **$**
Embassy Suites
1440 E. Imperial Highway
Tel: 310/640-3600 or 800/EMBASSY
www.embassy-suites.com
349 suites, 1 and 2 bedroom, next to I-105, 1 mile south of LAX in beach community of El Segundo. Five minutes to beach, 20 minutes to Downtown. Breakfast included, pool, exercise facilities. **$–$$**
Hampton Inn
10300 La Cienega Boulevard, Inglewood
Tel: 310/846-3200 or 800/HAMTON; fax: 645-6925
148 rooms. Free LAX transportation. Fitness center, spa, free continental breakfast. **$**

DOWNTOWN LA

The Downtown area usually caters to business travelers, but it also attracts shoppers with its jewelry, fashion and flower marts.

Luxury
Hotel Intercontinental at California Plaza
251 S Olive Street
Tel: 213/617-3300 or 800/327-0200; fax: 617-3399
www.interconti.com
Adjoins Museum of Contemporary Art and overlooks water court. Restaurant, lounge, pool, fitness center, free parking. **$$$**
The New Otani Hotel and Garden
120 S Los Angeles Street
Tel: 213/629-1200 or 800/421-8795, in California 800/273-2294; fax: 213/622-0980
www.newotani.com
Deluxe 414-room hotel with two shopping levels and a half acre Japanese Garden. Near the Music Center, court buildings and Little Tokyo. Airport bus service, restaurants, jacuzzi, courtesy coffee, kitchen units, babysitting, most pets OK, foreign currency exchange. **$$$**

Price Guide

The price guide indicates rates for a standard double room:
$$$ = (luxury) over $200
$$ = (moderate) $100–200
$ = (inexpensive) under $100

Regal Biltmore Hotel
506 S Grand
Tel: 213/624-1011; fax: 612-1545
www.thebiltmore.com
Dramatic interiors reflect the blending of classical architecture found in European palaces. Gourmet dining. It was here in 1960 that JFK named LBJ as his running mate and where the Beatles stayed on their first US tour. Restaurants, art-deco pool, jacuzzi, weight room, babysitting, foreign exchange. **$$$**
Westin Bonaventure
404 S Figueroa Street
Tel: 213/624-1000 or 888/625-5144; fax: 213/612-4800;
www.westin.com
Five glass towers housing 1,354 rooms around a six-story atrium. Famous filming location. 24-hour room service, business center. Airport bus service, restaurants, free use of adjoining fitness facilities, pool, babysitting, most pets allowed, foreign currency exchange. **$$$**
Wyndham Checkers Hotel
535 S Grand Avenue
Tel: 213/624-0000; fax: 626-9906

www.wyndham.com
European-style luxury with 158 rooms, good cuisine and world-class service. Restaurant, pool, jacuzzi, weight room, babysitting, most pets allowed, foreign currency exchange. Near airport bus service. **$$$**

Moderate
Figueroa Hotel Convention Center
939 S Figueroa Street
Tel: 213/627-8971 or (800) 421-9092, in California 800/331-5151; fax: 689-0305
Charming Spanish-style hotel one block from the Convention Center. Airport bus service, restaurants, patio dining, pool, jacuzzi, laundromat, free parking. **$$**
Holiday Inn Downtown
750 S Garland Avenue
Tel: 213/628-5242 or 800/628-5240; fax: 628-1201
www.basshotels.com
Close to the business district. Airport bus service, restaurant, tour bus pickups, free cable TV, giant screen TV in the lounge, pool, courtesy coffee, laundromat, kitchen units, free parking. **$$**
Hyatt Regency Los Angeles
711 S Hope Street
Tel: 213/683-1234 or 800/233-1234; fax: 612-3163
www.hyatt.com
443 rooms. In LA's financial/legal center, easy walk from the Convention Center and the Jewelry and California marts. Airport bus service, restaurants, jacuzzi, weight room, babysitting, most pets OK, foreign exchange. **$$**
Kawada Hotel
200 South Hill Street
Tel: 213/621-4455 or 800/752-9232; fax: 213/687-4455
www.kawadahotel.com
115 rooms. Centrally located near Angels' Flight. Free Downtown shuttle service. Room refrigerators, bar with "earthquake" art, exercise room, restaurants. **$$**
Los Angeles Marriott Downtown,
333 S Figueroa Street
Tel: 213/617-1133 or 800/228-9290; fax: 213/613-0291
www.marriott.com
Luxury hotel with 469 rooms in

four acres of landscaped grounds, near Music Center and Dodger Stadium. Executive floor, health club, business center, valet parking, airport bus service, restaurants, pool, courtesy coffee, babysitting, foreign currency exchange. **$$–$$$**

Radisson Midtown
3540 Figueroa Street
Tel: 213/748-4141 or 800/333-3333; fax: 213/746-325
www.radisson-midtown.com
Across the street from USC, 240 recently renovated rooms, walking distance to Coliseum and science museums. Pool, fitness center, shuttles, restaurant. **$$**

Wilshire Royale Hotel
2619 Wilshire Boulevard
Tel: 213/387-5311 or 800/421-8072; fax: 380-8174
www.hotelroyale.com
99 rooms. Art-deco landmark 10 minutes from Downtown. Restaurant, pool, spa. **$$**

Inexpensive

Best Western Executive Mid-Wilshire Hotel Inn
603 S New Hampshire Avenue at 6th Street
Tel: 213/385-4444; fax: 380-5413
www.bestwestern.com
All 9l rooms have a small refrigerator and cable TV. Airport bus service, pool, jacuzzi, weight room, laundromat, free parking. **$**

City Center Motel
1135 W 7th Street
Tel: 213/628-7141; fax: 629-1064
42 rooms. Within walking distance of Downtown and financial district. Airport bus service, direct-dial phones, Gray Line Tour buses pick up daily, pool, laundromat, free parking. **$**

Downtowner Motel
944 S Georgia Street
Tel: 213/627-2003; fax: 627-2005
Right in central Downtown. 40 rooms, free parking. Kitchenettes with refrigerators. Car rental. **$**

Inntowne Hotel Los Angeles
913 S Figueroa Street
Tel: 213/628-2222 or 800/457-8520; fax: 687-0566
168 rooms. Near Fashion Center. Airport bus service, restaurants,

cocktail lounge, laundromat, babysitting, free transportation within downtown, free parking. **$**

Jerry's Motel
285 S Lucas Avenue
Tel: 213/481-8181
10 rooms. Pool, car rental, laundry room. **$**

Metro Plaza Hotel
711 N Main Street
Tel: 213/680-0200 or 800/223-2223; fax: 213/620-0200
www.metroplazahotel.com
76 rooms. In Chinatown, near Olvera Street and Union Station. Laundry, sauna, whirlpool, restaurant, free parking. **$**

Milner Hotel
813 S Flower Street
Tel: 213/627-6981 or 800/827-0411; fax: 213/623-9751
www.milner-hotels.com
177 rooms. Opposite Broadway Plaza shopping center. Restaurant, free breakfast, free shuttle from airport, cable TV. **$**

Motel de Ville
1123 W 7th Street
Tel: 213/624-8474; fax: 624-7652
60 rooms. Restaurant, pool, car rental, LAX shuttle. **$**

Orchid Hotel
819 S Flower Street
Tel: 213/624-5855 or 800/874-5855; fax: 213/624-8740
63 rooms. Cozy. Laundromat. Transportation to LAX. **$**

Royal Host Motel
901 W Olympic Boulevard
Tel: 213/626-6255; fax: 488-3481
54 rooms. Kitchenettes, free coffee, pool, car rental, free parking. **$**

University of Southern California (USC) Summer Conferences
642 W 34th Street,
Tel: 213/740-0031; fax: 740-8488
Around 1,000 inexpensive rooms. Two miles from Downtown at the University of Southern California and near three museums. Cocktail lounge, pool, tennis, dining and recreational facilities, laundromat, kitchen units. **$**

Vagabond Inn
3101 Figueroa Street
Tel: 213/746-2531
www.vagabondinns.worldres.com
Near USC midway between

Coliseum, science museums and Staples Center. Minutes from Downtown and major attractions. Free coffee, pool, free parking, pets allowed, restaurant. **$**

HOLLYWOOD AND WESTSIDE

Luxury

The Argyle
8358 Sunset Boulevard
Tel: 323/654-7100 or 800/225-8637; fax: 654-9287
www.argylehotel.com
63 rooms, mostly suites. Art-deco landmark, formerly the Sunset Tower and onetime home of Jean Harlow, Clark Gable, Marilyn Monroe and Erroll Flynn. Restaurant, butler service, pool, fitness center. **$$$**

Beverly Hills Hotel
9641 Sunset Boulevard
Tel: 310/276-2251 or 800/283-8885; fax: 281-2905
www.thebeverlyhillshotel.com
200 rooms including bungalows whose high-profile, high-spending guests are given personal phone lines and gold keys engraved with their name. Bungalow 5 ($3,000 per night) has four bedrooms and its own pool. Twelve acres of tropical gardens, exotic flowers, and celebs galore. Restaurants, pool, fitness facilities and classy shops. **$$$**

The Beverly Hilton
9876 Wilshire Boulevard near Rodeo Drive
Tel: 310/274-7777 or 800/445-8667; fax: 285-1313; www.hilton.co
With 540 rooms, it's the largest hotel in Beverly Hills. Airport bus service, restaurants, pool, courtesy coffee, babysitting, foreign currency exchange. **$$$**

Century Plaza Hotel and Tower
2025 Avenue of the Stars, Century City
Tel: 310/277-2000 or 800/WESTIN-1; fax: 551-3395
www.centuryplazala.com
1,046 rooms. President Nixon welcomed the first astronauts back from the moon at a party here and Ronald Reagan kept an office in the tower. Sheer luxury all around. **$$$**

Chateau Marmont
8221 Sunset Boulevard
Tel: 323/656-1010 or 800/242-8328; fax: 323/655-5311
63 rooms, mostly suites. Legendary home of stars for 70 years and choice of today's younger movie set such as Johnny Depp, Matt Dillon, and Courtney Love. Dining room, pool, child care, fitness room. **$$$**

Le Dufy Hotel
1000 Westmount Drive
Tel: 310/657-7400; fax: 854-6744
A luxurious quiet hideaway near La Cienega. All 120 suites attractively decorated with contemporary art, kitchens, pool, sauna. **$$$**

Four Seasons Hotel
300 S Doheny Drive at Burton Way
Tel: 310/273-2222 or 800/819-5053; fax: 859-3824;
www.fshr.com
Almost 300 rooms and suites. Favorite of stars. Quiet residential neighborhood adjacent to Beverly Hills to which there is free transportation. Restaurants, business center, pool, jacuzzi, free coffee, babysitting, free parking, foreign currency exchange. **$$$**

Hollywood Roosevelt Hotel
7000 Hollywood Boulevard
Tel: 323/466-7000 or 800/950-7667; fax: 469-7006;
www.hollywoodroosevelt.com
270 rooms, a few inexpensively priced. Legendary Hollywood landmark with art-deco trimmings, palm-shaded pool, mezzanine museum. The first Academy Awards took place here and a (free) museum of movie memorabilia occupies the mezzanine. **$–$$$**

Hotel Bel Air
701 Stone Canyon Road, Bel Air
Tel: 310/472-1211; fax: 476-5890
www.bel-air.com
In 11 acres of landscaped grounds in secluded canyon. Among the 40 elegant suites and 52 rooms is Room 160, informally called the Princess Grace Suite, which was Grace Kelly's favorite. Room 138, the Swan Lake Suite, is favored for marriage proposals. **$$$**

Le Meridien
465 S La Cienega
Tel: 310/247-0400 or 800/543-4300; fax: 310/247-0315

www.le-meridienhotels.com
297 oversized rooms next to Restaurant Row, near Beverly Hills. Spa, pool, business center. **$$$**

Peninsula Hotel
9882 Little Santa Monica Boulevard
Tel: 310/551-2888 or 800/462-7899; fax: 310/788-2319
www.peninsula.com
Ultra deluxe in Beverly Hills; 196 rooms, suites, and villas. Villas from 580 to 2,250 sq ft. Spa, pool, roof garden; fine restaurants and bar. 24-hour room service and concierge; courtesy Rolls-Royce service. **$$$**

Sheraton Universal
333 Universal Terrace Parkway, on Universal Studio lot
Tel: 818/980-1212 or 800/325-3535; fax: 818/509-060;
www.sheraton.com
Luxury high rise with 440 rooms. Restaurant, health club, child care, pool. **$$$**

Price Guide

The price guide indicates rates for a standard double room:
$$$ = (luxury) over $200
$$ = (moderate) $100–200
$ = (inexpensive) under $100

Sunset Marquis Hotel and Villas
1200 Alta Loma Road
Tel: 310/657-1333; fax: 657-1330
www.srs-worldhotels.com
Secluded, elegant, Mediterranean hideaway, favorite of stars and musicians (even has recording studio). Near Sunset Strip. **$$$**

W Los Angeles-Westwood
930 Hilgard Avenue
Tel: 310/208-8765; fax: 824-0355
www.whotels.com
258 one- and two-bedroom suites. A hip, boutique feel, next to UCLA and near Beverly Hills. Caters to business clientele. 2 pools, restaurant, business and fitness centers. **$$$**

Wyndham-Bel Age
1020 N San Vicente Boulevard
Tel: 310/854-1111 or 800/424-4353; fax: 323/851-1800
www.wyndham.com
All-suite deluxe hotel with fine art in each suite, three phones and a TV

in the bathroom, valet parking, limo service to Beverly Hills and Century City, restaurants, pool, jacuzzi, kitchen units, free parking, foreign currency exchange. **$$$**

Moderate

Beverly Hills Plaza Hotel
10300 Wilshire Boulevard
Tel: 310/275-5575 or 800/800-1234; fax: 278-3325
116 luxury suites, with an elegant, modern European decor. In between Beverly Hills and Westwood. A small gem. Pool, jacuzzi, fitness center, restaurant and bar. **$$–$$$**

Carlyle Inn
1119 S Robertson Boulevard at eastern end of Beverly Hills
Tel: 310/275-4445 or 800/3-CARLYLE; fax: 310/859-0496
32 suites. European-style hotel with restaurant, spa, fitness center, afternoon tea, free breakfast. **$$**

Doubletree Los Angeles-Westwood
10740 Wilshire Boulevard
Tel: 310/475-8711 or 800/222-TREE; fax: 310/475-5220
www.doubletreehotels.com
295 rooms. Walking distance of Westwood Village and UCLA. 10-minute drive to Rodeo Drive. Cable TV and complimentary newspapers, restaurant, swimming pool, jacuzzi, babysitting, free parking. **$$**

Holiday Inn (Brentwood)
170 N Church Lane
Tel: 310/476-6411; fax: 472-1157
www.basshotels.com
Close to Getty Center and UCLA, shuttle to Getty, Westwod, Brentwood. Great views. Just off 405 freeway. Exercise club, pool, fitness center, restaurant. **$$–$$$**

Holiday Inn (Hollywood)
2005 N Highland Avenue
Tel:(323/850-5811); fax: 876-3272
www.basshotels.com
Located one block from Hollywood Boulevard and Hollywood Bowl, 1 mile to Universal Studios. 470 rooms, 10 equipped of visitor with disabilities, 23 floors. Pool, rooftop restaurant, babysitting, laundry, pets allowed. **$$**

Hotel Sofitel
8555 Beverly Boulevard
Tel: 310/278-5444 or 800/521-7772; fax: 310/657-0389

www.sofitelbeverlyhills.com
311 deluxe rooms, renovated in 1998. The charm of a French Chateau and Pierre Deux decor. Across the street from Beverly Center, near Restaurant Row, Melrose Avenue. Fitness club, pool, sundeck, spa, restaurant/bar. **$$–$$$**

Inexpensive
Banana Bungalow
2775 Cahuenga Boulevard in Hollywood Hills
Tel: 323/851-1129 or 800/4-HOSTEL; fax: 851-156
www.bananabungalow.com
Popular youth hostel chain. Poolside bungalows, weight room, restaurant, laundromat, movie theater, free transport to airport, beach, and Disneyland. **$**
Best Western Hollywood Plaza Inn
2011 N Highland Avenue
Tel: 323/851-1800 or 800/445-4353; fax: 851-1836
www.bestwestern.com
80 rooms. Centrally located and conveniently close to the Hollywood Bowl and Mann's Chinese Theatre. Restaurant, pool, jacuzzi, free coffee, laundromat, car rental and free parking. **$–$$**
Beverly Laurel Motor Hotel
8010 Beverly Boulevard
Tel: 323/651-2441 or 800/962-3824; fax: 651-5225
Friendly family-run place near to Farmers Market, museums, and Beverly Center mall. Pool, coffee shop, room refrigerators. **$**
Brentwood Motor Hotel
12200 Sunset Boulevard
Tel: 310/476-9981 or 800/840-3808; www.bmhotel.com
20 quaint rooms, close to Getty Center, UCLA, Brentwood, and Santa Monica. Refrigerators, free parking and continental breakfast; e-mail, voice mail, and fax services. **$–$$**
Century City Inn
10330 W Olympic Boulevard
Tel: 310/553-1000 or 800/553-1005; fax: 277-1633
34 rooms. Homestyle elegance. Courtesy coffee, complimentary breakfast, valet parking, refrigerator, microwave, coffee maker, kitchen units, **$**

Crest Motel
7701 Beverly Boulevard
Tel: 310/931-8108 or 800/367-1717; fax: 805/371-8868
28 rooms. Within walking distance of shopping, Farmers Market, and restaurants. Pool, free parking. **$**
EconoLodge Hollywood
777 N Vine near Universal Studios
Tel: 323/463-5671 or 800/446-3916, from California 800/628-3353; fax: 323/463-5675
www.econolodgehollywood.com
Free breakfast, pool, free parking, laundry. **$**
Hollywood Hills' Magic Hotel
7025 Franklin Avenue, near Magic Castle and Yamashiro restaurant
Tel: 323/851-0800 or 800/741-4915; fax: 323/851-4926;
www.magichotel.com
Inexpensive with pool, apartment-sized suites, free parking. **$**
Hollywood Orchid Suites Hotel
1753 N Orchid Avenue
Tel: 323/874-9678 or 800/537-3052; fax: 323/874-9931;
www.orchidsuites.com
40 rooms, mostly suites. Pool, free parking. **$**
Ramada Inn Hollywood
1160 N Vermont
Tel: 323/660-1788; fax: 663-8069
www.ramada.com
130 rooms. Pool, whirlpool, excercise room, car rental, babysitting. **$**
TraveLodge Hollywood
1401 N Vermont
Tel: 323/665-5735 or 800/578-7878; fax: 323/665-0879
www.travelodge.com
70 rooms. Pool, free coffee, car rental, free parking. **$**

THE COAST

Luxury
Beach House Inn
1300 The Strand, Hermosa Beach
Tel: 310/374-3001 or 888/895-4559; fax: 310/372-2115;
www.beach-house.com
Gorgeous Cape Cod-like small hotel, on beach, all suites with fireplaces, wet bar. Free continental breakfast and dip in the ocean. **$$$**
Fairmont-Miramar Hotel
101 Wilshire Boulevard,

Santa Monica
Tel: 310/576-7777 or 800/325-3535527-4727; fax: 458-7912
www.fairmont.com
This historic hotel has landscaped grounds, pool, health club, coffee shop. **$$$**
Hotel Oceana
849 Ocean Avenue, Santa Monica
Tel: 310/393-0486; fax: 458-1182
www.hoteloceana.com
63 suites. Mediterranean-villa like, across from ocean, walk to pier and promenade. Room service by Wolfgang Puck Café. Pool, laundromat, fitness center, car rental. **$$$**
Inn at Playa del Rey
435 Culver Boulevard, Playa del Rey
Tel: 310/574-1920; fax: 574-9920
www.calendarlive.com
Romantic getaway in quiet beach town just north of LAX. 5 miles south of Santa Monica. 21 rooms and suites, private garden with hot tub, overlooks 300 acres of wetland sanctuary. Beach chairs, bikes and towels provided. **$$$**
Loew's Santa Monica Beach Hotel
1700 Ocean Avenue
Tel: 310/458-6700 or 800/235-6397; fax: 310/458-676
www.loewshotels.com
350 rooms. This was the first luxury hotel in LA to be located on the beach when it opened in 1989. Pools, whirlpool, restaurants, health club. **$$$**
Malibu Beach Inn
22878 Pacific Coast Highway
Tel: 310/456-6444 or 800/4-MALIBU; fax: 456-1499;
www.malibubeachinn.com
44 rooms near the pier, with fireplaces, fitness center, free breakfast, café, babysitting. **$$$**
Marina Beach Marriott Hotel
4100 Admiralty Way, Marina del Rey
Tel: 310/301-3000 or 800/228-9290; fax: 310/448-4870
www.marriott.com
Deluxe hotel with 370 rooms, 5 miles north of LAX overlooking the marina. Courtesy airport bus, highly-rated restaurants, pool, baby-sitting. **$$$**
Marina del Rey Hotel
13534 Bali Way
Tel: 310/301-1000 or 800/882-

4000; fax: (310)301-8167
www.marinadelreyhotel.com
153 rooms. restaurants, pool, free
parking, car rental, shuttle to LAX.
$$$

Ritz-Carlton Marina Del Rey
4375 Admiralty Way
Tel: 310/823-1700 or 800/241-
3333; fax: 310/823-2403
www.ritzcarlton.com
Elegant hotel on the Marina, with
306 rooms and every amenity. **$$$**

Shangri La Hotel
1301 Ocean Avenue, Santa Monica
Tel: 310/394-2791
www.shangrila-hotel.com
Art-deco landmark opposite
Palisades Park. Walk to pier and
promenade. Rooms, suites, 2
penthouses. Kitchenettes,
laundromat, free parking. **$$$**

Shutters on the Beach
1 Pico Boulevard, Santa Monica
Tel: 310/458-0030 or 800/334-
9000; fax: 458-4589
www.shuttersonthebeach.com
Jacaranda in the blue stone
driveway, pricey contemporary art in
the lobby. Great views, luxurious
rooms. Pool, whirlpool, several
restaurants. One of the most
popular hotels in LA. **$$$**

Moderate

Barnabey's
3501 Sepulveda Boulevard,
Manhattan Beach
Tel: 310/545-8466 or 888296-
6838; fax: 545-8621;
www.tarsadia.com
European-style inn featuring 120
rooms with Victorian period
antiques. 5 minutes to LAX.
1 mile from beach. Indoor pool,
whirlpool, restaurant/bar/afternoon
tea. **$$-$$$**

The Georgian
1415 Ocean Avenue, Santa Monica,
Tel: 310/395-9945 or 800/538-
8147; fax: 451-3374
www.georgianhotel.com
Built in 1933 in art-deco style with
84 rooms, most with ocean view,
sited on an old speakeasy. Former
hideout for stars and mobsters.
Renovated in 2000. Across from
Palisades Park, with flower-filled
marble lobby, free shoe shine,
morning paper. **$$-$$$**

Holiday Inn Express
737 Washington Boulevard,
Marina del Rey
Tel: 310/821-4455 or 800/821-
8277; fax: 310/821-8098
www.holidayinnmarinadelrey.com
68 rooms, mostly suites. Childcare,
outdoor spa, free breakfast, car
rental, free parking. **$$**

Inn at Venice Beach
327 Washington Boulevard,
Marina del Rey
Tel: 310/821-2557 or 800/828-
0688; fax: 827-0289
Country decor. Breakfast served in
cobblestone courtyard cafe. **$$**

Malibu Country Inn
6506 Westward Beach Road
Tel: 310/457-9622 or
800/FUN'N'SURF; fax: 457-1349
www.malibu.org
16 room B&B, overlooking the
ocean. Pool, restaurant. **$$**

Price Guide

The price guide indicates rates for
a standard double room:
$$$ = (luxury) over $200
$$ = (moderate) $100–200
$ = (inexpensive) under $100

Marina Pacific Hotel and Suites
1697 Pacific Avenue, Venice
Tel: 310/452-1111 or 800/421-
8151; fax: 310/452-5479
www.mphotel.com
80 rooms, walk to beach and
boardwalk. Kitchenettes, laundry,
cafe, free parking. **$$**

Marriott Manhattan Beach
1400 Parkview Avenue,
Manhattan Beach
Tel: 310/546-7511 or 800/228-
9290; fax: 310/939-1486;
www.marriott.com
385 rooms, near Rosecrans
business/restaurant area, 1½ miles
to beach, 5 mins to LAX. Pool, health
club, shuttle to pier, restaurant,
business center, laundry, concierge,
9-hole par 3 golf course. **$$-$$$**

Portofino Hotel and Yacht Club
260 Portofino Way, Redondo Beach
Tel: 310/379-8481 or 800/468-
4292; fax: 310/372-7329;
www.noblehousehotels.com
165 rooms, on the water. Pool,

excellent restaurant, views over the
marina, bikes and access to Gold's
Gym nearby. **$$-$$$**

Venice Beach House
15 Thirtieth Avenue, Venice
Tel: 310/823-1966; fax: 823-1842
Pretty B&B near the beach built in
1911. Nine rooms, full breakfast,
some shared bathrooms. **$$**

Inexpensive

Best Western Gateway Hotel
1920 Santa Monica Boulevard
Tel: 310/829-9100 or 800/528-
1234; fax: 310/829-9211
125 rooms, restaurant. **$**

Best Western Sunrise Hotel
400 N Harbor Drive, Redondo
Tel: 310/376-0746 or 800/334-
7384; fax: 310/376-7384;
www.bestwesternwunrise.com
111 rooms. At the marina. Bike
rentals. Pool, spa, restaurant. **$-$$**

The Cadillac
8 Dudley Avenue, Venice
Tel: 310/399-8876; fax: 399-4536
www.thecadillachotel.com
40 rooms. Renovated art-deco
landmark. On beach, ocean views.
Fitness center, sauna, free coffee,
free parking. **$**

Carmel Hotel
201 Broadway, Santa Monica
Tel: 310/451-2469 or 800/445-
8695; fax: 310/393-4180
www.hotelcarmel.com
110 rooms, Old World charm, some
ocean views, airport transfer. **$-$$**

Hotel Santa Monica
3102 Pico Boulevard, Santa Monica
Tel: 310/450-5766 or 800/231-
7679
Kitchenettes, laundromat, free
breakfast. **$**

Santa Monica Pico Travel Lodge
3102 Pico Boulevard, Santa Monica
Tel: 310/450-5766
www.travelodge.com
87 rooms, kitchenettes, 8 miles
(13 km) from airport. **$**

VALLEYS

Pasadena

The Artists' Inn
1038 Magnolia Street, South
Pasadena
Tel: 626/799-5668 or 888/799-

5668, fax: 626/799-3678; www.artistsinns.com

An 1895 Victorian farmhouse with period furnishings converted into a romantic B&B. Check out the "Midweek Special." **$$$**

Holiday Inn Pasadena Convention Center Hotel

303 E Cordova Street
Tel: 626/449-4000; fax: 584-1390
www.basshotels.com

Adjoins Pasadena Convention Center and Civic Auditorium. Airport bus service, restaurant, pool, tennis, babysitting. **$$$**

Ritz Carlton Huntington Hotel

1401 S Oak Knoll Avenue
Tel: 626/568-3900 or 800/241-3333; fax: 626/668-3700
www.ritzcarlton.com

One of the world's top hotels since its founding 87 years ago. Elegant suites, cottages, tennis courts, pool, gourmet restaurants, free transportation to Downtown. **$$$**

Pasadena Hotel

76 N Fair Oaks Avenue
Tel: 626/568-8172 or 800/653-8886; fax: 793-6409
www.pasadenahotel.com

12 rooms. Late 19th-century elegance, centrally located near Old Town (including the nightlife sounds). Recently renovated. Restaurant and lounge, free breakfast. **$$**

Pasadena Inn

400 S Arroyo Parkway
Tel: 626/795-8401; fax: 577-2629.
65 rooms. Near Huntington library. Pool, restaurant, Airport transfer. **$**

Super 8

2863 E Colorado Boulevard
Tel/fax: 626/449-3020
www.super8.com

70 rooms, renovated 1999. Near Santa Anita racetrack. Pool, free breakfast. **$**

San Fernando Valley

Universal City Hilton and Towers

555 Universal Terrace Parkway
Tel: 818/506-2500; fax: 509-2031
www.hilton.com

450 rooms. Near Universal Studios. Pool, whirlpool. gym. **$$$**

Burbank Airport Hilton

2500 Hollywood Way, Burbank
Tel: 818/843-6000 or 800/HILTONS;

fax: 818/842-9720
www.hilton.com

500 rooms. Across the street from the Burbank Airport with free connecting bus. Restaurant, pool, jacuzzi, laundromat, babysitting, car rental, free parking, foreign currency exchange. **$$**

Warner Center Marriott

21850 Oxnard Street,
Woodland Hills
Tel: 818/887-4800 or 800/228-9290; fax: 818/340-5893
www.marriott.com

460 rooms. Near Warner Center Business Park and the Promenade Shopping Mall. Airport bus service, restaurants, pool, jacuzzi, laundromat, babysitting, free parking, foreign currency exchange. **$$**

Comfort Inn

2300 W Colorado Boulevard,
Eagle Rock
Tel: 213/256-1199; fax: 255-7768
www.comfortinn-er.com

58 rooms. It's an easy journey to the Rose Bowl and Dodger Stadium, 7 miles to Downtown LA. Pool, spa, free breakfast and free parking. **$**

Holiday Lodge

3901 Riverside Drive, Burbank
Tel: 818/843-1121

28 rooms. Pool, air-conditioning, in-room spas, free coffee, parking. **$**

Santa Clarita Valley

Hyatt Valencia and Santa Clarita Conference Center

24500 Town Center Drive
Tel: 661/799-1234; fax: 799-1233
www.hyatt.com

244 rooms, close to Magic Mountain, in Downtown Valencia. Business center, currency exchange, pool, spa, fitness center, miniature golf. **$$**

Residence Inn Santa Clarita

25320 The Old Road
Tel: 661/298-2800; fax: 290-2802
www.residenceinn.com.

90 suites, close to Magic Mountain, 20 miles to Downtown LA. Free breakfast, room service, pool, exercise room, full kitchens. **$$**

Best Western Valencia Inn

24713 Championship Way
Tel: 661/255-0555 or 800/944-7446; fax: 661/255-2216
www.travelweb.com

184 rooms on 8 acres close to Magic Mountain, free continental breakfast, 2 pools, free parking. **$**

OUT OF TOWN

Anaheim/Buena Park

Disneyland Hotel

1150 W Cerritos, tel: 714/778-6600 or 800/642-5391
www.disney.go.com

1,350 rooms. Adjoins Disneyland. Pools, spa, 11 restaurants, tennis courts, airport transfer. **$$$**

Embassy Suites Buena Park-Disneyland

7762 Beach Boulevard
Tel: 714/739-5600 or 800/EMBASSY
www.embassy-suites.com

200 suites around open courtyard, walking distance to Knott's Berry Farm, a few miles from Disneyland. Gameroom, gym, pool, jacuzzi, restaurant, room service. **$$**

Holiday Inn Express

435 W Katella Avenue
Tel: 714/772-7755 or 800/833-7888; fax: 714/772-2727
www.holiday-anaheim.com

100 rooms. Pool, spa, fitness center, car rental. **$$**

Inn Suites Hotel Buena Park/Anaheim

7555 Beach Boulevard
Tel: 714/522-3366 or 800/842-4242; fax: 714/523-2883

70 small suites, walking distance to Knott's Berry Farm, Medieval Times, Wild Bill's. Pool, jacuzzi, restaurant, basketball court, exercise room, video arcade. **$$**

Sheraton Anaheim Hotel

1015 W Ball Road, eight blocks from Disneyland
Tel: 714/778-1700 or 800/325-3535; fax: 714/535-3889
www.sheraton.com

500 rooms, recently renovated. Pool, exercise room, games room, restaurant. **$$–$$$**

Convention Center Inn

2017 S Harbor Boulevard
Tel: 714/740-2500 or 800/521-5628; fax: 714/750-5676

222 rooms. Short distance to Disneyland. Pool, spa, restaurant, kitchenettes. **$**

Days Inn Main Gate/Convention Center
620 W Orangewood
Tel: 714/971-9000 or 800/999-7844; fax: 714/740-2065
www.daysinn-maingate.com
58 rooms, two blocks from Disneyland, across street from Convention Center, free shuttles, contintental breakfast, pool, spa, restaurant. $

Inn at Buena Park
7828 Orangethorpe Avenue, Buena Park
Tel: 714/670-7200 or 800/727-7205; fax: 714/522-3319
175 rooms. 8 miles (13 km) from Disneyland with free shuttle there and to Knott's Berry Farm. Pool, spa. $

Penny Sleeper Inn
1441 S Manchester Avenue
Tel: 714/991-8100 or 800/854-6118; fax: 714/533-6430
www.pennysleeperinn.com
200 rooms, recently remodeled. Pool, game room, Disneyland shuttle. $

Peter Pan Motor Lodge
1734 S Harbor Boulevard
Tel: 714/750-0232; fax: 750-5676
78 rooms. Pool, spa, kitchens. $

Ramada Main Gate/Saga Inn
1650 S Harbor Boulevard,
tel: 714/772-0440 or 800/854-6097; fax: 714/9991-8219
185 rooms. Pool, restaurant, laundry, shuttle. $-$$

Tropicana Inn
1540 S Harbor Boulevard
Tel: 714/635-4082 or 800/828-4898; fax: 714/635-1535
www.anaheimhotelsonline.com
200 rooms. Pool, spa, kitchenettes, Disneyland shuttle. $

Long Beach
Hotel *Queen Mary*
1126 Queens Highway, Long Beach
Tel: 562/435-3511
Expensive staterooms with period furnishings and original art as well as interior cabins. Hotel guests have free run of the *Queen Mary*, with its shops and numerous classy restaurants. $$$

Long Beach Hilton
2 World Trade Center
Tel: 562/983-3400; fax: 983-1200
www.hilton.com

300 rooms. 8 miles (13 km) from airport, three blocks to Convention Center/Aquarium. Pool, spa, restaurants. $$$

Guest House Hotel
5325 E Pacific Coast Highway
Tel: 562/597-1341; fax: 597-1664
Pool, deli-restaurant. $$

Hyatt Regency Long Beach
200 S Pine Avenue
Tel: 562/491-1234; fax: 624-6115
www.hyatt.com
521 rooms, walk to Convention Center, Aquarium, and Pine Street restaurants, Shoreline Village. Business Center, currency exchange, pool, jacuzzi, babysitting, exercise room. $$-$$$

Price Guide

The price guide indicates rates for a standard double room:
$$$ = (luxury) over $200
$$ = (moderate) $100–200
$ = (inexpensive) under $100

Long Beach Airport Marriot
4700 Airport Plaza Drive
Tel: 562/425-5210 or 800/228-9290; fax: 562/425-274
www.marriott.com
300 rooms. Pool, restaurant, sauna, whirlpool, gym. $$

Comfort Inn
3201 E Pacific Coast Highway
Tel: 562/597-3374 or 800/228-5150; fax: 562/985-3142
www.hotelchoice.com
68 rooms. 1½ miles (2.5 km) from beach, 3½ miles (5.6 km) to Convention Center/ Aquarium. Pool, whirlpool. $

Vagabond Inn
150 Alamitos Avenue
Tel: 562/435-7621 or 800/522-1555; fax: 562/436-4011
www.vagabondinns.worldres.com
61 rooms. Pool, kitchenettes, free breakfast. $

Catalina Island
Inn on Mount Ada
Avalon
Tel: 310/510-2030; fax: 510-2237
www.catalina.com
B&B with six gorgeous rooms, with private bathrooms. Georgian

Colonial home with spectacular views; former home summer home of William Wrigley, Jr. $$$

Banning House Lodge
1 Banning House Road
Tel: 310/510-2800; fax: 510-1354
www.catalina.com
A 1910, rustic B&B with Old California charm, it is tucked away at Two Harbors village on the north side of the island, with limited transportation to the main town of Avalon. A real getaway with only 11 rooms, all with private bathrooms. Hiking, biking, snorkeling and scuba in renowned sites, kayaking, or relaxing. $$

Best Western Catalina Canyon Resort
Avalon
Tel: 310/510-0325 or 800/253-9361; fax: 310/510-0900
www.catalina.com
Garden courtyard, day spa, restaurant, pool, jacuzzi, conference center, shuttle. $-$$

Zane Grey Pueblo
Avalon
Tel: 310/510-0966 or 800/ 3-PUEBLO; fax: 310/510-0151
www.virtualcities.com
17 rooms, on hill with views above Avalon. Hopi Indian-style pueblo built by author Zane Grey in 1926. Pool, shuttle, free continental breakfast. $-$$

Orange County Beach Communities
Four Seasons Hotel
690 Newport Center Drive, Newport Beach
Tel: 949/759-0808 or 800/332-3442; fax: 759-0568;
www.fshr.com
285 rooms. Deluxe. Next to Fashion Island Mall. One mile from beach. Pool, restaurants, fitness club, tennis. $$$

Ritz-Carlton Laguna Miguel
1 Ritz Carlton Drive, Dana Point
Tel: 949/240-2000 or 800/241-3333; fax: 949/240-0829
www.ritzcarlton.com
Enthroned on a clifftop over the ocean, one of the finest and most romantic hotels in the US. 50 miles (80 km) south of LA, 10 miles (16 km) south of Newport Beach. $$$

Waterfront Hilton Beach Resort
21100 Pacific Coast Highway,
Huntington Beach
Tel: 714/960-7873 or 800/822-
SURF; fax: 714/960-2642
www.hilton.com
300 rooms. At the beach. Pool,
spa, tennis, restaurant, handcap
facilities. **$$$**

Aliso Creek Resort
31106 Coast Highway,
Laguna Beach
Tel: 949/499-2271 or 800/223-
3309; fax: 499-4601
www.alisocreekinn.com
62 townhomes. Three miles (5 km)
from Downtown, three minutes'
from beach. Pool, spa, restaurant,
golf course. **$$**

Hotel Laguna
425 S Coast Highway,
Laguna Beach
Tel: 949/494-1151 or 800/524-
2927; fax: 497-2163;
www.hotellaguna.com
65 rooms. Old Spanish classic,
former movie star haunt. On beach.
Near Pageant of Masters.
Restaurants. **$$**

Radisson Inn
600 Marina Drive, Seal Beach
Tel: 562/493-7501 or 800/333-
3333; fax: 562/596-3448
www.radisson.com
On beach 8 miles from airport.
Pool, spa, airport transfer. **$$**

Newport Classic Inn
2300 W Coast Highway,
Newport Beach
Tel: 949/722-2999 or 800/633-
3199; fax: 631-5659
52 rooms. On bay, ½ mile from
beach. Restaurant, pool, sauna. **$**

Quality Inn
800 Pacific Coast Highway,
Huntington Beach
Tel: 714/536-7500 or 800/228-
5151; fax: 714/536-6846
www.hotelchoice.com
50 rooms. Near the beach. Spa. **$**

North County San Diego

L'Auberge Del Mar Resort and Spa
1540 Camino Del Mar
Tel: 858/259-1515 or 800/553-
1336; fax: 858/755-4940
www.sandiego.worldres.com
120 luxury resort, One block from
ocean. Full European spa, in the

heart of Old Del Mar. **$$$**

Four Seasons Aviara
7100 Four Seasons Point Drive,
Carlsbad
Tel: 760/603-6800; fax: 603-6801
www.fshr.com
331 luxury rooms including 44
suites, oversized rooms with
balconies. Views, fitness center,
spa, championship golf and tennis.
Excellent restaurant. **$$$**

Beach Club Del Mar
159 S Shore Drive, Solana Beach
Tel: 858/487-8343; fax: 451-6689
Privately owned condos on a bluff
above the ocean, gated, beach
access, tennis, pools. 90 minutes
to Disneyland, 20 minutes to
Legoland, Sea World, 2 minutes to
Del Mar Racetrack. **$$**

Best Western Beach Terrace
2775 Ocean Street, Carlsbad
Tel: 760/729-5951 or 800/443-
5415; fax: 760/729-1078
www.beachterraceinn.com
49 suites on the beach, ocean
views, fireplaces, free continental
breakfast, sauna, therapy pool,
near Legoland. **$$**

Holiday Inn Carlsbad
850 Palomar Airport Road
Tel: 760/438-7880 or 800/HOLIDAY;
fax: 438-1015
www.carlsbadholidayinn.com
150 rooms, 2 minutes to Legoland,
across street from Outlet Shopping
mall. Special Zoo, Wild Animal Park,
Sea World, Legoland packages.
Pool, laundry, restaurant. **$$–$$$**

The Inn at Rancho Santa Fe
5951 Linea Del Cielo
Tel: 858/756-1131 or 800/843-
4661; fax: 858/759-1604
www.theinnatranchosantafe.com
Charming, Old California country
inn. 90 units, most in Spanish
cottages scattered through 20
acres. Shuttle to private Del Mar
beach house, restaurants, access
to renowned Rancho Santa Fe Golf
Club. A tad out of the way – but
worth it. 30 minutes to Sea World
and Downtown; 20 minutes to
Legoland. **$$–$$$**

Days Inn – San Diego/Encinitas
133 Encinitas Boulevard
Tel: 760/944-0260 or 800/795-
6044; fax: 760/944-2803
www.daysinnencinitas.com

124 units near I-5, near beach.
Free continental breakfast,
8 minutes to Legoland, 30 minutes
to Sea World. **$**

La Jolla

La Jolla Beach and Tennis Club
2000 Spindthrift Drive
Tel: 858/454-7126 or 800/624-
2582; fax: 456-3805
www.ljbtc.com
90 rooms. On the beach, near Sea
World. Restaurant, pool, golf tennis,
some facilities for visitors with
disabilities. **$$$**

La Valencia Hotel
1132 Prospect Street
Tel: 858/454-0771 or 800/451-
0772: fax: 456-3921
100 rooms. A local favorite. Greta
Garbo used to stay here as did
Mary Pickford. Pool, spa,
restaurants. **$$$**

Hyatt Regency La Jolla
3777 La Jolla Village Drive
Tel: 858/552-1234 or 800/233-
1234; fax: 858/552-6066
www.hyatt.com
419 units located a few miles
inland, just off I-5, between
Downtown La Jolla and the
business/mall Golden Triangle.
Designed by noted architect
Michael Graves, includes 5
restaurants, giant fitness club. 12
minutes to Sea World Zoo. **$$–$$$**

The Lodge at Torrey Pines
11480 N Torrey Pines Road,
Tel: 619/453-4420 or 800/995-
4507, fax: 619/453-0691
71 rooms. Overlooks ocean and
18th green, one mile from beach,
10 minutes to Del Mar racetrack.
Pool, restaurant, golf. **$$**

Residence Inn by Marriott
8901 Gilman Drive
Tel: 858/587-1770 or 800/331-
3131: fax: 552-0387
www.residenceinn.com
287 rooms. Pool, spa, golf, tennis,
airport transfer. **$$**

La Jolla Beach Travelodge
6750 La Jolla Boulevard
Tel: 858/454-0176 or 800/578-
7878; fax: 858/454-1075
www.sandiego.worldres.com
44 units, pool, jacuzzi, air-
conditioning, restaurant. Ocean
views, Suites. **$–$$**

San Diego

Hotel del Coronado
1500 Orange Avenue, Coronado
Tel: 619/435-6611; fax: 522-8262
www.hoteldel.com
629 rooms, World-famous Victorian-
era landmark. Tennis court, pool,
spa, golf, beach, restaurants. **$$$**

Loew's Coronado Bay Resort
4000 Coronado Bay Road
Tel: 619/424-4000 or 800/815-
6397; fax: 619/424-4400
440 units, tennis, children's
programs, marina, five restaurants,
health club, views. **$$$**

San Diego Marriott Hotel and Marina
333 W Harbor Drive
Tel: 619/234-1500 or 800/228-
9290; fax: 619/234-8678
www.marriott.com
1,355 units on the waterfront.
Wonderful bay and city views.
Onsite restaurants and recreation.
Next to Convention Center. **$$$**

Westgate Hotel
1055 Second Avenue
Tel: 619/238-1818 or 800/221-
3802; fax: 619/557-3737
223 units, elegant European-style
hotel in the center of the theatre,
Gaslamp, and business area of
Downtown. **$$$**

Westin Horton Plaza
910 Broadway
Tel: 619/239-2200 or (800)643-
7846; fax: 619/239-0509
www.westin.com
450 rooms in Downtown.
Restaurant, pool, spa, lighted
tennis courts, health club. **$$$**

Catamaran Resort
3999 Mission Boulevard
Tel: 858/488-1081 or 800/422-
8386; www.catamaranresort.com
313 rooms on Mission Bay. Spa,
fitness center, watersports,
entertainment, moonlight cruises. **$$**

Embassy Suites
601 Pacific Coast Highway
Tel: 619/239-2400 or
800/EMBASSY; fax: 239-1520
www.embassy-suites.com
Next to Seaport Village, beautiful
hotel, all suites, free full breakfast
and happy hour cocktails. **$$**

Holiday Inn-Harbor View
1617 1st Avenue
Tel. 619/239-9600 or 800/366-
3164; fax: 619/233-6228
200 rooms. Close to I-5. Pool,
restaurant, laundromat. Shuttle to
airport, zoo, Sea World. **$$**

Horton Grand
311 Island Avenue
Tel: 619/544-1886 or 800/542-
1886; fax: 619/239-3823
www.hortongrand.com
132 units, elegant, historic
Victorian hotel, in Gaslamp District.
Fireplaces, antiques. **$$**

Ramada Hotel Oldtown
2435 Jefferson Street
Tel: 619/260-8500 or 800/255-
3544; fax: 619/297-2078
176 rooms. Pool, spa, restaurants,
kitchenettes, airport transfer
available. **$$**

Price Guide

The price guide indicates rates for
a standard double room:
$$$ = (luxury) over $200
$$ = (moderate) $100–200
$ = (inexpensive) under $100

U.S. Grant Hotel
326 Broadway
Tel: 619/232-3121 or 800/334-
6957; fax: 619/232-3626
www.grandheritage.com
Restored, grand old historic hotel in
heart of business/shopping/
nightlife. Near trolley and
Convention Center. **$$–$$$**

La Pensione Hotel
1700 India Street
Tel: 619/236-8000 or 800/232-
4683; fax: 619/236-8088
www.lapensionehotel.com
A wonderful little secret, San
Diego's best budget hotel,
in Little Italy surrounded by
cafes. Easy walk to Downtown and
harbor. Two blocks to trolley.
European-style guesthouse, 80
units. **$**

Qualty Inn and Suites Downtown Harborview
1430 Seventh Avenue
Tel: 619/696-0911 or 800/404-
6835; fax: 619/234-9416
www.sandiego.worldres.com
136 units, 24-hour airport/Amtrak
shuttle, free continental breakfast,
near Downtown. **$**

Villager Lodge
660 G Street
Tel: 619/238-4100 or 800/598-
1810; fax: 619/238-5310
Fully remodeled, Gaslamp area, walk
to Horton Plaza and Convention
Center. Cable, refrigerators,
microwaves, dataports. **$**

Inland and Mountains

Mission Inn
3949 Mission Inn Avenue, Riverside
Tel: 909/784-0300 or 800/843-
7755; fax: 909/341-6730
235 rooms and suites, fabulous
European-style historic landmark.
Many of the rooms have features
such as domed ceilings, wrought-
iron balconies, tiled floors, stained
glass. Various famous marriages in
the chapel. **$$–$$$**

Gold Mountain Manor B&B
1117 Anita, Big Bear
Tel: 909/585-6997 or 800/509-
2604; fax: 909/585-0327
www.goldmountainmanor.com
Historic log mini-mansion, rustic but
elegant – tasteful not kitschy. Six
great rooms with private baths,
fireplaces and Queen beds. Many
antiques. One block from national
forest, 1½ miles to lake. **$$**

Holiday Inn Big Bear Chateau
42200 Moonridge Road
Tel: 909/866-6666 or 800/232-
7466; www.basshotels.com
80 deluxe rooms, all with
fireplaces, some with two-person
jacuzzis. 1 mile to ski lift; 1 mile to
golf. Fitness center. 75 miles (120
km) to Ontario Airport. **$$** Summer
$$$ Winter

Knickerbocker Mansion
869 Knickerbocker Road, Big Bear
Tel: 909/878-9190 or 877/423-
1180; fax: 909/878-4248
www.knickerbockermansion.com
B&B set in a rustic old mansion on
two acres, eight blocks to town,
four blocks to lake. nine standard
bedrooms with private bath and two
large suites. **$$–$$$**

Lake Arrowhead Resort
27984 Highway 189
Tel: 800/800-6792; fax: 909/336-
1378; www.lakearrowheadresort.
com
177 lakeside rooms and suites,
water and alpine views. Pool,

jacuzzi, secluded beach, health club, spa, restaurant, walk to village. **$$–$$$**

Eagle's Landing B&B
27406 Cedarwood, Lake Arrowhead
Tel: 800/835-5085
Four varied rooms in this modern mountain chateau on the lake. Gourmet breakfast, close to all lake activities. **$–$$**

Palm Springs
Hyatt Grand Champion Resort
44600 Indian Wells Lane
Tel: 760/341-1000; fax: 568-2236
www.hyatt.com
Deluxe suites and villas, 5 pools, health club, spa, 12 tennis courts, 36 golf holes. **$$$**

Ingleside Inn
2000 Ramon
Tel: 760/325-0046
Greta Garbo slept here. Garden, antiques, pool, restaurant. **$$$**

La Mancha
444 Avenida Caballeros,
Tel: 760/323-1773 or 800/255-1773; fax: 760/323-5928
www.lamancha.com
100 rooms. Attractively furnished villas, emphasis on privacy. Pools, sauna, putting green, lighted tennis courts, croquet, restaurant. **$$$**

Marriott Desert Springs Resort and Spa
74855 Country Club Drive
Tel: 760/341-2211
www.marriott.com
884 rooms, five restaurants, business center. Pool, tennis, 36 golf holes. **$$$**

La Quinta Hotel and Resort
49-499 Eisenhower Drive, La Quinta
Tel: 760/564-4111
www.lqresort.com
Old Spanish California charm, a celebrity favorite, especially the bungalows. 20 miles from Palm Springs. Numerous swimming pools and spas, tennis and five restaurants. **$$$**

Two Bunch Palms Resort and Spa
67-425 Two Bunch Palms Trail,
Desert Hot Springs
Tel: 760/329-8791 or 800/472-4334; fax: 760/329-1317
www.twobunchpalms.com
Built by gangster Al Capone as a secluded playground for gangsters

and stars, it's one of the top spas in the US. Rooms, casitas, villas, mud baths, massages, amongst serene desert oasis. 45 minutes north of Palm Springs. **$$$**

Willows Inn
412 W Tahquitz Canyon
Tel: 760/320-0780 or 800/966-9597; fax: 760/320-0771
www.thewillowspalmsprings.com
An almost forgotten secret – historic Mediterranean villa, located in Old Palm Springs Village, with eight guest rooms featuring antiques, fine linens, fireplace, fine dining. Very private – open only to guests. Albert Einstein frequented; Lombard and Gable honeymooned here. **$$$**

Casa Cody
175 S Cahuila Road
Tel: 760/320-9346 or 800/231-2639; fax: 760/325-8610
Founded by Buffalo Bill's niece. Pretty, Southwest charm, 23 airy suites, many around pool. **$$**

Mojave Rock Cabins
Joshua Tree
Tel: 760/366-8455; fax: 366-1966
www.mojaverockranch.com
An hour north of Palm Springs at Joshua Tree, but too cool not to mention. A secret in the desert on 120 acres, it's part hotel, part wilderness, a real desert getaway. Four eclectic, hip, artful cabins, each with two bedrooms and courtyards, barbecues, pet quarters. TV/CD; otherwise, no civilization. **$$–$$$**

Villa Royale
1620 Indian Trail
Tel: 760/327-2314 or 800/245-2344; fax: 760/322-3794
Suites decorated in syles of different countries, fireplaces, intimate and excellent restaurant, charming courtyards, pool. **$$–$$$**

Desert Lodge
1177 S Palm Canyon Drive
Tel: 760/325-1356 or 800/385-6343; fax: 760/325-7124
www.desertresorts.com
50 rooms. Pool, spa, airport transfer. **$**

Vagabond Inn
1699 S Palm Canyon Drive
Tel: 760/325-7211 or 800/522-

1555; fax: 760/322-9269
www.vagabondinns.worldres.com.
120 rooms. Pool, saunas, coffee shop. **$**

Santa Barbara
El Encanto
1900 Lasuen Street
Tel: 805/687-5000 or 800/223-5652; fax: 805/687-3903
84 cottages and garden villas, many with fireplaces. Romantic landmark hideaway, old favorite of stars and presidents. In town. Excellent restaurant with views, pool, tennis courts. **$$$**

Four Seasons Resort Hotel
1260 Channel Drive
Tel: 805/969-2261 or 800/332-3442; fax: 969-4212;
www.fshr.com
234 rooms. Originally the famous Biltmore. Near beach. First class. Pool, restaurant, tennis. **$$$**

Hotel Santa Barbara
533 State Street
Tel: 805/965-4572 or 800/259-7700; fax: 962-2412
www.hotelsantabarbara.com
75 rooms, newly renovated. Mediterranean charm. Great location to shopping, wharf. **$$$**

Ojai Valley Inn and Spa
Country Club Road
Tel: 800/422-6524
www.ojairesort.com
Set in the rich, secluded hills of Ojai, 45 minutes southeast of Santa Barbara. 206 deluxe guestrooms and suites, overlooking one of the top golf and tennis resorts in the US. Playground for celebrities. Beautiful, serene setting. Golf, Three pools, hiking, biking, croquet. **$$$**

San Ysidro Ranch
900 San Ysidro Lane, Montecito
Tel: 805/969-5046 or 800/368-6488; fax: 805/565-1995
www.sanysidroranch.com
Luxury resort with a celebrated history. 500 rolling acres, 20 private cottages. Exclusive. **$$$**

The Upham
1404 De La Vina
Tel: 805/962-0058 or 800/727-0876; fax: 963-2825
www.uphamhotel.com
Built in 1871, this is Southern

California's oldest continuously operating hostelry. Charming garden cottages and main building furnished with antiques and period furniture. **$$$**

Fess Parker's Doubletree Resort
633 E Cabrillo Boulevard
Tel: 805/564-4333 or 800/879-2929; fax: 805/962-8198
www.doubletreehotels.com
Across from beach in spacious grounds. Restaurant, pool, spa, tennis, putting green. **$$–$$$**

Olive House
1604 Olive Street
Tel: 805/962-4902 or 800/786-6422; fax: 962-9983
www.sbinns.com
Early 20th-century Craftsman-style B&B near the Mission. Redwood paneling, private decks and hot tubs. **$$–$$$**

Cathedral Oaks Lodge
4770 Calle Real
Tel: 805/654-1965 or 888/298-2054; fax: 964-0075
www.ramada.com
100 rooms. Pool, spa, airport transfer. **$–$$**

Motels

If you're traveling by car, don't plan on spending a great deal of time in your room and want an inexpensive alternative to hotels, motels are the best solution. Whether set along busy Sunset Boulevard in Los Angeles or along the riverbank in a remote Southern Californian town, most motels provide parking space, at a premium in almost all of California, within a few paces of your room.

Motel quality tends to vary considerably, but you can usually expect clean and simple accommodation. This is especially true for most of the national chains. A restaurant or coffee shop, swimming pool and sauna are often found on the premises. Room facilities generally include a telephone, television and radio, but don't hesitate to ask the motel manager if you may inspect a room before taking it.

Other than their accessibility by auto, the attraction of motels is

their price. Motels in California range from under $50 to $100 per night, double occupancy. Following are the US/Canada no-cost 800/numbers of major chains. Dial (1) then 800 before the number. For toll-free numbers outside the US and Canada, please check directories on websites.

Price Guide

The price guide indicates rates for a standard double room:
$$$ = (luxury) over $200
$$ = (moderate) $100–200
$ = (inexpensive) under $100

NATIONAL MOTELS AND HOTELS

Best Western: 780-7234; www.bestwestern.com
Days Inn: 544-8313; www.daysinn.com
Doubletree: 222-TREE; ww.doubletreehotels.com
Embassy Suites: 326-2779; www.embassy-suites.com
Four Seasons: 819-5053: www.fshr.com
Hilton: HILTONS; www. HILTON.com
Holiday Inn: HOLIDAY; www.BASSHOTELS.com
Hyatt: 633-7313; www.hyatt.com
Marriott: 228-9290; www.marriott.com
Motel 6: 466-8356; ww.motel6.com
Quality Inn: 228-5151; www.qualityinn.com
Ramada: 272-623; www.ramada.com
Ritz-Carlton: 241-3333; www.ritzcarlton.com
Sheraton: 325-3535; www.sheraton.com
Travelodge: 578-7878; www.travelodge.com
Vagabond: 522-1555; www.vagabondinns.worldres.com
Westin: WESTIN-1; www.westin.com

Bed and Breakfast

Historical architecture – usually Victorian – and oodles of charm is what draws most people to bed and breakfast inns which resemble hardly at all their counterparts in England, where B&Bs tend to be inexpensive.

Many inns have shared bathrooms and only a few have TVs or telephones in the rooms. Call or write in advance – the inns are particularly popular on weekends and in the summer.

The **California Association of Bed and Breakfast Inns**, 2715 Porter Street, Soquel, CA 95073, tel: 831/462-9191; fax: 462-0402; www.cabbi.com, publishes an annual list of its members which can also be obtained from State Tourism offices, tel: 800/GO-CALIF for further information.

Specialty reservation services include: **California Riviera**, tel: 800/621-0500; www.calriv800. com for rooms along the coast of Southern California and **Bed and Breakfast International**, 1181 Solano, Albany, 94706, tel: 510/525-4569.

There are also a number of website travel services under "Bed and Breakfast inns" in the *Yellow Pages*.

Hostels

Hostels are clean, comfortable, and inexpensive (as low as $10 per night). Although suitable for people of all ages, they are definitely for the young at heart. Beds are provided in dormitory-like rooms. Hostelers carry their own gear (silverware, sleeping bag, towel, etc.) and are expected, following breakfast each day, to take 15 minutes to help clean up and perform other communal tasks.

Hostels are closed from 9.30am to 4.30pm, so most guests fill their days with nearby outdoor activities. Reservations are highly recommended.

Information is also available at www.hiayh.com, the website of Hostelling International-American Youth Hostels; www.hostels.com, the self-proclaimed "complete hostelling and budget travel resource;" and www.4hostels.com

American Youth Hostels
733 15th Street NW Ste. 840, Washington D.C. 20005
Tel: 202/783-6161; fax: 783-6171

Banana Bungalow
2775 Cahuenga Boulevard in
Hollywood Hills
Tel: 323/851-1129 or 800/4-
HOSTEL; fax: 851-1569
www.bananabungalow.com
Popular youth hostel chain.
Poolside bungalows, weight room,
restaurant, laundromat, movie
theater, free transport to airport,
beach, and Disneyland.

**Hostelling International - Central
California Council**
PO Box 3645, Merced, CA 95344
Tel: 209/847-4140

Colonial Inn Youth Hostel
421 8th Street, Huntington Beac
Tel: 714/536-3315
18 semi-private rooms near
Disneyland and Knotts Berry Farm.

Hostelling International
1436 Second Street, Santa Monica
Tel: 310/393-6263; fax: 393-1769
www.hostelweb.com
230 beds. Near the beach. Kitchen,
laundry room, TV, library.

Fullerton Hacienda AYH-Hostel
1700 N Harbor Boulevard, Fullerton
Tel: 714/738-3721
On the site of an old dairy farm, in
congenial, relaxed surroundings.
Close to Disneyland and a wide
variety of Orange County
attractions.

Hostelling International San Diego
655 Fourth Avenue, Suite 46, San
Diego
Tel: 619/338-9981; fax: 525-1533
www.hostelweb.com

Hostelling International San Pedro
3601 South Gaffey Street, San
Pedro
Tel: 310/831-8109

**Los Angeles International AYH-
Hostel**
3601 S Gaffey Street, Building
#613, San Pedro
Tel: 310/831-8109; fax: 831-4635
In Angels Gate Park, overlooking the
ocean Easy bus access. Kitchen, TV
room, library and laundry.

Share-Tel International Hostel
20 Brooks Avenue, Venice Beach
Tel: 310/392-0325
Students and international travelers
share fullsize apartments on a
weekly basis.

Where to Eat

How to Choose

Southern Californians dine out an
average of two or three times a
week and variety is one of the main
reasons. The most prevalent ethnic
food you'll encounter here is
Mexican, but the Golden State has
also been the birthplace of several
culinary trends over the years,
including Szechuan, sushi, and of
course, California cuisine.

The best-known of the celebrity
chefs are Wolfgang Puck (Spago,
Chinois on Main) and Joachim
Splichal (Cafe Pinot), but in a place
where achievement equals celebrity
there are many others.

The following list is a mere
sampling of some notable
restaurants across the city.

Price Guide

The price guide refers to a meal
for two without wine:
$$$ = $100 and above
$$ = $40–100
$ =   under $40

Restaurant Listings

BREAKFAST

Polo Lounge
Beverly Hills Hotel
9641 Sunset Boulevard
Tel: 310/276-2251
Expensive but worth it just to tell
the folks back home. **$$**

John O'Groats
10516 W Pico Boulevard
A cheerful, tiny place well known to
locals and appreciated by
everybody. **$**

Newsroom the Cafe
120 N Robertson Boulevard, West

Hollywood, tel: 310/652-4444.
Newspapers, CNN on the TV and
breakfast served all day. **$**

Original Pantry Cafe
877 Figueroa, Downtown
Tel: 213/972-9279
This longtime favorite, open around
the clock, is owned by LA's mayor
Richard Riordan. **$**

Pasadena Baking Co
29 E Colorado, Pasadena
Tel: 626/796-9966
Get an early start on exploring
Pasadena with some exotic waffles
or cranberry-stuffed French toast. **$**

Patrick's Roadhouse
106 Entrada, off the Pacific Coast
Highway
Tel: 310/459-4544
An unpretentious diner much
favored by some of the stars who
live nearby. **$**

Ye Olde Kings Head
116 Santa Monica Boulevard,
Tel: 310/451-1402
Those enormous English breakfasts
that last well into the day are a
specialty here and if you're still
hungry there are all those items for
lunch. **$**

DOWNTOWN LOS
ANGELES

Luxury

A Thousand Cranes
120 S Los Angeles Street
Tel: 213/253-9255
The classiest of three restaurants
in the New Otani Hotel, this one
overlooks the lovely third-floor
garden. Refined Japanese cuisine
with sushi and tempura bars and
tatami rooms. **$$$**

Cicada
617 Olive Street
Tel: 213/488-9488
A gorgeously decorated dining
room, in the classic Oviatt Building
(formerly Rex II Ristorante), serving
Northern Italian food. **$$$**

Water Grill
544 S Grand Avenue
Tel: 213/891-0900
Elegant, chic seafood specialist,
with major business and music
center-bound clientele. Great oyster
bar. Top notch. **$$$**

Moderate

Cafe Pinot
700 West 5th Street
Tel: 213/239-6500
A few steps from the Central Library, this California/French brasserie has outdoor tables under the trees. Try the oysters, endive salad and suckling pig with mustard sauce. Closed Sunday. **$$**

Ciao Trattoria
815 W Seventh Street
Tel: 213/624-2244
Unique pastas and daily specials, considered one of the best Italian restaurants in the city. **$$–$$$**

Ciudad
445 S Figueroa Street
Tel: 213/486-5171
Latin and Southwest cross, in a wildly artistic way. From Salvadoran *pupusas* (perfect cornmeal puffs with cucumber *curtido* and mango rocoto sauce) to Colorado lamb sirloin steak with sweet roasted poblano chili. Incredible desserts and liqueurs. The new darling of Downtown, from the Border Grill team. **$$–$$$**

Engine Co
#28, 644 S Figueroa near Wilshire
Tel: 213/624-6996
A classy dining place in an 85-year-old building that was once a firehouse. Traditional cuisine. **$$**

McCormick and Schmicks
633 Fifth Street
Tel: 213/629-1929
Rich, "men's club" decor, emphasis on seafood,with a booming happy hour at all locations. (Also in Beverly Hills, Manhattan Beach, Pasadena, Irvine.) **$$–$$$**

Stepps on the Court
350 S Hope St in the Wells Fargo building
Tel: 213/626-0900
Office workers by day, Music Center patrons by night. **$$**

Taylor's Prime Steaks
3361 W Eighth Street
Tel: 213/382-8449
Old school steakhouse, an LA favorite and USC tradition for years. Reasonable prices. **$$**

Inexpensive

Barragan's
1538 W Sunset Boulevard
Tel: 213/250-4526
Great Mexican and margaritas; 40 years of family management has perfected the recipes. **$–$$**

Boulevard Cafe
3710 Martin Luther King Boulevard
Tel: 213/292-7900
Southern cooking specializing in ribs, fried chicken chitlins and cornbread. No credit cards. **$**

Clifton's Cafeteria
648 S Broadway
Tel: 213/627-1673
This long-beloved but eccentrically decorated place goes back to Downtown's golden era. **$**

Cafe Capriccio
2014 N Western
Tel: 213/662-5900
Small, friendly place in Silver Lake. Try the Vesuvio chicken or the scampi **$**

Price Guide

The price guide refers to a meal for two without wine:
$$$ = $100 and above
$$ = $40–100
$ = under $40

Grand Central Market
317 S Broadway
Tel: 213/624-2378
Bustling shoppers, neon signs and varied produce – stalls offering fish tacos and other cheap street food. **$**

Harold and Belle's
2920 W Jefferson Boulevard
Tel: 323/735-9023
Huge portions of Southern Creole. Known for the best shrimp in the 'hood. Downhome atmosphere. **$**

Jacob's Cafe
4705 S Broadway
Tel: 323/233-3803
Diners feast on generous plates of fried chicken, catfish, or oxtails, while a jazz band plays. Opened in South Central LA in 1947, features a "Blues on Broadway" series once a month. **$**

Philippe The Original
1001 Alameda Street
Tel: 213/628-3781
A legendary deli that claims to have invented the French-dip sandwich. Always crowded. Near Olvera Street, Union Station. **$**

Woody's Bar-B-Que
3446 W Slauson Avenue
Tel: 323/294-9443
Soul food and some of the most celebrated barbecues in the city. **$**

CHINATOWN

ABC Seafood
708 New High Street
Tel: 213/680-2887
Great, authentic dim sum at extremely low prices. Excellent shrimp dishes, too. **$**

Empress Pavilion
Bamboo Plaza, 988 N Hill
Tel: 213/617-9898
An elegant Hong Kong-style place that packs them in at lunchtime for inexpensive dim sum. **$**

Mandarin Deli
727 N Broadway
Tel: 213/623-6054
It's worth going Downtown to sample these great Chinese dumplings. **$**

Ocean Seafood
750 N Hill
Tel: 213/687-3088
Steamed dumplings, meat-filled buns, dim sum, custard tarts. **$**

San Woo Bar-B-Que
803 N Broadway
Tel: 213/687-7238
Deservedly renowned far and wide for its roast duck. **$**

WESTSIDE AND COAST

Luxury

La Boheme
8400 Santa Monica Boulevard, West Hollywood
Tel: 323/848-2360
Dinner and Sunday brunch only in this cavernous, Gothic and romantic villa, with roaring fireplace and eclectic California-Asian cuisine. Romantic, some hidden booths. On a budget? Appetizers at the bar. **$$$**

Campanile
624 S La Brea
Tel: 323/938-1447
Inventive, delicious Mediterranean food loved by the celebrity crowd; memorable bread from LA's most famous bakery next door. **$$$**

Chinois on Main
2709 Main Street, Santa Monica
Tel: 310/392-9025
Wolfgang Puck's flavorful fusion of
East and West. **$$$**

Citrus
6703 Melrose Avenue
Tel: 323/857-0034. Tagged by
some as the best restaurant in
town. A crisp white and glass
restaurant is the setting for
renowned pastry-chef Michel
Richard's fabulous dishes. Allow
room for dessert. **$$$**

Dar Maghreb
7651 Sunset Boulevard
Tel: 323/876-7651
A popular tourist stop, this lushly-
decorated restaurant offers an
interesting Moroccan menu. **$$$**

DC3
2800 Donald Douglas Loop, near
28th Street
Tel: 310/399-2323
Overlooking tiny Santa Monica
Airport, a jazz group often plays
Wednesday–Saturday nights, free
kids' care Tuesday–Thursday.
Try salmon in Dijon cream sauce.
$$$

Les Deux Cafe
1638 N Las Palmas, Hollywood
Tel: 323/465-0509
Ultra hipsters at this unique French
spot in the middle of a parking lot.
The food is better than the service
– but that's still secondary to the
beautiful people. **$$$**

Diaghilev
1020 N San Vicente Boulevard
Tel: 310/854-1111
Romantic and elegant, this French-
Russian opulence is the only place
for vodka and caviar. Harpist from
Bolshoi, to boot. Constant raves; in
the Bel Age hotel. **$$$**

Le Dome
8720 Sunset Boulevard
Tel: 310/659-6919.
Famous place, famous menu,
famous patrons. **$$$**

Eurochow
1099 Westwood Boulevard,
Westwood
Tel: 310/209-0066
New stark white and temple-like,
it's an Italian/Chinese dream that
you meander into – intoxicating food
(and attitude). **$$$**

The Four Oaks
2181 Beverly Glen Boulevard (east
of Sunset)
Tel: 310/470-2265
Longtime romantic favorite, tucked
away in the trees of this canyon.
Serving exquisite Country French
cuisine by a caring staff. A hidden
jewel. **$$$**

Gaylord
50 N La Cienega Boulevard
Tel: 310/652-3838
On Restaurant Row, exquisite Indian
cuisine, part of the worldwide chain.
Excellent Sunday brunch. **$$$**

Gladstone's 4 Fish
17300 Pacific Coast Highway at
Sunset
Tel: 310/573-0212
Crowded and touristy but good for
sunset-watchers and seafood, of
which they serve 400 lbs per day
plus 140lbs of lobster. **$$$**

Granita
23725 W Malibu Road
Tel: 310/450-0488
Wolfgang Puck by the sea – a bit of
Spago and Cal-Mediterranean
cuisine. Plenty of star gazing. **$$$**

Hotel Bel Air
701 Stone Canyon Road
Tel: 310/472-1211
With swans on the stream and
power-eaters all around it would be
hard to find a more impressive
ambience. Terrific food, of course.
Jacket required. **$$$**

House of Blues
8430 Sunset Boulevard, West
Hollywood
Tel: 213/848-5100
Owned, like its cousins in New
Orleans and Boston, by Hard Rock
Cafe founder Isaac Tigrett it
combines soul (and other) food with
funky music. **$$$**

Jimmy's
201 Moreno Drive, Beverly Hills
Tel: 310/552-2394
Early 20th-century French decor
with abundant art on the walls.
Piano from 7pm, dancing 10pm.
Rack of lamb, Dover sole etc. **$$$**

Lawry's
The Prime Rib, 100 N La Cienega
Tel: 310/652-2827
Traditional steak house with huge
servings long favored by heavy
trenchermen. **$$$**

The Little Door
8164 W Third Street
Tel: 323/951-1210
Low-key romantic French country
hideaway with wonderful little patio
courtyard. Favorite of film industry
powerbrokers and stars. Discreet,
intimate, with attitude. **$$$**

Manhattan Wonton Company
8475 Melrose Place
Tel: 213/655-6030
Delicious New York-style Cantonese
food served indoors or in the
courtyard garden. Minced chicken
with scallions and pine nuts or the
shrimp in lobster sauce are good
choices. **$$$**

Matsuhisa
129 N La Cienega
Tel: 310/659-9639
Celebrated and celebrity sushi. **$$$**

Morton's
8764 Melrose Avenue, West
Hollywood
Tel: 310/276-5205
One of LA's celeb watering holes,
with food better than it has to be,
and although you'll probably be
seated in Siberia unless you're
somebody, you're really in the seat
for people-watching. **$$$**

Olive
119 Fairfax Avenue
Tel: 213/939-2001
Steaks and fish until 2am in a dim
atmosphere. **$$$**

L'Orangerie
903 N La Cienega Boulevard
Tel: 310/652-9770
Lobster souffle, caviar with eggs
and the like in elegant
surroundings. **$$$**

Pangaea
Hotel Nikko, 465 S La Cienega
Boulevard
Tel: 310/246-2000
Virtually part of the delightful
Japanese garden that fills the
hotel's ground floor. Asian cuisine,
fish especially good. **$$$**

Schatz-on-Main
3110 Main Street, Santa Monica
Tel: 310/399-4800
Famous less for its food than for its
founder Arnold Schwarzenegger. **$$$**

Spago
1114 Horn Avenue, Sunset
Boulevard, West Hollywood
Tel: 310/652-3706, and

176 N Canon Drive, Beverly Hills
Tel: 310/385-0880
All the old favorites that have
enhanced chef Wolfgang Puck's
worldwide reputation. **$$$**
Valentino
3115 Pico Boulevard, Santa Monica
Tel: 310/829-4313
The standard in fine Italian
restaurants for Southern California
– rave reviews for food, service,
and wine cellar. **$$$**

Moderate
Angeli Caffe
7274 Melrose Avenue, Hollywood
Tel: 323/936-9086
The original and last remaining of
the Angeli chain. Noisy, crowded
and tiny, but great fun. Angeli
serves up some of the best rustic
Italian cuisine in town. **$$**
Authentic Cafe
7605 Beverly Boulevard, Hollywood
Tel: 213/939-4626
Popular neighborhood restaurant,
serving an eclectic mix of
Southwestern, Italian and American
cuisines. No reservations, so
usually a wait, but worth it. **$$**
Border Grill
1445 4th Street
Tel: 310/451-1655
Some of the best modern-Mexican
cuisine around. Large choice of
delicious appetiziers. **$$**
Cafe Blanc
9777 Little Santa Monica
Boulevard, Beverly Hills
Tel: 310/888-0108
Asian-New French, full of creative
delights with gorgeous
presentations and a helpful staff.
Offers one of the best lunch deals
around. **$$**
Cafe Rodeo in the Summit Hotel
360 N Rodeo
Tel: 310/273-0300
The only place on this famous
shopping street where you can sit
at a sidewalk table and people-
watch. **$$**
Chart House
18412 Pacific Coast Highway,
Malibu
Tel: 310/454-9321
It just seems that there is one
every 10 miles along the California
coast. A staple through the 1970s

and '80s in Southern California,
their classic salad bar, steak, and
seafood menu remains as good as
ever – and although they've
expanded across the US, sitting
here they feel as much a part of
California as the Beach Boys. (Also
in Marina Del Rey, Redondo Beach,
Newport Beach, Dana Point,
Oceanside, Cardiff, La Jolla, San
Diego, and Coronado.) **$$**
Chianti Ristorante
7383 Melrose Avenue at Martel
Tel: 323/653-8333
Classic Italian and romantic with
private booths, low lighting and
murals of Italian countryside. Veal,
pastas, regional dishes, spit-
roasted meats and fowl. **$$**

Price Guide

The price guide refers to a meal
for two without wine:
$$$ = $100 and above
$$ = $40–100
$ = under $40

The Firehouse
213 Rose Avenue, Venice
Tel: 310/396-6810
Built in 1902 the building has
housed an antique shop and a
bakery before becoming a family-
style restaurant a decade ago.
Charboiled halibut, chicken fajitas,
spinach pancakes etc. **$$**
Geoffrey's
27400 Pacific Coast Highway,
Malibu
Tel: 310/457-1519
Stunning views and food over the
Pacific. California-Eclectic, popular
with Malibu jet-set. **$$–$$$**
Georgia
7250 Melrose Avenue
Tel: 323/933-8420
Elegant, upscale Southern and soul
food, popular with African-American
celebrities. Check out the fried
chicken, biscuits, and Bloody
Marys. **$$**
Hampton's Hollywood Cafe
1342 N Highland Avenue
Tel: 323/469-1090
Tasty fettuccine, every possible kind
of burger and veggie dishes, exotic
desserts. **$$**

Hirozen Gourmet
8385 Beverly Boulevard
Tel: 323/653-0470
All the Japanese dishes are good
but check out the crab cakes and
the seafood stew (*yosenabe*). **$$**
Inn of the Seventh Ray
128 Old Topanga Boulevard
Tel: 310/455-1311
Beautiful location, indifferent
vegetarian food. **$$**
Jiraffe
502 Santa Monica Boulevard,
Santa Monica
Tel: 310/917-6671
Innovative California cuisine at this
hip scene. Good wine list.
Interesting open architecture. **$$**
Kate Mantilini
9101 Wilshire Boulevard
Tel: 310/278-3699
In a distinctive-looking building, this
popular late-night spot serves
American dishes until at least
1.30am every night but Sunday. **$$**
Magic Carpet
8566 W Pico Boulevard
Tel: 310/652-8507
Yemenite cuisine: chicken schnitzel,
beef stew and tasty lentil soup. **$$**
Mexico City
2121 Hillhurst Avenue, Los Feliz
Tel: 213/661-7227
Retro-hip atmosphere. Cactus salad
and familiar south-of-the border fare
with the Plata Mexica offering a bit
of everything. **$$**
Miceli's Italian Restaurant
3655 Cahuenga Boulevard
Tel: 323/851-3344
Operatically-trained waiters
serenade as you eat classic Italian
food at this family-type spot. **$$**
Moustache Cafe
8155 Melrose Avenue
Tel: 323/651-2111
Longstanding favorite of the late
dining crowd who fill the attractive
patio and pick from a menu ranging
over grilled salmon, Thai noodles,
Moroccan cous cous and standard
French cuisine. It's all foreplay for
what they really come for – the
chocolate souffle dessert. In
Westwood also 310/208-6633. **$$**
Musso and Frank's
6667 Hollywood Boulevard
Tel: 323/467-7788
A menu of old faithfuls that's

basically unchanged since it began aeons ago when Hollywood giants could be seen through the gloom (some still can). **$$**

Red
7450 Beverly Boulevard
Tel: 323/937-0331
Smack in the middle of the nightlife strip. Hip joint, hipper bar, some outside seating. Chicken roasted in apple cider and thyme and chicken stew are tasty choices. **$$**

The Stinking Rose
55 N La Cienega Boulevard
Tel: 310/652-7673
Garlic soups, salads, entrees, desserts and drinks in half a dozen amusingly themed rooms. **$$**

Sunset Landmark
6525 Sunset Boulevard, Hollywood
Tel: 323/460-6778
Dinner menu is minimal (burgers, pasta) but diners are usually first in line for the popular pool tables with no time limit (formerly the Hollywood Athletic Club). **$$**

Taiko
11677 San Vicente Boulevard, Brentwood
Tel: 310/207-7782
First-rate Japanese cuisine includes 18 dfferent kinds of noodles and a vegetable sushi. **$$**

Taverna Tony
23410 Civic Center Drive, Malibu
Tel: 310/317-9667
Lively Greek place with patio dining and entertainment, including the famous regular faces. **$$**

Warszawa
1414 Lincoln Boulevard
Santa Monica
Tel: 310/393-8831
Eastern European delight, authentic and homey. Try the lamb dumplings and potato pancakes. **$$**

Yamishiro
1999 North Sycamore Avenue, Hollywood
Tel: 323/466-5125
Some claim it offers the nicest view in LA. Surrounded by Japanese gardens, this is a lovely place for dinner or drinks. **$$–$$$**

Inexpensive

Apple Pan
10801 W Pico Boulevard
Tel: 310/475-3585

Family-run for 50 years and still offering such old diner reliables as hamburgers and excellent pies. **$**

Barney's Beanery
8477 Santa Monica Boulevard, Hollywood
Tel: 323/654-2287
A newspaper-sized menu offering at least 200 international beers plus tables for a friendly game of pool. Casual, funky and fun. **$**

Benita's Frites
1437 Third Street Promenade, Santa Monica
Tel: 310/458-2889
Delicious Belgian frites with a choice of 20 tasty sauces. **$**

Bombay Cafe
12021 W Pico Boulevard, near Bundy
Tel: 310/820-2070
Delectable Indian food. **$**

Caffe Latte
6254 Wilshire Boulevard
Tel: 323/936-5213
Coffee roasted on the premises. Simple food with great sausages, cappucino pancakes. **$**

California Pizza Kitchen
207 S Beverly Drive, Beverly Hills
Tel: 310/854-6555
One of a chain and "the People's Spago", declares dining-out critic Merrill Shindler. **$**

Canter's Delicatessen and Bakery
419 Fairfax Avenue, near Third Street
Tel: 323/651-2030
Famous large and lively deli with classic 1950s interior. Open around the clock. **$**

El Coyote Spanish Cafe
73132 Beverly Boulevard
Tel: 323/939-2255
A long-standing landmark with unexceptional (inexpensive) Mexican standard items but great ambiance and unbeatable margaritas. **$**

The Gumbo Pot
6333 W 3rd Street
Tel: 323/933-0358
Hot Cajun, Oone of the dozens of great eating places in the Farmers Market. Note: the market closes early evening. **$**

Hollywood Hills Coffee Shop
6145 Franklin Avenue
Tel: 323/467-7678

Classic diner food, but come for the atmosphere. This is where young stars-to-be (and even some who are) meet, and where *Swingers* was filmed. **$**

Hu's Szechwan Restaurant
10450 National Boulevard
Tel: 310/837-0252
Hot, spicy, inexpensive Chinese. **$**

Nate 'n Al's
414 N Beverly Drive, Beverly Hills
Tel: 310/274-0101
A classic deli, with chicken soup, and brisket like your Jewish grandmother used to make – and the old waitresses act like her too! Local favorite, you never know who you might bump into. **$**

Original Tommy's
2575 W Beverly Boulevard at Rampart
Tel: 213/389-9060
Unpretentious hamburger stand with scores of imitators (all with similar names) and around a million customers a year. **$**

Pink's Famous Chili Dogs
709 N La Brea Avenue
Tel: 213/931-7594
Starting as a dime hot dog counter around 60 years ago, Pink's became a Hollywood legend, its stellar customers including Bruce Willis (who reportedly proposed to Demi Moore here). **$**

Real Food Daily
514 Santa Monica Boulevard
Tel: 310/451-7544
Spartan vegetarian, even vegan, cooking; no meat, no dairy. **$**

Red Lion Tavern
2366 Glendale Boulevard, Silver Lake
Tel: 323/662-5337
Rustic surroundings, waitresses in peasant dress, German beer and garlicky food to match. **$**

Rick Royce Premier Barbecue
10916 W Pico Boulevard
Tel: 310/441-7427
Unpretentious, white-washed room operated by the legendary Royce whose baby back ribs won a national contest. Chicken, swordfish and beef, too, and don't overlook the spicy sauces. **$**

Rita Flora/Kitchen
460 N La Brea at 6th Street
Tel: 323/931-9900

A combination restaurant/flower shop with sidewalk tables. Tasty fresh baked desserts. **$**

Rosalind's Ethiopian
1044 S Fairfax Avenue
Tel: 323/936-2486
Nigerian goat and ground nut stew are among the African specialties here. **$**

Roscoe's Chicken and Waffles
1514 N Gower Street, Hollywood
Tel: 323/466-7453
Homestyle Southern cooking, revolving around tasty, crispy chicken and fluffy waffles. They really do go well together, as well as the snappy waitresses. A Sharon Stone favorite. (Also in LA and Pasadena.) **$**

Taix French Restaurant
1911 Sunset Boulevard near Alvarado
Tel: 213/484-1265
An old reliable that's been around forever and has remained cosy and reasonably priced. **$.**

Uzbekistan
7077 Sunset Boulevard
Tel: 323/464-3663
Skewered meat and chicken eaten with the fingers and accompanied by wok-tossed vegetables. **$**

SOUTH BAY, LONG BEACH AND SAN PEDRO

Luxury

Chez Melange
1716 Pacific Coast Highway, Redondo Beach
Tel: 310/540-1222
Long the standard in the South Bay -- eclectic menu, a pioneer in inventive combinations. Good martini bar too. **$$$**

The Madison
102 Pine Avenue, Long Beach
Tel: 562/628-8866
Upscale steak, chop and seafood in an elegant setting, with attentive service. **$$$**

L'Opera
101 Pine Avenue, Long Beach
Tel: 562/491-0066
Locals rave about this touch of Italy, its atmosphere and service. **$$$**

The Sky Room
40 S Locust Avenue, Long Beach
Tel: 562/983-2703

Fabulous retro dinner nightclub, where stars once frolicked in the 1940s. Now renovated, but serving the old time Continental menu. On top of landmark "Breakers" building, with great views. **$$$**

Moderate

Il Boccaccio
39 Pier Avenue, Hermosa Beach
Tel: 310/376-0211
On the Promenade, this romantic jewel is known for inventive Italian – walk it off on the nearby pier. **$$**

Cheesecake Factory
605 N Harbor Drive, Redondo Beach
Tel: 310/376-0466
On the marina, where locals take visitors first. Extensive menu of salads, sandwiches, burgers, omelettes, etc., huge portions, and guess what's for dessert? **$$**

Price Guide

The price guide refers to a meal for two without wine:
$$$ = $100 and above
$$ = $40–100
$ =   under $40

Cucina Paradiso
1611 S Catalina Avenue, Redondo Beach
Tel: 310/792-1972
Delicious Italian trattoria. Make reservations in advance. **$$–$$$**

Encounter
Los Angeles Airport
Tel: 310/215-5151
Redesigned by the creative folks at Walt Disney Imagineering as a sort of *Star Wars* meets *The Jetsons*, and a menu by the renowned Chef John Sedlar (including Wasabi Caviar Pasta), this unique spot in the middle of LAX is a treat. **$$–$$$**

Gina Lee's Bistro
211 Palos Verdes Boulevard, Redondo Beach
Tel: 310/375-4462
Pacific Asian fusion. Possibly the best fish restaurant in the South Bay. Friendly service, upscale but casual. **$$**

Houston's
1550 Rosecrans Avenue, Manhattan Beach
Tel: 310/643-7211
Upscale American fare, with incredible ribs. Try the tasty artichoke dip. Nice bar. Also in Century City, Pasadena, Woodland Hills, and Irvine. **$$**

Kincaid's
500 Fishermen's Wharf, Redondo Beach
Tel: 310/318-6080
Best new South Bay restaurant features excellent steak, chops and fish in a dramatic waterfront room, bringing a touch of class to Redondo pier. **$$–$$$**

Michi
903 Manhattan Avenue, Manhattan Beach
Tel: 310/376-0613
Chic beach crowd grooving to California-Pacific-Asian menu and martinis. **$$–$$$**

Papadakis Taverna
301 W 6th Street, San Pedro
Tel: 310/548-1186
Prime Greek cuisine with lots of singing and dancing. **$$**

P.F. Changs
2041 Rosecrans, El Segundo
Tel: 310/607-9062
Chinese with California nouvelle overtones – upscale with popular bars. (Also in West LA, Santa Monica, and Newport Beach.) **$$**

Soleil
1142 Manhattan Avenue, Manhattan Beach
Tel: 310/545-8654
Eclectic-Mediterranean menu in a stylish bistro, with an excellent wine list. **$$**

Zazou
1810 S Catalina Avenue, Redondo Beach
Tel: 310/540-4884
Creative Californian-Mediterranean; intimate, noisy, fun. Stroll the quaint Hollywood-Riviera Village afterwards. **$$**

Inexpensive

Fish Tale
2050 Bellflower Boulevard, Long Beach
Tel: 562/594-8771
Seafood in nice surroundings. **$**

Ragin' Cajun
422 Pier Avenue, Hermosa Beach
Tel: 310/376-7878
Good, spicy Cajun, at reasonable prices. Always lively. **$**

SAN FERNANDO VALLEY

Luxury
Cafe Sierra
555 Universal Terrace Parkway, Universal City
Tel: 818/509-2030
In the soaring chrome and glass lobby of the Universal City Hilton, best known for Sunday brunch. **$$$**

Moderate
Bamboo Inn
14010 Ventura Boulevard, between Woodman and Hazeltine avenues
Tel: 818/788-0202
A good neighborhood place for Chinese cuisine. **$$**
Ca' del Sole
4100 Cahuenga Boulevard, North Hollywood
Tel: 818/985-4669
Authentic Italian in a Tuscan home-like environment – popular studio and network hangout. Nice patio. (Sister to Ca' Brea on La Brea.) **$$**
Moonlight Supper Club
13730 Ventura Boulevard, Sherman Oaks
Tel: 818/788-2000
A late-night supper club with singing waiters and a white-tuxedoed "big band" combo that inspires conga lines and other frivolity. **$$**
La Parrilla
19601 Ventura Boulevard between Reseda Boulevard and Van Alden Avenue, Tarzana
Tel: 818/708-7422 or
19265 Roscoe Boulevard at Tampa Avenue, Northridge
Tel: 818/993-7773
Authentic fun Mexican. **$$**
Sid's Seafood
21911 Roscoe Boulevard, Canoga Park
Tel: 818/887-1692
A family institution that is crowded every evening, especially for Wednesday's crab feast. Big portions, tip top service. **$$**

Tempo
16610 Ventura Boulevard between Havenhurst and Balboa boulevards, Encino
Tel: 818/905-5885
A Middle Eastern eatery with a special sabbath dinner every Friday night. **$$**
Ueru-Ka-Mu
19596 Ventura Boulevard, Tarzana
Tel: 818/609-0993
A typical *izakaya*, or Japanese drinking pub, specializing in the tiny dishes that suit serious sake drinkers. **$$**

Inexpensive
Art's Deli
12224 Ventura Boulevard, Studio City
Tel: 818/762-1221
Some say it's the best deli in LA; it's certainly the best deli in the Valley. Mile-high sandwiches, great knishes and stuffed cabbage. **$**
Rubin's Red Hot
15322 Ventura Boulevard, Sherman Oaks
Tel: 818/905-6515
A legendary hot-dog dispensary in unsurpassable Chicago style. **$**

Among the LA restaurants that have branched out into the Valley are **Pinot**, 12969 Ventura Boulevard between Coldwater Canyon and Fulton avenues, Studio City, tel: 818/990-0500 and **Posto**, 14928 Ventura Boulevard at Kester Avenue, Sherman Oaks, tel: 818/784-4400, a casual cousin of Piero Selvaggio's top-rated Valentino. (Both **$$**).
Beverly Hills' famed Bistro Garden is now the **Bistro Garden at Coldwater**, 12950 Ventura Boulevard, Studio City, tel: 818/501-0202, featuring modern continental cuisine from the longtime LA favorite. **Yang Chow**, LA's long-time top-rated traditional Chinese restaurant, has one branch in Chinatown at 819 N Broadway, tel: 213/625-0811, one in the Valley at 6443 Topanga Canyon Boulevard, Woodland Hills, tel: 818/347-2610, and one in Pasadena at 3777 Colorado Boulevard, 626/432-6868 (All **$$–$$$**).

For the budget conscious, look for one of several **Baja Fresh** or **Poquito Mas** locations in the Valley for good, cheap, fast Mexican food.

PASADENA

Luxury
Yujean Kang's
67 N Raymond Avenue
Tel: 626/585-0855
Well-presented nouvelle Chinese food. Also in West Hollywood. **$$$**

Moderate
Twin Palms
101 N Green Street
Tel: 626/577-2567
Californian food is good but secondary to the unique tent-like enclosed scene and be seen. Hot singles scene, live jazz, good Sunday gospel brunch. **$$**

Inexpensive
Clearwater Seafood
168 W Colorado Boulevard
Tel: 626/356-0959
Seafood, healthy vegetable dishes, some Japanese touches. **$**
Gordon Biersch Brewing Co.
41 Hugus Alley (between Colorado and Fair Oaks)
Tel: 626/449-0052
Great beer and good fod (try the garlic fries) in an upscale yet casual environment, popular with young singles. **$**

ORANGE COUNTY BEACH TOWNS

Luxury
Pascal
1000 N Bristol Street, Newport Beach
Tel: 949/752-0107
Rave reviews for this French Country stalwart, possibly the finest restaurant in Orange County. **$$$**
The Ritz
880 Newport Center Drive, Newport Beach
Tel: 949/720-1800
Old money dining – traditional fare classically served in a tremendous dining room. **$$$**

21 Ocean Front
2100 W Ocean Front,
Newport Beach,
Tel:949/673-2100
Overlooking the sea and near the
pier. Pasta, seafood, steaks. **$$$**

Moderate
The Cannery Restaurant
3010 Lafayette Street,
Newport Beach
Tel: 714/675-5777
Attractive surroundings in a former
canning plant by the harbor.
Seafood, steaks. Organizes
weekend cruises. **$$**
Cedar Creek Inn
384 Forest Avenue, Laguna Beach
Tel: 949/497-8696
Wide selection of American cuisine
plus evening oyster bar. **$$**
Five Crowns
3801 East Coast Highway,
Corona del Mar
Tel: 949/760-0331
Delighful food served in a beautiful
two-story building modeled after Ye
Olde Bell, England's oldest inn.
Dinner and Sunday brunch only. **$$**
Five Feet
328 Glenneyre Street,
Laguna Beach
Tel: 949/497-4955
Eclectic, incredibly inventive, and
always delicious Asian-French-
Pacific Rim cuisine. Hip, noisy, and
fun. **$$–$$$**

Inexpensive
Las Brisas
361 Cliff Drive, Laguna Beach
Tel: 949/497-5434
Beside the sea. Mexican cuisine. **$**
Crab Cooker
2200 Newport Boulevard (on the
peninsula)
Tel: 949/673-0100
Rustic local landmark, valued for its
fresh seafood and cheap prices (if
you don't mind the paper plates). **$**
Daily Grill
957 Newport Center Drive,
Newport Beach
Tel: 949/644-2223
In Fashion Island at Newport
Center. American cuisine. **$**

ANAHEIM

The Cellar Restaurant
305 North Harbor Boulevard,
Fullerton
Tel: 714/525-5682
Superb French cuisine and
expansive wine cellar 4 miles
(7 km) from Disneyland. **$$$**
Acapulco Mexican Restaurant
1410 Harbor Boulevard
Tel: 714/956-7380
Award-winning Mexican food across
the street from Disneyland. **$$**
The Catch
S State College Boulevard
Tel: 714/634-1829
Steak and seafood in '20s decor. **$$**

Price Guide

The price guide refers to a meal
for two without wine:
$$$ = $100 and above
$$ = $40–100
$ = under $40

Hansa House Smorgasbord
1840 S Harbor Boulevard
Tel: 714/750-2411
Scandinavian decor and cuisine
served in buffet style. **$$**
Minmi's Cafe,
1240 N Euclid Avenue
Tel: 714/535-1552
Frenchified cafe with family
ambiance and American food. **$**

Cafe Sitting

Santa Monica's **Third Street
Promenade**, a pedestrian-only
outdoor mall with sidewalk cafes,
restaurants and bars is always
interesting, but especially so in
the evening.
Other good people-watching
areas with groups of sidewalk cafes
are **Montana Avenue** between 12th
and 17th Street; **Melrose Avenue**
between La Brea and Fairfax in
West Hollywood; and **San Vicente
Boulevard** at Barrington in
Brentwood.
Some outdoor cafes worth visiting
are **Highland Grounds**, 742 N
Highland Avenue, tel: 323/466-1507
with its patio courtyard and music

most nights; the **Sidewalk Cafe**,
Ocean Front Walk, Venice,
tel: 310/399-5547, with nightly
music and a good view of the
boardwalk happenings.
Other interesting cafes are the **Hot
House Jazz Cafe**, 12123 Riverside
Drive, N Hollywood,
tel: 818/506-7058; the **Library Cafe**,
10144 Riverside Drive, **Toluca Lake**,
tel: 818/505-0930; **Little Frida's**,
8730 Santa Monica Boulevard, tel:
310/854-5421; the **Unurban Coffee
House**, 3301 Pico Boulevard, Santa
Monica, tel: 310/315-0056; and
Java Man, 157 Pier Avenue,
Hermosa Beach, tel: 310/379-7209.

Downtown Bars

Downtown's bars are usually
packed with business folk who work
nearby. Once deserted after working
hours, the area is now host to many
popular bars.
The Redwood House, 316 W 2nd
Street, is the hang-out for the crowd
from the *Los Angeles Times*.
Cicada, 617 S Olive, is frequented
by uppercrust business people. An
elegant spot, it mirrors the art-deco
ambiance of a 1930s cruise liner,
accompanied by a great martini.
Otto Rothschild's Bar and Grill,
135 N Grand Avenue, tel: 213/972-
7322, is where folk meet before
and after attending performances
at the Dorothy Chandler Pavilion.
Not far away at 613 S Grand
Avenue is the sports-minded
Casey's Bar and Grill,
tel: 213/629-2353, and, at No.
506 in the Biltmore Hotel, is the
Grand Avenue Bar, tel: 213/612-
1532, with all-star jazz at night.
Ever been to an elegant sports
bar? **Flower Street Cafe**, 615 S
Flower Street, tel: 213/623-4777 is
one you won't be embarrassed to
bring a date; if you really want to
impress though, the bar at **Tesoro
Trattoria** is almost as impressive
as the food. Excellent happy hour,
and wine list, too – at the **California
Plaza**, 300. Grand,
tel: 213/680-0000,
Great evening views can be had
from the 34th floor **Bona Vista Bar**
in the Westin Bonaventure Hotel,

404 S Figueroa Street. In Little Tokyo, the **Genji Bar**, 120 S Los Angeles Street (in the New Otani Hotel) has a piano bar.

Long-time favorite **Engine Co. No. 28**, 644 S Figueroa Street, tel: 213/624-6996, still holds its own among the after-work professional crowd, but the recent champion of happy hours is **McCormick and Schmicks**, 633 W. Fifth Street, tel: 213/629-1929, where the drinks are hand-shaken and only fresh juices are used.

AT THE BEACHES

Santa Monica has several good British-style pubs, the best being **Ye Olde King's Head** at 116 Santa Monica Boulevard, tel: 310/451-1402 which serves traditional British ale and lager, and the food is at least as good as in most English pubs.

The ever-popular Mexican bars include **Marix Tex Mex**, 8350 Santa Monica Boulevard, tel: 310/459-8596 whose superb margaritas are popular with young beachgoers, and the recently relocated **Rebecca's**, 101 Broadway, known for its upscale, creative Mexican menu (including tuna tartare and duck *rellenos*.

In Venice, the trendy strip is on **Abbott Kinney Way** and includes great restaurant/bars like **Hal's**, (California cuisine) at 1349, tel: 310/396-1035, and **Joe's** at 1023, tel: 310/399-5811. Joe's, in particular, is renowned for its New American fare and Sunday brunch, but both are filled nightly with *artistes and* movie types.

Down in the South Bay, the **Hermosa Beach Pier Promenade** has an armful of restaurants and bars for singles and families, with the nightife going strong at **Sangria**, tel: 310/376-4412, an upscale, restaurant with outdoor seating (and jazz regularly); **Aloha Sharkeez**, tel: 310/374-7823, the wild'n'crazy singles scene (good, cheap burgers and tacos, too), and **Brewski's**, tel: 310/318-2666, a microbrewery with outdoor patio and tasty American fare.

WESTSIDE DRINKING SPOTS

The **Cat 'n Fiddle**, 6530 Sunset Boulevard, tel: 323/468-3800 is a lively restaurant bar with an open patio. Jazz and/or blues on Sunday and Monday nights.

A survivor of an earlier movie era is the **Formosa**, 7156 Santa Monica Boulevard, tel: 323/850-9050, whose walls are lined with photos of the stars who used to come here. As it's near Warner-Hollywood Studios, some still do.

For a good game of backgammon or chess, stop in at the **San Francisco Saloon**, 11501 W Pico Boulevard, tel: 310/478-0152. Pool your game? Try **Cue's** on Wilshire Boulevard at Barrington Boulevard. The **Sunset Landmark**, 6525 Sunset Boulevard, tel: 323/460-6778, where stars John Wayne and John Barrymore got drunk together, is now an upscale bar and poolroom. **Tom Bergin's**, 1121 S Western Avenue, tel: 323/936-7151, is a traditional Irish pub dating back over 50 years.

Another great spot is **Musso and Frank's**, 6667 Hollywood Boulevard, tel: 323/467-5123, with reasonable prices, colorful waiters, and the best martinis in town.

Yamashiro's, 1999 N Sycamore Avenue, tel: 323/466-5125, is an upscale restaurant and relaxing bar with lush gardens that's perfect for an overview of Hollywood at dusk. Lower down, the **Cafe Mondrian**, 8440 Sunset Boulevard, tel: 323/650-8999, offers almost as good a view from its lounge patio.

Planet Hollywood, 9560 Wilshire Boulevard, Beverly Hills, tel: 310/275-7828 is where Forest Gump's box of chocolates and other movie ephemera can be found. **The Hard Rock Cafe**, 8600 Beverly Boulevard, tel: 310/276-7605, serves good burgers and, like others in the chain, is filled with rock memorabilia.

Westwood Brewing Co., 1097 Glendon near UCLA, tel: 310/209-2739 is a microbrewery with different beers and good food.

Culture

Ticket Agencies

Al Brooks Theatre Ticket Agency
900 Wilshire Boulevard #104
Tel: 213/626-5863
A Musical Chair
11677 San Vicente Boulevard
Tel: 310/207-7070
Front Center Ticket Services
1355 Westwood Boulevard #3
Tel: 310/478-0848
Ticketmaster
3701 Wilshire Boulevard
Tel: 213/480-3232;
www.ticketmaster,com
Ticket Time
11577 Olympic Boulevard
Tel: 310/473-1000
Tickets.com
An online ticketing website:
www.tickets.com

Nightlife

LA offers world-class operas and musicals, theater and symphonies as well as first-rate comedy and funky live blues, jazz, rock 'n' roll and discos.

Bars and clubs along the 8000 blocks of Santa Monica Boulevard in West Hollywood are predominantly for gays.

To track down other nightlife, refer to local newspapers as a guide to what's on in town. The Calendar section of Sunday's *Los Angeles Times* offers fairly complete listings of events in the area, but the two weekly free newspapers, the *LA Weekly* and less-popular *New Times* give hipper and more comprehensive details about local events including movie schedules and activities at the various music clubs. The concierges at most hotels are very knowledgeable.

Dance

The Music Center/Performing Arts Center Los Angeles
135 N Grand
Tel: 310/972-7211;
www.performingartscenterla.org
The western home of the Joffrey bi-coastal ballet company, which is most active in the spring.

The Shrine Auditorium
649 W Jefferson
Tel: 213/748-5116
The Shrine hosts the American Ballet Theater in March.

UCLA Center for the Arts
4405 N Hillgard, Westwood
Tel: 310/825-2101;
www.ucla.performingarts.edu
Famous ballet companies share this center for the arts with the UCLA Dance Company.

The **Wiltern Theatre**, tel: 213/380-2005; the **Veterans Wadsworth Theatre**, tel: 310/825-2101; **the Pasadena Civic Auditorium**, tel: 626/449-7360 and **Glendale's Alex Theatre**, tel: 800/233-3123, www.alextheatre.org also stage dance concerts semi-regularly.

For specific listings, consult the Sunday Calendar section of the *Los Angeles Times*.

Opera

Dorothy Chandler Pavilion
135 N Grand Avenue
Tel: 213/972-7211
The pavilion showcases the Los Angeles Civic Light Opera. The building is richly appointed with marble walls, sculptured columns, and crystal chandeliers.

The Wilshire Ebell Theater
4401 W Eighth Street
Tel: 323/939-1128
This Spanish-designed venue was built in 1924, and often hosts the Los Angeles Opera Theater.

Wiltern Theater
Wilshire Boulevard and Western Avenue
Tel: 213/380-5005
Built in 1930 and now a protected art-deco landmark, the Wiltern is also a venue for the Los Angeles Opera Theater and musical events.

Music

The 3,200-seat **Dorothy Chandler Pavilion**, part of the Music Center/Performing Arts Center of LA County complex, 135 N Grand Avenue, Downtown, tel: 213/972-7211 is the home of the Los Angeles Philharmonic, tel: 323/850-2000; www.laphil.org.

The June to September season at the **Hollywood Bowl** has nightly concerts: jazz, classical and pop. Park free at specific lots and take the roundtrip bus or take Bowlbus from 14 different locations. For information and reservations: tel: 323/850-2000, www.hollywoodbowl.org. Ask about free morning rehearsals.

Other local sounds include the **Santa Monica Symphony**, www.smsymphony.org, free at the Santa Monica Civic Auditorium, tel: 310/996-3620; and the **Pasadena Symphony**, tel: 626/793-7172.

There are also regular concerts at the **Greek Theatre**, tel: 323/665-1927; www.nederlander.com, in Griffith Park, the venerable **Palace in Hollywood**, 1735 N Vine Street, tel: 323/462-3000; www.hollywoodpalace.com, and the **Universal Amphitheatre** above Universal City, tel: 818/622-4440; www.hob.com.

Other spots for top acts include the **House of Blues**, 8430 Sunset Boulevard, tel: 310/848-5100; www.hob.com; the **Staples Center**, 1111 S Figueroa Street, Downtown, tel: 213/480-3232 (Ticketmaster); www.staplescenter.com; and the **Sun Theatre** in Anaheim, tel: 714/712-2700; www.sun-theatre.com.

For outdoor summer Sunday performances, check **Warner Park**, Woodland Hills. Tel: 818/704-1587 for schedule. Santa Clarita's summer concerts take place in **Old Orchard Park**, tel: 805/284-1460. In Thousand Oaks, the locale is **Conejo Community Park**, tel: 805/495-2163, and in Agoura Hills at **Chumash Park**, tel: 818/597-7361. In West Hollywood, **Summer Sounds** takes place every Sunday, featuring a variety from orchestra to swing, tel: 800/368-6020. **Polliwog Park** in Manhattan Beach hosts the Sunday Concerts in the Park on Labor Day, tel: 310/802-5408. In July and August, **Redondo Beach Pier** hosts free concerts Thursday and Saturday evenings, tel: 310/374-2171; www.redondo.com

Theater

With a score of openings every week at one or another of its little theaters, LA is the spawning ground for many of Broadway's famous shows. More than four million theater tickets are sold in LA every year and resident troupes often include famous actors, enjoying a hiatus from the camera by taking some meaty role in a 99-seat Equity-waiver production.

The Groundlings, 7307 Melrose Avenue, tel: 323/934-9700; www.groundlings.com, is a long-established venue and now under challenge from the breakway **Acme Comedy Theatre**, tel: 323/525-0202; www.acmecomedy.com.

But in addition to the dozens of tiny houses there are also the better-known **Shubert Theatre**, tel: 800/447-7400 in Century City, the **Mark Taper Forum**, the **Ahmanson**, tel: 213/628-2772; www.TaperAhmanson.com in the Music Center at 135 N Grand; and the **Geffen Theatre**, tel: 310/208-5454; www.geffenplayhouse.com, near the UCLA campus.

Repertory can be enjoyed at the **Cast Theatre**, 804 N El Centro, Hollywood, tel: 323/462-9872 and other theaters with a regular schedule include the **Wilshire Ebell Theatre**, West 8th Street, tel: 323/939-1128; the **Pantages**, 6233 Hollywood Boulevard, tel: 323/468-1770; www.nederlander.com (or Ticketmaster 213/480-3232); and the **James A. Doolittle**, 1615 N Vine, tel: 323/462-6666. Also, the **Los Angeles Theatre Center**, Downtown, tel: 213/485-1681; the **Canon Theatre** in Hollywood, tel: 310/859-2830; **Court Theatre** on La Cienega, tel: 310/289-2999, and **Actors Co-op**, in Hollywood, tel: 323/462-8460.

Further afield are the **Hermosa Beach Playhouse**, tel: 310/372-4477; www.civiclightopera.com; the **Cerittos Center for the Performing Arts**, tel: 800/300-4345; www.cerritoscenter.com; the **Santa Monica Playhouse**, tel: 310/394-9779; the **Back Alley**, 15231 Burbank Boulevard, Van Nuys, tel: 818/780-2240; the **Pasadena Playhouse**, 39 El Molino Avenue, tel: 626/356-7529; www.pasadena playhouse.org; and the **Thousand Oaks Civic Arts Plaza**, tel: 805/449-2700.

Productions at **Santa Monica's Highways**, tel: 310/453-1755, the **Bilingual Foundation for the Arts**, tel: 323/225-4044, north of Downtown, the **Japan American Theatre** and the **Vision Complex**, 4310 Degnan, Leimert Park, tel: 323/295-9685 are always worth seeing. Also try **Shakespeare by the Sea**, Point Fermin Park, San Pedro, tel: 310/548-7705; www.ghog.com/seashakespeare, Thursday–Saturday in mid-summer.

Look for listings in the free *LA Weekly*, widely distributed around town or call **Theater LA** on 213/688-ARTS; www.theatrela.org, which offers comprehensive listings.

For discounted tickets to LA theaters, tel: 213/688-ARTS.

Libraries

A restored 1920s Beaux Arts landmark, the **Los Angeles Public Library**, 630 W 5th Street, tel: 213/228-7000; www.lapl.org, has daily tours.

Two other libraries worth seeing are the **William Adams Clark Memorial Library** in an Italian Renaissance-style house at 2520 Cimarron Street at Adams Boulevard, tel: 323/731-8529; www.humnet.ucla.edu, west of Downtown LA, with its collection of 16th- and 17th-century editions of Shakespeare, John Dryden, Samuel Pepys, etc.; and the **Brand Library and Art Center** at 1601 Mountain Street in Glendale, tel: 818/548-

2051; www.library.ci.glendale.ca.us, an impressive mansion that's reputed to have the largest collection of music and art in Southern California. Closed Monday.

The **Richard Nixon Library and Birthplace**, 18001 Yorba Linda Boulevard, Yorba Linda, tel: 714/993-3393; www.nixon foundation.org has an edited version of the controversial former president's tenure in the White House, souvenirs of state, and the restored farmhouse where he was born in 1913.

Ronald Reagan Presidential Library, 40 Presidential Drive, Simi Valley, tel: 805/522-8444, www. reagan.utexas.edu houses records of the Reagan presidency.

Museums

California Afro-American Museum 600 State, in Exposition Park Tel: 213/744-7432; www.caam.ca.gov Treasures of African-American art, history, culture. Closed Monday.
California Institute of Technology 1201 East California Boulevard, Pasadena Tel: 626/395-6327; wwwcaltech.edu World-renowned home of scientific breakthroughs. Free guided walking tours of campus every weekday.
California ScienCenter 700 State Drive Tel: 323/724-3623 www.casciencectr.org This new Exposition Park museum, invites visitors to "come touch tomorrow," exploring such topics as electricity, gravity, computers and the immune system. Visit the Aerospace Hall's collection of airplanes, spacecraft and scientific exhibits.

The IMAX Theater shows stunning science, nature and travel films on an 80 by 60-ft (24 by 18-meter) screen, tel: 213/744-7400.
Carole and Barry Kaye Museum of Miniatures 5900 Wilshire Tel: 323/937-6464 www.caroleandbarrykayemuseumof miniatures.com Vast collection of miniature

mansions, palaces, and a store with pricey dolls.
Chinese-American Museum 423 N Los Angles Street Tel: 213/626-5240; www.camla.org Dedicated to the Chinese-American experience and history in this region. Opens fall 2001.
Craft and Folk Museum 5800 Wilshire Boulevard Tel: 323/937-4230; www.scf.usc.edu Ethnic textiles, pottery, jewelry.
Doorknob Museum 1228 W Manchester Avenue Tel: 323/759-0344 This one-room display also includes locks, doorstops and push-plates. Call for appointment.
Fowler Museum of Cultural History on the UCLA campus Tel: 310/825-4361 www.fmch.ucla.edu Colorful flags, ceramics, etc. celebrating cultural diversity. Closed Monday and Tuesday.
Frederick's of Hollywood Lingerie Museum 6608 Hollywood Boulevard Tel: 213/466-5151 Underwear through the ages, with a special celebrity collection. Open during normal store hours.
Geffen Contemporary 152 North Central Avenue, Downtown Tel: 213/621-2766; www.moca-la.org Hosts major exhibits in two city warehouses transformed into galleries by LA architect Frank Gehry. The space was planned to be temporary (originally called Temporary Contemporary), but was so popular they left it as is.
Gene Autry Western Heritage Museum 4700 Western Heritage Way, next to the zoo in Griffith Park Tel: 323/667-2000 www.geneautrymuseum.org Disney Imagineers designed the fascinating exhibits (including the shoot-out at the OK Corral) that bring the history of the West to life. Cowboys of early radio, motion picture and TV as well as the art of Frederic Remington and others. Closed most Mondays, except some holidays.

George C. Page Museum (La Brea Tar Pits)
5801 Wilshire Boulevard
Tel: 323/936-2230; www.tarpits.org
View the La Brea tar pits, discovered in 1906, as well as over 1 million Ice Age plant and animal fossils, including the remains of the imperial mammoth and a saber-toothed tiger. Short films of the excavation and a "tar machine."

J. Paul Getty Center
1200 Getty Center Drive
Tel: 310/440-7300; www.getty.edu
On top of the Brentwood Hills off I-405, this center houses almost all the Getty art collections in a fabulous multi-building complex with spectacular views of the sea. The collections include 18th-century European decorative arts; 13th- to 19th-century European paintings and drawings; medieval and Renaissance manuscripts; and American and European photographs. Free admission. Call for parking reservations first. Closed Monday.

J. Paul Getty Villa
(Closed until 2002)
Perched high on a cliff overlooking the Pacific Coast Highway between Sunset Boulevard and Topanga Canyon, this museum is a spectacular re-creation of an authentic 1st century Roman villa housing Greek and Roman antiquities. When the museum reopens, entry will be free, but you must call 310/458-2003 to reserve a parking space or get a pass from the driver on MTA bus 434.

Greystone Mansion
905 Loma Vista Drive, Beverly Hills
Tel: 310/550-4796; www.bhvb.org
Rare tours of the impressive mansion built in 1928 by oil millionaire Edward Doheny. Free. Grounds open daily. Park open 10am–5pm daily.

Grier-Musser Museum
403 S Bonnie Brae Street
Tel: 213/413-1814
Antique furnishings, artifacts in a restoted Queen Anne-style house.

Guinness World of Records
6764 Hollywood Boulevard
Tel: 323/463-6433
Speaks for itself!

Hollywood Bowl Museum
2301 N Highland Avenue
Tel: 323/850-2050
www.hollywoodbowl.org
Overview of great names and events from the Bowl's musical history.

Hollywood Entertainment Museum
7021 Hollywood Boulevard
Tel: 323/465-7900
www.hollywoodmuseum.com
Probably the best movie-museum in town; displays sets from famous radio and TV shows as well as other movie ephemera. There's also a dazzling six-minute show compiled from old film clips.

Hollywood Studio Museum
2100 N Highland
Tel: 323/874-2276
The yellow barn where most of *The Squaw Man* was filmed in 1913 was badly damaged by fire but is being restored. Open weekends.

Hollywood Wax Museum
6767 Hollywood Boulevard
Tel: 323/462-5991
Waxworks of the famous.

Japanese American National Museum
369 E 1st Street
Tel: 213/625-0414
In a renovated former Buddhist temple in Little Tokyo, closed Monday.

Latino Museum of History, Art and Culture
112 S Main Street
Tel: 213/626-7600
www.latinomuseum.org
Celebrating the heritage of Latinos and promoting their development in the Americas. Closed Wednesday.

Los Angeles County Museum of Art (LACMA)
5905 Wilshire Boulevard
Tel: 323/857-6000; www.lacma.org
A varied collection of fine arts from various corners of the world, outstanding temporary exhibitions and an outdoor sculpture garden. Jazz groups play on the patio some Friday evenings. Closed Wednesday.

Museum in Black
4331 Degnan, Leimert Park Village
Tel: 323/292-9528
Sculpture and African masks. Temporary exhibitions.

Museum of Contemporary Art (MOCA)
California Plaza, 250 South Grand Avenue, Downtown
Tel: 213/621-2766; www.moca-la.org
Devoted exclusively to art from 1940 to the present, the permanent collection includes paintings, sculpture, live performance and environmental works. Designed by Japanese architect Arata Isozaki, the building is an artwork in its own right. A shuttle connects it with the museum's satellite. Live jazz every Thursday evening, June–September.

Museum of Jurassic Technology
9341 Venice Boulevard, Venice
Tel: 310/836-6131; www.mjt.org
Wacky little museum that walks the line between a joke and a brilliant analysis of modern life. This eccentric place claims to have its roots in the natural history museums of the 19th century, which were part sideshow and part laboratory. Open Thursday–Sunday.

Museum of Neon Art (MONA)
501 W Olympic Boulevard
Tel: 213/489-9918
www.neonmona.org
The world's only museum devoted to neon, electric and kinetic art. Rotating (and glowing) exhibits. Closed Monday and Tuesday, and public holidays.

Museum of Televison and Radio
465 N Beverly Drive, Beverly Hills
Tel: 310/786-1000
Tapes of more than 75,000 TV and radio shows and commercials can be viewed here.

Museum of Tolerance
Simon Wiesenthal Center, 9768 W Pico Boulevard
Tel: 310/553-8403
www.wiesenthal.com
Technologically-advanced museum utilizes multimedia experiences to promote better understanding among all people. Videos about civil rights; hands-on exhibits including explanation of the LA riots; an absorbing Holocaust section taking visitors through an unforgettable piece of history. Closed Saturday and Jewish holidays.

Natural History Museum of Los Angeles County
900 Exposition

Tel: 213/763-DINO; www.nhm.org
Hands-on exhibits, games and fossil rubbings. Kids love it.

Observatory and Planetarium, Griffith Park
Tel: 323/664-1191
www.griffithobs.org
Moon and star viewing and a panorama of the city at night. Closed Monday September–June.

Petersen Automotive Museum
6060 Wilshire
Tel: 323/930-2277
www.petersen.org
Rare motorcycles, Indy racing cars, movie treasures, etc. Historically interesting even to the neophyte. Closed Monday.

Santa Monica Heritage Museum
2612 Main Street, Santa Monica
Tel: 310/392-8537
Period furniture and historical exhibitions in a century-old house. Open Thursday–Sunday.

Santa Monica Museum of Art
2525 Michigan Avenue, Building G1
Tel: 310/586-6488
www.nexvip.com/smmoa
Eclectic and contemporary, with loads of seminars, workshops, and exhibits.

Skirball Cultural Center
Sepulveda Pass
Tel: 310/440-4500; www.skirball.org
Depicts the Jewish experience in the Old World and the New. Closed Monday.

Southwest Museum
234 Museum Drive, near Pasadena Freeway
Tel: 213/221-2164
This museum's collections represent Native American cultures from Alaska to South America and include some of the finest examples of Indian art and artifacts in the United States. The museum itself, founded in 1907, is the oldest in Los Angeles.

Travel Town Museum
5200 Zoo Drive, Griffith Park
Tel: 323/662-5874; www.cityofla.org
Old locomotives, firetrucks and trolleys, plus rides on a miniature train. Open daily.

Wells Fargo Museum
333 S Grand Avenue
Tel: 213/253-7166
www.wellsfargo.com

A stagecoach, gold assaying tools and lots of fascinating Western history.

MUSEUMS FURTHER AFIELD

Anaheim Museum
241 S Anaheim Boulevard at Broadway, Anaheim
Tel: 714/778-3301
Historical and cultural northern Orange County artifacts housed in the 83-year-old Carnegie Library Building.

Bowers Museum of Cultural Art and Kidseum
2002 North Main Street, Santa Ana
Tel: 714/567-3600; www.bowers.org
This 1934 Mission Revival museum's collection, dedicated to the art of indigenous peoples, contains 85,000 pieces of art from the Americas, Pacific Rim and Africa.

Cabrillo Marine Museum
3720 Stephen White Drive, San Pedro
Tel: 310/548-7562
www.cabrilloaq.org
Thirty-eight tanks contain live sea animals and plants. Exhibits include a whale bone graveyard, tidepool touchtank and displays of California marine environments as well as multi-media shows and whalewatch and grunion programs.

Hobby City Doll and Toy Museum
1238 South Beach Boulevard at Ball Road, Anaheim
Tel: 714/527-2323
3,000 dolls from around the world, from a 5,000-year-old Egyptian relic to the present day.

International Printing Museum
8469 Kass Drive, Buena Park
Tel: 714/523-2070
1,000 items from 500 years of printing history. See the first American edition of the *Gutenberg Bible* and more than 150 working antique presses.

International Surfing Museum
4111 Olive Avenue, Huntington Beach
Tel: 714/960-3483
www.surfingmuseum.org
Surfing artwork, assorted artifacts

and a collection of antique surfboards and paddleboards.

Karpeles Manuscript Museum
465 Hot Springs Road, Santa Barbara
Tel: 805/962-5322
rain.org/~karpeles/sbfrm
Contains original draft of Bill of Rights along with manuscripts by Lincoln, Washington, Galileo, and many others.

Laguna Art Museum
307 Cliff Drive, Laguna Beach
Tel: 949/494-6531
www.lagunaartmuseum.org
Historical and contemporary American art on display.

Lawrence Welk Museum
8860 Lawrence Welk Drive, Escondido
Tel: 800/932-WELK
www.WELKRESORT.com
Memorabilia from the bandleader's life.

Long Beach Aquarium of the Pacific
100 Aquarium Way
Tel: 562/590-3100
www.aquariumofthepacific.org
One of the largest aquariums in the US, highlighting Southern California/Baja, Tropical Pacific, and Northwest Pacific. Open daily except Christmas.

Movieland Wax Museum
7711 Beach Boulevard, Buena Park
Tel: 714/522-1154
www.movielandwaxmuseum.com
Original sets, costumes and special effects, along with 270 wax replicas of Hollywood's biggest legends comprise one of the best shows of its kind you'll ever see.

Old Courthouse Museum
211 W Santa Ana Boulevard, Santa Ana
Tel: 714/834-5536; www.oc.ca.gov
This 1901 Romanesque building is the oldest courthouse in Southern California. Closed weekends.

Orange County Museum of Art
850 San Clemente Drive
Tel: 949/759-1122; www.ocma.net
2,000 modern and contemporary paintings, sculptures, photographs and works on paper by internationally known California artists. Closed Monday.

Orange Empire Railway Museum
2201 S A Street, Perris
Tel: 949/657-2605
www.oerm.mus.ca.us
One of the country's most extensive railroad museums. Trains run on weekends and you can ride the antiques. Museum open daily.

Palomar Observatory
scenic drive along San Diego County Road 56 to top of mountain
Tel: 760/742-2119
www.astro.caltech.edu
Contains America's largest telescope.

Planes of Fame
7000 Merrill Avenue, Chino
Tel: 909/597-3722
www.planesoffame.org
One of the first and largest west coast air museums, with over 30 flyable historic planes, including the B-25, P-38 Lightning, P-51 Mustang, and a Japanese Zero. Fly in one for a fee. See restorations in progress. Open daily.

Ripley's Believe It or Not
Buena Park at 7850 Beach Boulevard
Tel: 714/522-7045
www.movielandwaxmuseum.com
Oddities and scarcely believable artifacts. Open daily.

San Sylmar Tower of Beauty Museum
15180 Bledsoe Street, Sylmar
Tel: 818/367-2251
A private museum owned and operated by the Merle Norman Cosmetic Co., offers a world-class collection of antiques, vintage automobiles, rare musical instruments and music boxes. Tours require reservations, so call ahead. Open Tuesday–Saturday.

Stagecoach Inn Museum
51 S Ventu Park Road, Newbury Park
Tel: 805/498-9441; www.toguide.com
Pioneer house, adobe and Chumash Indian hut grouped around restored stagecoach stop.

PASADENA

A couple of famous houses are well worth inspecting, but they tend to close early.

Near the freeway is the 18-room **Fenyes Mansion**, 470 W Walnut, tel: 626/577-1660, the handsome home of the Pasadena Historical Society where in 1905 D.W. Griffiths shot one of his first films.

Half a block away is the impressive "California-style bungalow" built by the Greene Brothers, the **Gamble House**. Reservations are essential, tel: 626/793-3334; www.gamblehouse.org. Open Thursday–Sunday.

Just before the freeway is the **Norton Simon Museum**, 411 W Colorado Boulevard, tel: 626/449-6840; www.nortonsimon.org, which contains a world-renowned collection of Asian art. Closed Monday and Tuesday.

Also in Pasadena are the **Pacific Asia Museum**, 46 N Las Robles Avenue, tel: 626/449-2742, in a Chinese Treasure House built by in 1924. **The Rose Bowl**, tel: 626/577-3100; www.rosebowl.com, is the site of the Tournament of Roses annual football classic, while the Tournament House and headquarters for the Tournament of Roses is the old **Wrigley Mansion and Gardens**, 391 S Orange Grove Boulevard, tel: 626/449-4100, noted for its flowers. There are free afternoon tours some days.

For the **Huntington Museum** see *Gardens* section to follow.

Architecture

Bradbury Building
304 S Broadway
Tel: 213/626-1893
Century-old National Historic Landmark with ornate wrought-ironwork and elegant atrium designed by George H. Wyman, with the vision of mining tycoon Louis Bradbury.

Capital Records
1750 Vine Street, Hollywood.
Designed by Welton Becket in 1954 to resemble a stack of 45 rpm records, complete with stylized playing needle on top, it claims to be the first round building. (Beckett and associates also designed Century City with its twin triangular towers by Minoru Yamaskai.)

Carroll Avenue
Echo Park
Some of the elegant Victorian houses have been here since this was LA's first suburb; others have been brought from elsewhere. Moviemakers find them irresistible.

Chiat Day Advertising Agency Building
340 Main Street, Venice
Whimsically designed by LA's controversial architect Frank Gehry in the shape of a pair of binoculars. Also by Gehry is the remarkable but still-unfinished Walt Disney Concert Hall under construction Downtown on Bunker Hill. The building has caused much comment to date. (Chiat Day moved to Playa Del Rey in 1998.)

Coca-Cola Bottling Company
1334 Central Avenue
Designed by Robert Derrah in 1936, this is an outstanding example of Streamline Moderne. Shaped like an 1890s ocean liner, complete with porthole windows, ship doors, a promenade deck and catwalk. Derrah also built the **Crossroads of the World** at 6671 Sunset Boulevard, which opened in October 1936 as LA's first shopping mall. The central building is patterned after a ship on a world cruise, passing small shops (now offices) representing such architectural styles as Spanish Colonial, Tudor and French Provincial.

Crystal Cathedral
12141 Lewis Street, Garden Grove
Tel: 714/971-4000
Sunday morning services take place in this 12-story glass and steel church designed by Philip Johnson and there are guided tours of the 32-acre garden every day.

Doheny Hall
A Gothic style 1900 mansion owned by oil tycoon Edward Doheny, now on Mount St Mary's campus, West Adams Street.

The Dutch Castle
1366 Angelo Drive, Beverly Hills
Perched on the edge of a canyon, built in 1981 by designer Mark Nixon, is this 6,000-sq ft main house plus a 1,600-sq ft

gatehouse. Nixon's inspiration for the stepped gables were the 16th-century castles in Holland.

Ennis-Brown House
2655 Glendower Avenue
Tel: 323/668-0234
www.ennis-brown.org
One of Frank Lloyd Wright's better creations. Other Frank Lloyd Wright-designed buildings and homes in the LA area include: the **Barnsdall Mansion**; the **Storer House**, 8161 Hollywood Boulevard; the **Freeman House**, 1962 Glencoe Way, Hollywood; the **Sturges House**, 449 Skyeway Road, Brentwood; and the **Arch Oboler House**, 32436 Mulholland Drive, Malibu.

The Gamble House
4 Westmoreland Place, Pasadena
Tel: 626/793-3334
Built in 1908 by Charles Sumner and Henry Mather Greene with polished woods, Tiffany glass and leaded windows inspired by England's Arts and Crafts movement. Tours of interior by reservation only.

Los Angeles Theater
Broadway
A French Renaissance classic built by S. Charles Lee in 1931 with its art gallery, mahogany paneled ballroom, baroque ceiling, fountain and children's playroom. It premiered with Charlie Chaplin's *City Lights*.

Magic Castle
7001 Franklin, West Hollywood
A bizarrely neo-Victorian building. Nearby is **Yamashiro**, a former Japanese palace imported and reassembled as a restaurant.

Schindler House
835 N Kings Road, West Hollywood
Tel: 323/651-1510
The airy 1921 home of Frank Lloyd Wright's partner Rudolf Schindler.

Tail o' the Pup
San Vicente Boulevard near Beverly Boulevard
Behind the Hotel Sofitel is a steel-reinforced 17-ft (5.2-meter) hot dog, complete with mustard, designed in 1938 by Milton J. Black.

Watts Towers
1765 East 10th Street, Watts
Between 1921 and 1954 Simon Rodia created these fragile, lacy

107ft-high metal towers covered with plaster, bits of metal, seashells, ceramics, and glass.

The Witches House
516 Walden Drive, Beverly Hills
Designed and built for the Irwin Willat film company in Culver City by art director Harry C. Oliver, but moved here in 1929 because of traffic problems caused by sightseers. Oliver, who won an Oscar for design for the movie *Seventh Heaven*, also invented the machine that creates fake cobwebs.

Architectural Tours

Tours of some of LA's grand or architecturally interesting homes are available.

Frank Lloyd Wright's Hollyhock House, tel: 323/913-4157; and **Wright's Ennis-Brown House**, 2655 Glendower Avenue, tel: 323/668-0234. Check for times.

Streisand Center, 5750 Ramirez Canyon Road, tel: 310/589-2850, www.ceres.ca.gov/smmc/sccs. An environmental think tank situated on 22 acres (and in four houses) in Malibu. They were donated by Barbra Streisand to the Santa Monica Mountains Conservancy.

Whitley Heights, a movie star community before the heyday of Beverly Hills, is behind Hollywood between Highland Avenue and Cahuenga. Occasional tours are organized by the Whitley Heights Civic Association, tel: 323/874-6438.

Also check out **Architours**, a company for the serious architect buff or professional that can create a custom tour, tel: 888/6AR-CHITOURS or 323/294-5821.

Missions

From the beginning of California's history, the 21 missions set up along El Camino Real by Father Junipéro Serra and his successors have played an important role. Today they are major tourist attractions. The quintet between Santa Barbara and San Diego are San Buenaventura, San Fernando, San Gabriel, San Juan Capistrano, and San Luis Rey.

The Missions

San Buenaventura, Ventura, tel: 805/643-4318. Ancient paintings and original rafters. Open 10am–5pm Monday–Saturday; 10am–4pm Sunday. Closed holidays.

San Diego de Alcala, tel: 619/281-8449, www.bgmm.com. The first mission to be founded on California territory. In San Diego's Old Town area. Open 9am–5pm.

San Fernando Rey de Espana, 15151 San Fernando Mission Boulevard, tel: 818/361-0186. The 17th mission, founded in 1797. It was twice rebuilt after earthquakes (1806 and 1971). Thick adobe walls and classical arches. Statues of Serra and his successor, Father Lasuen. Open 9am–5pm daily. Closed Thanksgiving and Christmas.

Andres Pico Adobe, 10940 Sepulveda Boulevard, Mission Hills, tel: 818/365-7810, is the oldest home in San Fernando, built by San Fernando Indians in 1834.

San Gabriel Arcangel, Baldwin Park about 9 miles (14 km) east of Highway 10, tel: 626/457-3035, has unusual architecture, statues and paintings and a September festival to celebrate its 1771 founding. Open 9.30am–4.30pm daily. Closed Easter, Thanksgiving and Christmas.

San Juan Capistrano, tel: 949/248-2048, www.missionsjc.com. Near Laguna Beach. Father Serra's original chapel. Celebration every March 19 to recognize the return of the swallows. Open 8.30am–5pm daily. Closed noon–3pm Good Friday and Thanksgiving and Christmas.

San Luis Rey, north of Oceanside off US5, tel: 760/757-3651. Vestments and a two-day fiesta in June to celebrate its founding. Open 10am–4.30pm Monday–Saturday; noon–4.30pm Sunday. Closed Thanksgiving and Christmas.

Santa Barbara "Queen of the Missions," tel: 805/682-4149, has 60 Franciscan friars in residence. Open daily 9am–5pm.

Originally developed by Spanish clerics with virtual slave labor from local Indians, most of the missions were abandoned and fell into decay after the passing of the Secularization Act in 1834 and were forgotten for almost half a century. Helen Hunt Jackson's 1880 book about mistreatment of the Indians, *A Century of Dishonor*, revived interest in the buildings whose architecture thereafter became a much-emulated style.

Wineries

WINERY TOURS

At **Rancho Cucamonga**, www.citi. vu.com/cucamonga, 60 miles (100 km) east of LA, are the Galleano and J. Filippi wineries, almost the last in an area once busier than the Napa Valley. Tours on Sunday. Also, **Temecula Valley Vintners Association**, tel: 909/699-3626; www. temeculawines.org; 14 winieries and more coming in this valley an hour south of Riverside

Wineries and Vineyards of Santa Barbara County are one hour's driving time northwest of Santa Barbara in the Scandinavian-style town of Solvang, with its windmills and gas street lamps. There a scores of wineries within easy reach. Most offer free tasting, tours and grounds on which to picnic, if not restaurants on the premises.

Information from the **Santa Barbara County Vintners Association**, PO Box 1558, Santa Ynez, CA 93460, tel: 805/688-0881; www.sbcountywines.com

Movie Magic

See also *Starware* and *Bookstores* in the *Shopping* Section.

TV AND MOVIE SETS

The **EIDC Office**, 7083 Hollywood Boulevard, prints up a daily list of the average of 50 movie and TV productions that are being shot on LA streets everyday. Tel: 323/957-1000; www.eidc.com

The syndicated TV show *Baywatch* is filmed on various beaches between Santa Monica and Malibu but more often than not can be found at Paradise Cove, 28128 Pacific Coast Highway, a secluded private beach that charges a fairly hefty admission.

The CBS drama *Dr Quinn, Medicine Woman* had a permanent set on the Paramount Ranch which housed many Westerns for 70 years. Visitors are welcome. Tel: 818/597-9192 for directions and shooting schedules. To visit tapings of CBS TV shows, tel: 818/760-5000.

NBC Studio Tour, 3000 W Alameda Avenue, Burbank, tel: 818/840-3537. Visitors who pick up their tour tickets early in the day can usually also get free tickets for that day's taping of *The Tonight Show,* for which the line can begin at 4pm. You can also write three weeks in advance for tickets. Fee for tour.

Paramount Studio Tour, 860 N Gower Street. Two-hour walking tours of TV and movie sets. No reservations necessary; continuous tours 9am–2pm. Admission fee. To attend a TV show taping call for a reservation: 323/956-5575, for tour information call 323/956-1777. For information about attending TV tapings at other studios call **Audiences Unlimited** 818/506-0067.

Sony Pictures in the former home of MGM (10202 Washington Boulevard, Culver City) is closed to the public except for the studio audiences when TV shows are taped. Call for information 310/280-8000.

Universal Studios, 100 Universal City Plaza, Universal City, tel: 818/622-3036. For an hour and 45 minutes the hapless tour tram dodges an avalanche, parts the Red Sea, escapes a tourist-hungry King Kong and survives a major earthquake. Disembark to explore the largest film studio in the world, see stunt and animal shows, beam aboard the Starship Enterprise of *Star Trek* fame and take a runaway raft ride in jungly

Jurassic Park, where 40-ft (12-meter) dinosaurs threaten on all sides. Off-season hours: Box office 8.30am–4pm; Park 9am–7pm. Summer and holiday hours: Box office 7.30am–6pm; Park 8.30am–10pm. Discount for military personnel and their families. Tours are offered with English, Spanish, German, French, Japanese, and Korean.

Universal City Walk offers amusing shops of the souvenir type, good restaurants, sidewalk musicians and entertainers, B.B. King's Blues Club and a movie theater with a dozen screens. It was expanded in 2000 with more restaurants, ships, and an IMAX theatre. Admission free with parking validated for 90 minutes, otherwise a fee (except for moviegoers). Starline, tel: 323/463-3131 and Grayline, tel: 213/856-5900 operate tours to Universal City. The nearest MTA bus stop is at Lankershim and Ventura boulevards.

Warner Bros. VIP Studio Tour, 4000 Warner Boulevard, Burbank, tel: 818/954-1744. Home of Warner Bros. and Lorimar Productions. For the more serious student of movie and television production, this 12-person "golfcart tour" is unstaged and educational, and includes whatever may be on the day's production schedule, plus a look at the prop and special effects shops, a peek at a historical backlot and a visit to the studio museum. Two-hour tours by reservation only, weekdays 10am–2pm. No children under 10.

TV SHOW TAPINGS

If you write far enough in advance you can usually obtain free tickets for the taping of TV shows. Include date requested and send stamped-self-addressed envelope or International Money Order for stamps two or more weeks in advance. Some addresses are: *Jeopardy*!, Sony Pictures, 10202 W Washington Boulevard, Culver City, CA 90232.

The Price Is Right, CBS, 7800 Beverly Boulevard, Los Angeles, CA 90036.

The Tonight Show, NBC, 3000 W Alameda, Burbank, CA 91523.

Wheel of Fortune, PO Box 3763, Hollywood, CA 90028.

For other shows try calling **Audiences Unlimited**, 5746 Sunset Bouelvard, tel: 818/771-7195, which dispenses free tickets to select shows and viewing audiences.

HOLLYWOOD TOURS

Do-it-Yourself Tours

For those aspiring to drive around looking at moviestar homes, be warned that the maps widely available in Hollywood and from street vendors along the western stretches of Sunset Boulevard are not necessarily accurate. Biggest seller is the one published by Rockwell Enterprises of Carson, a company that has been around for many years. For an excellent website to discover the life and lives of Tinseltown check out www.seeing-stars.com

Grave Line Tours

Tel: 323/469-4149
www.lacoroner.com
Satisfy your most morbid curiosity with this award winning tour that features "Deathstyles of the Rich and Famous." From the back of a funeral limousine, see the sites of Hollywood's most notorious deaths, sins and scandals, including the restaurant where James Dean ate his last meal and where gangster Bugsy Siegel was shot.

The LA Conservancy

Tel: 213/623-2489
www.laconservancy.org
Conducts two-hour Saturday tours of the Downtown historic movie theatres, the unqiue Bradbury Building and Grand Central Market.

The Next Stage

Tel: 626/577-7880
Marlene Gordon's "the real LA."

Other companies that operate tours, not only to Hollywood but all over the city are:

Columbia Shuttle

Tel: 213/739-5757
www.tours-in-losangeles.com
City, stars homes, beach tours.

GrayLine

Tel 800/339-8421
www.grayline.com
Stars, city, Universal tours.

Guideline Tours

Tel: 800/604-8433
www.guidelinetours.com
Stars, city, nightlife, theme parks.

Helinet Aviation Services

Tel: 818/902-0229
www.helinet aviation.com
Operates helicopter tours of the city.

Hollywood Fantasy Tours

651 N Highland Avenue
Tel: 323/469-8184
2- to 5-hour guided tours of Hollywood and Beverly Hills in mini-vans.

LA City Tours

Tel: 888/800-7878
www.lacitytours.com
City and stars tours.

LA Nighthawks

PO Box 10224, Beverly Hills
Tel: 310/859-1171
Live shows, hot clubs.

The LA Showbus

11950 San Vicente Boulevard
Tel: 310/826-4665
Musical tours.

Royal Dynasty Tours

Tel: 888/900-8687
www.dynastytour.com
City, stars, beach, Getty tours.

Starline Tours of Hollywood

6925 Hollywood Boulevard
Tel: 323/463-3333; starlinetours.com
Tours for star fans in a minivan.

Sun and Adventure Tours

200 Wilshire Boulevard
Tel: 213/891-9408

Trolleywood Tours

6671 Hollywood Boulevard
Tel: 323/469-8184

MOVIE LOCATIONS

Scores of movies have been made, not only in Los Angeles but with the city (or one of its satellites) as the star itself. *Hollywood Hotel* (1937), *Hollywood Canteen* (1944), *Sunset Boulevard* (1950) *LA Story* (1991), and *LA Confidential* (1998) are only the obvious ones.

Others have included: *Singin' in the Rain* (1952), *Rebel Without A Cause* (1955), *Gidget* (1959), *The Long Goodbye* (1973), *Chinatown* (1974), *Beverly Hills Cop* (1984), *Die Hard* (1989), *The Player* (1992), *Short Cuts* (1993), *Mulholland Falls* (1996), and *City of Angels* (1998).

To avid moviegoers, many a street or local landmark is as familar as his own home. Here are some movies whose locations are easy to recognize:

Pretty Woman: Julia Roberts' seedy apartment was on North Las Palmas in Hollywood; she also tossed an escargot shell at Cicada restaurant, Downtown and shared a suite with Richard Gere at the Beverly Hills Wilshire, the same hotel where Eddie Murphy stays in *Beverly Hills Cop*.

Down and Out in Beverly Hills: Nick Nolte and Bette Midler lived on North Bedford Drive.

Fabulous Baker Boys: Michelle Pfeiffer crooned on top of a baby grand piano in the Cinegrill nightlcub at the Hollywood Roosevelt Hotel; other shoots there have included *Internal Affairs* with Richard Gere, *Beverly Hills Cop II* with Eddie Murphy, and the TV show *Moonlighting* with Bruce Willis and Cybill Shepherd.

Grease: John Travolta and Olivia Newton John frolicked at Rydell High, otherwise known as Venice High School.

Halloween: The midwest setting of this screamer is actually Orange Grove Avenue in Hollywooe, just north of Sunset. Jamie Lee Curtis was babysitting at 1530, her best friend was murdered at 1537.

Annie Hall: The final scene goodbye between Woody Allen and Diane Keaton was filmed at The Source, 8301 Sunset Boulevard (now the Cajun Bistro).

Back to the Future: Doc Brown's house is actually the Gamble House, a landmark in Pasadena.

Indecent Proposal: Robert Redford's estate is actually the Huntington Library in San Marino.

The Sting, *Ruthless People* and *Funny Girl*: all filmed at Santa Monica Pier.

Grand Canyon: Steve Martin lived in the Ennis-Brown House on Glendower Road in Los Feliz. Part of **Blade Runner** was also filmed in this Frank Lloyd Wright creation.

Nightmare on Elm Street: Freddie Krueger sliced up all those dreaming teenagers at the two-story white house at 1428 Genessee, just south of Sunset in Hollywood.

The Biltmore Hotel has been used many times, including **Vertigo**, **The Sting**, **Ghostbusters**, **The Poseidon Adventure**, **Splash**, **Chinatown**, **Bugsy**, and **A Star is Born**.

Lethal Weapon and **Mighty Joe Young** both rampaged down Hollywood Boulevard.

Blade Runner also filmed in the Bradbury Building, Downtown, 304 S Broadway, as did **Chinatown**.

The Graduate and **Secrets of the Lost Temple** were partially filmed at USC Doheny Library.

Rocky: Many of the fight scenes were at the Olympic Auditorium in Downtown LA.

Point Break: Keanu Reeves and Patrick Swayze surf near Manhattan Beach Pier; the footchase is through Hermosa Beach 30th Street area.

Father of the Bride: Diane Keaton and Steve Martin's home was on South El Molino in Pasadena.

The Bonaventure Hotel has served as location for a number of films, including **In the Line of Fire**, where Clint Eastwood and an assassin are trapped in a glass elevator; **True Lies** where Arnold Schwarzenegger rampages on a motorcycle; also **Blue Thunder** and **Rain Man**.

Sister Act: Whoopi Goldberg was filmed at the Hollywood Presbyterian Church on Highland Avenue.

Speed: Sandra Bullock drives a bus rigged to explode on the Century 105 freeway, the same freeway Mel Gibson crashes in a motorcycle chase for **Lethal Weapon 3**. Also in **Speed**, the Santa Monica Bus blows up at the intersection of Main and Rose.

Die Hard: The Nakatomi building is actually Fox Plaza Tower, in Century City on the former back lot of Twentieth Century-Fox.

LA Confidential locations included the Formosa Cafe, where Lana Turner is amusingly misidentified, Crossroads of the World on Sunset, where Danny DeVito's office was, and JandJ's Sandwich Shop on 6th Street Downtown, which served as the Night Owl Café, where the bloody murders take place.

The Music Box: This famous short that won Laurel and Hardy an Oscar was filmed on the stairway on Vendome Street in Silver Lake.

Casablanca: The famous final runway scene where Humphrey Bogart says goodbye to Ingrid Bergman is actually at Van Nuys Airport, near Hangar 6 . (You can also see the faux streets of Paris on the Warner Bros. tour – remember "We'll always have Paris…"

MOVIE PALACES

Notable movie theaters are the 1930s palaces such as the **Los Angeles Theater**, 615 S Broadway and the **Orpheum** and **United Artists** two blocks further down; **Mann's Chinese Theater**, 6925 Hollywood Boulevard, tel: 323/464-8111; and the beautifully restored **El Capitan**, 6838 Hollywood Boulevard, tel: 323/467-7674 and **Egyptian**, 6712 Hollywood Boulevard, tel: 323/466-FILM.

There are **multiscreen** complexes in Century City, at Universal City Walk, at the Beverly Center, at Sherman Oaks Galleria and many smaller ones around town.

Santa Monica's Third Street pedestrian mall features about a dozen screens in the three blocks between Broadway and Wilshire Boulevard.

The **"village" of Westwood**, near UCLA, has a group of about 10 movie theaters with the half-century-old **Mann's Village Theatre**, 961 Broxton, tel: 310/208-5576, a local landmark.

Consult the local free weeklies or the Los Angeles Times for listings and schedules.

Theme Parks

Castle Park
3500 Polk Avenue, Riverside off the 91 Freeway
Tel: 909/785-3000
Attractively landscaped family amusement park with videos, miniature golf courses, amusement rides, fountains and waterfalls.

Disneyland
PO Box 3232, Anaheim
Tel: 714/781-4560
www.disney.go.com
"The Happiest Place on Earth" features dining, shopping, entertainment and more than 60 adventures and attractions in eight magical themed lands. Recent attractions are The Hunchback of Notre Dame, Festival of Fools and Hercules, based on Disney movies. Write or call ahead if you can and ask for a map so that you can plan your strategy before you arrive. Open daily year-round. Winter hours: 10am–6pm Monday–Friday; 9am–midnight weekends. Summer hours: 8–1am daily.

The Disneyland Hotel is the headquarters of The Airport Bus, tel: 714/938-8900 or 800/772-5299 which operates between the park and LAX as well as Downtown LA, Universal City, Pasadena, and the John Wayne/Orange County Airport.

Knott's Berry Farm
8039 Beach Boulevard, Buena Park
Tel: 714/220-5200; www.knotts.com
A major Western-style park whose six themed lands – Ghost Town, Roaring '20s, Camp Snoopy, Indian Trails, Wildwater Wilderness, and Fiesta Village – are funkier and less automated than Disneyland. The 165 adventures and rides include the recent addition Perilous Plunge, a wild, wet attraction. A theater that books major stars and 26 shops also keeps visitors occupied. Winter hours: 10am–6pm Monday–Friday; 10am–10pm Saturday; 10am–7pm Sunday. Summer hours: 10am–11pm Sunday–Friday; 10am–midnight Saturday. Nearby are the **Movieland Wax Museum**, 7711 Beach Boulevard, tel: 714/522-1154,

www.movielandwaxmuseum.com.
Open daily all year, and **Wild Bill's
Wild West Dinner Extravaganza**,
7600 Beach Boulevard,
tel: 714/522-6414. Another nearby
dinner entertainment venue is
**Medieval Times Dinner and
Tournament**, 7662 Beach
Boulevard, tel: 714/521-4740,
which was humorously portrayed in
the Jim Carrey/Matthew Broderick
film *Cable Guy*.

Raging Waters
San Dimas
Tel: 909/802-2200
www.ragingwaters.com
A score of watery attractions for the
whole family.

Renaissance Pleasure Faire
Regional Park, San Bernadino
County
Tel: 800/52-FAIRE
www.recfair.com
Knights on horseback, Elizabethan
characters, arts and crafts, country
dancing. The main attraction is
when Old Master paintings are
reenacted by actual people. Open
weekends late April to late June.

Sea World of California
1720 South Shores Road,
Mission Bay
Tel: 619/226-3901
www.seaworld.com
Stars killer-whale *Shamu* in the
"New Visions" show. This park has
20 marine exhibits and attractions
and many live shows. Open
10am–5pm daily.

Sherman Oaks Castle Park
4989 Sepulveda Boulevard
Tel: 818/756-9459
Owned and run by LA Parks and
Recreation, including miniature golf,
arcade, batting cages. Open daily
10am–11pm.

Six Flags Magic Mountain
26101 Magic Mountain Parkway, PO
Box 5500, Valencia
Tel: 661/255-4100
www.sixflags.com
A 260-acre (105-hectare) theme
park half an hour north of
Hollywood, with over 100 shows
and thrill-seeker rides including the
world's largest dual-track roller
coaster, the Colossus; the Batman
ride described as resembling "a
ride on a high-speed ski chairlift

that spins upside down," Superman
– The Escape, and the newest ultra-
wet-your-pants-coaster, Goliath.
Open daily from Memorial Day to
Labor Day as well as weekends and
some holidays year-round. Nearby is
Hurricane Harbor, a waterpark with
14 attractions.

Universal Studios
see *TV and Film Sets* in *Movie
Magic*.

Wild Rivers Water Park
8770 Irvine Center Drive
Tel: 949/768-WILD
www.wildrivers.com
Family playground with 40 rides and
other attractions. Open mid-May to
September.

Children

Activities

Bob Baker Marionette Theater
1345 W First Street, Downtown LA
Tel: 213/250-9995
Open 10.30am Tuesday–Friday;
2.30pm weekends.

Fruit picking
Cherries, peaches, apricots, and
citrus fruits are some of the
summer products that visitors can
pick, at a nominal price, on various
orchards and farms in LA County.
Call for specific details: **PJK Cherry
Farm**, Gorman, tel: 661/337-6498;
Nessa Ranch, Leona Valley,
tel: 661/266-7116; **Zink's Ranch**,
Littlerock, tel: 661/944-1239;
Heritage Park, La Verne,
tel: 909/593-3862; **Betsy Young
Orchard**, Shadow Hills,
tel: 818/352-1366; **Orcutt Ranch**,
West Hills, tel: 818/888-6641,
www.cityofla.org.

Fisherman's Village
13755 Fiji Way, Marina del Ray
Tel: 310/823-5411
Pseudo-New England harbor with
fake lighthouse, themed shops,
good restaurants, fishing trips.
Open 10am–10pm daily.

Museums

Kidspace
390 South El Molino Avenue,
Pasadena
Tel: 661/449-9144
www.kidspacemuseum.org
Participatory museum where
children are encouraged to touch
and explore. Open daily except
Monday in summer; Wednesday and
weekends during school year.

Los Angeles Central Library
630 West 5th Street
Tel: 213/228-7000

Story theaters, video matinees and readings are among the special events produced for a young audience.

Los Angeles Childrens' Museum
310 N Main Street
Tel: 213/687-8800
Foam building blocks, finger painting, firetrucks, police motorcycles, art studio, do-it-yourself TV, and Sticky City. Apart from the attractions in **Griffith Park** listed, such as the Travel Town Museum, the Zoo and the Gene Autry Museum, there are also **pony and train rides** at 3300 Riverside, tel: 323/664-3266.

Los Angeles Zoo
Griffith Park
Tel: 323/644-6400; www.lazoo.org
Open daily 10am–5pm except Christmas.

Children's Restaurants

Ed Debevic's
134 N La Cienega
Tel: 310/659-195
Corny signs, hamburgers and bantering waiters and waitresses.

Encounter
Los Angeles Airport
Tel: 310/251-1515
Wild and space-age, with interior designed by Walt Disney Imagineering. A crazy spider-shaped building in the middle of the airport. It is a fun but upscale restaurant – you'll have to hold back the food fights at this one.

Zoos and Wildlife

Los Angeles Zoo
Griffith Park, 5333 Zoo Drive
Tel: 323/644-6400; www.lazoo.org
Features more than 2,000 animals and reptiles and 78 endangered species. Key exhibits: koala house, white tiger, gorilla troops, orangutan colony and walk-through aviary. The facility includes a complete children's zoo and an 80-acre main zoo. Open daily except Christmas.

San Diego Wild Animal Park
Off Interstate 15 east of Escondido, tel: 760/747-8702
www.sandiegozoo.org

1,800-acre (730-hectare) preserve where wild animals roam freely. Open daily. Entrance fee includes animal shows and monorail tour.

San Diego Zoo
Balboa Park
Tel: 619/231-1515
www.sandiegozoo.org
The zoo houses almost 800 different species. Open daily.

Beaches

With 72 miles (116 km) of coastline between Long Beach and Malibu there are plenty of beaches to choose from. Fifty million people visit them each year. **Surfrider Beach** at 23200 Pacific Coast Highway in Malibu is noted for predictably perfect waves. Teens head further north to play volleyball on **Zuma** at 30050 Pacific Coast Highway, tel: 310/457-9701, partying college kids further south to **Hermosa**, tel: 310/379-8471. Seekers of tidepools frequent **Leo Carillo**, grunion fans head for **Cabrillo** in San Pedro, tel: 310/832-1130 and those in search of seclusion favor **El Matador** at 32000 Pacific Coast Highway.

Snorkeling and scuba diving aficionados choose the underwater kelp forests and shipwrecks off **Catalina Island**. The shore is calm and virtually waveless at **Mother's Beach** at Admiralty and **Via Marina** in Marina del Rey.

Venice Beach has the additional delights of the living sideshow along the boardwalk and the adjoining **Santa Monica Beach**, tel: 310/578-0478 begins with the 90-year-old pier with its restaurants and amusement park.

For further information check out beaches at www.co.la.ca.us, or call **LA County Department of Beaches and Harbors**, tel: 310/305-9545.

For beaches featured in the TV show *Baywatch*, see *Movie Magic*.

Gardens

Exposition Park Rose Garden
701 State
Tel: 213/748-4772
Broad grass walkways firmly edged

with white concrete bands define 200 rectangular rose beds. This 7½-acre sunken garden, installed in 1926, is one of the city's oldest public gardens. Flowering period late April to early November, but peak bloom occurs between June and September.

Virginia Robinson Home
1008 Eden Way, Beverly Hills
Tel: 310/276-5367 for visiting hours
Multi-terraced Italian garden with statues, herb garden, etc.

Three attractive gardens can be found on the UCLA campus: **Mildred E. Mathias Botanical Garden**, Hilgared, north of Le Conte, tel: 310/825-1260, is an 8-acre woodsy area with 4,000 plant species: **Franklin D. Murphy Sculpture Garden** adjoining the Wight Art Gallery at the north end of the UCLA campus off Sunset Boulevard, tel: 310/825-9345, is a small park with a simple palette of plants and shade provided by flowering jacaranda and coral trees. More than 50 sculptures by Rodin, Henry Moore and Calder: UCLA **Hannah Carter Japanese Garden**, 10619 Bellagio Road, Bel Air, tel: 310/825-4574, is an ingenious adaptation of Japanese themes to the vertical topography of Bel Air. Garden artifacts include Buddha carvings, stone water basins, pagodas, lanterns, and more – all transported from Japan.

FURTHER AFIELD

Descanso Garden
1418 Descanso Drive, La Canada Flintridge
Tel: 818/952-4400
www.descanso.com
A camellia forest, Japanese garden and pretty walks are among the attractions of this tranquil place. Open all year, 9am–5pm.

Earl Burns Miller Japanese Garden
California State University at Long Beach, Earl Warren Drive, Long Beach
Tel: 562/985-8885
www.csulb.edu/~jgarden/
This garden has all the traditional

Japanese garden components – teahouse, stone lanterns, azalea, iris and pine – arranged with eminent grace. Landscape architect Edward R. Lovell visited Japan's Imperial Gardens for inspiration. Closed Monday and Saturday.

Huntington Museum and Botanical Gardens
1151 Oxford Road, San Marino
Tel: 626/405-2100
www.huntington.org
15 gorgeous gardens spread over 150 sweet-smelling acres with library and world-renowned art collection. Closed Monday.

Japanese Garden
6100 Woodley Avenue, Van Nuys
Tel: 818/756-8166
A 6-acre botanical delight, created in the early 1990s on the Donald C. Tillman Water Reclamation Plant. Morning tours visit three gardens in distinctly different styles. In summer there are "sunset" tours on weekdays. Reservations a must.

Los Angeles County Arboretum
301 N Baldwin Avenue, Arcadia
Tel: 818/821-3222
www.arboretum.org
Enormous collection of eucalyptus trees and 5,000 plant species.

Orcutt Ranch Horticulture Center
23600 Roscoe Boulevard, West Hills
Tel: 818/888-6641; www.cityofla.org
Citrus groves bounded by majestic and stately oaks, statuary and sundials. Open to the public on a weekend announced in June or July.

Rancho Los Alamitos Historical Ranch and Gardens
6400 Bixby Hill Road, Long Beach
Tel: 562/431-3541
www.ci.longbeach.ca.us./park/rancho
Former Spanish rancho and Bixby estate, with elegant gardens planted in the 1920s; monthly programs on agriculture, arts, culture and landscape design.

Santa Barbara Orchid Estate
1250 Orchid Drive, Santa Barbara
Tel: 805/967-1284 or 800/553-3387; www.sborchid.com
Thousands of flowers.

Sherman Library and Gardens
2746 E Pacific Coast Highway, Corona del Mar
Tel: 714/673-2261

Established in 1958 in memory of industrialist M.H. Sherman. A Discovery Garden recounts a history of herbs in scent and touch for the blind. The horticultural goal at Sherman is to produce glorious color all year long.

South Coast Botanic Garden
26300 Crenshaw Boulevard, Palos Verdes Peninsula
Tel: 310/544-6815
www.palosverdes.com
A former landfill now displaying fruit trees, roses, a desert garden with cactus, and duck-filled lake.

Parks and Houses

Charmlee Nature Preserve
2577 Encinal Canyon off Pacific Coast Highway
Tel: 310/457-7247
Lots of birds and a small nature museum.

Forest Lawn Memorial Park
1712 S Glendale Avenue
Tel: 323/254-3131 and
Hollywood Hills, 6300 Forest Lawn Drive, Hollywood
Tel: 323/254-7251
www.forestlawn.com
Two locations flanking 4,000-acre (1,600-hectare) Griffith Park, Glendale.

Greystone Mansion
905 Loma Vista Drive, Beverly Hills
Tel: 310/550-4654; www.bhvc.com
Rare tours of the impressive mansion built in 1928 by oil millionaire Edward Doheny; but the grounds are open daily.

Griffith Park
www.cityofla.org
A huge park in the hills above Los Angeles, Griffith Park comprises many picnic areas and hiking trails, the famous Hollywood sign, the 113-acre (46-hectare) Los Angeles Zoo and the Griffith Park Observatory, which features a planetarium and a spectacular view of the city. Rail buffs should visit Travel Town at the park's northwest corner, with its collection of vintage trains (rides on first weekend of each month). Heritage Square, a collection of old homes, is nearby but open only on weekends.

Lummis Home
43 Highland Park
Tel: 213/222-0546
Boulder and log cabin built in 1897 by Charles Lummis, founder of the Southwest Museum. Early California artifacts and garden of native plants.

Malibu Creek State Park
Malibu Canon Road
Tel: 818/880-0367 and

Topanga State Park
20829 Entrada, Topanga
Tel: 310/454-8212
www.cal-parks.ca.gov
Both offer miles of mountain trails with wildlife and great panoramic views. Decent walks.

El Pueblo de Los Angeles State Historic Park
800 N Alameda
Tel: 213/638-6987; www.cityofla.org
This historical 44-acre (18-hectare) Downtown park houses the city's first church, firehouse and theater. Its center is Olvera Street, a block-long pedestrian way lined with open-air stalls, cafes, restaurants, and gift shops. On Olvera Street are the Avila Adobe House, the city's oldest home, and the Visitors Center (tel: 213/628-1274), which shows a film about the neighborhood.

Will Rogers State Historic Park
off Sunset Boulevard, near the coast
Tel: 310/454-8212
www.cal-parks.ca.gov
The star's ranch house, plus a film of his life. Picnic area, polo field and walking trails.

SAN FERNANDO VALLEY

Los Angeles State and County Arboretum
301 N Baldwin Avenue, Arcadia
Tel: 626/821-3222
www.arboretum.org
This 127-acre (51-hectare) county-run arboretum was established to house the extensive collection of the world-traveling horticulturalist Dr Saumuel Ayres. There are some 30,000 permanent plants on the grounds admired by half a million visitors each year. The peacocks are descendants of the original

three pairs brought from India more than 100 years ago.

Rancho de los Encinos State Historic Park

16756 Moorpark Street, Encino
Tel: 748/784-4849
www.cal-parks.ca.gov

Amidst the 5 acres (2 hectares) of manicured lawns, duck ponds, and eucalyptus and citrus groves is the De la Osa Adobe, built in 1849 and restored with period furnishings. A stone blacksmith shop and a two-story French provincial home, built by the rancho's second owners, are also located here.

Santa Susana Pass State Park

Chatsworth Park South Community Center, Chatsworth
Tel: 310/455-2465
www.cal-parks.ca.gov

Three-hour conducted tour along part of the old Butterfield Stagecoach Trail. Open Sunday.

William S. Hart Ranch and Museum

near San Fernando Road exit of Antelope Valley Freeway
Tel: 661/254-4584
www.hartmuseum.org

Spanish Colonial house full of Western treasures bequeathed to the state by the silent screen cowboy.

Sport

Participant Sports

BALLOONING

Balloon rides are popular attractions. **Panorama Balloon Tours** launches hot-air balloons daily for flights that overlook the Temecula wine country or the Del Mar coastal valley or Palm Springs, tel: 800/455-3592; www.gohotair. com: **Skysurfer**, tel: 858/481-6800 also covers Del Mar, as does **Balloon San Diego**, tel: 858/481-4100 and **Balloon Flights**, tel: 858/350-7620: **Dream Flights**, tel: 800/933-5628, www.dreamflights. com, overlooks Palm Desert.

Other choices in Temecula include **Riders in the Sky**, tel: 909/944-1906: and **D&D Ballooning**, tel: 909/302-0448; www.hotairadventures.com: **SmileRides** offers balloon tours of the Simi and Antelope Valleys (north of LA), as well as Las Vegas. Check local phone books for other listings.

For trips over the Sierras contact **Sunshine Adventures**, tel: 800/829-7238. Also **DAE Flights**, tel: 951/676-3902 or **Above All Balloon Charters**, tel: 951/694-6287 or 800/942-7433.

BICYCLING

Pasadena operates an extensive cycling program and free bike maps are obtainable from City Hall, tel: 626/744-4755; www.ci.pasadena. ca.us.

For information about obtaining a free bike map for the LA County area, tel: 213/244-6539. For information about cycling in the **Santa Monica Mountains** – one of

the world's largest urban wilderness areas – tel: 805/370-2301; www.nps.gov/samo.

Organized bicycle adventures which include accommodation operate in San Diego and other parts of the state from **Imagine Tours**, tel: 800/228-7041. **Mammoth Mountain Bike Park**, tel: 800/228-4947 offers 50 miles of cycling trails and stunt tracks. Closes in October for the winter.

FISHING

California's **Department of Fish and Game**, tel: 916/653-7664; www.dfg.ca.gov, oversees fishing areas at wildlife and ecological reserves in various parts of the state and offers a free copy of its magazine, *Outdoor California* (call 1-800-THE-WILD).

One day in June and another in September each year are "Free Fishing Days" when a license is not needed to fish.

GOLF

Greater Los Angeles Area

Brookside Golf Course
1133 N Rosemont Avenue, Pasadena
Tel: 626/796-8151

DeBell Golf Course
1500 Walnut Avenue, Burbank
Tel: 818/845-0022

Griffith Golf Courses
4730 Crystal Springs Drive
Tel: 213/664-2255

Industry Hills Golf Club
1 Industry Hills Parkway, City of Industry
Tel: 818/810-4653

Los Verdes Golf Course
7000 W Los Verdes Drive, Rancho Palos Verdes
Tel: 310/377-7370

Rancho Park Golf Course
10460 W Pico Boulevard, Beverly Hills
Tel: 310/838-7373

Also see: www.golfersweb.com, and the LA County Parks site, www.parks.co.la.ca.us

Orange County
Costa Mesa Golf Course
1701 Golf Course Drive,
Costa Mesa
Tel: 714/540-7500
Newport Beach Golf Course
3100 Irvine Avenue
Tel: 714/852-8681

San Diego County
Torrey Pines Golf Courses
11840 North Torrey Pines Road,
La Jolla
Tel: 800/985-4653 or 858/
452-3226

HORSEBACK RIDING

Horses to ride in LA's **Griffith Park** can be rented at several nearby stables among which are **Bar S Stables** in Glendale, tel: 818/242-8443; **J.P. Stables**, tel: 818/843-9890 and **LA Equestrian Center**, tel: 818/840-8894, both in Burbank; and **Sunset Ranch Stables** in Hollywood, tel: 323/469-5450. In winter, most stables close around mid-afternoon.

SKIING

Within 2–3 hours' driving from Los Angeles are:
Bear Mountain
PO Box 6812, Big Bear Lake, CA 92315
Tel: 909/585-2517
www.bearmtn.com
Mount Baldy
PO Box 459, Mount Baldy, CA 91759
Tel: 949/981-1234
Mount Waterman
817 Lynn Haven Lane, La Canada Flintridge, CA 91011
Tel: 626/440-1041
Mountain High
PO Box 428, Wrightswood, CA 92397
Tel: 760/249-5808
www.mthigh.com
Ski Sunrise
24501 Big Pines Highway,
Wrightwood, CA 92397
Tel: 760/249-6150
www.skisunrise.com

Snow Forest
400 Cherry Lane, Big Bear Lake, CA 92315
Tel: 909/866-8891
Snow Summit
880 Summit Road, Big Bear Lake, CA 92315
Tel: 909/866-5766
www.snowsummit.com
Snow Valley
PO Box 2337, Running Springs, CA 92382
Tel: 909/867-2751 or 814/867-2751; www.snow-valley.com

SURFING AND WATER SKIING

Lessons and equipment hire are available from **Ski Surfshop**, 1765 Artesia Boulevard, Manhattan Beach, tel: 310/379-2312: **Becker Surfboards**, 301 Pier Avenue, Hermosa Beach, tel: 310/374-7626; www.beckersurf. com, or **Action Water Sports**, 4144 Lincoln Boulevard, Marina del Rey, tel: 310/306-9539; www.action watersports.com

OTHER WATER ACTIVITIES

Operating out of Lake Isabella, three hours north of Los Angeles, is **Kern River Tours**, tel: 760/379-4616, www.kernrivertours.com. **Aqua Adventures Kayak School**, tel: 619/272-0800; www.aqua-adventures.com, is in San Diego, and **Paddle Power Inc.**, tel: 949/675-1215, which offers kayak lessons and rentals, is in Newport Beach.

TENNIS

In **Griffith Park**, just off Riverside Drive, are four free courts that don't require reservations, tel: 323/662-7772; **Tennis LA**, 5880 W Third Street, tel: 323/936-9900, has 16 courts to rent; **Studio City Golf and Tennis**, 4141 Whitsett Avenue, Studio City, tel: 818/769-5263, has 20 lighted courts; the

Racquet Center of Universal City, 10933 Ventura Boulevard, Studio City, tel: 818/760-2303, also has 20 courts.
Public courts (reservations advised) include **Poinsettia Recreation Center**, 7341 Willoughby Avenue, tel: 213/876-5014; **Pacific Palisades Recreation Center**, 851 Alma Road, tel: 310/454-5445; **Cheviot Hills Recreation Center**, 2551 Motor Avenue, tel: 310/836-8879; and **Westwood Recreation Complex**, 1350 Sepulveda Boulevard, Westwood, tel: 310/575-8299.
Also, **Century City Tennis Club**, 2040 Avenue of the Stars, tel: 310/282-0762; **Beverly Hills Tennis**, 325 S La Cienega Boulevard, tel: 310/652-7555; and **Plummer Park Tennis**, 1200 N Vista, West Hollywood, tel: 323/876-8180.

Spectator Sports
BASEBALL

The baseball season runs from April to late September. In Southern California, the **Los Angeles Dodgers** play at Dodger Stadium, 1000 Elysian Park Avenue, tel: 323/224-1448; www.dodgers.com to an average of 2.6 million fans each year. The **Anaheim Angels** play at Anaheim Stadium, 2000 Gene Autry Way, tel: 888/796-4256; www.anaheim angels.com. The **San Diego Padres** play at San Diego's Qualcomm Stadium, tel: 619/29-PADRES; www.padres.com
If the Dodgers, Angels or Padres have winning seasons, they could enter the Fall Classic (the World Series) and play until mid-October.

BASKETBALL

The regular National Basketball Association (NBA) season runs from October to April, with championship playoffs continuing in June.
The **Los Angeles Lakers** (www.nba.com/lakers), which has won many world championships and qualified for the playoffs 19

times in 20 years, and the **LA Clippers** (www.nba.com/clippers) play at the Staples Center, Downtown at 1111 S Figueroa Street, tel: 213/480-3232 (Ticketmaster); www.staples center.com.

The **USC Trojans**, tel: 213/740-GOSC; www.usctrojans.com, are playing at the Los Angeles Sports Arena, 3939 South Figueroa, until their own new arena is finished in 2002; and the **UCLA Bruins** play on campus at Pauley Pavilion. For tickets tel: 310/825-2101; www.uclabruins.com

FOOTBALL

USC, tel: 213/740-GOSC; www.usctrojans.com, at the Coliseum, and **UCLA**, tel: 310/825-2101; www.uclabruins.com at the immense Rose Bowl in Pasadena, where the Pac-10 and Big-10 teams battle every January 1 right after Pasadena's glorious annual Rose Parade, unless one of them is in the National Championship Game, which rotates among top bowls (the Rose Bowl will host the championship in 2002. For January 1 Rose Bowl tickets tel: 626/577-3100).

The **NFL** has gone from the LA scene for several years. However, the **Arena Football League** is relatively new, with the Los Angeles Avengers the local representatives. They play indoor on a smaller field than the NFL, but with rules that encourage a faster and higher-scoring game.

The Avengers play at the **Staples Center**, 1111 S Figueroa Street, Downtown, tel: 213/480-3232 (Ticketmaster); www. laavengers. com

HOCKEY

California has two professional hockey teams: the **Los Angeles Kings**, who play at the Staples Center, 1111 S Figueroa Street, Downtown, tel: 213/480-3232 (Ticketmaster); www.lakings.com; and the younger **San Jose Sharks**,

who play at the San Jose Arena. The hockey season runs from October to April.

SOCCER

LA's Galaxy, tel: 877/3-GALAXY, www.lagalaxy.com, one of 12 teams in the MLS (Major League Soccer), debuted in a winning game in April 1996 at Pasadena's Rose Bowl, its home field.

HORSE RACING

Southern California has three tracks to choose from:
Hollywood Park, tel: 310/419-1500; www.hollywoodpark.com in Inglewood hosts thoroughbred racing from April to July and harness racing in November and December.
Santa Anita Park, tel: 626/574-7223; www.santaanita.com in Arcadia hosts thoroughbred racing from October to mid-November and December to late April.
The season at the **Del Mar Thoroughbred Club**, tel: 858/755-1141; www.dmtc.com, about 30 miles north of San Diego, runs from mid-July to early September.

GENERAL

True sports fans can save a bundle by attending college or high school events such as **basketball** games at Crenshaw High School, tel: 213/296-5370; **volleyball** at USC, tel: 213/740-GOSC or UCLA, tel: 310/825-2101; **football** at Occidental College, tel: 213/259-2677; **baseball** at USC, tel: 213/740-GOSC; **softball** at UCLA, tel: 310/825-2101 or San Pedro High School, tel: 310/547-2491 or **tennis** at Peninsula High School, tel: 310/377-4888.

Also worth checking out is the **Fila Summer Pro Basketball League**, at the Pyramid Arena at Cal State University Long Beach, which features NBA and collegiate stars during July, tel: 562/445-4646.

Shopping

Where to Shop

LOS ANGELES CITY

For intrepid shoppers, Southern California can be right up there with Paris and Hong Kong. No matter what your taste or budget, you are bound to find what you're looking for. A recent press release by the tourist bureau claimed that the area is becoming "the unofficial seamstress to the casually-clad masses."

Much of the high-class fashion, of course, can be found along that glitziest shopping street, Beverly Hills' renowned **Rodeo Drive**. While Rodeo has now become quite a tourist trap, with more people window-shopping than buying, some of the world-class shops along the drive include **Chanel**, **Armani**, **Ungaro**, **Alaia**, and **Bottega Veneta**. Rodeo Drive's luxurious amenities were increased by 40 percent a few years back with the ingenious addition of a new street, **Two Rodeo** (or **Via Rodeo**), a curving, cobble-stoned walkway lined with such top-name stores as **Tiffany**, **Christian Dior**, and **Cartier**, whose classy emporiums feature granite colonnades and copper-toned roofs. An underground parking lot offering free valet parking feeds shoppers right into the middle of the street.

Nearby in the 9500–9700 blocks of **Wilshire** are the big department stores: **Neiman-Marcus**, tel: 310/550-5900; www. neimanmarcus.com; **Saks Fifth Avenue**, tel: 310/275-4211; saksincorporated.com; and **Barneys New York**, tel: 310/276-4400; www.netcity.com/barneysny.

Another collection of good, large shops (including **Nordstrom**,

Robinsons-May and **Barnes and Noble**) is in the **Westside Pavilion**, 10800 W Pico Boulevard, tel: 310/474-6255; www.westside pavilion.com. It is open until 9pm on weekdays.

A trip down **Melrose Avenue** is a must. First there's the **Pacific Design Center – The Blue Whale –** with its 200 designers showrooms at the corner of San Vicente, tel: 310/657-0800; www.pdc. digitalhousing.net, and then there are several blocks of raffish shops between **Croft** and **La Brea**. Some of Southern California's best people-watching goes on here, and there are plenty of little cafes to serve as rest stops. Those into avant-garde high fashion can go to **Maxfield** near Doheny and Melrose, an austere temple of haute style, where stars like Jack Nicholson, Robin Williams, and a host of rock 'n' rollers find labels like **Gaultier**, **Lagerfeld**, and **Katherine Hamnett**.

For a change of pace you might want to browse among one of the country's largest collections of antique books at the **Heritage Book Store** in the 8500 block of Melrose, where an extensive autograph collection includes those of Mark Twain and Charles Dickens. There are **antique** stores along La Brea in the 300–600 blocks and many others at the Santa Monica Antique Market, 1607 Lincoln Boulevard.

Although trendy shopping streets like **La Brea** and **Santa Monica's Third Street Promenade** and **Montana Avenue** (antiques, home furnishings) have not lost their luster, there always seems to be a thriving newcomer. A recent addition is Venice's **Abbot Kinney Boulevard** which was named for the visionary developer who created Venice at the beginning of the 20th century. Palm trees have been planted and set off art galleries, restaurants, clothing and jewelry stores.

Lively **Chinatown**, rife with the aromas of herbs, dried fish, ginseng, and ginger is the primary source of Asian imports. Try **F. See On Company**, 507 Chungking, tel: 213/628-3532 for teak furniture and porcelain; **Fongs**, 939 Chungking, tel: 213/626-5904 for antiques, cloisonne, figurines, handpainted bottles; and **Win Sun**, 951 Chungking, tel: 213/680-9862, for jade and opal jewelry. All three are in the **Chungking Mall**. Try **Hong Kong Gifts**, 470 Gin Ling, tel: 213/617-9008 for silk jackets and kimonos; and **Shanghai Corner**, 951 Sun Mun, tel: 213/628-1697 for inexpensive porcelain, slippers, toys, herbs, ginseng, ginger – the smells in Chinatown.

Don't forget that for mall lovers, Southern California is a shopper's Valhalla. One of the Southland's most famous landmarks, the outstanding former Uniroyal tire plant beside the Santa Ana Freeway in the City of Commerce has re-emerged as the **Citadel Outlet Collection**, www.citadelfactory stores.com, an enticing shopping plaza whose 42 stores spread around a tree-flanked courtyard. The mind reels at the number of mega-malls dotted throughout the region: **Century City**, **Beverly Center**, and **Topanga Plaza** among them. But you might want to devote some time to the huge **South Coast Plaza**, 3333 Bristol, Santa Ana, tel: 949/435-8571; www.southcoast plaza.com, said to be the richest in the country and whose 350 shops include **J. Crew** (of mail-order fame), **Armani**, **Rizzoli bookshop**, a **Museum of Modern Art giftstore**, **Joan & David**, **Yves Saint Laurent**, and the West Coast's first **Calvin Klein Boutique** to name just a few, as well as a wide range of good eateries.

Downtown LA's Fashion District is dominated by the **California Mart**, tel: 213/630-3710; www.californiamart.com, which houses more than 1,000 showrooms in more than 1 million sq ft of space. Although primarily for wholesalers, the Mart is open to the public on the last Friday and Saturday of each month.

FURTHER AFIELD

The **San Fernando Valley** is renowned for its malls, the most famous and biggest of which are the **Glendale Galleria** (270 stores, www.glendalegallerica.com), the **Northridge Fashion Center** (212 stores), and the **Sherman Oaks Fashion Square** (140 stores).

A little further afield, in addition to Orange County's **South Coast Plaza**, are the **Del Amo Fashion Square** in Torrance, www.netstyle. com/southbay/shopppingcenters/ delamomall, and the 200 specialty shops in a Mediterranean-village type atmosphere of Newport Beach's **Fashion Island**, 1045 Newport Center Drive, www.fashion island-nb.com

Because of its upscale nature, the **Palm Springs** region is understandably one big shopping area, with the **Desert Fashion Plaza**, www.desert-resorts.com, on Palm Canyon Drive possibly outclassed by Palm Desert's nearby **Town Center**, www.desert-resorts.com, where around 130 shops and an outdoor ice-skating rink are flanked by several major department stores.

Equally attractive is the charm and ambiance of **Santa Barbara**'s **Paseo Nuevo Shopping Center**, a cheerful Spanish-style courtyard adorned with tile, ornamental ironwork and bright flags. Yet another era is evoked by **San Diego**'s **Gaslamp Quarter**, a 16-block, 38-acre district recommended for arts and crafts. In addition to San Diego's **Seaport Village**, www.spvillage.com, and the multilevel **Horton Plaza**, www.hortonplaza.com, the city is also just a short hop away from the Mexican border town of **Tijuana**, where there are different souvenirs and lower prices.

Starwear

Among the stores that specialize in selling castoffs from stars' wardrobes are **StarWares**, formerly in Santa Monica but now an Internet store only, www.starwares. com; **Baby Jane of Hollywood**, 7985 Santa Monica Boulevard, W Hollywood, tel: 323/848-7080, www.babyjaneofhollywood.com;

Jean's Stars Apparel, 12616 Ventura Boulevard, Studio City, tel: 818/760-8872; the nearby **Reel Clothes**, 13607 Ventura Boulevard, Studio City, tel: 818/990-2443; and **Studio Wardrobe**, 1125 N. Highland Avenue, Hollywood, tel: 323/467-9455.

Quite often the clothing consists of garments used in various productions and comes directly from studio wardrobes, as at **It's A Wrap**, 3315 W Magnolia Boulevard, Burbank, tel: 818/567-7366; www.itsawrappws.com. **Universal City Walk**, tel: 818/622-9841; www.mca.com/citywalk, by Universal Studios, sells movie souvenirs.

Markets

El Mercado, 3425 East 1st Street, Boyle Heights, is a marketplace located in the heart of the Latino community – an area rife with great multicolored murals.
Farmers Market, Fairfax and 3rd Street, tel: 323/933-9211, www.farmersmarketla.com, has unlimited free parking, shops, a post office, market stalls, scores of counters for daytime eating. Stars are sometimes spotted.
Grand Central Market, 317 S Broadway, tel: 213/624-2378. This bustling and noisy 80-year-old landmark is one of the liveliest and most colorful places in town.
Rose Bowl Flea Market, Pasadena. Second Sunday of each month. Open 9am–3pm.
Westwood Farmers Market, open 2–7pm Thursday. About 70 stalls and live jazz.

Star Supermarkets

Some of the supermarkets in which celebrities pick up their groceries include **Hughes**, 23481 West Malibu Road in Malibu; **Brentwood Country Mart**, 225 26th Street, Santa Monica; and **Gelson's Market**, 15424 Sunset Boulevard, Pacific Palisades.

Bookstores

Acres of Books
240 Long Beach Boulevard, Long Beach
Tel: 562/437-6980
Owners claim that their half a million books take up six miles of shelving.
Bodhi Tree Bookstore
8585 Melrose Avenue
Tel: 310/659-1733
www.bodhitree.com
Eastern and Western religions, occult, psychology, metaphysical.
Book Soup
8818 Sunset Boulevard
Tel: 310/659-3110
Specialties include art, cinema, and music.
Children's Book World
10580½ W Pico Boulevard
Tel: 310/559-2665
Almost 50,000 titles for kids plus storytelling and author events.
Cinema Collectors
1507 Wilcox Avenue
Tel: 323/461-6516
Variety of stills and posters for sale.
The Cook's Library
8373 West 3rd Street
Tel: 323/655-3141
Famous cookery authors plus books about ethnic cuisine, herbs and "recipes by outlaws."
Dutton's Brentwood Books
11975 San Vicente Boulevard
Tel: 310/476-6263 or 800/286-READ; www.duttonsbrentwood.com
Thousands of titles in all categories, CD-Roms, "bookish antiques," and free author readings ands literary events two or three times each week.
C.G. Jung Bookstore
10349 W Pico Boulevard
Tel: 323/556-1196
www.junginla.org
Specializing in works of psychology, religion and fairy tales.
Larry Edmunds Book Shop
6644 Hollywood Boulevard
Tel: 323/463-3273
The most likely place to find that rare, regular or obvious book about the movies. Also, thousands of stills.
Samuel French Bookshop
7623 Sunset Boulevard

Tel: 323/876-0570
www.samuelfrench.com
Enormous selection of plays, filmbooks, tomes on acting, directing and screenwriting.
Soap Plant
4633 Hollywood Boulevard
Tel: 323/663-0122
Pop culture, alternative literature, offbeat toys. The perfect place to find a quirky gift for a friend.
Traveler's Bookcase
8375 W 3rd Street
Tel: 213/655-0575 or 800/655-0053; www.travelbooks.com
Travel books and accessories, maps, language tapes.
Vedanta Bookshop
1946 Vedanta Place, Hollywood
Tel: 323/960-1736 or 800/816-2242; www.vedanta.com
Meditation and spiritual matters including titles on Eastern philosophies.
World Book and News
1652 N Cahuenga Boulevard
Tel: 323/465-4352
Open 24 hours. Science fiction, mystery and suspense.

Clothing Sizes

This table gives a comparison of American, Continental and British clothing sizes. It is always best to try on any article before buying it, however, as sizes may vary.

Women's Dresses/Suits

American	Continental	British
8	40/36N	10/32
10	42/38N	12/34
12	44/40N	14/36
14	46/42N	16/38
16	48/44N	18/40

Women's Shoes

American	Continental	British
5½	37	4
6½	38	5
7½	39	6
8½	40	7
9½	41	8

Men's Suits

American	Continental	British
34	44	34
–	46	36
38	48	38
–	50	40
42	52	42
–	54	44
46	56	46

Men's Shirts

American	Continental	British
14	36	14
14½	37	14½
15	38	15
15½	39	15½
16	40	16
16½	41	16½
17	42	17

Men's Shoes

American	Continental	British
6½	39	6
7½	40	7
8½	41	8
9½	42	9
10½	43	10
11½	44	11

Festivals

Calendar of Events

More than 170 festivals take place each year in the Los Angeles area. Current ones are listed in the "Calendar" section of the *Los Angeles Times*, the *LA Weekly* or *Los Angeles Magazine*.

Here are just a few of the most popular events.

January

Bob Hope Chrysler Golf Classic
Palm Desert
Tel: 760/346-8184 or 888/MR-BHOPE; www.bhcc.com

Buick Invitational
La Jolla
Tel: 800/888-BUICK
PGA golf tournament.

International Film Festival
Palm Springs
Tel: 760/322-2930 or check www.psfilmfest.org for information

Martin Luther King Celebration
Long Beach
Tel: 562/570-6816
www.golongbeach.org
Music and guest speaker.

Oshogatsu Festival
Tel: 213/628-2725
Japanese New Year celebrations.

Renactment of 1847 American Military occupation of Mission San Luis Rey
Oceanside
Tel: 760/757-3651
Living history event with period costumes.

Southwest Arts festival
Indio
Tel: 760/347-0676 or 800/44-INDIO; www.wartsfest.com

The Tournament of the Roses Parade
Pasadena
Tel. 626/449-4100,
www.tournamentofroses.com
January 1. Make reservations for grandstand seats 5-6 weeks ahead. Parade begins 8.40am.

Whale Watching
Santa Barbara
Tel: 805/963-3654, or
Long Beach
Tel: 800/228-2546

February

Afrikans Are Coming
Los Angeles
Tel: 818/361-7075
African-born master drummers and dancers.

Bob Marley Reggae Festival
Long Beach
Tel: 562/436-3661
Celebrating the famous reggae star's birthday and music.

Charles Dickens Festival
Riverside
Tel: 800/430-4140
www.pe.net/dickens

Chinese-American Expo
Pomona
Tel: 818/285-6500
Ethnic music, dances, traditional arts.

The Chinese New Year Parade
Chinatown
Tel: 213/617-0396
An annual fest where the theme is determined by whichever animal (chicken, rabbit, dragon) is celebrated that year. Also in San Diego, 619/234-4447.

Desert Circuit Horse Show
Palm Springs
Tel: 760/775-7731
www.palmsprings.com
International jumping competition, 1,400 exhibitors.

Festival of the Whales
Dana Point
Tel: 714/496-1555 or 800/290-DANA; www. dpfestivalofwhales.com
Crafts, rides, food.

Flying Leap Storytelling Festival
Solvang
Tel: 805/688-9533
Storytellers from around the world gather.

Frank Sinatra Celebrity Invitational
Palm Desert
Tel: 800/377-8277
Celebrity and amateur golf event with entertainment and fashion show.

Juan de Anza Pageant
Calabasas
Tel: 818/880-0350.
Long Beach Symphony Pops
Long Beach
Tel: 562/436-3203; www.lbso.org
Mexican Mardi Gras
Olvera Street
Tel: 213/625-5045
www.olvera-street.com
The traditional pre-Lent celebration
on LA's oldest street.
**National Date Festival/Riverside
County Fair**
Tel: 800/811-FAIR; www.datefest.org
Produce and date exhibits; camel
and ostrich races, rodeo, music
pageant, carnival.
Queen Mary **Scottish Festival**
Long Beach
Tel: 562/435-3511
www.queenmary.com
Pipe bands, Highland dancing.
The Southern California Boat Show
Los Angeles Convention Center
Tel: 213/741-1151; www.scma.com
Taste of Huntington Beach
Food, music, dancing.
Toshiba Senior Classic
Newport Beach
Tel: 800/94-COAST
Senior PGA golf tour stop.
Valentine's "Sweetheart Dance"
Catalina Island
Tel: 310/510-1520
At the historic Casino Ballroom.
Winter Barrel Tasting
Temecula
Tel: 800/801-WINE
Barrel tastings and food, meet
winemakers.

March
Asian Pacific Festival
Santa Monica
Tel: 310/453-1755
Performance art, dance and
theater.
Azalea Festival
Los Angeles
Tel: 213/563-5443
Horse show, car show, parade and
carnival.
Country Folk Art Show
Pomona
Tel: 818/634-4151
Entries from all over the country.
Country Music Festival
Avalon

Tel: 310/510-1520
Catalina's two-day celebration.
Cowboy Poetry and Music Festival
Santa Clarita
Tel: 661/286-402
Foreign Film Movie Marathon
Santa Monica
Tel: 323/856-7707;
www.afionline.org
The American Film Institute screens
many of the year's foreign film
classics.
Indio PowWow
Tel: 760/342-5000
Pageantry and tradition of American
Indian dance, foods, crafts.
International Film Festival
Santa Barbara
Tel: 805/963-0023
www.sbfilmfestival.org
International Orchid Show
Santa Barbara
Tel: 805/967-6331
www.sborchidshow.com
Los Angeles Marathon
Tel: 310/444-5544
Through the streets of LA.
**Nabisco Dinah Shore LPGA
Celeb Pro-Am**
Rancho Mirage
Tel: 760/324-4546
Ojai Film Festival
Tel: 805/604-1210
www.filmfestival.ojai.net
Return of the Swallows
San Juan Capistrano
Tel: 949/248-2047
Parades and dances to celebrate
the few birds that now turn up.
St Patrick's Day Parades
Held all over the city. The grandest
is always in Downtown Los
Angeles.
St Patrick's Day Parade
Old Pasadena
Tel: 626/796-5049
Salute to Mexico, Imperial
Tel: 619/355-1324
Music, dance, food.
Santa Monica Festival
Tel: 310/458-8350
Multicultural performing arts
festival, including workshops,
crafts, and food.
Taste of Solvang
Tel: 805/688-6144 or 800/468-
6765; www.solvang.org
Beer gardens, "the world's largest
Danish pastry" entertainment.

Village Arts and Crafts Fair
San Clemente
Tel: 949/361-0735

April
Annual Flower Show
Coronado
Tel: 619/437-8788 or 800/622-
8333; www.coronado.ca.us
Flowers, art in the park and antique
car show.
Art and Photo Show
Encinitas
Tel: 760/436-9236
Works inspired by Quail Botanical
Gardens.
Avalon Harbor Underwater Cleanup
Catalina
Tel: 310/510-2595
Only time scuba allowed in Avalon
Bay.
Avocado Festival
Fallbrook
Tel: 760/728-5845
Arts, crafts, entertainment in
avocado capital, including tours of
packing houses.
Brentwood Art Festival
Los Angeles
Tel: 818/797-6803
Bunka-Sai Festival
Tel: 310/618-2930
www.tcac.torrnet.com
Torrance
Japanese cultural celebrations,
Country Music Festival
Avalon
Tel: 310/510-1520
Catalina Island's two-day
celebration.
Easter Sunrise Services
Hollywood Bowl
Tel: 323/850-2000
Services begin at dawn in the city's
most popular amphitheater.
Grapefruit Festival
Borrego Springs
Tel: 800/559-5524
Arts and crafts, car show,
entertaiment, rides.
Jewish Festival
Tel: 805/957-1115; www.sbjf.org
Santa Barbara
Ethnic food, dancing.
LA Fiesta Broadway
Los Angeles
Tel: 310/914-8308 or 888/
296-7966
Immense annual street festival.

LA Independent Film Festival
Tel: 888/386-8497; www.laiff.com
Features, documentaries, shorts.

Mainstreet Marketplace
La Quinta
Tel: 760/564-3199
www.lqchamber.org
Reggae music, arts and crafts,
street fair.

**Major League Baseball's
Opening Day**
Tel: 323/224-1448
www.dodgers.com
For the Dodgers at the Dodger
Stadium, and the Angels at
Anaheim Stadium, tel: 888/796-
4256, www.anaheimangels.com

Newport Beach–Ensenada Race
Tel: 714/771-0691; www.nosa.org
More than 500 boats take part.

Orange Blossom Festival
Riverside
Tel: 909/715-3400 or 800/382-
8202); www.orangeblossomfestival.org
Citrus celebration including
fireworks, entertainment, carnival.

Ramona Pageant
Hemet
Tel: 909/658-3111
America's oldest outdoor pageant,
about California's Mission Indians.

Renaissance Pleasure Faire
San Bernadino
Tel: 800/52-FAIRE; www.recfair.com
Costumed performers, musicians,
arts and crafts, merchants.

Russian American Festival
West Hollywood
Tel: 310/858-1990. Food, music,
arts and crafts.

Scandinavian Festival
Thousand Oaks
Tel: 805/493-5151
Traditional costumes, music,
dancing, and food.

Sony Art Walk
San Diego
Tel: 619/615-1090
Visual and performing artists and
self-guided tours of Downtown.

Spring Art Festival
Pasadena
Tel: 626/797-6803
Arts, crafts, music and food.

Spring Garden Show
Costa Mesa
Tel: 949/435-2167
Garden clubs, horticultural
societies, nurseries all join forces.

Strawberry Country Jamboree
Vista
Tel: 760/724-8822
County fair with blacksmiths, butter
churning, and entertainments.

Sunfest
Palm Springs
Tel: 760/325-8979
Street entertainment, art shows.

Taste of Ventura County
Oxnard
Tel: 805/985-4852 or 800/
994-4852
Food, wine, music, games.

Tennis Tournament
Ojai
Tel: 805/646-7241
www.ojaitourney.org
Top juniors through college.
Prestigious tournament.

Thoroughbred Racing Season
Opens at Hollywood Park in
Inglewood
Tel: 310/419-1500
www.hollywoodpark.com

Toyota Grand Prix
Long Beach
Tel: 562/436-9953 or 800/752-
9524; www.longbeachgp.com
Longest street race in the US.

Ventura Music Festival
Tel: 805/648-3146
International music in historic and
cultural settings.

May

Affaire in the Gardens
Beverly Hills
Tel: 310/550-2648
Two-day art show with music, food.

Aloha Concert Jam
Long Beach
Tel: 909/606-9494
www.alohaconcertjam.com
Two days of the best Hawaiian
entertainment, outrigger canoe
races, hula, lei-making, food.

Arts in the Country Festival
Temecula
Tel: 909/695-2787
Month-long art exhibit, music,
dance, children's activities.

Boat Ride and Harbor Tour
At the port in San Pedro during the
Annual World Trade Week
Tel: 888/288-9242

California Strawberry Festival
Oxnard
Tel: 805/385-7578

www.strawberry-fest.org
Entertainment, arts and crafts,
food.

Catalina Blues Festival
Tel: 888/25-EVENT
www.catalinablues.com

**Catalina Island Old Boys Rugby
Tournament**
Tel: 310/510-2848
www.larugby.com

Cinco de Mayo
Celebrations in LA
Tel: 213/625-5045
San Diego, tel: 619/296-3161;
Oceanside, tel: 619/757-7011;
Calexico, tel: 619/357-1166; and
Riverside, tel: 909/340-5906

Conejo Valley Days
Thousand Oaks
Tel: 805/371-8730
www.cvdbbq.loop.com
Deep-pit barbecue, classic car
show, carnival, parade, rodeo.

Day at the Docks
San Diego
Tel: 619/294-7912
Sportfishing and festival

**ESPN Pro Beach Hockey
Tournament**
Huntington Beach
Tel: 310/419-3262
Month-long event.

Fiesta Days
Hermosa Beach
Tel: 310/376-0951
www.fiestahermosa.com
Crafts, entertainment, and food.

Fillmore Orange Festival
Tel: 661/524-1500
www.fillmoreca.com
Carnival, entertainment, train rides.

Garden Tour
Ojai
Tel: 805/646-8126

Indian Hill Pow Wow
Drake Stadium
Tel: 310/206-7513
Gathering of Native American tribes.
Dances, arts, crafts, ethnic food.

Italian Street Painting Festival
Santa Barbara
Tel: 805/569-3873
www.rain.org/~imadonna/

Lobsterfest
Yorba Linda
Tel: 714/777-3018
All you can eat fresh Maine lobster
and barbecue steak; country music,
dancing.

May Trout Classic
Big Bear Lake
Tel: 800/4BIGBEAR
Fishing competition.

Memorial Day Parade
Canoga Park
Tel: 818/884-4222
Bands, floats, marching groups.

National Orange Show
San Bernardino
Tel: 909/888-6788
Annual event since 1911. Carnival, entertainment, animals

Old-Fashioned Days
Altadena
Tel: 626/794-3988
Classic cars, bands, crafts.

Orange County Art and Jazz Festival
Anaheim
Tel: 714/541-ARTS; www.anaheim.net
Music, car show.

Ramona Pageant
Hemet
Tel: 909/658-3111 or 800/645-4465; www.ramonapageant.com
Continues from April.

Renaissance Pleasure Faire
San Bernadino
Tel: 909/880-3911 or 800/52-FAIRE; www.recfair.com
Continues from April.

Scottish Festival
Costa Mesa
Tel: 949/998-7857
Pipes and drummers, dancing, athletics.

Strawberry Festival
Garden Grove
Tel: 714/638-0981
Crafts, rides, food, talent show.

Street Faire
Downey
Tel: 562/923-2191
Arts and crafts, classic cars, food.

Westwood Sidewalk Arts and Crafts Show
First weekend of the month on the sidewalks of Westwood
Tel: 310/475-4574

June

Annual Del Mar Fair
Tel: 858/755-1161
www.delmarfair.com
Flower show, livestock, entertainment, food. Usually to July 5.

Beachfest
Long Beach
Tel: 949/376-6942
www.beachfest.com
50 bands on five stages, "World's largest chili cook-off."

Concours D'Elegance
Huntington Beach
Tel: 714/375-5023
www.hbonline.com
Exotic, classical cars.

Concours on Rodeo Drive
Beverly Hills
Tel: 310/248-1000
www.beverlyhillscc.org
Classy cars with affuent drivers. Food and music.

Father's Day Vintage Car Show
Thousand Oaks
Tel: 805/497-1955

Gay and Lesbian Parade
West Hollywood
Tel: 310/289-2525

The Great American Irish Fair and Music Festival
Santa Anita Racetrack
Tel: 818/501-3781
www.irishfair.org
Dance, crafts, music, food, and good rides.

Greek Theatre's Outdoor Concerts
Griffith Park
Tel: 323/665-1927
www.nederlander.com
From June to September all types of musical concerts are performed under the stars.

Hermosa Beach Open
Tel: 310/577-0775; www.avptour.com
Professional volleyball and entertainment.

Hollywood Bowl Arts Fair
Hollywood
Tel: 323/462-2355
Arts, crafts, food, entertainment.

Indian Fair
San Diego
Tel: 619/239-2001
Native American festival. Jewelry, children's crafts, art demonstrations.

Juneteenth Cultural Celebration
Oceanside
Tel: 760/722-1534
www.oceanside-ca.com
African-American fiesta with arts and crafts, music, entertainment, and food.

Los Angeles Child's Day Celebration
Exposition Park
Tel: 213/765-5366
Art, crafts, performances.

Meet the Grunion
Cabrillo Marine Aquarium, San Pedro
Tel: 310/548-7562
Nighttime aquarium visiting, and watch the silvery fish come up on the beach to spawn.

Open Sky Music Festival
Big Bear Lake
Tel: 800/4BIGBEAR
Acoustic, folk, jazz and blues; New Orleans-style food.

Palos Verdes Street Fair
Tel: 310/377-8111
Rides, entertainment, food, crafts.

San Fernando Valley Fair
Burbank
Tel: 818/557-1600
Livestock, entertainment, food, crafts.

Santa Monica Pier Twilight Dance Concerts
Tel: 310/458-6900
www.calendarlive.com/smpier/
Free Thursday night shows – from blues to swing to rock – from late June through August.

Salute to Recreation Family Festival
Northridge
Tel: 818/756-8060
Four-day program with International children village, four stages with music, Hawaiian village, crafts, card show, carnival.

Sawdust Festival
Laguna Beach
Tel: 949/494-3030
www.sawdustartfestival.org
Arts and crafts, food, entertainment. June–August.

Scottish Highland Games
San Diego
Tel: 619/645-8080
www.sdhighlandgames.org
Dancing, piping and drumming, athletic, sheep dog trials.

Strawberry Festival
Idyllwild
Tel: 909/659-3259
Food, rides, music.

Summer Food and Wine Festival
Costa Mesa
Tel: 714/435-2167

Summer Solstice Parade
Santa Barbara
Tel: 805/965-3396
www.rain.org/~solstice
Fantastic costumes, music, mimes, dance.

Temecula Valley Balloon and Wine Festival
Temecula
Tel: 909/676-6713

Village Arts and Crafts Fair
San Clemente
Tel: 949/361-0735.

The Whale Fiesta
Cabrillo Beach
Tel: 310/548-7563
Artists create freestanding whales out of anything they can get their hands on, including metal, wood, fiberglass and even trash. Country bands and strolling singers entertain.

Wine Festival
Ojai
Tel: 805/646-1109; www.ojai.org

July

Air Fair
Torrance
Tel: 310/325-7223
Warbirds, military displays, skydiving, food and rides

Blue Torch Pro of Surfing
Huntington Beach
Tel: 949/215-8008
www.bluetorch.com
World championship tour event.

Cajun and Zydeco Festival
Long Beach
Tel: 562/427-3713
Food, dance, music.

Colorado Street Bridge Celebration
Pasadena
Tel: 626/441-6333
Entertainment and food on the famous landmark.

Del Mar Fair
Continued from June.

ESPN B3
Oceanside
Tel: 760/721-1101
Skateboard and bike stunts, in-line skating competition.

Festa Italia
Santa Monica
Tel: 310/535-2416
Italian cuisine, music, entertainment.

Festival of Arts and Pageant of the Masters
Laguna Beach
Tel: 949/494-1145 or 800/487-3378; www.foapom.com
Exhibits, artwork, and the famous annual display of living artworks.

Fila Summer Pro Basketball League
Long Beach
Tel: 562/445-4646
The Pyramid Arena at CSLBU features NBA and collegiate stars for month long league

Fleet Week
San Diego
Tel: 619/236-1212
Naval celebration with ship tours, parades, air shows.

Greek Festival
Santa Barbara
Tel: 805/683-4492
Music, dancing, ethnic cuisine.

Hollywood Bowl Summer Festival
Hollywood
Tel: 323/850-2000

July 4 Firework Displays
Tel: 213/624-7300
From dawn – Santa Monica presents a "Dawn's Early Light" show at the Pier – till after dusk, fireworks are blasting everywhere in the city. July 4 Celebrations also at Pomona, tel: 909/563-5443; Huntington Beach, tel: 714/374-1535; Newport Beach, tel: 714/644-1190; Santa Barbara, tel: 805/966-9222; Coronado, tel: 800/622-8300; Pasadena, tel: 818/795-9311; Ventura, tel: 805/654-7830; Torrance, tel: 310/618-2930; Northridge, tel 818/349-5676; La Crescenta, tel: 818/248-4957; Fullerton, tel: 714/738-6589; Riverside, tel: 909/683-7100; Big Bear, tel: 800/4BIGBEAR; Temecula, tel: 909/694-6480; Catalina, tel: 310/510-1520; Two Harbors, tel: 310/510-0303; Oxnard, tel: 805/985-4852; and Solvang, tel: 805/688-6144. Fireworks beside the *Queen Mary* at Long Beach, tel: 310/435-3511

LA Latino Film Festival
Tel: 323/469-9066
www.latinofilm.org
Features, documentaries, shorts.

Los Angeles Open
UCLA
Tel: 310/825-2101
www.mercedez-benzcup.com
ATP men's tennis tour stop.

Lotus Festival
Los Angeles
Tel: 213/485-1310
Celebrates Asian-Pacific culture with ethnic food, flower shows, dragon boat racing.

Malibu Festival of Arts and Crafts
Tel: 310/456-9025

Old Miners Days
Big Bear
Tel: 800/4 BIGBEAR
Historic gold discovery celebration, chili cook-off, fair, cowboy shootout.

Orange County Fair
Costa Mesa
Tel: 714/708-3247; www.ocfair.com
Carnival rides, big-name entertainment, livestock, etc.

Panasonic Shockwave Beach Games
Huntington Beach
Tel: 949/366-4584
World-class extreme sports festival; also tel: 949/215-8008 for US Open surfing and bodyboarding event.

Salsa Festival
Oxnard
Tel: 805/385-7545
www.oxnardtoursm.com
Salsa, crafts, food, music.

Sawdust Festival
Laguna Beach
Tel: 949/494-3030
Arts and crafts show continues through August.

Semana Nautica
Santa Barbara
Tel: 805/965-0509
www.sbontours.com
Multisports festival on land. sea and in the air.

Symphonies Under the Stars at the Hollywood Bowl
Tel: 213/876-0232.

US Open Sandcastle Contest
Imperial Beach
Tel: 619/424-3151
www.ci.imperial-beach.ca.us

Village Arts and Crafts Fair
San Clemente
Tel: 714/361-0735

August

African Marketplace and Cultural Fair
Los Angeles
Tel: 323/734-1164
Music, food, entertainment, seminars.

Bayfair
San Diego
Tel: 619/225-9160; www.bayfair.com
Powerboat racing and family festival.

California Beach Party
Ventura
Tel: 805/654-7830
Surfing, fashion show, food, entertainment.

Catalina Ski Race
Long Beach
Tel: 714/894-3498
Waterski racing to Catalina Island and back.

County Fair
Ventura
Tel: 805/648-3376; www.vcfair.org
Rodeo, horse show, concerts.

Great Labor Day Cruise
Costa Mesa
Tel: 714/826-1948
Cars, hotrods, arts and crafts, food.

Gourmet Food and Wine Tasting Festival
Torrance
Tel: 310/540-5858
First Saturday in August.

GTE Summer Classic Equestrian Event
Huntington Beach
Tel: 714/536-5258
Southern California's best jumping horses.

Hungarian Festival
Los Angeles
Tel: 213/463-3473
Gypsy music, folk dancers, goulash, bazaar.

International Family Festival
Westchester
Tel: 310/202-2850
Carnival, parade, petting zoo.

International Sea Festival
Long Beach
Tel: 562/570-3100
Boating, swimming, fishing events.

International Short Film Festival
Palm Springs
Tel: 760/322-2930
www.psfilmfest.org
Short films from around the world.

International Surf Festival
Tel: 310/545-5621
The best wave riders in California strut their stuff on Hermosa, Manhattan and Redondo beaches.

Japanese Festival
Los Angeles
Tel: 213/687-7193
Parade, arts and crafts, martial arts, etc.

Jazz Festival
Long Beach
Tel: 562/436-7794
www.longbeachjazzfestival.com

Jazz in the Pines
Idyllwild
Tel: 909/659-4885
Continuous jass at three venues; swing dance.

Latin America Festival
San Diego
Tel: 619/296-3266
Crafts, artists, entertainment, food.

Longboard Surfing Contest
Oceanside
Tel: 800/350-7873
Legends of surfing.

Los Angeles Open
Manhattan Beach
Tel: 213/480-3232 (Ticketmaster)
WTA professional women's tennis tour stop.

Manhattan Beach Open
Tel: 310/577-0775
www.avptour.com
The Wimbledon of volleyball tournaments.

Old Pasadena Summer Fest
Tel: 626/795-9656
Arts, food, music, crafts.

Old Spanish Days Fiesta
Santa Barbara
Tel: 805/962-8101
Five days of parades, dancers, carnival, rodeo.

Pow Wow
Costa Mesa
Tel: 714/663-1102
www.powwows.com
Native American arts and crafts.

Summer Art Show
Westwood
Tel: 626/797-6803
Fine arts and crafts, food, rides.

Taste in San Pedro
Tel: 310/832-7272
Multicultural food and drink celebration.

World Bodysurfing Championship
Oceanside
Tel: 800/350-7873

September

Arts Festival
Manhattan Beach
Tel: 310/545-5621
Music, dance, theater, visual art.

Art Festival in La Jolla Village
Tel: 888/ART-FEST
200 artists from around the nation; entertainment, local cuisine, children's activities.

Barstow Rodeo Stampede
Tel: 760/252-3093
PRCA rodeo with all the trimmings.

Bluegrass Jamboree and Banjo-Fiddle Contest
Julian
Tel: 760/765-1857
www.julianca.com
Bluegrass, antiques, wine tasting.

Bowful of Blues
Ojai
Tel: 805/646-7230
Worldclass blues musicians.

Chinese Moon Festival
Chinatown
Tel: 213/617-0396
Musicians, dancers, poets, martial arts.

Danish Days
Solvang
Tel: 805/688-6144
www.solvang.org
Music, folk dancing, parade.

Fiesta Hermosa
Hermosa Beach
Tel: 310/376-0951
www.fiestahermosa.com
Crafts, entertainment, food.

Harbor Day Festival
Chula Vista
Tel: 619/426-2882 and at Oceanside
Tel: 760/722-1534
Tall ships, maritime displays, entertainment.

International Jazz Festival
Santa Barbara
Tel: 805/969-2858

KLON Jazz Festival
Long Beach
Tel: 562/985-1686
Top blues musicians.

Laguna Beach Film Festival
Tel: 949/499-1313
www.lagunabeachfilmfestival.org

LA's Birthday Party
Olvera Street
Tel: 213/625-5045
Sept 6: festivities and fiestas.

Los Angeles County Fair
Pomona, 30 miles E of Downtown
Tel: 909/623-3111; www.fairplex.com
Competitions for the biggest pigs,
tastiest apple pie, best livestock.
Educational displays and a petting
zoo for the kids, and thoroughbred
horserace betting for the grownups
– a true country fair.

**Mexican Independence Day
Celebration**
Santa Monica
Tel: 310/458-8688

NASCAR LA Street Race
Downtown
Tel: 310/444-5544
World-famous stock-car racing.

**Philippine Arts and Culture
Festival**
San Pedro
Tel: 213/389-3050
www.vconline.org
Dance, music, theater, film.

Port of LA Lobsterfest
San Pedro
Tel: 310/366-6472
www.lobsterfest.com
Entertainment, crafts, lobster
calling contest.

Route 66 Rendezvous
San Bernardino
Tel: 800/TO-RTE66
Vintage car cruise and street fair.

Sandcastle Contest
Newport Beach
Tel: 949/729-4400
All levels of experience.

San Diego Street Scene
Tel: 619/350-3333
www.street-scene.com
Food, music and entertainment.

**Simon Rodia Watts Towers
Jazz Festival**
Los Angeles
Tel: 213/847-4646; www.cityofla.org
Also gospel, R&B, arts and crafts.

Taste of Newport
Newport Beach
Tel: 800/94-COAST
www.newportbeach.com
Foodtasting, top entertainment.

**Temecula Valley International Film
Festival**
Tel: 909/699-8681
Independent film festival.

October

AFI Film Festival
Hollywood
Tel: 323/856-7707; www.afifest.com
Features, docs, shorts, animation.

**Arts Festival and Old
Hometown Fair**
Manhattan Beach
Tel: 310/545-5621
Music, dance, theater; 10K race,
crafts, beer garden.

Borrego Days Desert Festival
Borrego Springs
Tel: 800/559-5524.
Parade, crafts, entertainment, rides.

Buccaneer Days
Two Harbors, Catalina Island
Tel: 310/510-0303.
Treasure hunt, costume contest.

Cabrillo Festival
San Diego
Tel: 619/557-5450
Re-enactment of Cabrillo's landing;
ethnic food stalls.

Calabasas Pumpkin Festival
Calabas
Tel: 818/225-2227
www.pumpkin-festival.com
Crafts, food and 30 tons of
pumpkins.

Catalina Island Jazz Festival
Avalon
Tel: 818/347-5299 or 888/330-
5252; www.jazztrax.com

Charity Pro Rodeo
City of Industry
Tel: 626/961-6892
Pony rides, petting zoo, food,
western wear.

**Edwards Air Force Base Open
House**
Palmdale
Tel: 661/277-3510
Open house and air show.

Farmer's Fair and Exposition
Perris
Tel: 909/657-4221
Top entertainment, PCRA rodeo,
carnival.

Foreign Film Movie Marathon
Santa Monica
Tel: 310/856-7707
American Film Institute screens the
year's foreign film classics.

Great American Irish Fair
Orange County Fairgrounds
Tel: 714/284-9558
www.irishfair.org
Dance, music, food, pubs, rides.

Grape Harvest Festival
Rancho Cucamonga
Tel: 909/987-1012
www.ranchochamber.org
Arts and crafts, pie-eating contests,
carnival rides.

Halloween Carnival
West Hollywood
Tel: 310/854-7400
Outrageous costumes, parade.

Harvest Festival
Irvine
Tel: 949/552-7336
Arts and crafts, carnival, petting zoo
pumpkin decorating.

Health Fair
Thousand Oaks
Tel: 805/499-1993
Health exhibits, screenings,
demonstrations.

The International Festival of Masks
Hancock Park
Tel: 323/934-8527
Last Sunday of October, initially this
was a Halloween parade, later
became a mask parade to celebrate
LA's ethnic diversity.

LA International Short Film Festival
Hollywood
Tel: 323/663-0242
www.lashortfest.com
Under 60 minutes, all genres.

Lemon Festival
Goleta
Lemon foods, childrens' rides,
music.

**Long Beach International Film
Festival**
Tel: 562/938-9687

Moon Festival
San Diego
Tel: 619/578-1282
Chinese cuisine, entertainment.

Motorcycle Weekend
Palm Springs
Tel: 760/323-4141
Bike show, party, chili cook-off.

Oktoberfest
Huntington Beach
Tel: 714/895-8020
Torrance/Alpine Village
Tel: 310/327-6560
Santa Barbara
Tel: 805/967-0754
Big Bear
Tel: 909/866-4607 and
Carlsbad
Tel: 800/227-5722
German beer, bands, dancing.

Pioneer Days
Twentynine Palms
Tel: 760/367-3445
Rodeo, carnival, Country & Western
dancing.

Redondo Beach Lobsterfest
Tel: 310/376-6911
www.lobsterfestival.com
Top classic surf bands, food, party,
and plenty of you-know-what.

Richmond Street Festival
El Segundo
Tel: 310/322-1220
Arts, crafts, music, food.

Sabor de Mexico
Huntington Park
Tel: 323/585-1155
Celebration honoring Mexican
heritage, music, food, crafts.

Scandinavian Festival
Santa Monica
Tel: 213/661-4273
Folk dancing, arts and crafts.

Shipwreck
Long Beach
Tel: 562/435-3511
The Queen Mary is transformed into
a haunted Halloween celebration for
the entire family.

Street Fair
Escondido
Tel: 760/745-2125
Arts and crafts, food, music.

Studio Art Tour
Ojai
Tel: 805/646-8126
Self-guided tour of 24 artists'
studios.

**Taste of Ventura County Food and
Wine Festival**
Channel Islands Harbor
Tel: 805/985-4852

Village Celebration
Westwood Village
Tel: 818/797-6803
Arts crafts, food, entertainment.

Western Days and Rodeo
San Dimas
Tel: 909/592-3818
PRCA Rodeo, parade, street dance,
crafts, car show.

November

Asian Pacific American Festival
Santa Monica
Tel: 310/453-1755
Theater, performance and visual art
with an emphasis on Asian
concerns.

Chrysler Grand Prix
Palm Springs
Tel: 619/323-3332
www.palmsprings.com
Vintage sports cars race through
the streets.

**Day of the Dead (Dia De Los
Muertos) Celebrations**
Olvera Street
Tel: 213/624-3660
San Diego
el. 619/296-3266
Latin American festival with parade.

Death Valley 49ers Encampment
Death Valley
Tel: 760/852-4524
Old West entertainment, fiddlers
competition, cowboy poetry.

The Doo Da Parade
Pasadena
Tel: 626/449-3689
A crazy array of local wackies who
parody all the hoop-la surrounding
the local Christmas parades as well
as poking fun at topical events in
the news.

Fall Art Festival
Pasadena
Tel: 626/797-6803

Festival of Lights
San Diego
Tel: 619/296-3161
Celebration includes dance
performances from around the
world, nativity lighting.

Golf Cart Parade
Palm Desert
Tel: 760/346-6111
Decorated golf carts, floats, bands.

Holiday Bazaar
Vista
Tel: 760/724-8822
Arts and crafts, llama and pony
rides, food.

Hollywood Christmas Parade
Tel: 323/469-2337
Held annually the Sunday after
Thanksgiving down 3¾ miles (5 km)
of Hollywood and Sunset
boulevards. Lots of celebrity "grand
marshalls" and usually one million
spectators. The parade, started
long ago, in 1931, is telecast live
and begins at 6pm.

LA Poetry Festival
Tel: 323/255-5223
www.lapoetryfestival.org
International poets, readings,
various venues.

Mariachi Festival
East LA
Tel: 213/485-2437; www.cityofla.org
Music, dance, costumes, food.

Mexican Day of the Dead
Mission Hills
Tel: 818/344-7017

**Plein Air Painters of America
Festival**
Catalina Island
Tel: 310/510-1552
Sale and show, dinner.

Poinsettia Festival
Encinitas
Tel: 760/943-1950
Holiday craft fair, music and beer
garden in the world poinsettia
capital.

Turkey Trot
Torrance
Tel: 310/618-2930
Family running events.

Winterfest
Solvang
Tel: 805/688-8620
Danish village celebrations late
November through Christmas.

December

Christmas Tree Lighting
Beverly Hills
Tel: 310/248-1000
Celebs and entertainers on hand.
Also at Costa Mesa
Tel: 949/435-2100
More than 10,000 lights. Carolers.

Christmas Open Houses
Heritage House, Redlands
Tel: 909/826-5273
Victorian-style celebrations
Rancho Los Cerritos, Long Beach
Tel: 562/570-1755
Mexico-style with pinatas.

Christmas Parades and festivals
Every week, everywhere.
Coronado
Tel: 800/622-8300
Santa Barbara
Tel: 805/862-2098
Long Beach
Tel: 562/434/3066
San Diego
Tel: 619/239-2749
Corona del Mar
Tel: 949/673-4050
Whittier
Tel: 562/696-2662
La Canada
Tel: 818/760-4289

Downey
Tel: 562/923-2191
Temecula
Tel: 909/694-6480
Palm Springs
Tel: 760/778-8415
Harvest Festival
Pomona
Tel: 707/778-6300
Art and crafts, strolling players.
International Tamale Festival
Indio
Tel: 760/342-6532 or 800/44-
INDIO; www.tamalefestival.org
Traditional foods, arts and crafts,
dancing, games.
Light Festival
Griffith Park
November 26–December 26.
Crystal Springs Road sparkles with
a full mile of spectacular light
displays, by car or via foot.
Lighted Boat Parades
San Pedro; tel: 310/832-7272
Oxnard; tel: 805/985-4852
Ventura; tel: 805/644-0169
San Diego; tel: 619/236-1212
Santa Barbara; tel: 805/564-5524
Huntington Beach; tel: 949/840-
7542
Newport Beach; tel: 949/722-1611
Oceanside; tel: 760/722-1534
Long Beach; tel: 562/435-4093
Naples; tel: 562/987-2674
Marina Del Rey; tel: 310/821-7614
New Year's Eve
Pine Avenue, Long Beach
Tel: 562/436-4259
Street performers, and great laser
light show.
New Year's Eve Gala
Catalina Island
Tel: 310/510-1520
In the world-famous Casino
Ballroom.
Pier Lighting and Fireworks
Manhattan Beach
Tel: 310/802-5408
Traditional songs, Santa, great
fireworks show from the pier
(lighting and fireworks may be on
different nights).
Queen Mary **Tree Lighting**
Long Beach
Tel: 562/435-3511
Old-fashioned holiday tradition.
Una Pastorella **the Shepherds' Play**
Santa Barbara
Tel: 805/966-9719.

Further Reading

Background Books

Adventures in the Screen Trade,
William Goldman (Warners, 1983)
The Big Sleep, Raymond Chandler
(Knopf, 1939)
California Coastal Access Guide,
the California Coastal Commission
*California: A Guide to the Golden
State*, the Federal Writers Project
(Hastings House, 1939)
California Southern Country, Carey
McWilliams (Duell, Sloan Pearce,
1946)
California's Missions, Ralph B.
Wright (Hubert A Lowan, 1978)
City of Quartz, Mike Davis (Verso,
1990)
L.A. Confidential, James Ellroy
(Warner, 1997)
L.A. Shortcuts, Brian Roberts and
Richard Schwadel (Red Car Press)
The Last Tycoon, E. Scott Fitzgerald
(Scribner, 1941)
*Los Angeles A to Z: An
Encyclopedia of the City and
County*, Leonard Pitt and Dale Pitt
(University of California Press,
1997)
*Los Angeles: An Architectural
Guide*, David Gebhardt and Robert
Winter (Gibbs Smith, 1994)
*Los Angeles Stories: Great Writers
on the City* edited by John Miller
(Chronicle Books, 1991)
The Loved One, Evelyn Waugh
(Doubleday, 1948)
The Missions of California, Melba
Levick and Stanley Young (Chronicle
Books, 1988)
Play It As it Lays, Joan Didion
(Farrar, Straus and Giroux, 1970)
Post Office, Charles Bukowski
(Black Sparrow Press, 1971)
The Real Oscar, Peter H. Brown
(Arlington House, 1991)
Tales from the Hollywood Raj,
Sheridan Morley (Viking Press, NY
1983)
Two Years Before the Mast,
Richard Henry Dana (New York
Heritage Press, 1841)

The Zoot Suit Murders, Thomas
Sanchez (E.P. Dutton, 1978)

People

*All the Stars in Heaven: Louis B
Mayer's MGM*, Gary Carey (E.P.
Dutton, 1981)
*An Empire of Their Own: How the
Jews Invented Hollywood*, Neil
Gabler (Doubleday, 1989)
Contemporary Architects (St
James Press, 1987)
Goldwyn, A. Scott Berg (Knopf, 1989)
*The Great Movie Stars: The Golden
Years*, David Shipman (Crown,
1970)
Hedda and Louella, George Eells
(G.P. Putnams Sons, 1972)
*Hollywood's Master Showman:
The Legendary Sid Grauman*,
Charles Beardsley (Cornwall Books,
1983)
Julia Morgan, Sara Holmes Boutelle
(Abbeville Press, 1988)
*Life and Good Times of William
Randolph Hearst*, John Tebbel (E.P
Dutton and Co, 1952)
The Life of Raymond Chandler,
Frank McShane (E.P. Dutton and Co,
1976)
*Norma Jean: The Life of Marilyn
Monroe*, Fred Lawrence Guiles
(McGraw Hill, 1969)
This is Hollywood, Ken Schessler
(Universal Books, 1989)
*Vamp: The Life and Times of Theda
Bara*, Ron Genini (McFarland Press,
1995)
*William Mulholland: A Forgotten
Forefather*, Robert William Matson
(Pacific Center for Western Studies,
1975)
Will Rogers in Hollywood, Bryan B.
and Frances N Sterling (Crown,
1984)

Geography and Natural History

*California Patterns: A Geographical
and Historical Atlas*, David
Hornbeck (Mayfield, 1983)
*California: The Geography of
Diversity*, Crane Miller and Richard
Hyslop (Mayfield, 1983)
The City and the Country, Harry
Ellington Brook (Kingsley, Barnes
and Newner, 1987)

Coast Walks, John McKinney
(Olympus Press, 1988)
Natural Los Angeles, Bill Thomas
(Harper and Row, 1989)
Southern California: Off the Beaten Path, Kathy Strong (Globe Pequot Press)
Walking Los Angeles: Adventures on the Urban Edge, John McKinney
(Harper Collins West, 1994)
Walks of California, Gary Ferguson
(Prentice Hall Press, 1987)

Places

California Public Gardens, Eric Sigg
(John Muir Publications, 1991)
The City Observed: Los Angeles,
Charles Moore, Peter Becker, and
Regula Campbell (Vintage, 1984)
Day Hikes Around Los Angeles: 45 Great Hikes, Robert Stone, (Day Hike Books, 2000)
Downtown Los Angeles: A Walking Guide, Robert Herman (City Vista Press, 1996)
The Encyclopedia of Hollywood,
Scott and Barbara Siegel (Facts on File, 1990)
Guide to Frank Lloyd Wright's California, Zimmerman (Gibbs-Smith)
Hollywood Death and Scandal Sites, E.J. Fleming (McFarland and Co., 2000)
L.A Bizarro: The Insider's Guide to the Obscure, the Absurd and the perverse in Los Angeles, Anthony R. Lovett and Matt Maranian (St Martins, 1997)
Los Angeles: An Architectural Guide, David Gebhardt and Robert Winter (Gibbs-Smith, Salt Lake City, 1994)
Out with the Stars, Jim Heimann
(Abbeville, 1985)
Street Gallery: Guide to 1000 Los Angeles Murals edited by John Miller (Chronicle Books, 1991)
The Ultimate Hollywood Tour Book,
William A. Gordon (North Ridge Books, 1994)
World Cities: Los Angeles edited by
Maggie Toy (Academy Editions, 1993)

History

City of Nets: A Portrait of Hollywood in the 1940s, Otto Friedrich (Harper and Row, 1986)

City-Makers, Remi Nadeau
(Doubleday, 1948)
A Companion to California, James Hart (Oxford University Press, 1978)
History of the San Fernando Valley,
Frank M. Keffner (Stillman, 1934)
Hollywood: The First Hundred Years, Bruce T. Torrence (New York Zoetrope, 1982)
Indians of Early Southern California, Edna B. Ziebold (Sapsis, 1969)
L.A Lost and Found: an architectural history, Sam Hall Kaplan (Crown, 1987)
Los Angeles, 1781–1981 (California Historical Society) Oil!,
Upton Sinclair (R. Bentley, Cambridge 1980)
The San Fernando Valley, Past and Present, Lawrence C. Jorgensen
(Pacific Rim Research, 1982)
Santa Monica Pier: A History from 1875–1990, Jeffrey Stanton
(Donahue Publications, 1980)
A Short History of the Movies,
Gerald Mast (University of Chicago Press, 1971)
The Times We Had: Life with William Randolph Hearst, Marion Davis (Bobbs Merrill, 1975)
Yesterday's Los Angeles, Norman Dash (E.A. Seamann Publishing, 1976)

Other Insight Guides

Apa Publications' incomparable range of more than 500 Insight Guides, Insight Compact Guides, Insight Pocket Guides and Insight Maps include the following titles relating to destinations in California:
Insight Guide: Southern California is a scenic and comprehensive account of the towns, the beaches, the movie stars and the missions of the southern part of the state.
Insight Guide: Northern California performs the same service for the northern sector of the state, combining insightful text and stunning photography.
Insight Guide: California brings together in one volume all that is best in this dynamic state.

Insight Guide: San Francisco focuses on California's other great city, capturing the city's timeless allure in entertaining text and eye-catching photographs.

Insight Compact Guide: Los Angeles is the ultimate portable guide, packing in a remarkable amount of information, pictures and maps into an easily carried and very affordable guidebook.

Insight Pocket Guide: Los Angeles provides personal recommendations from a local host to help you make the most of a short stay, and includes a full-size fold-out map.

Insight Map: Los Angeles combines clear, detailed cartography with essential information about the city, and a laminated finish makes the map durable and easy to fold.

Other Insight Guides to look out for include the following titles, all following the lavish format of the present volume: *American Southwest*, *Pacific Northwest*, *Seattle*, *Wild West*, and *US National Parks West*. A special volume, *USA On the Road*, provides practical itineraries for touring the entire country, including one for California's great coastal drive.

ART & PHOTO CREDITS

Picture Spreads

Cartographic Editor Zoë Goodwin
Design Consultants
Carlotta Junger, Graham Mitchener
Picture Research
Hilary Genin, Susannah Stone

Index

Numbers in italics refer to photographs

Feedback

We do our best to ensure the information in our books is as accurate and up-to-date as possible. The books are updated on a regular basis, using local contacts, who painstakingly add, amend and correct as required. However, in a fast-changing world, some mistakes and omissions are inevitable, and we are ultimately reliant on our readers to keep us in the picture.

We would welcome your feedback on any details related to your experiences using the book "on the road". Maybe we recommended a hotel that you liked (or another that you didn't), as well as interesting new attractions, or facts and figures you have found out about the country itself. The more details you can give

us (particularly with regard to addresses, e-mails and telephone numbers), the better.

We will acknowledge all contributions, and we'll offer an Insight Guide to the best letters received.

Please write to us at:
Insight Guides
APA Publications
PO Box 7910
London SE1 1XF
United Kingdom
Or send e-mail to:
insight@apaguide.demon.co.uk

❋ INSIGHT GUIDES

The world's largest collection of visual travel guides

Insight Guides – the Classic Series
that puts you in the picture

...ka	China	Hong Kong	Morocco	Singapore
...sace	Cologne	Hungary	Moscow	South Africa
Amazon Wildlife	Continental Europe		Munich	South America
American Southwest	Corsica	Iceland		South Tyrol
Amsterdam	Costa Rica	India	Namibia	Southeast Asia
Argentina	Crete	India's Western	Native America	Wildlife
Asia, East	Crossing America	Himalayas	Nepal	Spain
Asia, South	Cuba	India, South	Netherlands	Spain, Northern
Asia, Southeast	Cyprus	Indian Wildlife	New England	Spain, Southern
Athens	Czech & Slovak	Indonesia	New Orleans	Sri Lanka
Atlanta	Republic	Ireland	New York City	Sweden
Australia		Israel	New York State	Switzerland
Austria	Delhi, Jaipur & Agra	Istanbul	New Zealand	Sydney
	Denmark	Italy	Nile	Syria & Lebanon
Bahamas	Dominican Republic	Italy, Northern	Normandy	
Bali	Dresden		Norway	Taiwan
Baltic States	Dublin	Jamaica		Tenerife
Bangkok	Düsseldorf	Japan	Old South	Texas
Barbados		Java	Oman & The UAE	Thailand
Barcelona	East African Wildlife	Jerusalem	Oxford	Tokyo
Bay of Naples	Eastern Europe	Jordan		Trinidad & Tobago
Beijing	Ecuador		Pacific Northwest	Tunisia
Belgium	Edinburgh	Kathmandu	Pakistan	Turkey
Belize	Egypt	Kenya	Paris	Turkish Coast
Berlin	England	Korea	Peru	Tuscany
Bermuda			Philadelphia	
Boston	Finland	Laos & Cambodia	Philippines	Umbria
Brazil	Florence	Lisbon	Poland	USA: Eastern States
Brittany	Florida	Loire Valley	Portugal	USA: Western States
Brussels	France	London	Prague	US National Parks:
Budapest	Frankfurt	Los Angeles	Provence	East
Buenos Aires	French Riviera		Puerto Rico	US National Parks:
Burgundy		Madeira		West
Burma (Myanmar)	Gambia & Senegal	Madrid	Rajasthan	
	Germany	Malaysia	Rhine	Vancouver
Cairo	Glasgow	Mallorca & Ibiza	Rio de Janeiro	Venezuela
Calcutta	Gran Canaria	Malta	Rockies	Venice
California	Great Barrier Reef	Marine Life ot the	Rome	Vienna
California, Northern	Great Britain	South China Sea	Russia	Vietnam
California, Southern	Greece	Mauritius &		
Canada	Greek Islands	Seychelles	St. Petersburg	Wales
Caribbean	Guatemala, Belize &	Melbourne	San Francisco	Washington DC
Catalonia	Yucatán	Mexico City	Sardinia	Waterways of Europe
Channel Islands		Mexico	Scotland	Wild West
Chicago	Hamburg	Miami	Seattle	
Chile	Hawaii	Montreal	Sicily	Yemen

Complementing the above titles are 120 easy-to-carry Insight Compact Guides, 120 Insight Pocket Guides with full-size pull-out maps and more than 60 laminated easy-fold Insight Maps